FULL CIRCLE
The Long Way Home From Canada

Ulrich Steinhilper

FULL CIRCLE

THE LONG WAY HOME
FROM CANADA

Ulrich Steinhilper

&

Peter Osborne

Published in 1992 by
Independent Books
3, Leaves Green Crescent
Keston
Bromley BR2 6DN
Great Britain

First published 1992 by Independent Books

Translated from the original German '...und Gott Lenkt'
by Ulrich Steinhilper & Eugen Geiger

Edited by Carol Osborne
David Hough & 'Bill' Osborne

A catalogue record for this book is available from the British Library

ISBN 1 872836 02 X

Printed and bound in Great Britain by Hartnolls Ltd, Bodmin, Cornwall.

CONTENTS

Introduction:

Chapter 1:   In Safe Custody Again   Page 7

Chapter 2:   Return To Canada... But Where?   Page 18

Chapter 3:   Quiet Days   Page 29

Chapter 4:   Back and Forth to Fort Henry   Page 40

Chapter 5:   Fort Henry   Page 49

Chapter 6:   Bad Boys to Gravenhurst   Page 65

Chapter 7:   The 'Africans' are Coming!   Page 81

Chapter 8:   Gravenhurst Also Gets Going   Page 92

Chapter 9:   *Ehrenwort* - 'Parole'   Page 106

Chapter 10:   Spirit - Mind - Body   Page 115

Chapter 11:   Shackles and Tunnels   Page 130

Chapter 12:   The Snow Tunnel   Page 143

Chapter 13:   The Exchange Commission Visits   Page 169

Chapter 14:   *Wunderzange* - Miraculous Cutters   Page 170

Chapter 15:   A Great Risk in Broad Daylight   Page 182

Chapter 16:   POW Exchange - Information   Page 194

Chapter 17:   The Secret Code   Page 208

Chapter 18:   Worrying About Germany   Page 222

Chapter 19:   Into a Different World   Page 236

Chapter 20:   Pitiful People   Page 255

Chapter 21:   *...und Gott Lenkt...*   Page 270

Chapter 22:   The Situation Gets Difficult   Page 288

Chapter 23:   Discharged Into a New World   Page 299

Chapter 24:   The War Was Lost... But...   Page 313

Chapter 25:	Do We Still Have a Chance?	Page 325
Chapter 26:	Forlorn - Forgotten - Homeward	Page 339
Chapter 27:	Discharge - Retrospection - Prospects	Page 351
Epilogue		Page 357
Appendix I:		Page 368
Appendix II:		Page 376

PHOTOGRAPHS & PLANS

The Route of Our Escape	Page 14
Camp 31 - Fort Henry	Page 26
Fort Henry	Page 27
One of our famous *Puppkameraden*	Page 34
The Route Taken by Peter Krug	Page 60
Peter Krug in His *Luftwaffe* uniform	Page 61
POW Photos of Peter	Page 61
An Earlier Picture Having Just Been 'Fished Out'	Page 62
Camp 30 Bowmanville	Page 66
The Theatre at Bowmanville	Page 67
Schiller Behind Barbed Wire	Page 67
The Kitchen at Camp 30	Page 68
A Canadian Inspection	Page 68
'Escape Ringleaders' - Newspaper Cutting	Page 72
Toronto Daily Star	Page 75
Toronto Daily Star	Page 76
Toronto Globe & Mail	Page 77
Camp 20 Gravenhurst	Page 82
A View of The Camp	Page 83
The Edge of Lake Muskoka	Page 84

North Africa 1941   Page 93

After The *'Sollumslacht'*   Page 95

General Rommel   Page 96

Abitur zeugnis   Page 99

Theatre Costumes   Page 101

Gravenhurst May 1943   Page 104

Gravenhurst May 1943   Page 113

A Group Photo With a Purpose   Page 133

Officers At Gravenhurst   Page 141

Plan of Gravenhurst Showing The Snow Tunnel   Page 144

Toronto Daily Star   Page 161

The Montreal Daily Star   Page 162

The Gazette   Page 163

Die Wunderzange   Page 178

'The Most Beautiful Fence In All Canada'   Page 185

Plan of Fifth Escape   Page 186

A *Fistball* Game in Progress   Page 187

The Swedish Boat *Gripsholm*   Page 195

My Official Promotion to *Hauptmann*   Page 199

The Original Receipt For My Accordion   Page 201

The Original Typed Message Home   Page 203

The Reverse of Above   Page 203

Wilke's Original Letter   Page 204

The Secret Code - My Letter & Transcript   Page 213

Detail of The Decoding Process   Page 214

The Message Revealed   Page 215

Officers at Gravenhurst   Page 225

A View of The Camp   Page 226

The T+ Ice Hockey Team   Page 227

The Small Pavilion in Which I Was Held   Page 237

The Main Building of The Westminster Hospital   Page 243

The White Door Which Led to C Ward   Page 243

Tailfingen Sept/Oct 1943   Page 253

The Back of C Ward   Page 276

The Sunrooms of Upper and Lower B Ward   Page 285

General Hans von Ravenstein   Page 307

Officers at Bowmanville - Schweizer   Page 310

Camp Grande Ligne   Page 329

RMS Aquitainia   Page 336

My Certificate of Discharge   Page 354

Reverse of Above   Page 355

Filming at Hawkinge   Page 363

By the Replica of von Werra's '109   Page 364

Outside The Museum   Page 365

The Cemetery at Hawkinge   Page 366

The Remains of The Farmhouse as We First Saw It   Page 368

The Entrance to The Cellar   Page 369

The New House   Page 370

Some of The Builders   Page 370

The Log Stables   Page 371

Vegetable Production   Page 372

The Small Animals and Their Keepers   Page 373

The Plough Team   Page 374

Major Wüstefeldt   Page 374

INTRODUCTION

This is the last book in the series of three which cover my experiences in World War Two. It has been very hard work for all concerned but we are confident that the end product is the justification for it. What we have produced, both in English and in German, is what we believe to be a unique record of some, hitherto largely unreported, aspects of that war. To produce it we have drawn on the numerous letters I wrote at the time, a journal also hand-written then, and other letters and documents which were saved by my parents. This has resulted in what we believe is the most accurate and factual record of life in Allied POW camps.

To add to this the last two books were first published in German and read by many, many people who were directly involved in the events recorded in them. This has resulted, over the years, in more information coming forward and in some cases minor points being changed. The English language versions of my books have, therefore, benefitted from this and they are as accurate an account of those six years as it is possible to produce.

We have received lots of letters as a result of the publication of the first two books, *'Spitfire On My Tail'* and *'Ten Minutes To Buffalo'* and it has been a pleasure to read them all. What is most rewarding is that so many people have found so many diverse things of interest in these two books. This last volume will cover other aspects of the war and is by no means simply a repeat or extension of what has already been read. We can say now that some people will find this book exciting and others will be appalled by some of the things they read, all we can say is that it is all true and is written down having taken very great pains to research and cross-reference the material. For reasons which will emerge in the text I can say that parts of this book were very, very hard for me to write. I had to return to a time in my life which I had tried hard to forget. I hope you will find the effort was worthwhile.

Ulrich Steinhilper

1992

CHAPTER ONE

IN SAFE CUSTODY AGAIN

We were firmly taken care of in the Central Office of the American Border Police in Watertown. My friend Hinnerk Waller and myself, former *Oberleutnants* of the *Luftwaffe* and pilots in 3rd Squadron J.G. 52. We had both become victims of the "Battle Britain", Hinnerk in September and myself on 27th October 1940. Consequently, we were prisoners of war. The British had problems both of supply and also feared an imminent invasion and so sent us overseas to Canada in January 1941. The majority of the German POWs in England who were fit enough to be transported went in that first shipment.

Having escaped from Camp 30, at Bowmanville in Canada, Hinnerk and I had managed to cross the frozen St. Lawrence into the USA, but due to incredibly bad luck we'd been caught. Sometimes left alone, sometimes in the company of the policemen, we were still wondering what had happened. That evening, the evening of Sunday 22nd February 1942, we had been arrested by two American Policemen in Watertown, not far away from the St. Lawrence. It was, for me, the third escape attempt and we had been excellently prepared and, because of this, it was all the more difficult to understand how they had picked us out. We had been amongst many people walking on the sidewalk next to a main highway and doing nothing suspicious. It looked like bad luck and we had to accept it philosophically. After all we could not change the situation. Again it was our fortune, like with all the other POWs, to be taken care of by destiny and the will of others, not guided by our own decisions. Later in the evening we were moved to Ogdensburg, to the headquarters of the Border police.

Even though it was past midnight, we were not yet tired enough to leave unanswered the question of how we had been arrested, but the police would tell us nothing. However they would not stop their never-ending questions about our precise route of escape. They wanted to know again and again how we could have got to the crossing point so quickly and across the ice on the St. Lawrence without breaking it and falling through. Soon it became clear that behind all these questions was the hunch that after leaving our Canadian camp at Bowmanville, at the other side of Lake Ontario, we had been helped by a 5th Column. Such was the title attributed to the German underground organisation in the USA and Canada which the Allies were convinced operated; they always thought we had received secret help.

The officers of the border patrol were so keen to question us that it looked like they were out for special monetary reward, otherwise we could not understand why they doggedly kept to their line of questioning. Sometimes we had a very nice conversation with these people, but they soon came back to the same questions. I imagine they thought they were quite smart but we, the old POWs, were too hard-boiled. Interrogations, which had started soon after I had come down on my parachute in England and which peaked in the British interrogation camps, had been quite a good training for this. Compared with those professionals in the camps, these policemen were amateurs.

The conversation in general was agreeable and made a change for us, so we didn't want to stop it completely. We politely tried to avoid the interrogation attempts, but when they became too direct we told them clearly that if they continued we would have to stop the otherwise interesting exchange.

Meanwhile, after one and a half years as POWs, we each thought of ourselves as something of a philosopher. The old timers (those that had been POWs for some time) had learnt to open their mouths only if they thought they had something reasonable to say; there was no place for idle chatter. We had learnt that within a camp we could only live together peacefully if everybody refrained from opening his heart and mouth, letting thoughts wonder around too freely. Only a few people had been given sensible occupations at this time, some of them having already served two years as prisoners. But for everybody else there was just the utterly predictable routine within the fence, everybody knowing each other too well. Necessity dictated therefore that within the camp it was best not to talk too much. That was the way to avoid disturbing the other human beings within the fence.

For a time, at least, Hinnerk and I had broken the routine by planning and executing our escape and it would still be a while before we returned to the camp and that soul destroying routine. It was late but the questioning continued, even the Boss - that's how the other officer grades referred to the chief of the Border Police office in Ogdensburg - began to realise there was going to be no result and around two o'clock it was abandoned. But hats off to the Boss, rather than let us go to bed hungry, he sent some messengers out to a nearby place to get us some sandwiches and a coca-cola. However, he had to borrow the money for that from his junior officers!

After eating our impromptu meal we were warned not to attempt any further escapes. They cautioned us that the border patrol was excellently equipped to deal with the cold conditions and therefore any attempt would be quickly thwarted. We were not planning anything so rash. It would have been senseless to run away without equipment and without being prepared, into the cold winter with so much snow. But our guards were still occupied by the thought of the help by the 5th Column.

We were to remain under close guard but we much preferred this to being handcuffed; so many times we had been treated like criminals. They didn't seem to be able to make the distinction between those of their own society who were thieves and murderers and the POWs who were officers and, as such, subject to our codes of conduct and behaviour. We were taken up two floors into a large clean room where we saw three single beds. Next to us, in the third bed, would lie a patrolman who, together with a second border policeman, would alternate keeping a wakeful watch. They both looked really good with their wide brimmed hat, their red uniform jacket, breeches, brown long leather boots, patent leather Sam Browne belt and the heavy Colt revolver and bright cartridge cases in loops on the belt. They really looked as though they'd stepped out of a movie.

We were treated as prisoners, first class. This could clearly be read from a paper notice on the wall. The people who illegally crossed the border were divided into different classes: 'Undesirable immigrants, sailors who had 'jumped ship', soldiers, soldiers who had deserted, people who were avoiding their taxes, workers without official permit, thieves, murderers, pocket-pickers, smugglers.' Each one of them had his place on this list. For each class of them, the cells, the toilets, the washrooms and the equivalent meals, according to class, were prescribed.

We could not complain about our shower and washroom, which was faced with dark marble. We were classified as undesirable immigrants and it was explained to us we were, therefore, first class. With that, we were not given the worst standard of living. The two border patrolmen really liked to explain every detail to us. They thought we would never have seen such showers and washing facilities in Germany and imagined they had to explain to us how to use it in detail. This was very important for them and they showed us with consummate pride how to change the mixture from hot to cold. They were a bit disappointed when we mentioned that this kind of mixer was in common use in Germany and we already had used them during our *Luftwaffe* training. We wondered what kind of primitive race they thought we were.

Besides the showers and other items of immediate interest both the patrolmen were keen to talk to us on a wide range of subjects and here there was no hint of subtle interrogation. They, themselves, were very proud of their free country and their way of life. We didn't think we were *Nazis*, but were now used to the idea that all Germans were labelled as such. We were not about make any attempt to defend the record of Hitler and his acolytes, but we felt it was fair to defend many of the better inventions of our new state. For instance the *Kraft durch Freude* which was a way for many ordinary people to take a holiday. We cited the health system and many other things which during the last few years had really improved. We said we did not understand very much about politics, but that there were things that everybody could and should admire. When we discussed these subjects we never lacked an interested audience.

Because of such discussions, we were marked as politically dangerous and, subsequently, all German officers in Canada were contained within the camps for the duration of the War. They were never, not even on a voluntary basis, let out to work outside the camps. The idea was that we should be prevented from making contact with the local population and corrupting them with our evil *Nazi* ideas. We talked to our two patrolmen rather too long, and slowly our attention began to wander and fatigue took over. In spite of the physical stress which we had undergone previously, it took a long time until we fell asleep on our mattresses.

Next morning, when rising, only one patrolman appeared, a new face. From a neighbouring snack bar he got us a very good breakfast and, until the appearance of the Boss, we again talked with this new man. Apparently he had been well schooled, in High School probably. He was a Southerner who talked very slow and we could understand him very well. He had good manners and was very well turned out. He had served in the US Navy, spoke some Spanish and French and, before moving north, he'd served on the Texan/Mexican border and was an amateur pilot. He had just received his basic pilot's licence and was very fond of flying. He had a special admiration for the German *Luftwaffe* and was specially pleased to be able to chat to two former pilots. However, like all Englishmen and Americans, he thought the Spitfire was the best plane in the world. We tried to argue against this and things at times got rather heated. We agreed that with the new Merlin III engine the Spitfires could fly higher and could turn tighter but there were other considerations like speed, weaponry, control of the guns etc. etc. We had to defend what we saw as the superior features of the '109. It was a lively exchange.

Meanwhile, the Boss had come into the office but waited for a suitable time to interrupt. He then said we were to be individually interviewed by him and he left with Hinnerk. When he returned he had a very long face but I was unable to talk to him as I was immediately ordered in for my turn. Apparently the Boss liked to impress by being a little theatrical and gravely announced, "Now, I have to make a very sad announcement to you. You are a Canadian Prisoner of War and you have come into this country without permission. After you were taken into custody by the police here, you showed forged papers. Your illegal entry to the USA would not be a problem but because of the false papers, you will be put in front of a civil court and you will be put into jail. After your time in jail, we will then send you back to Canada."

Now I understood why Hinnerk had come back with such a long face. That was going to hit us hard. Had we been arrested as simple civilian illegal immigrants with false papers I would have accepted time in jail. At least for a while, we would have been out of range of any large scale search for us from Canada and maybe, in the meantime, we would even have had a chance to be forgotten by everybody. But now, to have to serve a jail sentence and then to be sent back was bad news.

Actually, Hinnerk and I had prepared for the eventuality of being arrested as civilians, that is not being recognised officially as Prisoners of War and being put to jail because of forged papers. We didn't know the likely outcome of anything like this because, to date, nobody had had that experience. We didn't know what the official American line would be. The Watertown Police and the Border Police had discovered our false papers but they knew at one and the same time we were escaped POWs. The question was how would the American and Canadian administrations handle our case? There was no doubt that an intensive dialogue was in progress, but first jail and then back to the camp - that didn't sound too good.

In my interview I declared right away I wanted to talk to a representative of Switzerland, our protecting power. The Boss enjoyed that, knowing that I'd had been hit hard by the thought of serving time in a civilian jail. A 'protecting power', he said, was unknown to him. For the USA I was a civilian with false papers. I told him that for my case there were certain paragraphs within the Geneva Convention. He continued with his dramatic act, telling me that there wasn't a United States Geneva Convention and they didn't have to comply with the international convention because they were not signatories. I knew this wasn't true, but he just kept up the act and it soon became clear he was only trying to put me under pressure.

Again, he and the others only wanted to know how and where we had crossed the river and how we had continued on to Watertown. The fact was that von Werra, Manhart and now we had crossed the St. Lawrence and the border in about the same area. The administration in the USA and Canada were more or less certain that their suspicion that we had been helped by a 5th Column in that particular area were correct. The real reason was much less dramatic and was certainly free of intrigue. According to our own calculations the St. Lawrence around that area was flowing slower. That meant that it would be the first section of the river to freeze with the approach of winter and the last section to remain traversable with the approach of the spring. It also had the advantage of being fairly narrow so a crossing would not take hours.

The Boss persisted with his idea that better cooperation, as he called it, would be helpful to us in any civil court proceedings. However, my answer to the subjects - time of escape and route of escape - stayed the same and I didn't give him any further information. After about one hour of continued discussions and further questioning, the phone rang. The discussion was in American slang and I really didn't understand anything. After the end of the phone call, and without any further discussion, the Boss declared there would be no civilian court. The decision had now been made and he had been informed on the phone that without any further proceedings we would be turned back and sent to a Canadian POW camp. That was a relief. There was no doubt the threat of the civil court and period in jail had been a ploy by this sly old fox to put us under pressure and to try to extract information about our route. Fortunately we had stuck it out, but it hadn't been easy. From now on we could talk freely and the Boss was a better listener.

I think this meant as much change in mood for the officers of the border patrol as it did for us. The Boss said he knew the German armed services and even called them by their German name *Deutsche Wehrmacht*. He also said that we, the *Nazi* officers, were not of the old school which he had come to know at the end of the first War in 1918 when he was in the occupation army in the Rhineland. I was surprised by his remarks. I agreed we didn't have terribly good haircuts and, of course we were dressed in our escape clothes, but I didn't think the image we apparently portrayed was sound enough evidence on which to base such a judgement. Actually I was rather proud of our haircuts which had been the product of the enterprise of a few prisoners, 'self improvers' in the art of *coiffeur*, within the camps. I was also at pains to point out that if he wanted to know why our hand baggage was in such a terribly disorganised state he'd better contact the police in Watertown who were the authors of it. I asked if he couldn't accept we hadn't wanted to look like officers, but were more keen to fit the part of sailors for our cover.

Without much comment on those propositions the Boss went on to mention the 'housewife'[1] which had been discovered in my kit. The German stamp on it *Kameradenhilfe* (literally comrade help - sent to the camps from Germany) had been covered by myself with a glued paper label on which was my false name. The Boss asked, "Where did you get this bloody name, Paul Sumser, when there are so many other German names?" I had to grin. If I had explained to him how carefully the names had been selected and in how many countries they were acceptable he would have been impressed by the quality of such a name. As it was, conscious we should give as little as possible away, I kept my own council.

He was keen to talk of his own experience during his time in Europe. With great pride he pointed to a framed paper on the wall which recorded the wounding of Corporal David Benjamin in the Great War. He said, "That was me. I was wounded twice." I imagined from his name that he was Jewish and he made the comment that the Jews were a stumbling block in existing American policy. There was already some anti-semitic feeling and now there was the problem of the immigrants from Germany who were, at one and the same time, Jews and Germans. In one way he said he could understand Hitler's attitude towards the Jews[2] but in other fields he did not like what was apparently happening. He said he had really got to like the Germans and, using the proper German word, there was nothing better than *Gemütlichkeit* (the word used to express a state of friendliness - similar to the French *bonhomie*). Also nothing compared, in his opinion, with a good *Biergarten*!

His general view was that the poor German people were being ruined by the Nazis. He claimed they would suppress and corrupt everyone, even small children who were already being drilled as soldiers. As we were then talking in general terms I felt I could reply more expansively and talked of *Kraft durch Freunde* again and of the interesting social ideas like *Arbeitsdienst* (labour service) where youngsters had, normally, to perform their service in an area of Germany previously unknown to them. In this way they learned much about Germany and the other peoples of the country. Also I strongly advocated the good German family life and what a good building block this was for the country as a whole. It was clear to me we would win the war and that Germany would become Europe, including England, and in that state Europe would become united and very strong. When that had been done we would be able to show the world what kind of people we were and what could be achieved.

Even though Mr Benjamin had been to the Olympic Games in Berlin in 1936 he didn't waver from his point of view. The American press had, apparently, successfully convinced him that we, the Germans, had now become a race that goose-stepped everywhere and who would't eat, drink or go dancing unless the appropriate orders were issued. His arguments so simplified the situation that his ideas, at least with me, fell on stony ground. He continued to describe the qualities of the immigrant Germans and asked

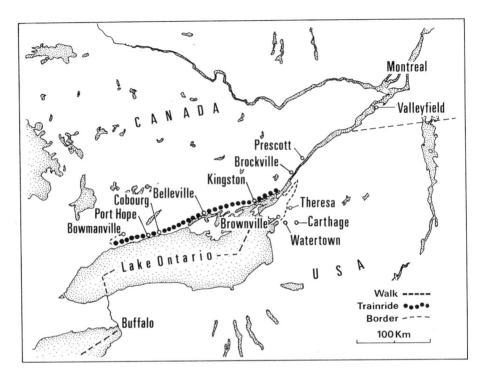

The route of the escape, from Bowmanville to Watertown.

why we had become so different from those good people. He said a German resident of Ogdensburg had, just the night before, asked if there was anything he could do for us, so good natured, he maintained, were the American Germans. Again I could not comment because I didn't think the German people who had remained at home were too different.

We did agree, however, on the positive influence of the Germans and, in particular, the German officer corps in the early days of the 'New World' and in the battles with, for instance, Mexico. Also, that German 'know how' and hard working attitudes had played an important part in the steady increase in American economic and commercial strength. But then this was, again, all in the past. We did agree it was a shame that we two peoples had been pitted against each other as enemies, but that really was the measure of our agreement. In his view the modern Germans had been totally corrupted by the influence of Hitler and the Nazis.

I changed tack slightly and made my point that at least our escapes had shown to the large number of ex-patriot Germans who lived around

Ogdensburg we had not lost our courage or sense of duty; nor were we incapable of acting upon our own initiative. He didn't seem overly impressed and brought the Japanese into the discussion. His view was that in declaring war on the USA they had prodded the sleeping tiger and the nation was now arming quickly. He had no doubt that the great American war machine would not be turned off until both Japan and Germany capitulated. I could not believe that the Americans could contemplate a repeat of the Great War and face the fantastic losses which had been taken by all sides in 1918. For my part I didn't believe this policeman had a true appreciation of the military potential of Germany and Japan.

Our exchange was interrupted when the door was opened and a man was ushered in accompanied by a border policeman. He was a civilian and wore a strange leather jacket, very colourful. On one side of the breast there was a large eagle embroidered in yellow silk. The Boss didn't seem so surprised, he was expecting this man and formally introduced him. His name was, I think, Evans and he was the proprietor of a private flying school in Ogdensburg. I gave him my name and reached out my hand to the gentleman. First cigarettes were offered and we made some 'small talk' but soon we got to the subject. The flyer said that he'd opened his school quite recently and only a short while ago had acquired some training aircraft. He was very inexperienced, he said, and when, the day before, he'd heard of two German pilots being held in Ogdensburg he thought he'd ask for some advice. He felt that because of my training and experience I might be able to offer him some tips. I have no doubt his approach was completely genuine, but we had become so conditioned to watch for subtle interrogation techniques that I had to be very guarded in my answers. It looked so much like the introductions I had experienced from the RAF intelligence officers in Kent and later in 'The Cage'.

I realised it was now about eighteen months since we'd been shot down and I was conscious we probably didn't have any crucial military information but I'd still be careful. The flyer was sensitive to my mood and quickly tried to put me at my ease by saying he wasn't looking for any military secrets. He said he only wanted me to answer when I was completely happy to do so but Mr Benjamin was disappointed with my obvious mistrust. Really, in their eyes they had not been asking for anything secret but then they hadn't had our conditioning. Apparently the flyer had just closed a lucrative contract with the American government for the basic training of American military pilots. He wanted to make a success of it even though he had very little previous experience. I was concerned about my orders to keep quiet on military matters and therefore had little to say, even thought it was obvious from their questions they didn't even know the basics of aviation training. It wasn't just my reluctance to answer because of any military content but in many cases I just didn't know the information they wanted; very fundamental items like the technical specification for training aircraft, the maintenance schedules and how many hours should be flown with pupils before they were sent solo. It was a little depressing for me to see how little he knew; he had, for instance, never flown anything other than the basic training aircraft nor did he have anything like an instrument or multi-engine rating. Nonetheless he was obviously determined to capitalise on this opportunity and to make as much money as possible from this war. I suppose it is indeed an ill wind which blows nobody any good.

Before too long they realised it was wearing for me to keep saying 'No' and so we changed the subject and started to talk about the American fighter planes. I knew a little bit about the Curtis P 36 and P 40, a few examples of which had flown in France and, in England, and had actually been in combat. Mainly from heresay I could report on their performance and advantages. But then, inevitably, the conversation came to the Spitfire, and clearly their view was there was nothing to touch it and the debate started again. This time I was unable to hold back and said that despite all the apparently technical superiority of the Spitfire I had shot down at least three of them and at least one Hurricane and a Blenheim. This, I added, was not in home defence, but in aggressive action in British airspace. They wanted to hear much more from me on this but I didn't want to go any further. Realising there was little point in continuing the flyer politely thanked me for my help, such as it had been, and left. The Boss also now seemed to be content and let me return to the room.

Reunited with Hinnerk the policemen soon appeared again to take photographs, not for official records but for their private albums and, in particular, for that of Mr Benjamin. He showed us a remarkable collection of photographs and newspaper articles about the German POWs who had been his 'guests' since we first arrived in North America. He was especially proud of the photographs and reports about Franz von Werra. Franz had promised him that when he returned to Germany[3] he would send him a postcard. This reality we could now admire. When showing the picture of Manni Manhart he pointed out the uniform which Manni had managed to change to a more civilian appearance. After Manni had been recaptured he had pinned on his Iron Cross First Class which he'd carried along in case he had been arrested and needed some proof he was a POW. To the Boss this picture together with Manni and his Iron Cross held great meaning, he was very proud of it. This was a little surprising to me but then in my estimation his special interest was linked to his First War experience and the Iron Cross then.

With our 'photo call' over we were fingerprinted and it became clear that we would now be entered on the American police records along with other 'criminals'.

Notes on Chapter One

[1] 'Housewife'- a small bag usually made of cotton cloth which contains items like needles and thread for personnel to effect basic repairs to uniforms and equipment.

[2] This was of course with regard to the expulsion of the Jews from Germany. At that time nobody outside the *Reich* had any idea of the more sinister policies that had already been initiated.

[3] Franz von Werra was held in Ogdensburg on his successful 'home run'. At that time the USA was not in the war and whilst the diplomatic wrangles took place he was able to flee to South America and then home. He was a man of his word because he not only sent the postcard to Mr Benjamin, but also to Squadron Leader Boniface at RAF Hucknal where he had tried to steal a Hurricane when he escaped from Swanwick in England.

CHAPTER TWO

RETURN TO CANADA... BUT WHERE?

On Monday afternoon, 23rd February 1942, it really looked like we were going back to Canada. Our new guard was introduced to us and it was difficult to appreciate the size of this fellow, he was so huge. He had an imposing presence. Casually dressed in a white and green football sweater of his college, his manner was quiet and easy. He took us to the American immigration office where we were asked to take an oath and were then questioned about our families as far back as our grandparents. We were questioned by an officer by the name of Hermann Kull and he behaved as though he could only speak very broken German and was anything but sympathetic towards us. We knew, from Manni Manhart who'd been there before us in January, Kull could speak what had been his mother tongue fluently. Every now and then he would forget his theatrical role and phrases would flow easily and give him away. We didn't give him any opportunity to continue his show and refused to speak anything but English. A friendly secretary who had to take notes of the proceedings for the official record of this 'show' gave each of us a document of expulsion. Quite correctly, she described it as a souvenir of American bureaucracy. Finally we were declared officially expelled from the United States.

Our genial giant now took us to the gangway which led to the ferry which crossed the St Lawrence from Ogdensburg to Prescott; thereby not only crossing the river but also the Canadian - American border. The people waiting for the boat couldn't take their eyes off us, everyone knew we were the escaped German officers and they wanted to take a good look at their first real 'Nazis'. As we went aboard our friendly football player was exchanged for Hermann Kull for our trip back to Canada. We just ignored him and had no reason to speak to him at all. Besides, still being red-blooded young men, our attention was completely taken by a group of young girls who were in a boisterous mood and creating quite a racket. They tried hard to speak to us but Herr Kull kept us completely segregated.

As the ferry docked we could see our reception was an officer of the RCMP and he immediately took us to the Canadian Customs house. Here too everybody seemed to recognise us for who we were and the girls from the ferry became very much bolder and came to our window to flirt. That was at least a happy distraction from the terrible depression which was dragging both of us down. There was no changing the situation and the only thing to do was to brace up and put on our best Monday faces. We watched as the head customs officer, an elderly man with grey hair, enjoyed taking the girls' identity cards and even managed to impose some control on their bubbling energy. In front of our door a noisy but happy atmosphere was prevailing. We could watch and enjoy it but for us there was nothing to celebrate. Our brief period of control over our future had gone and now we would have to wait for what crumbs might fall from the table of fate.

Gradually the hubbub outside died down as the girls left with many a backward glance and inviting look. It was well meant by them but really only helped to drive us further down. It reminded us both of what we were missing, losing so much of our youth behind the wire. The customs man came in and we soon realised he was a well-meaning Irishman who had a job to do. He was refreshingly detached from his job and didn't try to make it a personal crusade or try to score any political points. He just said, "I don't blame you for escaping, I blame those who let you escape." That was his point of view and he even gave us a newspaper article in which we could finally read about how and why we were recaptured. Here, at last, were the real circumstances.

'On Saturday Patrolman John A. Berow got a hot telex which announced two escaped German officers, Waller and Steinhilper, were being searched for. Sunday evening Berow went on his way to start duty at 8.00pm. Stopping to buy something he was approached by two tramps with strong accents who had first asked him and then asked two boys for a highway...'

What bloody bad luck again! For such a long time our comrades in the camp had covered our escape by walking the dummies along during the rollcalls. From Wednesday until Saturday there was no alarm and no search. It looked like they had stopped using the dummies a day too early, whilst we were still in the border area and we'd been caught. We could sympathise with our comrades in the camp as they would have been faced with a difficult decision of when to stop parading the dummies. They knew if we were captured the Canadians would not necessarily announce it immediately, but would be more interested in how our escape had been kept unobserved. That would mean the dummies would be discovered and would be of no further use. We couldn't blame them for blowing our cover on the Saturday.

But what a stupid and heartbreaking coincidence! Why did we have to ask this policeman for the highway to Carthage? Why was it one of the few officers who had seen the telex at that time? It was a bitter irony and a quirk of fate that could easily have driven us crazy. How lucky we'd been to think of this fresh escape trick, painting the fence in the camp. How well our good luck had held whilst we climbed the wire and when we were out, getting the trains so early and finding the right place to jump down. It had even held when we'd been crossing the cracking ice of the St.Lawrence and, finally, finding the correct way on the road, marching three nights through the icy cold and the blizzard. All that ended because we asked that policeman for the highway to Carthage. It was hard to take.

The Irishman looked at our false papers with a magnifying glass. A complete set had been given to him by the Americans: our identity cards, together with our letters of recommendation and references. Answering questions on where we had received such papers I told him the truth, mainly to avoid him jumping to conclusions. Our experts inside the camp were safe, they'd not been discovered or stopped anyway. After examining them with his magnifying glass he came to the conclusion that if they were indeed 'homemade' it was excellent work. Too bad Hannes Kauter, our good man on the drawing board, and Hans Berthel, our expert in painting, could not hear that compliment. With that remark it was no surprise that in the same newspaper we could also read that the American police in Boston were looking for the 1st Officer of the S.S. 'Filey Bird' of the Cunard-Red-Star-Line. They wanted to find out from him how we had got possession of those papers.

Too bad that the reports in these newspapers which came into our hands were very much censored, but this was understandable of course. We really could have learnt more about how our escapes could be improved. All in all, it was surprising to see how difficult it was for the other side to unravel the complex story we had woven. After some time, a police corporal arrived who was going to take us in his patrol car to Brockville. He told us he'd only spent a very short time in this area. Formerly he'd been on duty in a little town where many Germans and Italians were living. During this war he'd had the most disagreeable task of putting so many of these people into internment camps. He also knew of the town of Kitchener which, at the end of the First War, had changed its name from Berlin to Kitchener. He said out of the 35,000 inhabitants of the town almost 30,000 were Germans. There, he said, it could easily happen that one could walk through the streets without anybody speaking a word of English, impossible for him to understand anything.

The effect of his alarm siren on the way was impressive. The driver only had to get the thing going and the road in front of us cleared as though by magic. I told the corporal I'd like a siren just like that to install once I got home. He laughed and we continued our pleasant exchange but soon the ride with our amiable policeman was over and again we were pitched into a new environment. The police in Brockville were rough folks, right away pushing us into cells and slamming the iron doors. My room was in a terrible state, apparently my predecessor had had some kind of mental seizure and must have been incredibly strong. The furniture was no longer useable, even the frame of the iron bed had been twisted and torn apart. In the next cell, there appeared to be a lone prisoner who, about every 15 minutes, sounded-off in horrible curses. He howled and raged for about two minutes and then changed abruptly to singing popular songs. Then, after some repetition, there would suddenly come howling and crying like an animal which had been stabbed. The policemen in the guardroom in the front must have had nerves of steel or they were totally insensitive. They talked quietly amongst themselves and *'didn't even ignore him'* (*a direct translation of a popular, if somewhat "tongue-in-cheek", German saying*).

At the other side of our cell we could look through the keyhole of an adjoining door. There a young boy of, at most, 16 years was in his khaki uniform. Really he didn't look old enough to be a soldier, more like a child that had dressed-up. He began a loud and realistic military drill with his companion in the cell, a civilian with a broom in his hands as an improvised rifle. Amazingly, the young soldier had a voice that reminded us of our *Oberfeldwebel* (sergeant major) when we'd done our basic training and could have commanded a regiment on parade. However, in this environment, his loud voice sounded inappropriate and funny. The young soldier looked clean, whilst his 'trainee' looked really down at heel. His lank hair was hanging across his eyes and his front teeth were missing, probably the result of a fight or falling down drunk; we really were in wonderful company!

Suddenly there was a whispering through the keyhole; it was the boy soldier. "Where are you from?" he asked. I was pleased with the opportunity of a conversation, but only replied, "From Bowmanville." He said he was from Toronto and had been jailed there for overstaying his leave for five days without permission. "The damn police had me without my furlough papers," he said. "Have you anything to smoke?" he asked. I replied we hadn't and added we were German prisoners of war and everything had been taken away from us. That finished things there and then and he withdrew from the keyhole to carry on a hushed conversation with his 'trainee'.

As we did not get anything to eat, we asked for the left-overs of chocolate and figs which should have still been in our bags. That didn't seem to make much impression and certainly nothing was forthcoming, they let us wait until ten o'clock before they opened the cell door. Who should enter now but the Canadian Lieutenant Chin from Bowmanville, accompanied by two sergeants of the Veterans Guard. They were armed to the teeth and their behaviour was really very rough. We could understand their attitude and, no doubt, had we been in their position we wouldn't have been inclined to be very friendly. Certainly we could imagine we were not Bowmanville's most favourite sons! Within three months I had been out three times and secretly the two of us were scared of what might befall us on the way back. How well I remembered the threats made to me by the guards after my second escape. They told me they were fed up with always being ordered out of their beds because of me and having to spend the night searching the countryside. They had made it quite clear to me that if they found me outside the wire, or anywhere near it, they would shoot first and ask questions later. I think we were both justifiably worried whether they would shoot us *while trying to escape'* or whether we might just disappear. We were a real nuisance for them anyway, there was no denying that, but that was part of our duty as officers, not just to escape but to tie down as much as possible of the enemy forces and we'd achieved that handsomely.

Our hope was that the newspapers reporting we'd been captured alive would make it more difficult for us to disappear again. But there still lurked the spectre of a staged escape attempt with the predictably fatal consequences. Certainly they had managed to cover their tracks very well with the shooting of Martin Müller from Camp W at Neys and Alfred Miethling and Herbert Löffelmeier from Camp X at Angler without apparent repercussions. Hinnerk and I spoke openly about these thoughts and resolved we would be very careful and try to react intelligently in any suspicious circumstances.

We didn't know if Lieutenant Chin had been specially chosen for the duty but they couldn't have given the job to anyone more terrifying in appearance. He was huge, about 2 metres high (approx 6ft 8"), and certainly weighing about 120 kilos (approx twenty stones). Without any reason we could see, he continuously brandished his heavy gun in front of our noses. "You see this," he said as he towered above us, "if you try anything, you'll never see Germany again." Part of his demonstrative aggression, we could see in his face, was because he himself was still worried something unpredictable would happen and that made him nervous and a great potential danger to us. After this first tough show he next asked us for our parole for the duration of the journey, to give our word as officers not to attempt to escape. We said he'd already shown us his pistol and told us we wouldn't see Germany again if we misbehaved so we asked why he thought he needed our parole. It obviously wasn't the answer he wanted and quickly gave orders for the rest of his men to draw their pistols.

We began to wonder about their standard of training in weapons. Certainly with our infantry training we wouldn't have been waving obviously loaded weapons about with such apparent abandon. If we'd had to have drawn a gun it would have been in very exceptional circumstances and it would not have been pointed anywhere else but at the floor. It was another aspect with caused us great anxiety. Frequently at the change of guard at the camp stray shots had been fired by the inept handling of loaded and unsecured weapons. There was no doubt they were a real danger to us and, for that matter, to themselves. Our estimate of the situation was, fairly, that there was nothing but murder in their eyes and with this in mind we would have to be always on our guard.

The question of the parole was one which again had become ridiculous. I'd had the same experience with the Captain who led the guards who'd gone to Montreal to collect me after my second escape. He had launched into a great show of aggression and power and then asked me to give my parole. If Lieutenant Chin had just acted reasonably we would have given him our parole and we could all have undertaken the return a little more peaceably and with minimal stress. It just demonstrated that even the military did not appreciate we were not common criminals but officer prisoners of war.

Soon, outside of the police station, two newspaper reporters appeared but Lieutenant Chin was having no truck with them. He bawled at them in a military fashion and they beat a hasty retreat. After dark we got into the old station wagon with which I was now familiar. Nothing was said, no explanation of where we were bound; it looked grim. Lieutenant Chin and the driver sat up front with Hinnerk and myself between them and behind us sat the two sergeants, who were still brandishing their revolvers, even though we had begun the drive. This kept much of the terrible tension high and it came to a head when at about eleven o'clock, without any announcement, we stopped in the middle of a pitch-black forest. As Lieutenant Chin got out Hinnerk and I tried to communicate our anxiety by subtle looks and gestures. Softly I whispered to Hinnerk, *"Höchste Wahrschau!"* (take great care). We didn't want to sell our lives cheaply and we had already agreed that if the end really looked like it was coming we would fight with our bare hands rather than passively submit to summary execution. So charged was the atmosphere that we, ourselves, almost started on the principle 'the best defence is attack', but fortunately we recognised our error before it was too late. It was just a routine *'Pinklepause'* (equivalent to 'taking a leak'). They'd just stopped to relieve themselves. We relaxed as some of the tension evaporated from the situation. It would have been tragic if a fight had got started, no doubt there would have been serious injuries, if not fatalities on both sides. It served to clear the air a bit, with us realising that if our guards had not used an opportunity like this then they were unlikely to be looking for a chance to do away with us secretly.

In spite of the darkness, we could recognise some of the road signs and saw we were driving through Gananoque and, not much later, shortly before arriving at Kingston, we turned off to the left. Now it became clear why when Lieutenant Chin had reverted to rapid slang we had at least caught the name 'Fort Henry'. It was clear we weren't going back to Bowmanville at all, or at least not immediately. How would we possibly be accepted there? Rumour had it Fort Henry was then exclusively populated with civilian internees, not the military. If we were to stay there permanently, what kind of people would civil internees turn out to be? The military structure had little to recommend it for the most part but two advantages were familiarity with the ordered life and discipline. How would we fare amongst civilians? We couldn't speculate and, besides which, we had heard another rumour that a further shipment of German officers had arrived in Canada. Could it be these had displaced the civilians?

Shortly before midnight, we arrived and our question was soon to be answered. We were driven through gateways in the very thick stone walls into the inside of the fortress. After a heavy gate had been closed behind, we were driven into a large inner space which was lit brightly by electric searchlights all around. The grey walls were also brightly lit and, in strange contrast, nice soft white snow flurries were falling from the blackness of the night. Through another gate and we came to the final stop. Immediately a sergeant major started to shout, just like our *Oberfeldwebels* would have - it seems to be their place in the world. First, in a voice that could probably be heard outside the walls, he told Lieutenant Chin where his quarters would be and where he could sleep. Then, without breaking his high volume flow, he shouted to the two Sergeants that he was especially well prepared for us. Mr Foresight, we soon learnt his name, told us right away he had nothing but hatred for Germans and, therefore, he would treat us accordingly.

For the night he took everything away from us only letting us keep the flannel pyjamas which we, fortunately, had pulled on as underwear. He didn't even allow us to eat our own chocolate or dried figs which were still in our kit even though, as we would say, *"Nasenlöcher rauchten"* (literally 'nostrils were smoking' - a reference to vehemently angry protests). We argued that since breakfast with the Border Police, in Ogdensburg, we'd had nothing to eat. Each of us got a blanket and we were left alone in our cells with a wooden bed with no mattress. The guards were expressly told by Mr Foresight to keep the heating to a minimum only - he said it would be good to keep us cool, and then he disappeared. Briefly, in our pyjamas, we were taken to the courtyard to a cold water butt for a wash and from then onward we were freezing through all the night, but we were used to that.

The next morning we were woken by a terribly badly blown bugle. Badly blown as it was it was at least a German reveille and some little comfort as it reached us through the thick iron doors. Out of our small windows in the doors, we could look across the upper level of the fortress, across the handrails on the walkways and into the inner courtyard of the stone fortress. On the walkways and in the courtyard we could see many men with red round spots on their backs and red stripes on the trousers. They were milling around and running back and forth, looking for all the world like a crowded beehive. This turmoil looked almost frightening, they were all running quickly and throwing their arms around their bodies, apparently it was very cold.

"Man Uli!", called Hinnerk through the wall, "look down there at these poor fellows. Apparently they do what they like with the *Zivilinternierten*," (civilian internees). Outside, at a distance of about ten metres in front of the window, a man was passing by on the walkway. So he would see us, we were shouting, *"Wir sind auch Deutsch!"* (We also are Germans). Somewhat surprised, he stopped and tried to look from the outside through the gate at the windows in the cell doors. "Where you come from?" he asked in a heavy Frisian dialect. Hinnerk, himself a native of the same part of Germany, replied immediately in the local dialect and from that moment they couldn't be stopped. I hardly understood a word of their chatter but Hinnerk told me the man hadn't been able to tell much, in any event he was quickly pushed aside by one of the sentries. After this, the sentry came so close to the barred door to our cells that no further conversation was possible. Through the wall, Hinnerk was calling over to me what the man, a sailor, had told him. Really all it told us was that they knew all about us and most of the prisoners there were seamen from steamers.

We couldn't glean much from the guards, either they were stupid or they really were 'in the dark.' News of our presence soon seemed to have spread throughout the camp and prisoners constantly wandered near to the entrance to the cells to be shooed away by the irritable guards. Some way away a group of them gathered, in a reasonably straight line, and threw up the *Nazi* salute for our benefit. Although, in our time, this had not much been used in the military we responded so they'd be sure they knew our nationality.

Having made their point they dispersed and a nice kind young fellow

Camp 31 - The old Fort Henry, Kingston. This served as a German officers camp from July 1940 - 20 November 1941. From then on it was used for non-military internees. Our casement was on the left of the top picture.

appeared. He also wore the distinctive prison overalls and delivered two trays to the guards, our breakfast! The guards brought them through to our cells and we could savour this present from the prisoners. It really was the best breakfast we'd had all through our time as prisoners. Hinnerk and myself were famished and ate it all, even though it was a huge amount. Much later we would learn about the background of this famous kitchen at Fort Henry. In the meantime we were visited by the camp's interpreter and Hinnerk tried to give him a note of thanks to pass on to the other internees, but he'd have none of it.

We didn't manage to make contact with the camp's inhabitants before our transport arrived again at about nine o'clock. Outside the fortress beautiful winter sunshine was shining and the air was wonderfully warm. As we were driven back on the Highway Number 2, from Kingston to Bowmanville, we marvelled at the change in the landscape. Nobody who is used to European conditions would believe that just a few days before such ferocious snow storms had been raging and the going had been so terrible. Then, however,

Another view of Fort Henry taken in 1987. The soldiers are students rehearsing for the annual Historic Military Display.

there had been quite a difference in our situation. We had been on the freight train and, later, on foot. Now, on this most beautiful day, we were being driven along comfortably seated in a warm and windproof station wagon.

Jürgen von Krause probably had been right - it probably would have been better to wait for summer. When I had originally planned the escape I had asked Jürgen to partner me but he had honestly felt the chances of success were reduced by the winter conditions and favoured the summer. Hinnerk and I had chosen to continue in winter because of the possibility of crossing the St Lawrence on the ice. On reflection it had been very hard on us, but we'd almost succeeded. It had just been real bad luck that had defeated us, not the weather. I honestly addressed myself to the case and had to conclude we had just used up too much luck in crossing the fence as painters without being shot. Only in this kind of superstitious way could I make the books balance, as it were.

At around two o'clock, we arrived in Bowmanville. It had been a long journey because they couldn't drive very fast on the icy roads. Inside the camp there was no snow whatsoever. After the heavy snowfalls, it had become really warm and everything thawed quickly. It was almost unbelievable that within a distance of a few hundred kilometres there existed such a difference in weather conditions.

We were immediately taken to the Canadian Commandant who, of course, was unknown to us. Colonel Bull, the original Commandant, had been replaced by the army chiefs in Ottawa because of our escapes and I suppose we felt a little guilty about that. Colonel Bull had been a fair man and it wasn't his fault we'd found our ways out. The new man read out our punishment. We both got four weeks of solitary confinement in the detention block, the maximum allowable under the Convention, and right after this we were searched. First, every item of our clothing and then after this the thorough body search. This was undertaken with a certain vigour and enterprise that could no longer be termed as proper humane treatment.

CHAPTER THREE

QUIET DAYS

The detention barracks were outside the main compound of the camp and, to our surprise, were already occupied by two men, *Oberleutnant* Lüderitz and *Oberleutnant* Siegfried Schmidt. They were in their cells due to the discovery of a tunnel. When thinking back to our escape, whilst painting the fence, we'd just got to the ground outside the wire when we'd had a bad surprise. Two Canadian workers had arrived, right next to us, and were occupied digging around for the end of a tunnel. They had successfully located it in the end and appropriate steps were taken by the Canadians to fill it in. The entrance had been known to the guards for a while but, not wanting to venture into it, they didn't accurately know its extent and it was only by digging outside the fence that it was located.

This tunnel had been considered likely to be the most successful by us. It had been dug outwards from the central air box of the air-conditioning and heating systems in the basement of Building 2, our block. The large steel container was where the tunnel had its entry and had been started. Access to the tunnel within the air box was only possible by rope through a large vertical air duct which was leading up to the first floor dormitory. When entering and leaving there was therefore no danger of discovery and, also, there was no need for the transportation of the soil because the air box was big enough to hold it all; generally speaking ideal conditions.

The only way this tunnel was likely to be discovered was when moving earth. One side of this huge air box formed part of the washroom wall in the cellar of the building. It was only made of thin steel sheet and when transporting the earth into the container there was always some noise within the washroom as the stones and soil grated on the metal. Therefore one of our men, part of the digging team, always had to be in the washroom and his job was to be alert for the Canadians *Frettchen* (little ferrets, as we called them). When there was cause for alarm, a coded knock on the steel ensured the earth movements were stopped. In a way the digging in Building 2 was a bit dangerous because this building was known to be the home of the 'bad boys' and the *Frettchen* singled us out for special attention and frequent searches. They were far from stupid and after a while they naturally became suspicious because there always seemed to be someone shaving or washing their hands. We were clean people, but this was a bit much!

Against all odds it had gone well until the tunnel, by our calculations, was below the fence. It had reached a length of 14 metres and, as our building was close to the fence, that was sufficient. Everything looked good, but then bad luck began to dog progress and things happened quickly. First, our most important radio receiver was discovered. The Canadians, when seeing this technical masterpiece, found it difficult not to show their admiration for our ingenuity. All the parts had been made by hand - except for the valves of course - which we couldn't make. They had been stolen by our mail officer who, for the purpose of censoring and checking of the arriving parcels, had been outside the fence. He had taken the opportunity to steal the valves from a radio and an amplifier out there. Out of cigarette boxes, which were then still made of thin tin sheet, we had fabricated the variable condensers, painstakingly cut with nail files and nail scissors. All the coils had been made from stolen wire and the membranes for the headphones also owed their origin to the multi-facetted tin cigarette box.

This masterpiece was designed by *Luftnachrichtenoffizier* (Luftwaffe communications officer) Anton *'Tönnes'* Noewer, under the supervision of *Oberleutnant* Niehoff. Both of them were designing and calculating as well as building, and overcame the problem of the lack of proper parts by more invention. For instance, the variable resistors were made out of porridge bowls which were filled with salt water. Two large nails were designated plus and minus and put into the salt water. By altering their distance apart the resistance was changed.

'Tönnes' had already built three sets, all of which had been discovered, but again and again he found the strength and commitment, not only to find the raw materials but also to improve each successive design. However, he had to pay for his success and was often the subject of close scrutiny by the Canadians. He was well known for his advance announcement of his arrival, calling out, *"Ich werde verfolscht!"* (I am being followed!) as he was in full flight from the *Frettchen*. We had become accustomed to hearing his warning and then to have him hurtle past, hotly pursued by one or more Canadians. Fortunately on each occasion he had at least been able to deposit the precious valves in safe hands as he ran, and later to build from them again. What these receivers meant to us can only be appreciated by somebody who has been a prisoner himself and so far away from home. The discovery of this, the latest receiver, was because our own *Wächtern* (watchers) had been taken by surprise by a fast spot-search. After that discovery, our building was watched still closer.

The searches inside the camp were intensified when they discovered that all the toilets in Building 4 were unserviceable because they were full of lime. This lime came from a tunnel which had been started in Building 4, but the Canadians were soon convinced that it was coming out of our building and was being transported to No. 4. For them it was clear that inside the camp the Germans were digging. Building 2 was closest to the fence and, not coincidentally, where the 'bad boys' were living. It was proof absolute for the Canadians that we were digging. The process by which their suspicion had been arrived at was faulty but the net result was correct. There was a tunnel creeping out from our building and it was this combination of circumstances which had led to its discovery. Perhaps our dedicated cleanliness had also contributed.

One day, just before Hinnerk and I escaped, several *Frettchen* appeared under the guidance of the famous Staff Sergeant Rule and they began probing the walls in the cellar with iron bars and little apparent regard for potential damage. They eventually hit the sewerage system and the whole cellar was flooded. After four days searching, they discovered the fresh earth inside the air-box and, of course, also the tunnel leading out of it. However, they didn't discover how we were getting into the ducting. Apparently, they could not conceive the idea that we were entering vertically by rope from the first floor.

Initially, the Canadians only had a single guard, including the night, close to the inspection hatch in the cellar ducting which lead into the air-box. They just wanted to prevent anybody getting to the entrance of the tunnel. Schmidt and Lüderitz now tried a desperate last-minute attempt. They entered quietly from the top to find out whether it would be possible to start digging at the end of the tunnel and, in one night, get out to the surface. They got in unobserved and were working for about four hours, but they didn't reach the open. The ground on top of the tunnel was much harder than they'd expected and they had about two and a half metres more to get through to the top.

With such heavy work, some noise was unavoidable. The Canadian guard in the cellar heard it and got reinforcements, a sergeant taking the dangerous job of actually entering the tunnel. Schmidt and Lüderitz were both suddenly flooded by bright light from a powerful torch and there was no other way out but to be taken into detention. When we met them there on our return, they had about another 20 days to serve. As usual, the guard in the detention barracks tried to stop any conversation amongst ourselves, but after a few days they became more tolerant. Hinnerk and I had much to discuss with our fellow would-be escapers. They related to us their very special rendezvous below the ground and we, on our side, could appraise them of what had happened inside the camp after they had been taken out to the detention barracks.

They didn't know the Canadians had tried to open the tunnel outside the fence with dynamite. They tried several times with progressively higher charges, but all they succeeded in doing was blowing all the windows out of the outer face of Building 2, but the tunnel remained intact; no wonder the two tunnellers couldn't break through with their crude tools. It had been at that stage the labourers had been brought in to dig for the tunnel by hand and it was them who gave us such a shock as we alighted on the outside of the fence on our escape.

Of course, they wanted to know from us how we had got out of the camp, but we stayed really cautious. It was almost certain that the Canadians had put some sentries into the guard house who would understand German. This probably had some influence on the apparent relaxation of the *'no talking'* rule between prisoners from cell to cell. When taking our exercise together in a fenced enclosure adjacent to the block we had little chance of being overheard and felt more confident about security but still not completely safe. We wanted to be careful and ensure we didn't give away our *'neue Tour'* (new route) to anyone. We therefore agreed that when we returned to the camp they would be the first to hear the details. We hinted it was something special and they were happy to wait.[1]

The guarding of the detention barracks had been considerably strengthened. Two sentries were posted in the passage in front of the cells and, outside, the detention barrack was now completely surrounded with barbed wire. At night, both in front and behind, sentries were stationed and each night, at around eleven-thirty, the Canadian Adjutant appeared. Using his flashlight to illuminate our faces he would make us say at least one complete sentence to be absolutely certain that we were awake and really present. This behaviour was understandable as it soon became clear the Canadians still had no idea how and when the two of us had left the camp, but that didn't last long as far as they were concerned.

In the evening the alarm siren was going again and, unfortunately for us in the detention barrack, we had no idea what was going on and, of course, the guards wouldn't tell us anything about it. But the next morning, we had the solution. In came *Oberleutnant* Fritz Oeser and *Oberleutnant* Hans Fiebig. They really had performed their escape with courage. After my second escape the barbed wire had been increased by the heap, but still Fritz had patiently cut his way through. When out and right under the eyes of a guard on patrol, he had crossed a well lit roadway. Hans Fiebig had followed, a minor miracle that they both made it; either the guards were half asleep, a little drunk, or a combination of both. They made a clean break but, unfortunately, both had been caught again very soon.

Their goal had been the aerodrome of Oshawa but they had become lost during the night. According to their report, the weather that night had deteriorated terribly. It had rained all night and really heavy rain too. They said it was like someone pouring buckets over them and they were soon soaked to the skin. We could verify this by their appearance when they were brought in - they looked like a pair of half-drowned cats which had been dragged from a muddy ditch. They had separated and Fiebig was recaptured in the early morning near Oshawa. Fritz Oeser, however, had cleverly entered the aerodrome. Unfortunately, he was discovered just as he was about to pull on the overalls of a flying instructor.

Just the fact that they could penetrate the perimeter of a Canadian military airport again caused the Canadian press to ask for better guarding of installations and for the beefing-up of security in respect of the German POWs. Of course, as always, this escape had been known to the smart newspaper reporters who really seemed to have a sixth sense where our activities were concerned. If nothing else this once more illustrated how we were having an effect on the military resources, tying down more men and equipment, just to keep us in camp.

Now we were six in the detention barracks, a small but strong crew. Schmidt and Lüderitz were first to leave and then, because we were then longest serving in the cells, we got the only two tables; a small luxury in the bland detention block. More important, however, was that via Schmidt and Lüderitz we could send the important news inside the camp that the Canadians had not been informed by ourselves how we had got out of the camp or when. We were absolutely certain that they hadn't got a clue!

We could quiz the guards in the detention block from time to time and they told us the Canadian officer on duty on the Saturday, the day before our recapture in Watertown, had been 'busted' in rank. Apparently it was the new CO's opinion that he was responsible as the senior officer on duty and had not properly checked the refuse truck when it left. They were now convinced that this was when and how we'd left. The guards craftily suggested we could now own-up because the punishment on the Canadian side had already been metered out. It wasn't easy for us as officers to see a fellow officer, albeit a Canadian, unjustly punished, but what could we do? Tell them the truth? Tell them we'd climbed over the fences in broad daylight, three days before we were recaptured? The only thing we could do was ask the guards to tell him that we were absolutely certain that his punishment was unjustified; even that was possibly giving too much away.

Fritz Oeser told us in a low voice, almost laughingly, how our dummies

One of our famous Puppkameraden - the dummies who were 'marched' through in our places at roll call.

had been carried, supported below the arms of our colleagues, to five rollcalls. Only after everybody was certain we were far away were they 'withdrawn from the line'. Thus the ruse using the dummies was still completely unknown to the Canadians. Everything else would be recounted later, in detail, by Manni Manhart. We were, of course, really eager to find out the reason why the dummies had been withdrawn because that for us had been our undoing. In the end we didn't have to wait long because the Canadians did us a special favour. Apparently Manni had done something wrong again and he came out to us to the detention barrack. Hinnerk and myself had just had another five days to go when we had a wonderful surprise on a bright and sunny afternoon. Arriving outside the block was Manni in his best uniform.

He was soon marched into his cell and we were eager to chat but found, in contrast to the weather, he was terribly depressed. Apparently, during his absence at morning rollcall, a Canadian *Frettchen* had discovered a sharpened kitchen knife below his bed. This fact was recorded secretly and in the afternoon Manni was asked to see the Commandant, hence the best uniform. For his trouble he was given two weeks detention, even though he explained the knife was legitimately bought by him from the Eaton's catalogue for use as a carving knife. Manni remarked that the Commandant was obviously under pressure and just had to enforce this punishment and he also expressed some misgivings about the five of us being locked up together. Maybe he was just being a bit paranoid, but he wondered if his punishment had not been a means to get all the *'rotten eggs'* in one basket, then arrange something special for them.

Manni was put into the cell directly next to us, at the end of the passage and we could talk very discretely. This way I could get the story of our escape as seen from inside the wire. As a humorous fact he immediately reported that those fence posts chosen by us for painting could still be seen in their bright yellow colour which we'd daubed on in such quantity. Two days after our disappearance, still at that time apparently unknown to the Canadians, an officer and several guards had been seen standing by the posts and expressing their approval of this new aid to security; calling the attention of the guards, as it did, to this high risk spot. Something of an irony in a way!

We might not have got away completely, but we had apparently lifted morale in the camp by giving many of our colleagues something to laugh at every time they saw those big yellow bands around the posts. It certainly helped to lift us a little to hear of the amusement which had followed our escape, but the reality was that we were just back where we'd started after all that nerve-racking effort. Some measure of that tension which we had endured could be read into Manni's recalling what they saw of the escape. Everyone of our room had been so involved in the planning and execution of our escape that they were right there with us in spirit. Every pitch of the ladders, every move of the guards, caused terrible tension in those watching. In the end the strain had been too much and Manni said nobody could watch for long periods of time. Fortunately he had remembered the part he was to play if we were caught and held himself in readiness to make a dash for our packs if we lobbed them over the fence back into the compound. In these were our most valuable escape items including the false papers.

When the whole escape took so long, something like an hour under the close scrutiny of the guards, some of our colleagues had risked glances out of the window to see us still just a bit further on. Apparently the tension had been truly diabolical with some of our friends beginning to twitch uncontrollably and when the young Canadian guard approached us the atmosphere apparently nearly boiled over. Some, like Manni, were ready to dive out of the building and intervene there and then, but managed to control themselves. This wasn't helped by many of our comrades who didn't actually know of the attempt, but who saw us and recognised us whilst they were walking their 'rounds'. They had immediately diverted to our room to ask if we were mad! To cut a long story short, all the camp had started breathing easier when we were walking away on the other side. For them, as well as us, the immediate aftermath had had something of a dream quality about it. Nobody could really believe it had happened, even though so many had watched. Only a short time before they had been with us inside the room and now they watched us as, in broad daylight, we walked up the hill, through the meadow and then off out of sight in the apple trees.

Once clean away our good comrade Fehske became busy assembling the dummies for the first rollcall. Here our advanced planning began to pay handsomely: the folding frame on which the dummy heads were mounted allowed for them to be easily demounted and hidden. The 'handlers' had practised and become accomplished at marching with our substitutes, easily supporting the light frame and clothing under the arms. The dummies had proved to be good comrades to us, even in broad daylight, and didn't raise any suspicion. What had hastened their decision to stop using the dummies, explained Manni, was the persistence of first my own *Leibwächter*[2] and then the interest of Staff Sergeant Rule.

On Thursday, the day after I had escaped, my *Leibwächter* had appeared in our room to ask for me. Excuses had been made but nobody was wholly satisfied he was completely taken in. Then on Friday, Staff Sergeant Rule had asked Manni where I was and instructed him to tell me to report to the guardhouse to receive the wristwatch they had taken away from me in Montreal. When Manni himself tried to get it instead of myself they wouldn't let him have it. Then, in the afternoon, my body guard had appeared again, leaving instructions that I should finally come and get my watch. This time they said to him that I was at a birthday coffee party. He, apparently only half-jokingly, had asked if I had not escaped again.

Manni told that they thought all of this had been a trap. They had wondered if we had already been captured and now they wanted to discover how they were being duped at rollcall. The other logic they applied was that if we hadn't been captured by Saturday, then, looking at my travelling speed on former escapes, they felt almost certain we were well away from the border zone and, relatively speaking, out of immediate danger. Because the dummies and indeed the escape had worked so well they did not want to run the risk of compromising either for future use. Under the circumstances they made the best decision they could based on the information available at the time, but once Manni knew the consequences of that decision he felt very bad. The only consolation was that we were sure the Canadians had no idea how we'd escaped or that we had already been out three days before Saturday, the day they assumed we had got out in the refuse truck. It meant that *der Steinhilpersche Leitertrick* (Steinhilper's ladder trick) and the ruse with the dummies could be used again.

This not insignificant fact was mentioned by Manni when he told me that *Oberstleutnant* Gruber had ascribed a kind of copyright to me as the inventor and wanted to preserve this method of escape for future use. Even though some other pairs had asked permission already as to whether they too could try the painting escape they had been refused. I remembered my promise that if we were successful Reini Pfundtner was, in my opinion, first in the queue. I had promised that as a reward for his daring assistance in the Canadian Sergeant's uniform. I'd told him he would be next should we escape unscathed. I honestly felt we'd had our chance and luck or fate, call it what you will, had not continued to smile upon us. Perhaps someone else would have a better chance.

I, for my part, was totally fed up. The sequence of preparation, escaping and the gruelling test on the road outside only to return to the detention barracks had taken its toll. *Ich hat die Nase voll* (I'd had a nose full!) I was fed up and becoming depressed. However, a light was showing at the end of the tunnel - it would only be another five more days before we were released from detention. Then I would have access to all the facts and have the benefit of good council with my friends uninhibited by 'walls with ears'. I resolved it would be best to clarify things then.

Those last few days of the four weeks in detention passed so slowly, we could hardly stand the boredom. We were really longing for the return to normal, as much as moving from one form of confinement to another is normality. Only the man who has been in solitary detention can imagine how slowly time passes. Our day for release was a Sunday. Hinnerk had reached that conclusion by logging the days since our arrest. Our orderlies, who brought our meals from the camp kitchen, were sometimes able to carry messages and in this way we managed to pass one a slip which announced our imminent return.

On Saturday morning, as every morning, we waited for our morning exercise. It was only in the small high-fenced enclosure next to the detention block, but at least it was a small change from the four bare walls of our cells. Time wore on and the guards suddenly announced we would have to wait for a while. Apparently a Canadian General was to inspect us and our cells. This was not the first time and so we weren't too impressed, we just sat and waited. But the guards were not satisfied with that. They came with our better uniforms, which were kept in a special room, and asked us to put them on. They said they were sure we also wanted to appear nicely dressed when the General showed up. We became more interested; in earlier inspections from other high ranking officers we had been inspected in our training suit and plimsolls; so why the sudden interest in our sprucing ourselves up?

We duly changed and when ready we discovered this was another ruse. At ten o'clock the Canadian duty officer appeared and announced that we should get ready to be moved immediately. They told us all our property inside the camp had been packed and we should take from the cells only the clothing we weren't wearing. The books that belonged to the camp's library should be left. As our comrades had not been allowed to send much out to us, the few pieces were packed quickly and our journey could begin. In the short time before our actual departure it dawned upon us that we were another case like Manni. They had begun to realise that to get us away from the main body of the camp made things easier. Here, outside the fence, we were firmly in their hands and they could take any steps they liked without our camp leadership or our comrades coming to our assistance. So Manni had been right to be suspicious about his punishment after all. It had just been a means to get him out of the camp and in detention with us. All their 'rotten eggs' in one basket!

I soon finished my packing. My pyjamas, toilet articles and a few things to write with were all I had and I put these in my pillow slip. With this package under my arm and dressed in a good uniforms Hinnerk, Manni, Fritz Oeser, Fiebig and I left the detention barracks, eager to learn what was going to happen to us from now on. First, under very heavy guard, we were taken to the Commandant, again a new face behind the desk; the latest escape had probably caused the change. The new officer spoke to us coldly, "HQ Internment Operations in Ottawa have decided to take all five of you into a special camp as it is apparent that you do not appreciate the advantages of this camp and only misuse them to escape continually," he told us. Manni exploded angrily, shouting at him, "So now that's the real reason why you put me into detention!" It was quite understandable why he got so mad. First, he'd been falsely accused and punished, and now we were all to be relocated. Together, we now wanted to know where they were taking us.

By then we knew some of the Geneva Convention by heart and, accordingly, we argued we had the right, before being moved, to be told what the new destination would be. To our surprise we were answered quickly. Camp 31, Fort Henry. With that we were marched out and found the cars, including our luggage from inside the camp, well prepared and waiting outside the camp. We only had to step in and we would be on our way, reducing the chance of us making trouble to a minimum; we had to admire their planning. We naturally kicked up a fuss, cursing and protesting strongly and loudly, however, without any success.

Hinnerk and I had some memories about this Fort Henry and we knew what was coming. Some of our other comrades, officers who had formally been held there[3], had some 'rosy' descriptions of these isolated old walls. With what we knew from our first-hand experience we had some idea what was waiting for us. That this forbidding fortress was a great historical building for Canada wasn't much consolation. However, one thing did hold some curiosity for us, we were eager to learn whether the civilian internees would still be there or whether, in the meanwhile, the rumoured new transport of German officers had arrived from England.

Notes on Chapter Three

[1] When we did finally tell them the story upon our release they agreed that given the audacity of the escape and how relatively well things had gone outside we were damned unlucky to have been picked up.

[2] *Leibwächter* - Literally 'life watcher' - bodyguard. Because I had escaped twice I was singled out for special attention. I had Canadian 'ferrets' whose job it was to watch me and stay close all day. They were therefore nick-named my 'body guards'.

[3] Fort Henry was originally used to hold some of the officer prisoners whilst our group was away at the end of the world in Camp W Neys. They were transferred to Bowmanville at the same time as us.

CHAPTER FOUR

BACK AND FORTH TO FORT HENRY

Like dangerous criminals, the five of us were transported in a completely enclosed ambulance. Outside, the red cross on white background could be clearly seen. Behind us followed a staff car which was occupied by six men of the Veteran Guard, who were provided with machine guns, pistols and plenty of ammunition. Ahead of us was a Provincial Police car with two police officers, provided to speed us on our way with their siren in case of a traffic hold up. No doubt they were wary of the intervention of that marvellous figment of their imagination, 'The 5th Column' - now famous from newspaper articles. Next to our driver sat yet another guard with a machine pistol which we could see very well because he was between us and the only window - the windscreen. Bringing up the rear was a small truck with all of our luggage and the commanding officer of this little convoy seated beside his driver.

We thought the most desperate robbers could not have been guarded so closely. For five POWs, they used three drivers, one officer, two policeman and nine men as guards. On top of this, the ambulance served to help cover the identity of the convoy. They were really worried about the press reports about the 5th Column. On the way, not even a stop for a *'Pinklepause'* was approved for us. The guards did get one chance, but we had to sit and wait. Oeser eventually had such acute pains in the bladder he had to urinate on to the floor of the car, so intransigent were our keepers. Of course, he felt terribly sorry having to do that in front of us, but there had been no alternative. The whole scene seemed to us to be absolutely ridiculous. Our guards were behaving just as if they were moving the Emperor of China incognito. When driving through the city of Kingston we used only side roads because they were scared that we could get into a traffic jam on the busy main road.

It was three o'clock in the afternoon when we entered through the various doors and gates of the fortress. For Hinnerk and me that was the same as before, but this time we were taken to the ante-room of the cells without so much as a pause. The civil internees were looking at us with much surprise and astonishment. They were still dressed with the red points on their jackets and stripes down the trousers and were amused to see us in our officers' uniforms. We were greeted with a loud "Hello!", but that's where it had to stop for the time being. We would have no immediate opportunity to learn about each other or our new environment. After just a few steps, the door of the detention area was closed behind us and we were allocated our cells. It became clear we had to sit out the rest of our detention time there.

Hinnerk and I had only one more day to go and we really were looking forward to what would probably be the most interesting relationship with the civilian internees. We hoped very much that we would not be segregated from them when we were released. In the meantime, the conditions of the detention were, in our estimation, contrary to the Geneva Convention; the cells we occupied were the dark punishment cells of the former fortress. However, we were determined we wouldn't let our spirit be broken or morale decline and immediately saw a task for ourselves: to inspire these internees with our own courage and give them the right conditions and stability in their detention.

Whilst still in the cells we were visited by Mr Freudenthal, who had established himself as the *'Arbeitsminister'* (Minister of Labour) for the camp. He was clever and very astute, quickly telling us all we needed to know. Two of us would be getting out the next day and the camp was well prepared for us. He told us, however, that at that moment there were great difficulties with the so-called immigrants inside the camp. He left us to our thoughts with the new word *'Emigranten'* (immigrants), and we had to imagine what kind of people we would be with. Certainly we were a little apprehensive about the new situation - in the officers' camps we had never met anything like this.

In order now to describe things as accurately as possible I will quote verbatim from a report which I wrote at the time and which was amongst the papers which survived my time as a POW in Canada.

REPORT

The civilian internees are mainly men of the German *Handelsmarine* (merchant navy), the majority being ordinary seamen. Others were *Auslandsdeutschen*, ex-patriot Germans living in foreign countries, for instance, from South Africa, South America and England. From their reports, we can ascertain that most of the seamen were on ships

Note: As this is a direct translation of the actual report which was written in the spring of 1942 it will be found that it is written more in the recent past than distant past. It was one of the original documents which came back to me in 1953.

which, during the autumn of 1939, had tried to break through back to Germany. Their steamers were caught near Ireland, off of the African coast or near to Norway. All men had originally been in British camps. After the Norwegian campaign, these camps got new additions from those sailors whose ships had been sunk during the campaign. Into the same camps, however, were brought German citizens who had been living in England and working there. Most of them had been interned from March to May 1940, because of the danger of espionage or sabotage which had been felt to be increasing by the British.

Amongst these internees also were many former German Jews and other people who had fled the *Reich*. Of course, this cocktail of people from very different backgrounds had been the cause of many internal difficulties in the British camps. Those difficulties mainly stem from economic imbalances and varying levels of previous social status. This manifested itself most in the canteens and the sick-bay area which haven't been too well controlled by the British guards and some terrible fights, even fist-fights, had erupted within those camps.

During the autumn of 1940, most of the internees in England were, like us, transferred to Canada. The first transport was brought together with the officers who later went to Fort Henry. The second transport consisted of two steamers one of which, the 'Andorra Star', was torpedoed. The survivors of this ship were returned to England and later, when they were ready again for transportation, were shipped to Australia. Those who arrived in Canada finally reached Camp Red Rock at Nipigon Bay. There, initially, the conditions must have been unbelievable. Amongst other things, these people were locked in their huts; they had to lie on the floor and did not even receive enough blankets to provide one per man. The oldest internee was Pastor Wehrhan from London, who was over 70; the youngest inmates were ship boys of hardly 14 years.

Conditions in this camp improved only slowly, basically according to the largesse of the Canadian Commanding Officer. The German camp leadership originally rested in the hands of *Kapitän* Scharf who, before the war, was with Lloyds as Captain of the Bremen. In the Norwegian campaign he had been captured with the supply ship 'Alster' on the way to Narvik.

Camp Red Rock had about one thousand inhabitants, German Jews, the immigrants, German citizens from England, German citizens from all over the world and the seamen in a colourful but explosive mixture. There were several fights, mainly because of the differing opinions about working conditions and how to facilitate the Canadians. Most of the problems had yet to be overcome and were still the basis for these brawls continuing. These conditions are not to be compared at all with military POW camps, where such difficulties do not occur because discipline is still maintained and there is also the military structure to solve and prevent such situations.

In this camp (Red Rock) an 'encouraging' notice from the Canadian Commandant had asked the inmates to participate in work, it was even said that this was based on remarks from the Swiss representative. It almost, apparently, led to a riot. According to this paper on the notice board, German officers were already voluntarily working by building canals and highways in Canada. However, the truth was known, even within that civilian internees camp. They knew we couldn't leave the camps because nobody wanted us to meet the Canadian civilian population. Now, after we had arrived at Fort Henry, we confirmed this. Just about everything we heard about Camp Red Rock was discouraging.

In September 1941 they were reorganised, with part of the complement, together with those immigrants who were not to be paroled, transferred to a camp named 'Q'. A few of the Jewish inmates and reliable immigrants were put into a refugee camp by the Canadians. This camp served as a holding area and rumours are circulating that some of these refugees were returned, in groups, to England to assist in the repair and reconditioning work in the destroyed English cities. *Lagerleiter* (camp leader) Scharf stayed at Red Rock with about six-hundred men.

Three-hundred and fifty internees, including about thirty-five remaining immigrants, were sent to Q. First they considered themselves of kind of an experimental group, but soon they enjoyed a German camp leadership with a clear line. Initially, the thirty-five immigrants were able to stay separate. They established their demarcation line by signing a declaration that they would give up any protection of the German *Reich* and, at the same time, declared they were available to work for the British. The new camp elected a Mr Witt as *Lagerleiter*. He had, apparently, been a reserve officer and also belongs to the SS. He established absolute authority and acted accordingly. From the beginning, the Canadians gave him orders to develop the camp to become a large POW camp. However, Witt insisted, according to the Geneva Convention, they should be paid for that and they asked for better conditions. It took a long time to convince the Canadians and all sorts of bully-boy tactics were applied meanwhile, including *Tabaksperre* (a ban on tobacco rations). But these men followed Witt's advice for two months and, in the end, the Canadian Commander was exchanged; the demands were accepted, and then the camp was developed and properly equipped. In the middle of November 1941 it was ready to accept POW soldiers. When those arrived, mainly submarine crews and flying personnel, the civil internees were regrouped and moved. Apparently Witt, together with about seven-hundred men, is staying in our former Camp W at Neys.

Mr Mayer, now camp leader of Fort Henry, was moved there on November 23rd 1941 with about three-hundred people, including the thirty-five immigrants. By profession, he is First Steward and he was democratically elected as leader in spite of there being six captains of commercial steamers in the camp. *Lagerleiter* Mayer has not accepted an easy task, but so far he is judged a good leader. Originally, he had myriad difficulties - for instance: inspection of the accommodation was terribly depressing, really just bare *Kasematten* (casemates[1]). They also felt as if they had been deserted by their former camp leader and, to complete the negative outlook, the news on the war was disappointing, especially from Russia. Everything conspired to disappoint this odd group of very mixed people. They were a really forlorn crowd with little hope for improvement. Initially, they didn't even care to do their own cooking and no initiative came from the group to improve their bad situation. The immigrants especially, now since the Russian offensive came to a stand-still, thought it was the end and apparently did everything to increase the depression. Mayer had no other choice but to try to discourage such discussions. That only changed markedly after Japan had entered the War and came in with their initial successes.

Slowly, very slowly, he was successful in waking up the forlorn heap. He started giving courses/lessons, the Boxing Club Condor was revived and the kitchen came under the direction of a former passenger steamer chief cook, who, by the way, later told us that he had cooked for Hitler himself on the *Aviso Grille*.

However, when Waller and myself were able to leave detention, our first impression about the spirit in the camp was excellent. We didn't feel anything more from these bad beginnings. In order to get ourselves fitted well into the camp, we met with Mr Mayer right away, although our three comrades still had to sit it out, grumbling in detention. We mentioned to him that we had to protest to the Canadian authorities about this transportation and imprisonment of POW officers into a civilian internment camp. We explained we had to do that, a matter of principle, even though our personal feelings were much different. We asked him to explain that to his people when they heard about our protests.

We would, in fact, be rather looking forward to meeting new people and experiencing the conditions under which they were held. He understood the situation and asked us to include in our written protest comment that being locked up together with the immigrants was dishonourable. Perhaps, in that way, he suggested, it would be in the interest of the camp to expel those alien elements. Naturally we immediately included his suggestion in our deposition which the five of us had begun to prepare in detention. With that we began to know each other better and to lay down some 'ground-rules'. In our estimation Mr Mayer was glad to have us inside the camp. He was certain that our presence in the camp would help lift morale even further.

The first days absolutely flew by, we were hardly conscious of the passage of time. The inmates of the camp were very respectful to us as German officers and never before had we been in a position to understand what a uniform could mean. These people, alone and feeling forlorn for years, suddenly saw our uniforms and had some tangible contact and bond with their home country again. We became very much aware of this responsibility and did almost everything and anything possible to repay their kindliness without forgetting, of course, our comrades still sitting in detention. During our time we were involved in two evening boxing championships, one variety show and we, for our part, contributed two piano evenings of popular music and two lectures on our war experiences.

One copy of our Bowmanville Camp weekly newspaper gave them the initiative to start a monthly periodical for Fort Henry and, given their resources, they did an excellent job. Naturally in a civilian internment camp, with its rather indiscriminate mix of people, there are many talents for a project like that. Daily, the German *Wehrmachtsbericht* (military report) was prepared by translation from the Canadian press and read to the crowd at lunch time. They did not have any home made radio for further news and therefore had to rely on the Canadian press.

On the Saturday when we had been taken into the fortress the internees gave the *'Emigranten'* a very bad time. They really wanted to get rid of them by all and any means, even some which appeared to be illegal. But all that developed was that these people, already discriminated against inside the camp, had to be guarded by the Canadians. Two sentries were placed in front of their *Kasematten* and when they were going to the wash-room, to meals or to movies, they were escorted by six khaki-clad soldiers.

The spiritual leader of this very mixed group was a Professor Putzi Hanfstaengl, of whom we had never heard. However, we were told by the inmates and also later by the Canadians that he had formally been famous as Hitler's favourite pianist. He had got into trouble with Hitler and therefore emigrated.

The immigrant group consisted of some *Hilfsmarine* personnel, German citizens who'd been living elsewhere in the British Empire, variety artists and even a seventeen-year-old exchange student who had been abroad at the outbreak of war. According to what was told to us, there was often a change in outlook and politics within the group and sometimes an expressed desire to change sides. However, the Canadians would not agree to that. For them, the conditions to which the immigrants had formerly given signature in Camp Q was the right line. When we appeared in the camp, they also wanted to make contact with us. But, knowing about the existing *'Hick Hack'*, we declined so as not to increase it by our involvement.

Our own living quarters were most comfortable. They had prepared a specially good *Kasematte* for Waller and myself, even a little wash-room and a small dining-room had been designated for ourselves. I have to make a special report on this because in Bowmanville, of course, there are the former officer inmates of Fort Henry who would not have experienced this degree of comfort. There was no comparison for us with the conditions that must have formerly prevailed when they had first arrived from Gravenhurst.

When comparing our conditions with those of the other inmates we felt a little guilty about our soft treatment. They had even decorated our little dining-room and our *Kasematte* very nicely. However, soon we also saw this effort bore fruit for the inmates themselves as they recognised that with some collective effort they could improve their own conditions. Soon they repainted their own large dining room with materials provided by the Canadians, also adding some pictures and covering all the tables with bright waxed paper and even curtaining the windows. This continued and extended as more paint and materials were supplied and the individual *Kasematten* were repainted inside.

Spring began and the warm sun improved the morale inside the camp even more. Even *Lagerleiter* Mayer celebrated with us and we smiled as we, and they, enjoyed this new and much improved situation. The sportsmen inside the camp did not need to be encouraged to do better, the meals had become excellent and the improved physical condition almost begged for increased physical exercise (no easy feat inside a fortress). The kitchen continued to better itself by leaps and bounds under the guidance of the specialists of the passenger steamers. They even began to produce good German sausages, under the supervision of a butcher from Ulm. The last essential operation, the smoking of the finished sausages, was done in an old wooden barrel.

Towards the end of our time at Fort Henry two transports delivered about another thirty men from England. They came mostly from one boat that had been captured whilst returning from Japan in July. The others were crewmen of the supply ships of the battleship Bismarck. Altogether they were in good spirit and brought some freshness to the camp. However, some of them seemed somewhat undernourished and they maintained this was due to England suffering the effects of the submarine blockade. For our part that was at least encouraging news.

Gradually, things continued to improve within the camp and the facilities got better. The Commandant announced that a large meadow outside the Fort was soon to become available to the inmates, initially as an addition to the daily exercise walk. If successful he promised for the future that this meadow would be for the internees for the complete day. They would only have to return to the Fort for their meals. Everything, of course, would be voluntary. We thought this would be a good idea and would be a wonderful aid to help improve everyone's health. Things were really looking up, hand-ball, boxing and chess tournaments as well as a good programme of lectures were in full swing when we were told we had to leave. As the only piano player in this camp (apart from Putzi Hanfstaengl who was ostracised in the immigrant group), I had been able to add to the musical entertainments. However, this would have to stop.

We were notified of our imminent departure with very little warning; we were ordered to be ready to depart within one hour. As

47

we packed we felt we were being taken away from a valuable and rewarding task. But there was no argument, we had to leave the camp. We left to hearty cheers from the inmates and our closing impression was that we'd helped in some small measure to give those lost people a new confidence and an identity. Perhaps this in itself was the most important reason why we were taken out of the community. We don't think we were removed and returned here to Bowmanville because our protest was successful. More likely, we think, that the new and increasing self-confidence within the camp was an effect the Canadians had not foreseen. However, we would enjoy the chance to be able to repeat such an exchange of thinking with the internees again.

That is now the end of this report.

Notes On Chapter 4

[1] Casemate - An armoured compartment in a ship or fortification in which guns were mounted.

CHAPTER FIVE

FORT HENRY AND THE CIVILIAN INTERNEES

After his last nine days of detention, Manni was released and moved into our *Kasematte*. There was plenty of space for that, but he didn't stay long. *Oberleutnants* Fiebig and Oeser had, during their time in detention, been informed that they had been promoted to *Hauptmann* (Captain)[1], but they were not to be released back into the camp. We were just preparing for the celebration of their promotion and release from detention, when Manhart, Fiebig and Oeser got their *Verlegungsbefehl* (travel orders) for Bowmanville. They had to pack and within two hours they were on their way.

Now there were only the two of us with the internees and with no idea how long it would be before we too were returned to Bowmanville. As Manni was collecting his few belongings I took the opportunity to ask him to officially inform *Oberstleutnant* Gruber, in Camp Bowmanville, that I did not want to hold any 'patent' on the so-called *Steinhilperscher Leitertrick*. I said that whoever would like to try could do it with my blessing and with all my best wishes.[2] It wasn't long after they got back to Bowmanville and delivered my message that someone did.

One day another camp inmate, stevedore by trade, came to us in our *Kasematte* with a Canadian newspaper in his hands. The Canadian censor had not been too careful and now he could show us some photographs of his uncle who lived in Detroit. He was very proud of the pictures, but what was of great interest to us was that we could read that another two *Luftwaffe* officers had escaped from Bowmanville: *Leutnant* Peter Krug and *Leutnant* Erich Boehle. Boehle had already been recaptured in the railroad freight yard in Toronto, whilst Krug had apparently separated from him and had reached Detroit. There he had cautiously approached Mr Stephan, a German restaurant owner who, during World War I, had been an *Unteroffizier* (Sergeant) in the German army. Stephan, to his cost, had agreed to help Peter and the police or FBI had got wind of this and searched Stephan's restaurant and home and, later, arrested him. Peter Krug, in the meantime, was already on his way on a bus with the money he'd been given.

Mr Stephan was well known by name in the internment and POW camps because of his generous sending of comfort parcels. It may have been in this way that Peter Krug had obtained his address. We were sure that Peter was going to make it back to Germany and that we could look forward to hearing of another successful 'home run'. The paper recorded that not only had Mr Stephan helped Peter Krug but now, whilst in detention, he refused to divulge any information to the police. We thought our inmate was justifiably proud of what his uncle had done, but I don't think any of us foresaw the outcome of the case. Unfortunately, we could not follow it or Peter's progress because the Canadian interpreter, who acted as censor, became more meticulous and cut the reports from the papers. However, this is not the end of this sad story and I will come back to it later.

Before continuing with our story I feel I must mention some of the people with whom we were interned in Fort Henry. To just call them *'The Civilian Internees'* would paint them all too grey and uninteresting, when in truth they were a wonderful collection of different characters, each with their own complicated story. There would just be no end if I tried to recall them all and, perhaps, these few represent a cross section of the colourful mixture. When reading what follows, one can perhaps understand why our time in Fort Henry was, for us, remembered as a time of recreation:

There was our *Arbeitsminister*, Mr Freudenthal. He was one of the few who had been in service amongst the younger people. Before his internment, he had served in the *Luftwaffe* and had become an *Obergefreiter* and a *Bordmechaniker* (flight engineer). After that, he had been ship's engineer. Given his past *Luftwaffe* service, he thought he had a special right and responsibility to be our protector. On the first Sunday, when still in detention, he delivered a most wonderful tray with strawberries and cream, and excellent coffee. Of course, this did not become a daily event, however, on this point, I would like to make one specific remark: We could genuinely complain about many things to do with the internment operations in Canada but, in our estimations, the food during the war was always excellent!

Then, I would like to mention Dr. Lachmann. During the First World War he was a German officer & pilot. For some years before his internment he had been an aircraft construction engineer working in England. Work prospects were better in England because of the early embargo on aircraft development and construction in Germany. Although he had been designing British war planes he said he'd never thought there could be a conflict between England and Germany.

Amongst other interesting things he had apparently designed and patented were the *'Lachmannsche Spaltflügel'* (Lachmann's leading edge slats), which Hinnerk and I knew well from the wings of the Me 108 and, later the 109. They were sections of the leading edge of the wings which came out at low speeds, for instance on landing or close to stalling, to change the angle of incidence of the leading edge and create more lift. For us it was most interesting to hear that he also had been working on the early designs of the Spitfire for Supermarine. He had also, he claimed, designed the four-gun hydraulic turrets which were to be installed in the British bombers. For his trouble he had been accused of espionage and interned.

He was a really interesting man to talk to but, unfortunately, soon after we came into the camp, he left. He had been lucky enough to become one of those to be sent back to a camp in England. When it was known that this was at his own request, the other inmates ostracised him until he left. However, we understood why he'd made the choice, he had a wife and children in England and he promised us that for the duration of the War he wouldn't work in the British arms or aircraft industry.

Another most interesting, worldly wise and much travelled personality was *'Schmuggler'* (smuggler). He came from Frankfurt am Main and, before the war, he had been smuggling alcohol and cigarettes between the USA and Canada in his own seaplane. But he had been caught and, at the end of his detention on remand, he had been sent to this camp of internees. He pretended that his imprisonment as an internee was, for the Government, a way of avoiding a long legal action by him. He had also tried to escape twice but had been unlucky, even though his goal, the USA, was much closer than ours. He said he still had good contacts in the USA, but it would be necessary to have plenty of cash to live well. He claimed that if he could put enough money together to make it worthwhile escaping he would simply bring pressure to bear, in the form of blackmail, on one of the officers amongst the present guard. He apparently knew his father from his former smuggling activities. The father had been a 'middle man' in Canada and had gone on to become a full Lieutenant-Colonel in Ottawa. *'Schmuggler'* had few doubts that neither the father nor the son would want the past associations brought to the fore.

We and our exploits must have impressed *'Schmuggler'* because, with great pride, he gave us the benefit of some of his experience and a few hints. In the main he was able to tell us which railroads were the best for making good time and distance. Even though Hinnerk and myself were still fed up and hardly planning another escape, we never knew for whom such information could and should become useful. So we listened carefully and took note.

There was the top apparatus gymnast, Sepp, a complete barbarian, who told us how he once he took a monkey home from his travels at sea. Here I have to comment that *'Affen'*(monkey) has a duel meaning in German - it can also be a reference to being really drunk. So it wasn't too unusual to hear an ex-sailor say he went home 'with a monkey' but there are no doubts that in this case it really was an animal which he had bought in Caracas. The animal occupied his father so much in the home that he didn't have time to go to church any more. "So," asked Sepp, "was that a useful present or what?"

Oder Luz was an older man who could only walk with a stick. He had already lived in England forty years and, according to him, he had been involved in the formation of British internment policy and had been actively fighting against Winston Churchill. Exile in interment was his reward.

The brothers Scheuerle, three of them, were almost indispensable for the upkeep and maintenance of the camp. They had been proprietors of a goldsmith firm in Edinburgh and came, originally, from Pforzheim, a town famous for goldsmiths in Germany. Although they had lived and worked away from Germany for a long time they still felt like *Wurttembergers*[3]. The oldest brother had become the camp carpenter. The middle one was a very talented artist, supplying many drawings and watercolours for the common rooms and for his friends. And the youngest, our age, was giving us lessons in English. Otherwise he was working at the only camp typewriter. Because of his bilingual ability he was responsible for camp correspondence and preparation of the newsheet. We had a very agreeable relationship with the three, spending many hours with them. They gave us a lot of information about the living conditions in England.

Of course there were also aspects of the camp and people which were not so pleasant. One man was known as 'King Kong' and had been Captain of a merchant ship. The story was that during the American prohibition he had been smuggling alcohol, camouflaged as normal freight, into New York. It was said he had, thereby, earned quite a substantial fortune. The story also went around that one day he surrendered his ship to get the monetary reward from the government. The rest of his crew had, apparently, been put into close detention. We could not verify the story but apparently there were enough who believed it and he was completely ostracised in the camp.

Another story which was, I thought, rather sad was that of an elderly man from the countryside around Darmstadt. In his Hessian dialect he very calmly told us his story. "*Ja, Herr Oberleutnant,*" he said, "I don't care, *I have my sheep safely and in the dry*[5]. Should we lose the War, I have a very fine big hotel in Edinburgh. If the British should lose, I will return to Darmstadt where I am the proprietor of a most beautiful farm." 'Well, what kind of morals are those,' we thought. We couldn't understand someone who was so completely and unashamedly mercenary. It didn't make us mad at him, rather more we pitied him.

A really special personality in our camp was old Pastor Wehrhan who, as I have mentioned, was more than seventy-years-old. Formerly, he had served as Pastor in St Petersburg, in Italy and, before his internment, he had been preaching in London. His wife and two daughters had been kept in a camp in England. One daughter was in separate internment, but three of his sons were soldiers, fighting on the Eastern Front. With all his will power he was trying to hold back the effects of ageing and would hear of nothing other than that we should soon win the war so he could be reunited with his family. In the meantime he was a great character who gave comfort to many.

Last, but by no means least, I should mention *'unser Kurt'* (our Kurt). He had been a stoker on a steamer and had, voluntarily, reported to us offering his services as our *Bursche* (batman). That didn't mean a cleaner in the prison, but one who attends to the uniforms and equipment of his officer. Initially, we weren't comfortable with the idea at all. It was unnatural to have a man who was older than us providing a service and we tried to do most things for ourselves. Kurt found this upsetting and once, when catching me mending my own socks, became very disconsolate. Standing formally in front of me he asked, "*Herr Oberleutnant*, don't you trust me?" I looked at him in surprise, he really meant it honestly and seriously. "Why?" I asked. "Because you're mending your socks yourself. Certainly I can do that just as well, even when not having been in service. You can rely on that!" was his sincere reply. That's the way he was. We were not supposed to touch anything or work with our own fingers. Our clothing, and especially our *Kasematte*, were kept in impeccable order by *'unser Kurt'* and not left less than completely tidy as we, left to our own devices, might have done from time to time. With that service, he made our time at Fort Henry something of a vacation.

Like most of the sailors, he had seen quite a bit of the world. He originally came from Berlin and had married in Hamburg. "If I wanted to," he once told us, "I could buy myself a coffee farm in Africa. I know very well how to treat the negroes. If I just wanted to, I could quickly become a millionaire but you know," he continued in his clipped Berlin dialect, "countries outside Germany, are just *Kanakerländer*[3] and I don't want to spend the rest of my life there." One thing Kurt could not understand was our interest in the boxing training. He was in the gymnastics club but we chose to train with the boxers. "That's no good!" he would say "You should do gymnastics. Look what wide shoulders and chest I have. Boxing is for rowdies - 'we' should stay away from them."

Yes, it was true, in order to really stay in condition, we trained with *Herr* Schulz, the chief trainer of the Boxing Club Condor, following his exercises and club hours. He was quite a dainty little man of about forty-five who would have not normally have been entrusted, inside an internment camp, to head a sport-orientated group of people and be expected to achieve marked discipline with these young people. First to actually bring them together and then lead them in a structured and very disciplined manner. We were firmly convinced that when, at a later date, we got home to Germany we would re-discover one of those young sportsman in a top-class boxing club. If that was the case we would be certain it would be due to the enterprise of *Herr* Schulz and all credit to him. The conditions for such intensive training were ideal. These young boys had nothing more important to distract them other than to become physically fit and get themselves to top form. Neither alcohol nor women could detract from this purpose and the number of cigarettes and volume of coffee were strictly rationed and prescribed by Schulz. In many ways an ideal training camp.

We ourselves were doing some training for our health. *Herr* Schulz was training his boxing boys for two hours per day and really got them into fine condition. Hinnerk and I were participating one hour daily and that was enough for us. In two boxing tournaments we saw boxing at its best; no madness at each other, no wild hitting, but really just good boxing. *Herr* Schulz ran both the training and the tournaments with an iron hand. It is especially important to control the spectators when watching boxing, when the blood is up it is all too easy for the controlled sport of the ring to spill out to become uncontrolled violence amongst those who watch. That is probably nowhere more important than with boxing and, at the same time, nowhere more difficult. His requirement was that anyone who laughed at the boys should step in the ring himself and do better, or should just stay away. Later, when I was boxing, I had the experience of being hit hard and having to retreat a little, only to be scorned and sneered at by the spectators. Nothing can be more frustrating and cause a more dangerous anger to well-up in a fighter than that.

We also had the experience of the Canadian Officers, as well as men of the Veteran Guards, coming to watch and, possibly for the first time, seeing what real sport boxing was about. We had to believe their only previous experience had been to witness brawls in bars and you can't imagine how mad *Herr* Schulz was at a suggestion the Commandant made: the Canadian wanted to blindfold the two boxers and let them flay away at each other in the ring until one was left standing and suggested this would be infinitely more amusing! Some time after the event, when *Herr* Schulz told me the story, the anger still flared in him, it had made a deep impression. He said he had, at the time, really told the Canadian Commandant what he thought of him, but it hadn't helped to assuage the deep annoyance he felt. In the end the incident was not in vain. After a while, when the Canadians had not been invited to spectate, the Commandant came forward with a new idea to bridge the gap. He suggested he would offer, as a prize to the winner of each tournament, a tour in a staff car through the nice and pretty town of Kingston. Of course, from then on, invitations were repeated.

In strong contrast to the affable Commandant was the camp's Sergeant Major Foresight. When Hinnerk and I had arrived from Ogdensburg he had clearly declared his hatred of all Germans and he found all and every means to bully and harass the inmates. However, *Herr* Freudenthal, our *Arbeitsminister*, read Mr Foresight clearly and knew him as the bully he was. He realised that like most bullies they usually have monstrous egos and the way ahead was to flatter the Sergeant Major's. Freudenthal knew that the NCOs, however senior, were not entitled to be addressed as 'Sir' and he played on this. He always snapped to attention and called the Sergeant Major 'Sir'. It was almost comical to see Foresight preening himself, his chest visibly swelling, and the net result was that our sly old fox got quite a few privileges for the camp - all for the price of humouring a bully.

Herr Dunkel from Nürnberg, another internee, wrote a little poem about our entry into the sports hall for a football match:

21:3:42 FORT HENRY

The Spirit is in the words:

(1)
We were playing volleyball,
the first game the weather allowed us,
We were feeling rather lame,
and heard the scoffing about us.

(2)
But at last a warm ray,
lit up the gloomy wall.
Tempers had begun to fray -
but now we were on the ball.

(3)
Here we were by choice of fate,
incarcerated fighters -
When there opened the big, wide gate,
and we found new boys beside us.

(4)
Virginal faces these were indeed,
with laughing lips and looks,
A happier welcome they received,
than many on our books.

(5)
And through the battle-grey's*
enlivening colour,
'Reds' & 'Blues' experienced
new valour.

(6)
The boys who tanned
the hides of Brits,
brought spring to us -
over, walls and ditch!

*Battle-grey - Luftwaffe blue - a reference to our uniforms.

Of course, we often talked about *ein Wiedersehen* (meeting again - a reunion) after the war in Germany, in Stuttgart, but we never did.

It was an interesting time for us but soon things began to change. During a long evening at the camp cinema, the Canadians searched our *Kasematte*. I suffered a heavy loss, all my POW mail, all my notes and newspaper clippings which I had collected and cleanly glued into some folders, had been confiscated by the guards. My most vociferous protests the next day didn't help and even in front of the Commandant the duty guards denied any knowledge of the papers. I was sure, therefore, that it had not been an official act of confiscation but more the acquisition by an individual of an interesting souvenir.

Soon afterwards our departure came as suddenly as our colleague's had come. *Unser Kurt* 'assisted' us with our packing which effectively meant he did it all. Rather touchingly he gave us each a tiny ship in a bottle as a farewell gift to 'his officers'. As we finally left, he had tears in his eyes and later, apparently felt so attached to us that he even sacrificed one of his ration of POW cards to write to my mother.

The actual packing and departure were quite exciting because we were very closely supervised by the Canadian interpreter and two other guards. There existed, inside the camp, a small supply of real Canadian and American Dollars as distinguished from the specially printed camp money. The excitement began when, at many the farewell handshake, and there were a lot of those, real dollar bills were pressed into our palms. We had already each sewn three individual Canadian Dollars into our uniforms and then, at the handshakes suddenly five single Canadian Dollars came into our hands and one bill of US $20.00! These would be of inestimable value to us if we were to make another escape attempt or, if not, to someone who would.

As we actually left, the camp's loudspeaker system was playing German marching music. It was a suitable finale to what had been an education and a rest for us. After a few short steps the gates of the fortress crashed shut behind us and once more we entered the staff car.

In spite of the feeling of genuine sorrow at having to leave our new friends we were looking forward to joining our colleagues in camp. The camp would mean up-to-date news for us and new faces. We had learnt, meanwhile, that some survivors of the Bismarck and the famous submarine commander, *Kapitän* Otto Kretschmer, had arrived. However, as we left Fort Henry we didn't know where we were going, this time the Canadians obstinately refused to tell us - Geneva Convention or not. However, from our contact in the fort with internees freshly arrived from England it was clear a new transport of German officers had come with them and had been sent to Bowmanville. It was our conclusion, therefore, that so far only one camp for officers existed in Canada and that was Bowmanville.

Feeling very tense and anxious, we followed the directions which the cars took after leaving Kingston. First we were following the King's Highway Number 2, which was, by then, well known to us and seemed to indicate Bowmanville would be our destination. Soon there was no more doubt, we knew the road now, and our spirits lifted. We were certainly on our way back to Camp 30. On the way we stopped for fuel at the big Canadian air-training centre at Trenton. It had been Trenton I had passed on the train during my second escape. I remembered seeing the small aircraft on their night training exercises and felt a nostalgic pang of loss because of my enforced withdrawal from flying, but we were not even allowed to step out of the car. How much we would have loved just to see a few aircraft and, more practically, we were really in need of a toilet.

Having time to look about us on the journey we became well aware of how the climate changed as we neared Bowmanville. The countryside became greener and even some of the trees were coming into leaf and blossom, April in Canada. What a difference to Kingston where the meadows had just started to grow and become green. How would it look at Lake Superior now, in the former Camp W? Hundreds of miles away it could still be locked in snow. Such contrast in one land; what a great country this Canada was.

When we could see the camp from the outside and saw how our comrades there were already lying out and enjoying the sun, we knew we'd soon feel at home again. Our good feelings were soon dampened as we learned that *Oberstleutnant* Gruber was surprised by our arrival. He said the camp would be overcrowded, the new transport, a group of one hundred and fifty officers from England, had filled every place. He was doubtful if we would be exactly welcomed in our old rooms. However, when finally allowed in we were well received. My *Stubenältester* (room elder - room leader) had made my bed personally. It was then moved, simply for convenience, to provide a seat in the middle of the room and it was time for the stories to flow.

Hinnerk was equally well received in his own building and especially in his room. He was immediately required to update everyone and he, like me, was also anxious to know what had been happening in the month or so we had been away. We were invited for coffee, building by building, and probably had too much for our systems, but it was plentiful. All over the place, we were accepted and well received with great friendship and had, time and time again, to relate everything which had happened to us since we walked away through the orchards above the camp. It was understandable, we had not only escaped but had been going through something entirely new to them at Fort Henry.

In gratitude and in great respect of those honest people we had left in Fort Henry, fellow Germans, we were able to do something good for them. We had left our own books there, and now the German camp leadership, at our request, made a camp-wide collection and in the end we had a shipment of more than five-hundred good books for Fort Henry. We also sent a good mixture of musical instruments, fiddles, trumpets and whatever was necessary to a camp orchestra, even though this meant a sacrifice for some of us at Bowmanville. Certainly there was a need for these for us, but we judged the immediate need at Fort Henry to be the greater.

That having been done and our story having been widely told we could catch up on the news important to us. Peter Krug and Erich Boehle, both comrades from 'W' had indeed escaped. Peter, well known to me from the train transfer to Bowmanville, had successfully crossed the fence with two ladders and got away with Erich. The *Steinhilperscher Leitertrick* had triumphed again and this time with lighter, professionally built ladders. They had, this time, busied themselves fitting a new lamp to the fence and hooking up the necessary wiring to supply it. Once more it had been the sheer audacity of the escape that had not raised the suspicion of the Canadians.

They had apparently casually gone about their work and finally shouldered their ladders and calmly walked away just as we had. However, there should be no doubt that in spite of this *'Neue Tour'* which had been pioneered and tested by Hinnerk and myself it had still taken exceptional courage to carry it through. We could attest to the incredible strain which is generated by being in a position to be shot without warning and to be right under the Canadian guards' guns in broad daylight[6]. They, like us, had crossed two fences, each more than two and a half metres high with just two ladders and their courage.

Erich Boehle, meanwhile, was already sitting in the new detention block which had been rebuilt inside the main camp fence. Peter Krug was still at large in the USA and the subject of feverish searches. Every now and then articles would be overlooked by the camp censor and we could follow the hunt. The recapture of Krug had already been reported several times, but again and again it transpired that the press had got it wrong and he was still on the loose. They had captured people by the dozen but after normal checking they became aware the American police had arrested the wrong people. This game was to the immense enjoyment and delight of all the inmates, but somewhat to the chagrin of the Canadians. Given the time Peter had been out I was optimistic that he had already reached neutral Mexico.

It was with great pride that Hinnerk and I surveyed the yellow bands we had painted around the fence posts. They beamed their bright colour, 'Good quality paint,' we thought. As prisoners took their rounds for exercise we could witness the friendly smile the yellow rings brought to their faces each time they passed. It was doubly amusing to observe that the Canadians still thought it a very good idea to focus attention on this vulnerable spot on the fence. It was amazing they still had not the slightest inkling that these marvellous security aids had been painted on by two prisoners whilst they

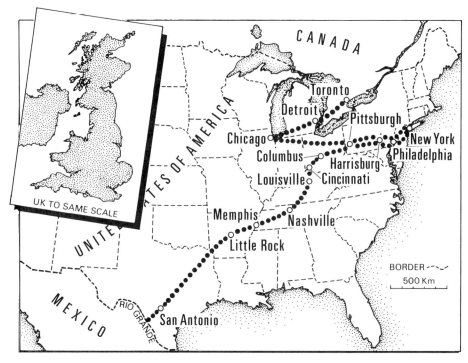

*The route taken by Peter Krug. The outline of Britain is
inset to illustrate the distances involved.*

escaped in broad daylight. An humorous irony we could enjoy at their cost!

Unfortunately, Peter Krug was not yet safe. After a brilliant accomplishment in getting as far as San Antonio, to the actual border between Texas and Mexico, he had been arrested. He now also felt the fickle nature of fortune. It was by pure coincidence that he was caught in a cheap hotel by a routine police search. On advice to be well equipped when crossing the borderline, he had purchased a revolver. When this was found in his possession the police suspicion was really raised. They arrested him and he was later identified and began the long journey back to our camp.

Brave Mr Stephan, Peter's benefactor in Detroit, had attracted much publicity during his trial and was well known to all. Possibly because of this he was sentenced to death for high treason, but this was later commuted to life imprisonment after a personal appeal to the president. In the end it made little difference because he was to die in prison. During the trial Peter Krug was transported to Detroit and, because he was judged so dangerous he was handcuffed and his legs were shackled.

One good thing was that because Krug and Boehle had, like Hinnerk and

Peter Krug in his Luftwaffe uniform.

myself, carried their ladders far away from the camp, *der Steinhilpersche Leitertrick* could be repeated. Again, this time in late April, *Leutnant* Dr 'Doc' Wagner[7] and my former 'Staff Sergeant', Reini Pfundtner, were on a work detail measuring the height and width of the fence. The actual time spent crossing the fence was becoming shorter with each attempt but, unfortunately, after this third successful escape, the Canadians found the ladders and that was the end of this kind of escape. The finding of the ladders was to lead to no small difficulties, not only in the camp's carpenter shop, but also in the tailor shop. Naturally it wasn't hard to prove that the ladders had been made in the carpenters shop and the civilian overalls had been run-up in the tailor's shop.

'Doc' Wagner and Reini Pfundtner had received dollars to use on their escape. They were, therefore, able to travel in comfort by express train across Canada, first to the Niagara Falls where the border crossing seemed to be too difficult. Then they returned to Ottawa where they *'tried their luck'*

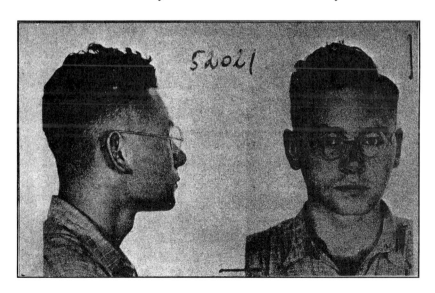
Peter Krug borrowed some glasses and had a radical change of hairstyle for these POW photos.

*A much earlier picture of Peter Krug on the harbour side near Margate
having just been 'fished out of the drink'!*

with a Vichy French Ambassador. However, he was no friend to them and told the police behind their backs and they were arrested.

Much later I was to learn from Peter Krug that Stephan had put him in touch with a real German underground movement within the USA. This organisation had handed him over from county to county, each having a sub-organisation. He had to be very clever to avoid the clutches of the police and his route, principally by omnibus, led criss-cross through the States, until finally, literally in sight of his final goal, he was recaptured.

Our dummies, our foldable *Pappkameraden*, had done their duty standing in for the missing men at each of these escape attempts. They had been duly marched past in the middle of the rows of five and were still unknown to the Canadians. Again it was to us who remained inside the camp to judge when we would withdraw the substitutes and in that way announce that someone else was out. Doing this properly ensured they would remain undiscovered and available to support any further escapes.

For my part I'd had enough, *'die Nase voll'* (totally fed up). So much planning, so much stress, so much time in solitary confinement and so much hardship on the road had taken its toll. If others wanted to try I would help, but for me it was over for a while.

Notes on Chapter Five

[1] Perhaps it should be mentioned here that at home in Germany our promotions went on normally. When everything went well, we were officially informed by the Red Cross and the agreement was that our Canadian POW pay was raised.

[2] It is worth remembering that in Canada as well as in Britain an escape could only be attempted with the permission of *der Ausbrecherkommittee* (escape committee of senior officers which had been installed by our own German camp leadership). They decided who would try the next escape attempt and to what degree the resources within the camp could be directed to support them. Some judgement of the level of discipline within the camps can be gained from this.

[3] *Wurttembergers* - Residents of the Württenburg state in southern Germany. Today Stuttgart is the capital of Baden-Württenburg as it is now called.

[4] *'I hab mei Schäfle im Trockena!'* (I have my sheep safe and in the dry) - a

colloquial expression meaning one has one's affairs in order - particularly financial affairs.

[5] *Kanakerländer* - A derisory term for foreign lands. Perhaps a British equivalent of the time would have been 'Wop' or 'Wog' countries.

[6] Even now, over fifty years later, it still makes my heart race to think of it.

[7] 'Doc' Wagner - an Austrian who, before the War and afterwards, was a lawyer in Vienna. He was also one of the five who escaped from Swanwick in England with Franz v. Werra.

CHAPTER SIX

BAD BOYS TO GRAVENHURST

Really I'd had it. I really did have *'die Nase voll'* - a nose full of the strange and repetitive bad luck which ended all my escape attempts. I was also disappointed that my attempts to fulfil what I saw as my duty as a soldier and as a POW were not totally successful, although I was sure I had kept significant numbers of the enemies forces tied down looking for me.

On the 26th February, 1942, I wrote to my mother from the detention block at Bowmanville after our return from Watertown. I believe that things written at the time more encapsulate the feelings and are not subject to the ravages of time like the memory.[1]

> *'... with diligence and care and everything I could do myself, I have tried to fight against fate here. If heaven had wanted me to succeed, it would have been possible. However, I now think that I have fulfilled my duty as well as I could but complete success was not meant for me. Perhaps another one is luckier than myself. I now write to you after it's behind me, but also to show that I am neither a softy nor unreasonable. I am not and I will not be "a good boy" for them!'*

In spite of Bowmanville being overcrowded, my old comrades had accepted me back into the fold. Now, with a good conscience, I wanted to take advantage of all that this camp had to offer. It would be a good mixture of sport and lessons, exercise of the mind and the body. There were of all kinds of opportunities; our hunger strike at Camp W, prompted by the poor conditions, was now paying long term benefits.

There was a large exercise and soccer ground, a swimming hall and, in the area of the ice hockey field, we were building a tennis court. All kinds of lessons were available and the library was bigger and got better and better, together with our selection of musical instruments. It was my intention to be as fit as possible physically and also in spirit. Then, after our liberation, I would return home to serve our country again.

What had been started in England with just a few books and some musical instruments and continued in the *Wildnislager* (wilderness camp) Camp W at Lake Superior had now really developed in Bowmanville. *Der Schweizer*

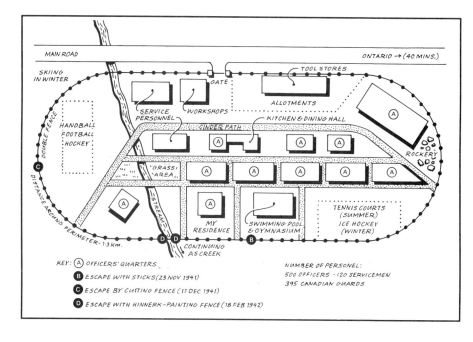

Camp 30 Bowmanville

Bürger (The Swiss citizen), Professor Boschenstein, lived in Toronto and busied himself obtaining books, science material and apparatus, sports equipment and instruments for music in many different Canadian camps. He understood the importance of the YMCA as well as the Red Cross procuring this equipment for the POWs. If you had to be imprisoned there were worse places than Bowmanville.

However, after a few days my positive outlook was dampened. Hinnerk and myself had been returned from Fort Henry at the end of April and it was soon the beginning of May. At that time we learnt that it was planned for some people to be taken out of Bowmanville. The first list of those to leave, names with no destination, was already circulating. When studying this list there was no doubt that the less liked, the 'Bad Boys,' were to be removed. Almost all the escapers were on the list and also those who had been tunnelling or who had been involved in other incidents. Certainly, the Canadian *Frettchen*, who understood German, had put many names on this list. Peter Krug was the only exception, staying in Bowmanville while the court proceedings against Mr Stephan were still active. He was still being regularly taken to the USA in order to give evidence in the court proceedings. Bowmanville, being close to Toronto, was convenient.

*The theatre at Bowmanville ready for the 'Wishing Concert'
by the band '13 Raven' led by Hans Poser.*

Schiller behind barbed wire.

It was clear why I was on this list, as well as Manhart and Hinnerk Waller. However, before being transported, I wanted to take the opportunity to do something which was of special interest to me. In the last transport from England, which arrived in April, was an officer of the Bismarck. After the

The kitchen at Camp 30 was quite outstanding

A Canadian inspection of the swimming pool.
All part of the original facilities

jig-saw of fragmented information we had managed to collect after censorship I finally wanted to know from *Kapitänleutnant Freiherr* von Müllenheim-Rechberg what really had happened. After a little asking around, I soon found his building. He and his room-mate, a *Luftwaffe Major*, were living in a quite comfortable two-bedded room. The *Major* told me that the *'Kaleu'* (short for *Kapitänleutnant*) was walking, probably near the kitchen building.

Sure enough I met him there and introduced myself, asking politely whether he would give me his story about the Bismarck; if not then, perhaps at some other time. My impatience, I explained, was born of my hardly having arrived from Fort Henry to learn we were going to be moved again. He just walked away, murmuring he had told the story several times and now was preparing a thorough presentation. At that time I couldn't understand the arrogant way he treated me. I tried to press him, explaining again that I was soon to be taken from Bowmanville, but he just continued his walk without a backward glance. It wasn't until many years later my eyes were opened[2].

From Bowmanville, we were transported to Camp 20 Gravenhurst, about one hundred and fifty kilometres to the north. We travelled in small groups by truck and only after arriving there did we realise what had happened to us. There was simply no comparison with Bowmanville. Gravenhurst had, a long time before, been a sanatorium for patients with tuberculosis. In the meantime it had decayed and looked ready for demolition. The rooms were on three floors and were narrow and also in very bad shape. The dining room and kitchen were in a wooden building separate from the living quarters. For our service personnel, the staff company of NCOs and enlisted men, another wooden building was just being built. Where would we find space for giving lessons and instructions? Where could we practise our sports and games? There were almost no books and only a few musical instruments. There was no doubt the Canadians were intent on really *'dropping us in it'*.

Of course, for them it was only important that this camp was surrounded by the 'most beautiful fence in all of Canada.' It was a very heavy chain-link fence some three metres high and topped with barbed wire, the individual wires of which were about five millimetres in diameter; impossible to cut with any normal pair of pliers. More importantly for them, this camp had been built on rocky ground, close to Lake Muskoka. For people who knew Norway, it looked like the hard coastline of many of the fjords and inlets, barely enough soil for grass and trees to grow. Certainly tunnelling would be limited to a few well defined places.

However, escaping was, at the beginning, not a subject for discussion, our morale was at zero. Even electing a camp leadership was difficult because of doubtful seniority and remained in abeyance for some time and that gave us no arbitration or decision-making machinery. That, in turn, didn't make the task of room allocation any the easier, but we got by.

Initially, we really were down in morale though it soon became clear there was no other way of helping ourselves other than by doing it ourselves. We moved onto the third floor, into a small room which could hold about four or five people. It was a little room in a corner joined to a balcony with a view of Muskoka Lake. This balcony had to be shared with the next room, in which there were four *Afrika Korps* officers with *Oberleutnant* Dr Paul Huppert as *Stubenältester* (room elder).

Our *Stubenältester* was *Hauptmann* Peter Döring a long-range reconnaissance pilot. Before the French campaign, he had come down in Belgium and been taken prisoner. During the evacuation at Dunkirk, he had some terrible experiences. The British troops, as is well known, had to leave many of their own men and those of their allies in the port and on the sands. However, they all took along the few German POWs they had, even under most risky conditions. Peter had to sustain an attack of our own Stukas after being locked in an abandoned railway freight car and feared for his life. When that threat had passed he was taken to the harbour at Dunkirk and was transferred from one burning ship to another until, finally, he landed in England.

He was good friends with another room-mate, *Hauptmann* Eberhard Wildermuth. They had served in the same regiment before the war before both transferred from the army to the *Luftwaffe*. Eberhard came from Bad Cannstatt and was a fellow *schwäbischer Landsmann*, a native of southern Germany. On 12th August 1940, as pilot of a Junkers 88 bomber, he had attacked the docks at Portsmouth with his unit, KG 51 *Edelweissgeschwader* (Edelweis Wing). He had, in spite of protection by fighters and by *Zerstörerschutzes* (Messerschmitt Me 110 'Destroyers'), been shot down along with ten other Ju 88s of this Wing. The *Kommodore* of the wing, *Oberst* (Colonel) Dr Fisser, was among those shot down and was killed.

We also had our youngest room-mate, our tall and lean *Leutnant* Benjamin Rudolf Theopold. He had been caught as a pilot of a Heinkel 111 on 16th August. His *Geschwader*, KG 55, had attacked ports and docks and the coast of Sussex, near Brighton. In this attack alone, the British fighters had shot down six aircraft of KG 55. Another victim of that day, a Reserve Officer *Leutnant* Vater, joined us later at Gravenhurst. He had been a master at a secondary school and more or less treated us all as *junge Dachsen* (young whippersnappers), but he was always friendly and full of good advice.

In a way it was good that the distribution of prisoners into the various rooms took time because of the lack of leadership. It kept us very busy with a relatively undemanding task and that helped to bridge the gulf between our comfortable existence at Bowmanville and the bland existence we now faced. A report in a newspaper under the date 19th May, which we discovered by coincidence, confirmed how our selection had been made (see page 72).

Of course it was understandable that the Government in Ottawa had to do something in order to quieten down the excited population. The public only had what the press was reporting in their own sensational style on which to base their opinions. When looking at the headlines of the newspapers which reported our recapture at Watertown and, earlier, my adventures to Niagara and Montreal, the key words were *Nazi* and *Hun* (see articles reproduced in 'Ten Minutes To Buffalo' pp 213-214, 215-216 (Niagara) 281-283 (Montreal) and 410 (Watertown). Given that since about 1933 the public had seen film on the cinema newsreels of the rallies at Nuremburg and the parades at the 1936 Olympic Games in Berlin, they quite naturally equated the *Nazis*, our political leaders, with the military parades and by association branded all Germans and, in particular, all military personnel as *Nazis*. Because of the press abuse of the terms *Nazi* and *Hun* it was quite easy for the public to become concerned about such *'monsters'* being at large.

However, the perplexing aspect of this for the Canadian population was that, on the one hand, the German soldiers who were fighting in Europe, Africa and Russia, as well as the POWs were called *Nazis* and *Huns* in the Canadian and the American press. That was fine as a simple concept, a strange marauding tribe of fanatics trying to conquer the world, led by the arch-*Nazi* Adolf Hitler. But then, on the other hand, came the question, 'If that is what they are why are they treated so *'soft'* in the camps? Why are they *'allowed'* to escape?' If they were to understand that at all they would have to embrace the idea that it was the duty of the officer POWs to escape. It was a condition of the Geneva Convention that creature comforts should be provided. And to understand that they would have to address the new equation: officers are soldiers, soldiers are people, civilised people negotiate treaties. Civilised people or *Nazis*? Soldiers or dangerous fanatics? Which reporter could write about that dilemma and not risk the sack. Which newspaper could print it without fearing an outcry? A similar unwritten veto required a complete absence of reports on the conditions provided in Germany for the numerous Allied POWs.

The tone and feeling of the press towards us can be felt in the article from The Toronto Daily Star of 23rd February 1942 which is copied, verbatim, beginning overleaf and is reproduced on pages 75 & 76. A similar article from Toronto Globe and Mail is more legible in its original state and is reproduced on page 77.

ESCAPE RINGLEADERS SENT TO NEW CAMP

By H. R. ARMSTRONG

Ottawa, Ont., May 19—As a result of repeated escapes from the German officers' prison camp at Bowmanville, a group of prisoners has been transferred to another camp, it is learned.

The official reason given for removal to a more northerly Ontario camp is "overcrowding" at Bowmanville. It is learned, however, that those moved are considered to be ringleaders in escape plans.

The transfer is considered to be one means of reducing the likelihood of further breaks from the Bowmanville camp. "A small number" has been moved, according to semi-official statement.

ORGANISED AID GIVEN NAZIS IN ESCAPE, U.S. CHIEF SURE

Amount of Equipment Indicates "Underground" System, He Declares

Awaiting return

Possibility of an "underground railway" assisting German officers in their escape from the Bowmanville internment camp was suggested today by Chief of Police Edward J. Curtin of Watertown, N.Y. Two officers who escaped from the camp last week were captured at Watertown last night. They are now being held at Ogdensburg N.Y. awaiting orders from the department of justice in Washington.

Chief Curtin said in his opinion the two prisoners could not have obtained all the equipment they had nor travelled such a distance without help. He said they had so much clothing they couldn't get it all into the one kit-bag they had.

Chief Curtin said he was amazed by the maps they had. Every town on both sides of the river between Watertown and Syracuse was marked and the maps also showed Lake Ontario the St. Lawrence river and the direction of the river's flow. Chief Cutin said.

"They had the whole area marked out," he said, "I suppose an aviator knows a lot about maps but it seems peculiar to me that war prisoners are able to get as detailed information about the countryside as these men had."

Neither prisoner would tell officers how they managed to travel nearly 200 miles after they escaped. Chief Curtin said, "They certainly didn't make the journey on foot," he asserted.

The prisoners told Watertown police they had escaped from the camp at 6 p.m. Their absence, according to officials, was not noticed until 10 p.m. roll call. The prisoners also claimed they had been away from the camp four days and had spent two days on a farm in New York state 20 miles from Brockville. Their story would place their escape on Thursday, a day before it was announced at Bowmanville.

An alert patrolman interrupted their trip to New York city. It was the third escape for the officers, Lieuts. Albert Henrick Waller and Ulrich Steinhilper and they would still be on their way if they hadn't worn so much clothing. Patrolman John Bero, off duty, was suspicious of the way the two were bundled up as they sauntered down the main street of Watertown. He called a fellow-officer and they escorted the two to police headquarters.

Military authorities at Kingston, who have jurisdiction over the camp said today there would be an immediate inquiry into the escape. They pointed out the prisoners may have obtained some of the supplies found on them from parcels sent into the camp by friends and organisations that provide supplies for war prisoners.

"It makes a man sick to think they could have got as far as they did," commented Patrolman Bero. "It was just a fluke that they were captured. I saw them walking along the street and thought there must be something wrong, they had so many clothes."

Say Method Was Secret

The officers refused to say how they escaped, except that they had got out by a "secret method." They told police they had walked across the St. Lawrence river ice in 15 minutes, without difficulty.

A map of New York city led police to believe they were headed there. They also had several other maps, some hand-drawn and others that appeared to have been taken out of Canadian school geography books. These included North and South America, the United States and the West Indies.

The Germans were well-equipped. They carried a brief-case and an overnight bag. In the bags were shaving outfits, chocolate bars, dates and pills which the Germans said were concentrated food, including dextrose and energy food.

Steinhilper had a Canadian dollar bill and two ten-cent pieces. On Waller police found four Canadian quarters and what police described as "two Canadian copper coins with the figure one on them which Waller said were of no value."

Posed as Swiss Sailors

The officers were posing as ship-wrecked Swiss sailors and police said they produced certificates to back up this story. Issued in Boston and dated Jan. 16 1942, they certified the bearers had been members of a ship's crew and were signed by the first officer.

Each wore an overcoat, two jackets, a sweater, two woollen shirts and woollen socks. The overcoats were worn over blue dungaree overalls, similar to those worn by mechanics. They had caps with ear-muffs and overshoes. In the opinion of Patrolman Bero, "they couldn't possibly have suffered from the cold."

The brief-case carried by one had a zipper top and both bags were of good leather. A well-worn blue cloth cover was around the brief-case.

"It was just sheer luck that I decided to stop them." Patrolman Bero said, "They were both in first-class physical condition and there was no indication they had suffered from the cold weather. They were both clean-shaven and their clothes were neat and clean and well made. They did not look as if they had been sleeping in anything other than a comfortable bed."

Patrolman Bero said he was sure the officers were headed for New York city. One claimed to have relatives in Reading, Pa. The hand-drawn maps, police said, were extremely well drawn. These included a map of the main highways in Canada and the United States.

From this report two things are obvious: First, how much the police in Watertown understood how to play up their *'alertness,'* how they had been on their guard. Policeman Berow didn't give any hint of how he, by sheer coincidence, was the officer who had received the description of the two of us the previous day. Or how lucky he had been that he, on his way on duty, was the guy of whom we had asked directions to Carthage. Secondly, and probably more important, is the great seriousness with which the underground movement, the *5th Column,* is described in Canada as well as in the USA. Now there was cause for concern for the public - not only were these Nazis and Huns walking away from the camps with alarming regularity but there, right in their midst, was an organisation of fanatics ready to help them when they got out!

This wasn't helped at all when, about six weeks after Hinnerk's and my escape, Peter Krug and Erich Böhle next used *die Leitertrick* and it was impossible for the Canadians to discover how they left the camp. The news exploded in the papers as the press demanded to know, on behalf of their concerned readership of course, how it was two more *Nazi* flyers could escape from Bowmanville without leaving a clue as to how they did it. Then, in the already intrigue-charged atmosphere, came the revelation that Peter Krug had actually succeeded in getting in contact with a real underground organisation. One sensational report was chasing the other. Now, for the first

ORGANIZED AID GIVEN NAZIS IN ESCAPE, U.S. CHIEF SURE

Amount of Equipment Indicates "Underground" System, He Declares

AWAITING RETURN

Possibility of an "underground railway" assisting German officers in their escape from the Bowmanville internment camp was suggested today by Chief of Police Edward J. Curtin of Watertown, N.Y. Two officers who escaped from the camp last week were captured at Watertown last night. They are now being held at Ogdensburg, N.Y. awaiting orders from the department of justice in Washington.

Chief Curtin said in his opinion the two prisoners could not have obtained all the equipment they had nor travelled such a distance without help. He said they had so much clothing they couldn't get it all into the one hand-bag they had.

Chief Curtin said he was amazed by the maps they had. Every town on both sides of the river between Watertown and Syracuse was marked and the maps also showed Lake Ontario, the St. Lawrence river and the direction of the river's flow, Chief Curtin said.

"They had the whole area marked out," he said. "I suppose an aviator knows a lot about maps but it seems peculiar to me that war prisoners are able to get as detailed information about the countryside as these men had."

Neither prisoner would tell offi-

PROVINCE WILL GET ESTATE OF $80,000

St. Thomas, Feb. 23—(CP)—All appeal in the Blanche K. Duncombe will case has been abandoned, according to the best information available here. Since there were no immediate relatives, the estate, consisting of approximately $80,000, passes to the province.

J. B. Davidson, solicitor for the executors, said no appeal was contemplated on the part of his clients. E. S. Livermore St. Thomas, retained by the Detroit beneficiaries, announced Saturday his instructions were not to proceed with the appeal.

overnight bag. In the bags were shaving outfits, chocolate bars, dates and pills which the Germans said were concentrated food, including dextrose, an energy food.

Steinhilper had a Canadian dollar bill and two ten-cent pieces. On Waller police found four Canadian quarters and what police described as "two Canadian copper coins with the figure one on them, which Waller said were of no value."

Posed as Swiss Sailors

The officers were posing as shipwrecked Swiss sailors and police said they produced certificates to back up this story. Issued in Boston and dated Jan. 16, 1942, they certified the bearers had been members of a ship's crew and were signed by the first officer.

Each wore an overcoat, two jackets, a sweater, two woollen shirts and woollen socks. The overcoats were worn over blue dun-

ONTARIO

NEW YORK STATE

Lake Ontario

cers how they managed to travel nearly 200 miles after they escaped, Chief Cuttle said. "They certainly didn't make the journey on foot," he asserted.

The prisoners told Watertown police they had escaped from the camp at 6 p.m. Their absence, according to officials, was not noticed until 10 p.m. roll-call. The prisoners also claimed they had been away from the camp four days and had spent two days on a farm in New York state 20 miles from Brockville. Their story would place their escape on Thursday, a day before it was announced at Bowmanville.

An alert patrolman interrupted their trip to New York city. It was the third escape for the officers, Lieuts. Albert Henrick Waller and Ulrich Steinhilper, and they would still be on their way if they hadn't worn so much clothing. Patrolman John Bero, off duty, was suspicious of the way the two were bundled up as they sauntered down the main street of Watertown. He called a fellow-officer and they escorted the two to police headquarters.

Military authorities at Kingston, who have jurisdiction over the camp, said today there would be an immediate inquiry into the escape. They pointed out the prisoners may have obtained some of the supplies found on them from parcels sent into the camp by friends and organizations that provide supplies for war prisoners.

"It makes a man sick to think that they could have got as far as they did," commented Patrolman Bero. "It was just a fluke that they were captured. I saw them walking along the street and thought there must be something wrong they had so many clothes."

Say Method Was Secret

The officers refused to say how they escaped, except that they had got out by a "secret method." They told police they had walked across the St. Lawrence river ice in 15 minutes without difficulty.

A map of New York city led police to believe they were headed there. They also had several other maps, some hand-drawn and others that appeared to have been taken out of Canadian school geography books. These included North and South America, the United States and the West Indies.

The Germans were well-equipped. They carried a brief-case and an gaire overalls similar to those worn by mechanics. They had caps with ear-muffs and overshoes. In the opinion of Patrolman Bero "they couldn't possibly have suffered from cold."

The brief-case carried by one had a zipper top and both bags were of good leather. A well-worn blue cloth cover was around the brief-case.

"It was just sheer luck that I decided to stop them," Patrolman Bero said. "They were both in first-class physical condition and there was no indication they had suffered from the cold weather. They were both clean-shaven and their clothes were neat and clean and well made. They did not look as if they had been sleeping in anything other than a comfortable bed."

Patrolman Bero said he was sure the officers were headed for New York city. One claimed to have relatives in Reading, Pa. The hand-drawn maps, police said, were extremely well-drawn. These included a map of the main highways in Canada and the United States.

Two Escaped Germans Retaken at Watertown

Watertown, N.Y., Feb. 22 (Special).—Otto Steinhiller, 22, and Albert Waller, 24, German prisoners of war who escaped from Bowmanville prison camp on Friday, were recaptured here tonight, turned over to Canadian immigration authorities, and were believed to be back across the Canadian border on their way to Bowmanville by 10 p.m.

Admitting that they had made their escape from the Bowmanville camp by means of a "secret passage," the Germans refused to talk much with local police officials, other than to make the claim that if they could have reached New York City and Reading, Pa., respectively, they would have been "all set" for a permanent getaway. One of them claimed to have relatives in Reading.

When searched, the prisoners were found to be carrying no weapons, but, according to local police, were well supplied with what purported to be identifications. They carried identification certificates of shipwrecked Swiss sailors ostensibly issued by the first officer of the S.S. Fley Bird of Boston, Mass. They had maps of the St. Lawrence River area and were well versed as to directions and locations in this county where they were captured. They said they had worked briefly at a farm near Hammond, a short distance away from Watertown. They said they crossed the St. Lawrence River on the ice but would not say where.

An eagle-eyed officer returning to duty in his car, dressed in plainclothes, at 7:30 this evening, was the means of the capture of the escaped prisoners. Unarmed, he noticed the men dressed in dungarees and carrying a sack, talking to a young boy on the street. Getting another officer, who was armed, to accompany him he caught up with the men on the main business street.

The escaped Germans were "covered" with a gun and asked to produce their identifications. They claimed to have been in an accident, but their explanations being unsatisfactory they were taken in for investigation and questioning.

Bowmanville, Feb. 22 (Special).— What is believed to be the first instance of a reserve unit being called for active duty within Canada occurred yesterday at Bowmanville when thirteen men of No. 4 platoon, 32nd Infantry Reserve, Veterans Guard of Canada, were summoned for duty in connection with the alleged escape of two German officer prisoners from Internment Camp 30, formerly the Boys' Training School. It is believed that some men from Port Hope platoon of the 32nd have also been called to Bowmanville.

TORONTO GLOBE AND MAIL - FEB. 23rd 1942

time, it was confirmed that a German 5th Column actually existed. 'The Underground Railway' they called it, an organisation which had assisted Peter Krug all the way to the Mexican border. Reports confirmed that restaurateur, Max Stephan, had been under observation from the FBI in Detroit, even before being contacted by Peter Krug. Soon after Stephan had turned Peter Krug over to the German secret organisation, he was arrested and put in front of a court.

All of America breathed easier when, finally, Peter was captured and positively identified in San Antonio; once again, however, after a stupid coincidence rather than special police work. The court proceedings against Mr Stephan, when they finally started, made the headlines with charges of high treason. But right on the heels of this news came the announcement of a new search, this time Reini Pfundtner and 'Doc' Wagner had, within just sixteen minutes, crossed the fences with the *Leitertrick*. Once more the hunt was on as again two *Nazis* walked away from Bowmanville and vanished into the vastness of Canada.

These two were off to a really good start as well, both of them spoke good American slang. Reini had been an exchange student in New York pre-war and 'Doc' had been a ski instructor and had an agency for *Tracht,* traditional Austrian costume like the *Dirndl*. They also had on them a vital ingredient for success - enough dollars to ride on the railroad. They were only caught because they placed their trust in the French Vichy Ambassador in Ottawa by asking him for help. This time the two ladders had been found and it at last dawned on the guards in the camp what had been going on. There were those yellow rings on the posts, then that matter with the lamp on the fence, and of course, the last coup was measuring the height and width of the fence. Once the first seed of thought had been sown they understood rather quickly and, of course, felt rather silly. Naturally the truth of the matter was kept from the newspapers. How could Canadian officialdom have faced down the hue and cry that would have arisen if it had been made known that six prisoners had just climbed over the fences in broad daylight and walked away.

The change of commanders in Camp Bowmanville was not enough for the excited population. Those escape ringleaders had to be taken to another place where they would be kept in safety.

Notes on Chapter Six

[1] This is possible only because my parents kept all my POW correspondence, postcards and letters. Monthly, four cards and three letters were permitted.

[2] In the year 1988, when I learned that von Müllenheim-Rechberg had written a book about the Battleship *Bismarck*, I bought one and started to read. I wanted, finally, to know what had really happened. The more I read, the more I understood. There was an example of one of the people who apparently could forsee the outcome of Hitler's leadership and yet did nothing. Someone who so hated the *Nazis*, but rose to become adjudant on the *Bismarck*, the capital ship of that regime. I encourage everyone to read this book and to judge for themselves how plausible it is.

CHAPTER SEVEN

THE "AFRICANS" ARE COMING!

We had only been in Gravenhurst for a few days and were still busy furnishing our new accommodation. In a new camp this not only meant the making up of our bunks, it also meant everything else had to be made again from scratch. Everything had to be organised again: the dining room, the day room, sports areas indoors and outdoors, library, music room, laundry and washing facilities etc. etc...

We had done it for the first time in England, then in Camp W in the wild west of Canada and then Bowmanville had just been brought up to standard by us, only to find we would have to start again in Gravenhurst. Although officers had been imprisoned there for some months from August 1940, they were later transferred to Fort Henry. When Fort Henry was designated for German internees they were moved to Bowmanville, arriving at about the same time we were brought back from the wilderness at Neys. When we arrived everything looked deserted and decayed, no signs that it had once been a clean sanatorium for lung complaints.

Admittedly, the surrounding countryside was beautiful; Lake Muskoka, by which Gravenhurst lay, was a weekend and recreation area for the residents of Toronto. For us this beautiful countryside was also painful as it strengthened our homesickness and our desire for freedom, especially at the weekends. Then the excursion boats would pass very close to the camp and in the evenings they were brightly lit with strings of coloured lights. What a comparison with the black-out in Europe! The bands on board always played extra loudly when near to the camp, often sounding, to us, like deliberate mockery. The British national anthem was sung with great gusto before the ships entered the Gravenhurst harbour, which further rubbed salt in the wounds. During the daylight hours we could watch the fast motor boats that bustled about within sight of the camp with great interest. In Gravenhurst there were several wharfs and boat yards which not only built large vessels, but also the smaller fast ones. Later during the war, it was said, parts for warships were built there, the size only being limited to that which could readily be transported by rail after construction.

Some of our officers now found themselves back in the place where they had been imprisoned for the first time in Canada, after having arrived from England. They had hidden some tools in partition walls and other secret spots

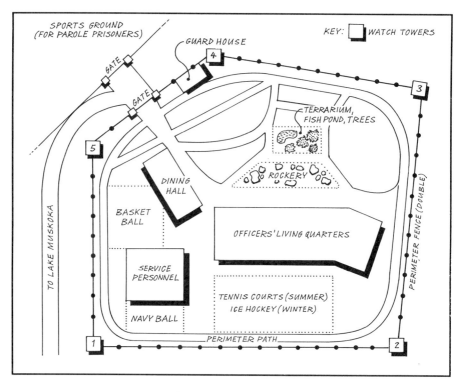

Inside the map:

SPORTS GROUND
(FOR PAROLE PRISONERS)

GUARD HOUSE

KEY: □ WATCH TOWERS

GATE

GATE

4

3

TERRARIUM,
FISH POND, TREES

5

ROCKERY

TO LAKE MUSKOKA

DINING
HALL

BASKET
BALL

OFFICERS' LIVING QUARTERS

PERIMETER FENCE (DOUBLE)

SERVICE
PERSONNEL

TENNIS COURTS (SUMMER)
ICE HOCKEY (WINTER)

NAVY BALL

PERIMETER PATH

1

2

Camp 20 Gravenhurst

before they had been transferred to Fort Henry and, in time, these were
recovered. During the extensive searches other items were also found which
had most probably been hidden by other internees before their departure.
Oberleutnant Niehoff, our Air Communications Officer and radio builder was
returning to Gravenhurst, having been there in the early days. We didn't
have a camp radio any more, but it wasn't long before he got to work
constructing a receiver. He lived only two doors away, a room, like ours,
which had a view of the lake. It was only a short time before our room was
also busily involved in the construction work, manufacturing the parts that
he had designed. Once more tin cans were arduously cut up to exact
specifications and coils were rolled from stolen wire.

Richard Marchfelder, *Leutnant* and pilot of a Me 110 with III.ZG 76, had
been shot down in August of 1940. He was most probably here in
Gravenhurst with us because, being a Bavarian with a typically *Bayerisch* dry
wit, had always openly voiced his opinion towards our guards when he
disliked something. Very early after arrival in Gravenhurst he was selected

*A view of the camp looking towards the main accommodation block.
Our room was immediately below the white dot.*

to be our *'Filmoffizier'*. As such he had the responsibility to safeguard and show the films that were provided by the YMCA. *Rima* (from **RI**chard **MA**rchfelder), as we called him, was proud of the fact that he was able to select exactly the right film for our taste, whether it was a 'Western' or 'Ann Sheridan' he was showing. The atmosphere that prevailed in the darkness of the room was most amusing. The Western films always had those famous scenes when there was a scuffle in the saloon, and a piano fell from the upper balcony into the fighting masses below. Of course this became predictable and the audience became so practised that at the crucial moment we would chorus as one: "The piano!...The piano...!" and then it would fall, right on cue!

When the hero, predictably, went closer to his 'beloved' to give her the first kiss, the audience would call: *"Brust!... Brust! ... "* (literally 'Breast...! Breast!...) It actually had nothing to do with the tempting curves of the American film star, rather more it meant: "Courage!...Courage!...go at it young man!" In these scenes one never had to wait too long. Being able to predict what would happen next was all part of the fun.

The edge of Lake Muskoka. This picture, taken in 1953, shows the 3 metre diving board which was all that remained of the original 5 metre tower. In the background is one of the guard towers slowly rotting away.

Rima also had an important role in the supply of radio parts. As in Bowmanville, we could make many of the parts but not the valves and this is where *Rima* knew how to help. Regularly, various parts of the projector's amplifier went defective, valves, transformers, condensers and whatever else we needed to be able to construct the radio. We needed the radio so badly to be able to hear Germany, to hear German news transmissions especially. Beyond that he was always supporting morale with his humour. He was an excellent artist and cartoonist and almost every Sunday a new cartoon was pinned to our notice board. It became part of our Sunday routine to go to the board to see his latest cartoon interpretation of events in the news or in the camp.

The valves that *Rima* had been able to secure were not always quite what we needed for our amplifier, but that was no problem, the radio was redesigned to suit the valves. We were lucky in another way; one of our comrades had to go to hospital in Toronto and while he was there in the hospital he was able to steal valves of exactly the type of which we were so badly in need. Again this required a change of specification but, of course, Niehoff could do this with ease!

At the end of May, without any advance notice, we were woken up one morning by the sound of German soldiers' songs previously not heard in the camp: *'Die blauen Dragoner sie reiten, mit klingendem Spiel durch das Tor!...'* (The blue dragoons ride, with ringing music through the gate...) What was this? The Canadians had informed our camp leader - at the time it was *Korvetenkapitän* Baumann - that we would be getting reinforcements, POWs from the *Afrikakorps*. It had all sounded very vague and indefinite but now it came to fruition. Out of our bunks and into Sunday uniform as quickly as we could was the order of the day and we just managed to get to the camp gate in time. The singing of the one hundred and fifty officers and enlisted men had been so loud, especially at this early hour - well before our normal waking time - it could be heard from miles away. It was a sight for sore eyes as they came marching in their khaki uniforms, the men from the *Afrikakorps*, of whom we had read so much in the Canadian newspapers, especially about *General* Erwin Rommel.

"Look at those soldiers!" some of us said, "when you see this, you can forget all our camp problems!" Honestly, how these young men came marching in! Some only wearing shorts and shirts with breast pockets, all in khaki, just like the English, some of them wearing *'Afrikamützen'* (Africa issue soft caps). Many had types of uniform we'd never seen before, making a real impression, but what had they gone through? There were all kinds of uniform combinations to be seen; some didn't even have shoes - they were marching barefoot - others were only dressed in pyjamas. It was unbelievable, we had to ask ourselves, 'How long have they been prisoners of war?'

Singing, their heads up high, they came marching along and once more the order was given: *'Ein Lied!'* ('Sing!'). Up to just before reaching the camp gate they sang and then came the command: *"Kompaniiie haaalt!"* There they stood like one man! They were still soldiers and they'd made their point, but then the more mundane human activities took over. Baggage had to be unloaded and they had to be searched, one by one in the open, before they were allowed to enter the camp. It was lucky for them it was the end of May 1942 and it was a warm, sunny day.

Once all *'Afrikaner'* were inside the camp, short welcoming speeches were held. A small stocky *Major* spoke for the *'Khakisoldaten'*. He had marched with them but, it transpired, had not commanded them in the field. He was *Major* Meythaler (nick-named *Korkweschte* for reasons which will be explained later) who began his speech in a genuine *pfälzichen* (Rhineland) dialect: *'Die Herre aus Afrika grüsse die Herre in Kanada!'* ('The men from Africa greet the men in Canada!') and already smiles spread across the faces at the sound of the distinctive pronunciation; there were to be many more anecdotes concerning *'Korkweschte'*. After the speeches were over the distance between us and the *'DAK' (Deutschen Afrikakorps)* was broken and a wave of helpfulness took over. *Kapitän* Baumann appealed to all to absorb the new comrades into the existing rooms with good heart. This worked well without further instructions and the 'newcomers' were provided with underwear, trousers and jackets to wear, or at least as far as our own supplies would allow.

One of the 'newcomers', *Oberleutnant* Dr. Paul Huppert [from the *'Oasenbataillon z.b.v. 200* (z.b.v. - 'special forces')], recalls his arrival as follows:

> *'On the second day of Whitsun 1942 we arrived with the Canadian National Railway in Camp '20', having come from New York. The camp inmates, dressed in their best uniforms, were lined up to welcome us. (The majority of uniforms were Luftwaffe and in Kriegsmarine, particularly white, with caps and all medals and honours.)*
>
> *For the 'newcomers' a fine sight that I will never forget. For 'die Alten' (the old-timers) a first confrontation with the war front and above all our incredible clothing which had partially been given to us by the South Africans after our having been robbed. Because we were really full of lice, almost everything we had worn had to be burnt or washed and we were given odd pieces of uniform from the 'old' camp inmates.'*

The *DAK* prisoners had experienced a small *'Weltreise'* (a world cruise): in March approximately three-hundred officers and eight-hundred enlisted men were collected from various camps around Cairo and had been embarked on boats at Suez. Their odyssey then took them through the Suez Canal, along the east coast of Africa to Durban. There they were unloaded and transported by rail to a tent camp near Pieter Maritzburg in South Africa.

There were many tales to be told of the long sea voyage. During the ship's passage, Albrecht, who had been an officer in the Merchant Navy and had become a prisoner while Harbour Master in Bardia, was apparently very much in evidence. Like Franz von Werra, during the journey from England to Canada, Albrecht had been entirely 'at home' on the *'Louis Pasteur'* that had been converted to a troop transporter. To the consternation of the crew and the guards, he was regularly found in almost all parts of the ship.

It was said that rumours were circulating that the Germans would seize the boat en-route. Apparently because of this, once, in middle in the night, the German prisoners were suddenly awakened and were herded into other rooms within the boat. Most of them were only able to take very few of their belongings along. Because it was so hot in the Red Sea, many had slept in their pyjamas or just in their underwear. Afterwards this was all that they owned. The guards, who were not British, had taken everything that had been left back in the cabins and regarded it as their 'loot'. Upon reaching Durban many prisoners disembarked with only a blanket to cover themselves. The scene was so sad that the waiting reporters of the South African newspapers were ashamed to take any photos. It was then the South African soldiers helped out and gave the prisoners pieces of their uniforms that were still in good condition and clean.

After approximately six weeks in the tent camp, they were shipped from Durban to Cape Town (Simonstown) on board the *'SMS Amsterdam'*. There, at the beginning of May, they were transferred to the 82,000 ton *'Queen Elizabeth'* and again some more pieces of clothing went missing. *'The Queen'*, as she was affectionately known by the crew, had been converted to a troop carrier 'for the duration' because she was too fast for the conventional U Boats to catch and really required little or no escort. First the journey took them to Rio de Janeiro and there the boat anchored for twenty-four hours. Then the journey continued northwards, along the east coast of America until New York was reached on 22nd May. On 24th of May the transport was then sorted out. The officers were split into two groups, the larger group together with their assigned orderlies, going to Gravenhurst. At the same time the smaller group, including the *Generale* von Ravenstein and Schmidt, were transported to Bowmanville.

During these boat passages, *Major* Meythaler had been very concerned about his *'Kameraden zur See'* (comrades at sea). In the course of the regular lifeboat drills everybody had to put on their *'Kork-Schwimmweste'* (cork swim vests). According to reports given by other passengers because *Major* Meythaler was short and stocky the addition of the life jacket made him look a sight. Nonetheless he was conscientious about wearing it during these exercises, although many had it that this owed more to the fact that he was a non-swimmer than any special sense of duty. Apparently one day he mislaid his swim vest and asked several people, once more in his distinctive dialect, if they'd seen his *'Korkweschte'*. From then on he had his nickname of *'Korkweschte'* and never lost it. (This can only be pronounced properly in the *Pfälz* dialect[2], otherwise it would be *Korkweste*.)

Being equivalent to *Korvetenkapitän* Baumann in rank, but the longer serving officer, the Canadian Commander appointed *'Korkweschte'* Meythaler as the senior German officer and spokesman at Gravenhurst. However *Major* Meythaler didn't care for this. He saw himself as a soldier and thought the position of *Lagerleiter* (camp leader) needed a political touch, especially as he spoke little or no English. The debate continued with the Canadians and even between the German Officers, but it didn't change things. In the end he resigned himself to the fairly rigid concept of *'Befehl ist Befehl'* (an order is an order) albeit that in the unusual circumstances of the camps it was not always advisable to do so. First he didn't seem to see how potentially dangerous it was when the Canadians did not want to stick completely to the Geneva Convention or when trouble amongst our camp-mates started, principally over rooming. Again he seemed to dismiss the internal disputes of who should be with whom as petty and also wanted to distance himself from the other inmates who were stupid enough to go on escaping. *"Don't they realise that escaping in this huge country is senseless! All this trouble!"*

Try as he would to keep himself from these issues it soon involved him. The Catholic priest, Hans Frense, being a military priest, was graded as a staff officer and, therefore, was entitled to live in the so-called *'Stabsoffizierszimmer'*, the staff officer room on the first floor. For the sailors and the airmen, Frense was something completely new, a priest prisoner of war. His *DAK* co-prisoners reported how bravely he had taken to his fate and many admired how jovial he was for a priest. Because of his openness he was very much liked and he was also not afraid to join one of the numerous *'Skat'* [3] schools and Bridge clubs that existed. In connection with this it must be said that he never went as far as some of the other POW comrades, who had started playing *'Skat'* while still in England, continuing during the boat passage to Canada on board the *'Duchess of York'*, and went on with almost fanatical fervour at Gravenhurst, Camp W and Bowmanville. This did happen and those comrades didn't fare at all badly during the lengthy time of imprisonment, having such a distraction

He also participated in sporting activities, especially playing *Faustball* (fistball - a variation of volley ball), which was admired by many, but living together with others was a problem. I am writing this because it shows, I think, how banal difficulties can arise during imprisonment, even when physical well-being is not lacking. *'Herr Pfarrer'* (Father) was disliked in the *'Stabs'* room because he was telling jokes the whole time, and these were not to the taste of everybody in the room, particulary because, being staff officers, they were generally regular career officers who are not exactly renowned for their sense of humour. Also, in other aspects he did not quite reach the standards of the room.

The results were, that his *Kollegium*, his room-mates, politely asked him to look for another room to live in. And now I will quote the words of another comrade so as to make clear where the problem lay:

> "The *'Korkweschte'* decided that the new room for him was to be the small hole in which 'Doc' Wagner and I lived. There he could *pfürzen* (fart) undisturbed (this being one of the reasons for him being transferred) and also he could drink the sacramental wine, which the Canadians had provided, for all of us. 'Doc' Wagner and I had to move out, the 'Doc' moved into the room where Reini Pfundtner lived and I moved in with 'Quex' Kuhnt and Tochtermann. Because of a lack of space I had to make do with a hammock. My revenge: I stole two bottles of *Pfarrer* Frense's excellent sacramental wine and drunk down my worries. This, my disgraceful deed, was never discovered."

Here we have reached one of the most difficult tasks that the German camp leadership had. Originally *Major* Meythaler just wanted to overlook the various disputes in the different rooms. In purely military terms soldiers should go where they are sent, but that was not a solution for the long term. He got fed up with all these little quarrels and one day decided to nominate a substitute for his position, *Major* Wüstefeld. He was to be responsible for the 'everyday business' and *Korkweschte* remained a sort of figure-head in the background.

With a more sympathetic eye it was soon realised that from time to time changes were necessary in the rooms. There were certain types that just would not fit into any group. For various reasons they did not seem to be able to blend in, to be capable of the necessary compromises. Because of this, about every six months the *Stubenälten* (room elders) gathered and then, with great dedication, 'transfers' were discussed and decided.

We had no wish that anybody be transferred out of our room but of course, we were just as vulnerable as all the others. And it was only the *Kampfgeist* (fighting spirit) of our room elder, Peter Döring, that we had to thank for not getting one of the *Unbeliebten* (unloved ones) put into our room. Over and over it could be seen that certain types had to leave one room after the other and finally never found a place to live, totally rejected. After extremely long discussions, the *Ältestenrat* (committee of the camp elders) came up with the idea to put all these special cases, about fifteen of them, together in one room. It was a difficult decision to impliment, but it was 'the' solution and from then on this room became renowned for its prodigious number of fights, while the rest of us lived in relative peace.

Actually it was astonishing how seldom the undercurrent of emotional depression broke through. Although we were well fed and had, in general, very good living conditions, we also had a strong feeling that we were in isolation, of no further use, outcasts. It was most probably the *zusammenhalten* (comradeship) of common purpose which kept us sane. The enforcement of measures to protect one's own interests and the readiness to run risks from the moment of capture until the final discharge helped to counter those feelings. It was only because of this imposed sense of purpose, on our otherwise apparently worthless existence, that one managed to maintain one's own dignity.

Naturally there were happenings here in the camp which, in normal life, would have just been overlooked, but for us it was a source of continual amusement. For example, our *Stubenältester*, Peter Döring, had read to his surprise, in Eaton's mail order catalogue, that one could buy a nightgown for $1. We all had reasons to be satisfied with the quality of Eaton's goods: One comrade had bought a pocket watch for $1 and, although the watch was made of steel, it ran exactly to the minute. One winter the watch fell into ice cold water and it was spring before he found it again. He oiled it, wound it up, and it ran as precisely as before - therefore Peter ordered his nightgown for $1. When the parcel arrived, and he was able to unpack it under the eyes of the nosy room-mates, this piece of clothing turned out to be a voluminous, white giant of a nightshirt; it absolutely swathed him in material. Nonetheless he wore it for years, most probably to annoy all of us, and many a time it was especially amusing to watch him climb into the upper bunk wrapped in his gigantic nightshirt.

We, and the inmates of most of the other rooms, had modified these double bunks in the very early days. We had altered them in such a manner that the upper mattress could be lowered at an angle as a back rest during the day time. Other than that, the furnishing of the rooms was Spartan in its simplicity. Tables and seating had been made using boards, poles and beams that had been 'recycled' from elsewhere in the camp and, in particular, from the neighbouring attic where we hung our clothing. We were lucky to have this attic room on the same floor as we were and close, only ten metres away. In our rooms there were hardly any wardrobes, and that's where the attic was so handy, for hanging our clothes.

However, we continuously suffered from one big nuisance: we were bitten to excess by bugs. Even today nobody really knows where they came from. Our *DAK* colleagues wanted to accept the responsibility for having brought the bugs into the camp, but there was no hard evidence it was the truth. It took us ages to get rid of them and we tried all means available. At first we boiled all our furniture, wooden bed legs and everything that could be got into the big kettle down on the ground floor, but it didn't cure the problem. Our comrade, Wildermuth, was especially plagued in our room, perhaps because he was the only non-smoker; he must have tasted especially good for the bugs because they wouldn't leave him alone. He even tried the trick of putting the legs of his bed in tin cans filled with water and some chemicals, but it didn't help at all. The bugs just let themselves drop from the ceiling onto him (and all of us as well!).

We finally discovered that one of the partition walls, made of fibre board, was absolutely full of these unfriendly insects. We carefully tore it out and equally carefully burnt it, making sure that the bugs were burnt with it. After that we went on detailed hunts to catch the last few that had escaped and in this manner we managed to overcome the plague of bugs.

Notes on Chapter Seven.

[1] Albrecht - In Gravenhurst he was an important wrestler and later trainer.

[2] Dialects - Here it is worth remembering that at this time actual dialects were more prevalent in countries rather than regional accents. My friend Hinnerk Waller came from North Germany, the Friesland area, and could slip into a very Dutch-sounding dialect which was virtually incomprehensible to me. My *Schwäbisch* was equally foreign to him. It is something which improved communications and travel have reduced and may not be so familiar to younger readers.

[3] Skat - a card game very popular in all services within *Die Wehrmacht*.

CHAPTER EIGHT

GRAVENHURST ALSO GETS MOVING...

The *'new'* camp leader, *Major im Generalstab* (General Staff), Wolfgang Wüstefeld, was respected from the beginning. Prior to his capture, on 23rd November 1941, he was *Ia Führungsgehilfe im Stabe des Deutschen Afrika Korps - DAK* (Ia Assistant to the Leader in the Headquarters of the German Africa Corps) with *General* Erwin Rommel, later with *General* Crüwell. Captured together with him were: *Hauptmann* Neumann, Chief of the *Funkkompanie* (radio) of the DAK, *Leutnant* Wagner, also *Funkoffizier*, *Oberleutnant* Pelzelmayer and *Oberleutnant* Schurich, both *Verbindungsoffiziere* (liaison officers) of the *Flak* for HQ DAK. *Major Diplom Ingenieur* (diploma engineer) Heinrich Keil had also been captured from the staff of the *Oberquartiermeister* (Quartermaster of the DAK). *Major* Wüstefeld was to remain the titular leader of the camp until September 1944, when a more senior ranking officer, *Oberst Freiherr von* Dobeneck, arrived.

The great respect Wüstefeld commanded meant he could depend on the informal assistance of numerous officers. It was of immeasurable help to the camp in redirecting the competitive efforts of *Das Heer* (the army), *Kriegsmarine* and *Luftwaffe* into controlled and mutually advantageous channels. At first, Wüstefeld was assisted by *Hauptmann* Brückmann and then later, also in the role of interpreter, by *Panzeroffizier Leutnant* Dr Kopp with the *Juristen* Dr Liese as his *Adjudant*. Liese and Kopp were, at the same time, also the *Postoffiziere* (post officers), the officers who were always present when the Canadian intelligence officer opened our mail for control purposes. Controls which we were to find, in time, were not always successful in finding everything that was concealed in the parcels and gifts, particularly, as we will see later, in my case.

Besides the Catholic military priest we also had a Protestant (Evangelical) vicar, *Oberleutnant* Seifert. He wasn't a military vicar, but had been captured as an officer of the reserves. Both clergymen held services for the inmates of the camp. The units of the *DAK* that were present at Gravenhurst were a colourful mixture. There were units from the 15th *Panzer Division*, the 21st *Panzer Division*, 90th *Leichten* (light) *Division*, the *Oasen* (oasis) *Bataillon z.b.V. 200*, and also the *Marine-Versorgungseinheiten* (navy support units). As well as the usual mixed bunch from scattered *Panzer,*

Schützen (infantry), *Artilleristen, Pioniere, Flak,* some *Marineflieger* (navy pilots), and a few of the daring *Strafbattallion 900* (punishment battalion) who had managed to escape death. One famous man amongst this wide range of military men was *Hauptmann,* later *Major,* Bach (formally a Protestant vicar), commander of *Schützenregiment 104* (infantry regiment 104). With his troops he had defended the extreme forward position at the Halfaya Pass until he ran out of ammunition. With this action he had been able to prevent the advance of the British for a very long time. In June 1941 he was decorated with the *Ritterkreuz* (Knight's Cross) but sadly he was one of the few that was not able to experience the return home.

North Africa June 1941: In the Command Post Halfaya-Pass after the Sollumschlacht (the battle for Sollum): from left General Rommel, Major Wüstefeldt , General Gause, Hauptmann Bach.

On his arrival in Canada he was obviously very ill but, being the fighter he was, he held out against it. Great efforts were made through the International Red Cross to get him exchanged for equally ill British prisoners, but all in vain. After being operated on in Toronto for a carcinoma in his intestines he died in the camp on 22nd December 1942, six months after arrival in Canada. After his death his best friends, comrades of the

DAK, laid him out with much reverence in Camp Gravenhurst. Officers of the *Afrika Korps* stood vigil at his coffin until the funeral, with full military honours, was held at the Memorial Cemetery in Gravenhurst. Because I was in detention again at this time I was not able to attend, but I was told the Canadians provided a guard of honour, showing great respect for an outstanding soldier. *Major* Bach was buried beside the soldier Erich Ertz, who had died in June. My previous *Staffelkapitän*, *Major* Robitzsch, who had also been shot down over England, carved two very nice crosses for both graves.[1]

Theo Schwabach, a POW from Karlsruhe, *Oberleutnant und Batterie Chief I.Abteilung Flak Regiment 33*, was also awarded the *Ritterkreuz* on 30th June 1941. It was common practice in Africa and elsewhere that the 88mm Flak guns were involved in ground action, shooting at enemy tanks at zero elevation.[2] Schwabach and his battery were in an open desert position and destroyed numerous British tanks during their attack in the *Sollumschlacht* (the battle for Sollum). He had waited so long to give the command *"Feuer frei!"* ("Fire at will!") that the first round from every one of his 88mm *Flakgeschütze* were hits. He had, in the course of talks he gave and in personal conversations, made it very clear how important the roll of the accurate 88mm *Flakgeschütze* had been when fortified positions had to be taken during the invasion of France and how this weapon became the scourge of the enemy tanks during the African campaign.

At a talk some time later, I was sitting beside him and I will never forget Schwabach's disgust when we heard from another *Flak Hauptmann* how he been taken prisoner. After the landing of the Allies in North Africa in 1943 he was *Batterie Chef* of a 105 mm *Flak Batterie*. "As nine Sherman tanks came rolling towards our four dug in *Geschütze* (guns) and opened fire," he said, "we had no other choice than to get out of our trenches, hands raised, and surrender." Schwabach got up in front of the large audience and said furiously, "Actually this man should only have reported how the landing took place! Now I know why this war could no longer be won! With my *Batterie* in the desert, we were on the open ground with no protection and opened fire on more than forty British tanks that were rolling towards us! After we had managed to finish off more than half of them, the rest turned around! And what do our soldiers do to-day?!" There was no way that I, or anyone else, could comfort him. For days he walked his rounds along the fence with a very serious look on his face, immersed in his thoughts. It was a while before he was himself again.

In addition to the doctors, Eitze and Heitsch, that were already in the camp, there came doctors Gress, Fritz and Laubscher. From then on it was

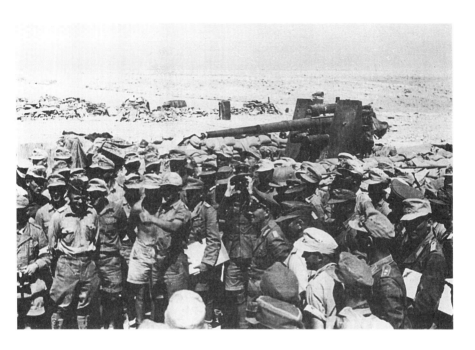

North Africa 1941: After the "Sollumschlacht" in June of 1941, German 8.8cm Flak. Front left with the dark cap Oberleutnant Schwabach, General Rommel in the midst of soldiers of the DAK.

almost possible to run the medical centre in three full shifts. But for the time being we didn't have that many soldiers needing medical care and it was something of a miracle that Jupp Bürschgens, an *Oberleutnant* and pilot with the *JG 26*, was able to hold his position as *Sani* (*Sanitätsgehilfe* - Medic) in the centre; perhaps it was because of his impish *Rheinischer* (Rhineland) humour and ebullient character that they kept him there.

Some parts of the medical centre had first to be rebuilt and repaired before they could be used. A much used part was the *Schwitz* (sweat bath - Sauna; part of the treatment of former TB patients when Gravenhurst was a sanatorium) which could have competed well with a public steam bath, such was its finished quality. In a basement room there were pipes laid on the floor and connected to the steam heating system. These pipes had very small holes drilled in them and one sat above this construction on a very crude wooden bench. When covered with a thick blanket or towels it resulted in profuse and very effective sweating. Dr Eitze was always fond of prescribing this treatment when one had caught a cold. Because I suffered several times

North Africa summer 1941: General Rommel in the harbour at Bardia with Oberleutnant zur See Albrecht (on the right) and Italian Navy Officers.

with angina[3], I was also subjected to this treatment, but without marked success. I mostly then resorted to an old *Hausmittel* (home made remedy), which helped me. Very hot boiled potatoes in a linen sack were laid on the neck, as hot as one could take, as a poultice until the ulcer was ripe and opened up inwards.

After the living quarter problems had been solved satisfactorily, we could turn our attention to other matters again. Our *Backschafter* (*Kriegsmarine* slang for 'service crew' - NCOs and enlisted men allocated to the camp to provide some services for the officers) finally moved into their wooden barracks which had just been completed. A group of officers under the leadership of *Hauptmann* Brückmann then set-to, renovating the rooms on the ground floor. These soon became the meeting place for entertainment, chess and card games. Anyone who saw the premises before and after the renovation must have believed in miracles. There had been dirty door frames, warped doors, rags and tatters hanging from the walls. I admit I wondered whether it was possible to do anything with these rooms in such a state.

Equipped with razor blades, the renovation troop started their work and scraped...and scraped...! First the walls were washed clean, then the door frames were scraped clean with the razor blades, centimetre by the centimetre. Under this appeared mahogany and maple wood frames which were then sanded down and covered with a coat of varnish; it was clear by then that the complete renovation was going to be worthwhile. After several weeks of work the official opening was celebrated in shifts, each party having saved their beer for the ceremony. The rooms were finally decorated and one could regard them as a sort of *gemütliche* (friendly) canteen.

The classrooms were installed in various corners of the buildings. They were not only partitioned off and renovated, but were also used intensively. Senior instructor and principal was *Reservehauptmann* (reserve captain) and *Landesforstmeister* (state forester) Dr Querengässer. It was said he had been predestined for the future German Colonies after the war had been won (such thoughts still existed). When listening to his forest speeches one realised that he knew a lot about the African and tropical forests and their trees. (After the war was over he spent several years as a forestry advisor in West Africa.) There were training courses offered for the *Abitur* (matriculation - equivalent to the A level GCE) in various grades. In charge of these courses was *Oberleutnant* Blume (*Studienrat* - senior teachers grade) and approximately fifty officers took part in these courses. The written examination tasks were submitted through the International Red Cross of Switzerland to the Ministry of Education in Berlin. From there the subjects for the written examinations were returned. The *Abitur* that was passed in this form was then later recognized by acting *Reichskulturminister* Rust and the individual officers acquired recognition in Canada. The teachers were *Studienräte* for general subjects, officers with interpreters' qualifications for languages and graduated chemists and physicists in their specialist fields.

I had passed *Abitur* at the end of my school time and soon participated in a technician course, the aim of which was the *Physikum*, the preliminary university examination course for machine design and construction. I was finally fed up with trying to escape and decided it was time that I continued my education. In this course, all subjects were taught that were in the curriculum at the *Hochschule* (high school). Our instructor, responsible for our relatively specialist course of instruction, was *Hauptmann* Kahlenberger. He, in civilian life, had instructed at a school for engineers and thus knew the broad subject outline. The special subjects, such as mathematics, mechanics, physics, material knowledge etc. were all taught by personnel who originated from technical occupations and by the specialists.

Here was a real advantage in the army having more reserve officers than the *Kriegsmarine* or the *Luftwaffe*. The reserve officers had been trained for the military and then returned to their full-time occupations. Now that the war had expanded so much, the government had drawn on more and more of its reserve officers, bringing them into full time service. Thus we had the benefit of professional people who knew about more than military tactics and warfare. I, as a young *Leutnant*, had helped to train a reserve *Nachrichtenzug* (communications platoon) whilst we were stationed at Böblingen near Stuttgart. These had been lawyers, doctors and accountants, all highly intelligent and professional men who really gave me a tough time in a good-natured way (see "Spitfire On My Tail" p 152).

Statics were instructed by Kahlenberger himself, but in knowledge of materials he took turns with the geologist, Dr Michels, who owned a pumice stone quarry in the Rheinland. Wood and forestry were instructed by Dr Querengaesser and *Forstmeister* (master forester) *Oberleutnant* Schnaidt who was, for me, a fellow and very sympathetic *Swabian*. Our forest specialists were not just theorists and concerned with the health and management of standing timber, but also very practical trained carpenters similar to the *Pioniere* (pioneers). Chemistry was instructed by *Leutnant* Kopp, physics by *Oberleutnant* Dr Braune and machine construction by *Major Diplom Ingineur* Keil. Of course the specialist teachers were also instructing in their subjects in other courses.

The forestry courses went over four terms in Canada and the courses were later recognized post-war. For example, the former Canadian POWs Kreisler and Wallbillich were able to continue their studies once back home and were later to become *Forstdirektoren* (forest directors). The *Förster* (foresters) shared the classroom in which the *Land und Forstwirtschaft* (agricultural and forestry management) was taught, together with the *Medizinern* (medical students) who were later given separate facilities. Because of a shortage of available rooms it was necessary that *Förster* and the *Mediziner* had to study in shifts, which was not always that easy. In later times, when we had that farm, the *Mediziner* could dissect sick piglets because it was said that the pig's organs and those of the human are similar, as is the basic structure of the body. With this, the agricultural and the medical students could happily cooperate together as well as with their shifts and shared facilities.

As far as foreign languages were concerned, there was an abundance of courses available. English and French were offered in several grades, for beginners, advanced and then English specialised. 'Doc' Wagner, who besides law, also instructed in American English and went so far as to teach his scholars American slang. Specialised English for technical, economic and the sciences was taught in modules. But not only these popular languages

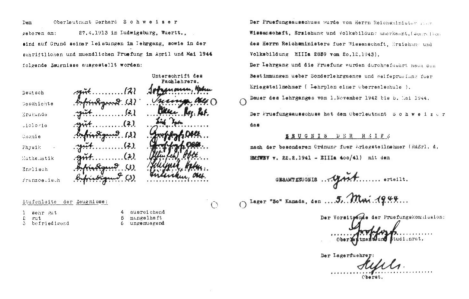

Abitur zeugnis: Final Report. This is how the 'metriculation' examination certificate looked in Canada. After some initial deliberations these were fully recognised after returning home.

were available - Spanish, Italian and even Russian were offered. *Sonderführer* (special leader) Schwochau, our professor for singing, not only gave singing instruction, but also, having been a singer at La Scala in Milan, was able to offer a course in Italian. Examinations as interpreters for English and French were taken and also recognised later. Exceptionally successful was our actor for ladies roles (in the camp theatre) *Quex* Kuhnt (his nickname came from the *Hitlerjunge* film *Quex*). He studied and learnt, entirely from books, Arabic and arabic script. Already, while still a POW in Canada, he prophesied that with this rare language, he would later work for the diplomatic service. And it actually happened, after the war he was in the diplomatic service for several years, at first in Cairo and later on as the Federal German Republic Ambassador in Abu Dabi.

In the subject of law there were excellent classes to be attended. Not only were there outstanding lawyers teaching, but also experienced Government officials were available. Dr Völker (the leading State Attorney), 'Doc' Wagner, *Oberleutnant* Fitschen and Dr Liese lectured on all themes of law that were necessary to cover the first term. In the subjects *Volks und Betriebswirtschaft* (political and business economics), *Oberleutnant* Dr Huppert led a *Handelshochschule* (trade high school) in Gravenhurst with great initiative. He wrote to his previous *Doctorvater* (university supervisor), Professor Dr Rössle, at the *Technische Hochschule* (TH) Munich, and asked him for his assistance. Rössle sent books and term schedules and initiated the necessary connection to the *Kuratorium für Fachliteratur* (Board of Trustees for Special Literature) in Berlin. From the course, participants received training and specialised books for their studies. Almost all scholars of Dr Huppert were *fernimmatrikuliert* (comparable with studying by correspondence course) with Professor Dr Rössle through our Dr Huppert's enterprise. A connection between the prisoner of war camp in Canada and *Heimat* (homeland) represented a great sustaining link for the POWs.

The training courses were verified at the end by a commission and the teachers involved. After the war many of these training courses were recognised and led to short studies. Of course at the time we didn't know this, we had no idea what the future held. The study of literature was also provided through the YMCA by the good work of Professor Dr Böschenstein, the Swiss citizen. In our camp we had a very good connection with him: *Luftwaffe Leutnant* Walter Stirnat had been a member of the same sailing club in Kiel together with Böschenstein and during his first visit to the camp he immediately recognised Stirnat. Although he was Swiss citizen, Böschenstein had studied *Germanistik* (German studies) in Kiel before the war.

Maybe this coincidence was why Professor Böschenstein paid many visits to our camp and regularly attended events held in the camp, calling it a *Kulture-Oase* (cultural oasis) in Canada. He was especially enthusiastic in his support of our camp theatre. He tried to fulfil almost every request we had in this respect, or at least whenever it was within his powers. He provided many costumes and decorations, items we would never have been able to make ourselves.

Walter Stirnat, himself an enthusiastic POW actor, wrote about these experiences:

> *"The camp theatre stood under the leadership of Dicken Bülk. Distinguished actors were: Quex Kuhnt (Joan of Arc), Thurz (also specialist for female roles), Zwarg (Tolstoi). My best role was the maid, Stiene, in the comedy 'Krach um Jolanthe' (Quarrel over Jolanthe). My partner was Hein Törber in the role of the farm hand Hannes. In this play I had to give him a kiss, which I did so*

'passionately', that he didn't have enough time left to take his pipe out of his mouth. The result was a broken front tooth which, to loud applause, fell clicking onto the stage. All the audience thought this was part of the play and were tremendously amused. "

Theatre costumes: In this group photo theatre costumes of various plays were being worn. Amongst others "A night in Venice". Front row: Beside the hangman: 'Stickel' Stirnat, 'Tolstoi' Doerwald, K.H. Thurz, who also looked good as a bar girl. Dressed as a nun is Leutnant Zwarg, to the extreme right is 'Quex' Kuhnt, (later Ambassador in Abu Dabi).

Besides 'Stickel' Stirnat, women's roles were also played very convincing by Karl Heinz Thurz. One time we decorated a room with paper chains and with coloured lights for Fastnachtszeit (carnival time before Shrove Tuesday). We also played music under the leadership of Oberleutnant Bärtling. Thurz sat behind the bar dressed as a barmaid; he really was a wonderful sight with his stuffed breasts and interesting coloured drinks he was pouring out, but nobody asked him to dance! - although many drinks had been 'saved', the right atmosphere never occurred.

As well as the theatre performances there were also other various musical recitals which were made possible after Professor Böschenstein provided us with more and more musical instruments. We had a large orchestra, under the leadership of *Oberleutnant* Pfanmüller, for the various works of chamber music. A brass and march music band played under *Oberleutnant* Bärtling, who also directed the ballroom orchestras, both large and small - all that was missing for the dancing were the real women!

A special experience were the singing recitals given by Professor Schwochau. He had not only been a tenor at La Scala, Milan, before the war, but was exceptionally proud of the fact that in 1937 he had been invited to sing in Westminster Abbey at the coronation of King George VI. Schwochau visited our room many times and, as time went on, we initiated a new feature on our *Veranda mit Seeblick* (veranda with view to the lake). Combined with a Sunday round (stroll around the inner perimeter) we began what we called *Kultur-frühstück* (cultural breakfast). He was one of our first guests, one of the people with whom we wanted closer contact. Another was Kilian Koll (pseudonym for the author Karl Bunje), who was many a time our guest. Schwochau and Koll, who had been captured as *Luftwaffe Hauptleute* (Captains), had a lot to talk about, especially Schwochau, who could report on his experiences outside of Germany in the times prior to *Machtübernahme* (take over of power by the *Nazis*).

Kilian Koll was from the older generation who had experienced the First World War and always calmed with the words *"...es geht alles vorüber"* ("with time all things will pass"). As the author of many folk plays and comedies he also had the right proportion of humour. He always liked to talk about *Nikolaichen* (little Nikolai) or his *Haus mit Schwein* (house with pig) in East Prussia, when he started talking about his wife at home, or when he enthusiastically talked about his *Tigerweibchen* (little tiger woman), it was always amusing to listen to. His book *Etappenhase* (a phrase meaning an 'old soldier' - a survivor) had already been filmed before the war and it was actually my contact with him which prompted me to put my experiences in connection with the various escape attempts to paper while still in Canada.[4]

Sport was also of very great importance. We had almost everything: light athletics which, because of the competitions that were continually being held, became very popular with all the camp inmates. Running events were always very competitive and difficult because the inside of our camp was really very small, but the enthusiasm of our ingenious sportsmen hardly knew any boundaries. There was a basket ball field built, a tennis court and a boxing ring all out in the open air and the gymnastic specialists struggled along on a lawn in the garden. With surprise I observed how the one time *Kapitän* of a *Hilfskreuzer* (fleet auxiliary cruiser) through months of intensive gymnastics got his oversize stomach to dwindle. But then this gymnastic group was led by a diploma sports teacher, Herrn Insinger.

Reini, Sergeant Rule during the pole painting episode and fellow escaper, was one of our most talented sportsmen. In the camp tennis tournament he almost always ended up in the finals against *Luftwaffe Oberleutnant* Ronge, who had been the Silesian youth champion. It was a real tennis festival when all the camp residents turned out with benches and deck chairs to surround the tennis court to watch the final match between the two of them. Reini, who had earlier been junior champion in the *Rot-Weiss-Berlin* (famous Berlin sports club), played very aggressive tennis during which his opponent managed to force him to make mistakes. These tennis tournaments were a very special event in the otherwise mundane POW camp life. Days before the tournament everybody was discussing it, who would win this time, Reini or would someone completely different make it to the finals? Reini also organised the ice hockey games. In Camp W (Neys) we had already begun to build the first ice hockey field when we were moved to Camp 30. In Bowmanville we created a very good ice hockey rink and then, in Gravenhurst, it was clear from the beginning that the tennis court had to be constructed in such a manner that it could be converted for ice hockey in winter and there was no other sport for which the Canadians were so helpful. Our guards were genuinely very sad that our POW camp teams weren't allowed to play against local ice hockey teams. Reini Pfundtner had already played ice hockey as a young boy, again for the *Rot-Weiss*, and had been a junior substitute for the 1936 German Olympic team. He was not only an expert player, but he also know how to train, both in winter and summer.

I played both tennis and ice hockey, but always had troubles with my left knee that had been severely strained during my parachute landing. It was also a handicap for me when doing light athletics.[5] I ran quite a lot to keep fit, nowadays known as jogging. Hinnerk and I had brought the enthusiasm for boxing with us from Fort Henry and we were therefore always helping to see that the right training equipment was obtained and set up. Before too long, 'Jupp' Bürschgens took over the responsibility for this sport because he knew far more about it than we did. We shared a cellar room with the wrestlers that were led by *Oberleutnant zur See* Albrecht. Only once did I get myself into a boxing match in public. My opponent was U-Boat *Kapitänleutnant* Esterer and naturally, during the fight, the spectators were immediately split into two groups. Here you had the *Kriegsmarine* and there the *Luftwaffe*. The *Afrikaner* didn't take sides initially, but then joined in with loud cheers and applause, especially every time that I took a hit.

On this occasion I discovered that my nature was not prepared for the rising rage in me. Every time that I received a stupid punch, the mob scoffed loudly! That was not at all good for my spirit and I became more and more annoyed every time I heard the applause for my opponent and started boxing without using my brain...just in temper. The result? I lost! Not through a K.O., but clearly by points!

So as not to admit that I had taken quite a beating, I plugged my bleeding nose and went straight to the tennis court to play a match there. Photographs exist, by coincidence, that were taken by a Canadian group photographer the next day. On these my 'boxing nose' can be clearly seen. From this *Krampf* (rubbish experience) I still have a slightly bent nose as an everlasting reminder. But this *Kampf* (fight) was also very educational; I continued boxing, but never again in front of spectators.

Gravenhurst May 1943. From left back row: Ltn. Theopold, Ltn. Vater, unknown, Obltn. Dr Liese, Hptm. Döring, Hptm. Wildermuth. Front row: Ltn. Becker, Obltn. Steinhilper (with boxing nose), unknown, Obltn. Niehoff.

Notes on Chapter Eight.

[1] Long after the War, in 1976, Walter Stirnat, who had in the meantime qualified as a pharmacologist, and Siegfried Tochtermann visited Canada and the two graves. They found them in an excellent condition. *Hauptmann* Neumann, (Staff DAK mentioned earlier on) had emigrated to Canada very soon after the war and had been taking care of the graves. During 1977 both graves were transferred to the German section for deceased POWs in the Woodland Cemetery in Kitchener (which had been called Berlin until 1918) in Ontario. Sadly the wooden cross from Major Bach's grave was badly damaged in 1978 when many graves were desecrated by vandalism in the course of Holocaust reprisals.

[2] Flak - It is worth remembering here that the *Flak Batterien* were *Luftwaffe* personnel. It may seem odd, but nonetheless true, that *Luftwaffe Flak* gunners, using the versatile '88s', were credited with thousands of tanks destroyed in all theatres during WW 2.

[3] Angina - It is common in German speaking countries to call all problems in the upper respiratory tract and throat, including ulceration, 'angina'. It does not have exactly the same cardio-vascular associations as it does in English.

[4] As fate would have it, in approximately 1965, when I was already working in the management level of IBM Germany, a young man by the name of Claus Bunje applied for a salesman job in Stuttgart. Being in charge of personnel I was able to direct the conversation and discovered with surprise he was the son of my one time fellow prisoner. We were able to hire Claus and he developed into a valuable asset for the company.

[5] This ultimately led to my having a hip replacement when I was sixty-six.

CHAPTER NINE

'EHRENWORT'(PAROLE)

It took a long time before we reached an agreement with the Canadians on our *'Ehrenwort'*('word of honour'). At first our intention was to be allowed to go for walks in the beautiful surroundings of the camp and the idea was that we would give our *'Ehrenwort'*, our parole, that during such excursions no escape attempts would be made. At last the day came when a large number of POWs gathered at the gate and waited to taken for a walk by a Canadian officer and two guards. But the guards were armed and that finished it for us; when we gave our word of honour there was no need for weapons. "Then you won't go!" was the Canadians' answer. Result - no walk.

After further discussions we reached an agreement: one unarmed Canadian officer would lead and two veteran guards would bring up the rear. In this manner we then enjoyed many beautiful walks in the charming rocky landscape along Lake Muskoka. Being knowledgeable, by virtue of my rural upbringing, of the various berries and wild fruits which grow, I was able to open my comrades' eyes to the wealth of varieties which grew in the surrounding areas. This naturally led to an application to the Canadians for us to look for the good berry-growing areas and then, the next day, for us to go straight to our destination. In such cases our whole room was equipped with the necessary tins for collecting the fruit. Half an hour marching to the site, one hour berry picking and half an hour's march back to the camp. No way were we allowed to exceed the two hours without penalty.

Most of the times we had a wonderful harvest, whether it was wild strawberries in summer, and the blue berries or wild cherries or even blackberries in autumn. In the course of these walks we were not allowed to be led through populated areas. Contact with the local residents was to be strictly avoided. One time one of the locals was very inquisitive and approached our group unnoticed from behind. Upon reaching the rear Canadian veteran guard, he spoke to him with great concern, telling him it was unthinkable to let so many Germans walk through the country side and with guards which were unarmed! The guard tried to calm him down, and some of our group listened in on this conversation:
"Yes, but what will you do if they suddenly decided to flee, simply run

away! You don't even have a pistol to shoot at them!" The guard replied, "They're on parole!" "What's that?" asked the local. It wasn't at all easy to explain to him. Then the guard had an idea and answered: "If they give their parole, that's like money, that's even better than money!" I don't know whether that nosy citizen understood what the guard had said but, in the meantime, the Canadian officer in the lead had caught wind of the discussions going on in the rear. He immediately dropped back and asked the man from Gravenhurst to leave immediately.

During these walks we also realised how many fish were swimming in the various pools that we passed, it was a pity that we couldn't go fishing there. Interesting also were the paths that we used, you could hardly go twenty metres in before you were lost in the midst of the virtually untouched forest. It was definitely most interesting to experience the beauty of the wild Canadian country side in this manner. Also completely new for us were the lorries full of pickers that arrived from Toronto in the best berry picking times. The guards told us that many of these pickers just boarded the lorries in the morning in Toronto to pick on their own account, but the majority were naturally picking for the lorry owners.

During these excursions we also went through and around a farm many times, the buildings had been burnt down and it was abandoned. The farm consisted of pastures, fields with good soil, shrubs and properly husbanded woods. Many of our farmers' boys crumbled the good soil through their fingers and, in their mind's eye, saw heards of fat Frisian cows chewing on the rich cud. One side of it was bordered by a beautiful bubbling stream to supply copious fresh water and to go around the whole farm perimeter we needed the complete two hours of our word of honour walk.

After the Canadians realised that we kept to our word, we were also allowed to go swimming in the lake immediately adjacent to the camp. A floating rope was the border of the area that we were allowed to swim in, but it was large enough for us to mark a twenty-five metre long lane and also a field for water polo. The sport divers, under the leadership of *Major* Müller, constructed themselves a diving board and a sort of tower to dive from. We had people amongst us that then, in summer, spent two hours from ten till twelve in the morning and again two hours in the afternoon in the water. The swimmers had their problems in winter: they had no opportunity to do any training and if they had no substitute sport they accumulated a layer of body fat.

Water polo was popular in the season, but during the games there was always a problem for the referee because he couldn't see what was happening under the brackish water in the depth of the lake. Many a shot at the goal never happened because the thrower was suddenly attacked from below by mysterious 'dark powers' that pulled him down into the depths!

Also on *'Ehrenwort'* we were allowed to make a soccer field on the open ground across from the camp gate. In the summer months it was used for football and handball and during the second winter we used it as our ice hockey field. There were always more and more newcomers who wanted to take a try at this *Kampfsport* (combat sport). In the beginning we had sufficient skates for all who wanted to play, but we didn't have enough protection for the shoulders, the face or legs. Injuries were, therefore, not only to be found amongst the goal keepers. One time during the winter, when the lake was frozen over, the Canadians allowed us go skating on the lake. Hardly had we been allowed to start than the POWs spread out all over the lake, assisted by the high speeds attainable on ice. On the shore there remained a very nervous guard team. They were all very pleased and relieved when they counted us all back in without any 'losses'. Canadian citizens had also been skating on the lake at that time and contacts had inevitably been made with them. It was, therefore, the one and only time we were allowed out on the lake skating. Each of us that had missed this one time opportunity was very sorry afterwards.

On the Canadian side our *Pferdedieb* (horse thief - see 'Ten Minutes To Buffalo') came to Gravenhurst as the interpreter and was now also the Intelligence Officer. Already in Camp W he had really 'shone' because of his *'excellent'* German. On the notice board could be read another example of his *'exemplary'* German in a written instructions: *"Wenn das kanadische Kommandant sich macht seine Nummer, müssen die German Officers Salut schiessen"*. This means, when directly translated,: "When the Canadian Commander makes himself his number, must the German officers fire salute." What he was actually trying to say was: "When the Canadian Commander takes the roll call, then the German Officers should stand to attention and salute".

In the meantime it had become obvious that he secretly had great respect for us Germans. Personal conversations took place and we found out his background which had remained a bit of a mystery. In Camp W at Neys he had most probably kept his own counsel, being afraid of what his fellow Canadians might think. Our *Lagerleiter* at Neys, *Oberstleutnant* von Wedel, had been a cavalry officer on the eastern front during the First World War. At the time he was stationed in the Ukraine and there he had established his billet in the large estate of Graf Tschramshenkow, father of our *Pferdedieb*. It seemed *Pferdedieb's* admiration for us went back to those days with von Wedel. In the course of the fighting between the Red and the White our

Pferdedieb was a White Russian officer and was injured, ending up in the military hospital where an English nurse took care of him. They later married and afterwards, because in the view of his family he had married 'below himself', they packed him off to Canada. There he barely made his living by dealing with horses, that's where his nickname *Pferdedieb* came from. Even after becoming an intelligence officer he couldn't stop dealing and trading. [1]

My initial report on Gravenhurst would not be complete without something which *Oberleutnant* Schnabel once wrote. He had already managed to escape in England, together with *Hauptmann* Wappler. Their outstanding effort entailed stealing a training plane and trying to fly to France. They got it started OK and actually took off but because of strong head winds they ran low on fuel and were forced to make the heart-breaking decision to turn back, making an emergency landing in England.

Schnabel managed to get exchanged from Canada back to Germany and upon his return home he wrote a report on Gravenhurst to my parents.

Oberleutnant Heinz Schnabel   Postmark: Zwickau 04/8/44
Altenburg/Thüringen
Bruehl 3

REPORT

On living in Prisoner of War Camp "20" Gravenhurst/Canada. Only for family members of the prisoners of war! Duplication or publication in any form forbidden!

THE CAMP

The camp lies in Ontario, approximately 150 kilometres north of Toronto. It lies between the small summer excursion town of Gravenhurst and the Muskoka Lake. This lake is approximately 50 kilometres east of the Georgian Bay of Lake Huron. At its closest the shore of Lake Muskoka is only 300 metres away from the camp fence, therefore, there is an excellent view. The lake lays in mountainous, partially rocky countryside covered with low to medium high mixed forests, similar to the areas around the German *Mittelgebirge*. These forests continue inside the camp in the form of thinner leaf trees. Therefore the open areas of the camp, also due to the care of the German prisoners, has a park like atmosphere. The camp perimeter is five cornered and the path on the inside of the fence is almost 400 metres long.

Because all the buildings - consisting of one large stone house in which the officers are accommodated and where the classrooms are, one large mess-hall with built on kitchen (officers' dining room) and one double walled large winter barracks for the enlisted men - are within the fence, the available open area for the 300 officers and 100 enlisted men is very restricted.

To make the greatest use of the open area, it has been sectioned as follows: Half of it has been cultivated with much effort of the German prisoners, there are lawns, flower beds, paths and a rock garden also. Two artificial ponds have been made and they contain various water animals that have been caught in the lake.

As a showpiece, raised in the middle of it all, there is a home-made terrarium, in which a number of various snakes and frogs are making each other's lives difficult. To the side of the *'garden'* is the light athletics corner with high and long jump and shot putting facilities. That was the front side of the camp towards the gate.

In the rear, towards the lake, the following miniature sports fields have been created: a fistball corner, a 'navy ball' corner, a basket ball corner, together with a home-made free ring and a high horizontal bar for gymnastics. Immediately outside the camp lies the football ground, again made by us. On this ground it is only possible to play football and hand ball under 'special guard'[2] and at certain times. Down at the lake it is possible to swim outside the camp fence, but again fenced in with barbed wire and under 'special guard' during the summer months only. The sport officer controls all the sport activities. The following ball games are played very extensively: handball, fistball, basketball, navy ball. Also gymnastics and light athletics are popular.

To bring some entertainment and diversion into the monotonous life in camp the following institutions have been founded: a symphony orchestra of approximately 50 officers, a ball room and entertainment orchestra and a brass band for march music also exists.

Every Sunday morning a military parade in the best uniform is held. It is always accompanied by marching music and the German camp leader holds a short speech in which special events of the past week are commented upon and then the speaker reads the programme for the coming week.

From time to time, musical evenings are held, during which a large variety of our German musical treasures are played.

Occasionally an entertainment evening is also held. On these evenings the ballroom and entertaining orchestra are the central focus and various comrades bring all kinds of short acts and routines to amuse the audience.

Several times we also had a theatre evening in which even the female roles were played to their best by the officers. Films, provided through the Y.M.C.A., are at first censored by the camp. If they pass then they are shown for all the POWs.

GENERAL

Concerning the relationship with the *English* (n.b. actually Canadian - *'English'* is a figure of speech) Camp Commander it must be said, as can be read in this report, we try to do everything under our own administration, through which the possibilities of running into conflict with the *English* is reduced to an absolute minimum. Because the *English* want to be sure that their soldiers are treated well in the German prisoner of war camps and they know that reports of bad treatment would sooner or later reach Germany and therefore could be the cause for retaliation. They provide, sometimes after long discussions and disputes, whatever is required for life in the camp. I emphasize again, that they do not do it because of the Geneva Convention, but only for the benefit of the English prisoners in Germany, which we know only too well from the times before Dunkirk.
The attitude of the *English* Camp Commander is, of course, of great importance. Certain regulations exist governing the treatment of POWs and this, in general, does not lead to too great difference in the essentials of everyday life. So treatment in the various camps is almost the same.
For everybody who, based on my report, gains the impression that life as a POW is ideal, I wish to remind them that a prisoner is lacking everything because one essential ingredient is missing - he is lacking freedom. This cannot be compensated for, not even with the greatest amount of comfort. To this comes an extra burden for the German Officer POWs in Canada, that they in no way have the freedom of movement the prisoners of war in Germany are used to (it was not uncommon for Allied POWs to 'work out'). The complete life takes part behind barbed wire. The walks that have been recently introduced take place on special paths, that more or less lead through the wilderness. One has no opportunity to observe the normal hustle and bustle of life.

ORGANISATION

Life in the camp is set up in such a manner that we can approach the *English* closely to exert the necessary pressure for our requirements. At the top we have the German Camp Leader, who has the final decision in all matters. He names a Deputy Camp Leader who is responsible for everyday matters in the camp and the traffic with the *English*. At his disposal he has a German adjutant, an interpreter and an officer responsible for all written matters (also POW Officers). This so-called camp leadership also has officials in charge of: press, canteen, laundry, music, lessons, stage, sport, kitchen, film, workshop and mail. There is also a Company Commander for the 100 enlisted men and non-commissioned officers in the camp. In this manner it is guaranteed that life in camp can take place with the least disturbance and the best results can be achieved in all matters.

LESSONS AND TRAINING COURSES

We spared no effort to provide all possibilities for a systematic working atmosphere. For this purpose the following training courses were initiated: Two classes for taking the *Abitur* (matriculation) with approximately 30 in each class. The aim was to achieve the *Reifeprüfung*, the end of school certificate proving an attained level of education. We received confirmation from the *Reich* (Government) that the examinations would be fully recognised. One class began their written examinations in April of this year, and the second will follow in August. A Technical Working Group has done preparation work for the preliminary examinations with a type of Technical High School as target. It is not yet certain whether the examinations can be held in the camp. I have myself participated in this training course and know from experience that excellent work is being produced.

A Legal Working Group is busy with the preparations for the studies of law and also providing exercise for those who had already started studies of the same. Again there are excellent instructors amongst the imprisoned officers.

A large number of foreign language courses in English, French, Spanish, Russian, Italian and Latin are being offered for all stages in the language concerned. The aim of these courses is the Certified Interpreter examination. Almost every officer is taking part in one or other course. An agricultural group of specialists is trying to work out theoretical courses and also practical courses for the training to become a farmer.[3] A Trade High School serves to instruct those officers with previous knowledge in this branch.

Shorthand lessons were also given in some groups. To keep up the interest in common subjects continually talks are being held by guest speakers on subjects like hunting rights, reports of experiences, economic, political and state sciences.

PRESS, SPORT, ENTERTAINMENT

The Press Officer has the task to prepare a daily news bulletin compiled from all the newspapers available in the camp. This is then read out loud during the midday meal.

CONCLUSION

Practically speaking, the walks are not at all different from the complete life in the camp. As far as the atmosphere is concerned the camp is excellent. Characteristic of this is the tone of the enemy press. When one of their readers asked whether it is possible to politically influence the German prisoners of war in their camps the reply was: "The same as a leopard cannot change his spots so the Nazi[4] officer cannot change his political thinking..."

With this I give you the assurance, that the comrades are waiting longingly, but with iron discipline for our final victory, which would give them their long awaited freedom.

Gravenhurst 1943 - From left to right: Rudolf Theopold, Hinnerk Waller, myself, Eberhard Wildermuth, Ltn. Vater, 'Jupp' Bürschgens, Hannes Strehl, 'Fürst' Büchler, Karl Stix.

Notes on Chapter Nine

[1] In 1944 he not only arranged for us to get the farm, but also the white horse "Maxi". The story of the acquisition of the farm doesn't fall into my time at Gravenhurst, but it is still well worthwhile reporting it in detail. This we have done in appendix one at the end of the book. The reports and photos from comrades are the basis for this.

[2] Schnabel was apparently not allowed to report in detail on our parole and therefore twice mentioned the 'special guard'.

[3] For the report on the training courses, for example the agricultural, one has to bear in mind that Schnabel was reporting on the situation during the winter of 1943/44, before the farm was acquired - hence the use of the word *theoretical*.

[4] *Nazi* officers - see also Appendix 2, the report and exchange of correspondence with the Watertown Daily Times in 1985.

CHAPTER 10

SPIRIT - MIND - BODY

The *Afrikaner* had been well absorbed into camp life and the summer suddenly returned to Gravenhurst, more or less missing spring altogether, and suggesting that even the seasons shared the Canadians' habitual lack of punctuality. Actually we could have properly enjoyed our wonderful *holiday resort* but, as *Oberleutnant* Schnabel wrote: "... a prisoner is lacking everything because one essential ingredient is missing - he is lacking freedom."

Although the birch, beech and maple trees seemed to have opened their buds overnight, and the brown glimmering green became lighter day by day to brighten our world. One should remember that at the time we were young men between twenty and thirty and not of the type that was prepared, by training or philosophy, for a life of almost monastic seclusion. However, it was our lot and we made the best we could out of it all. To help cope, various different life philosophies were created and were then discussed in detail.

Many were glad that their wives at home knew that they were in a safe place and not in the front line. Others, like myself, felt free not having any family ties of that kind; even my girlfriend of the time had become engaged to someone else whilst I was in Bowmanville. Others had preserved relationships and were glad of that firm connection as an anchor. Some were even thinking of having a marriage ceremony in absentia, which was not impossible, everything you needed to know about this being published in the German Red Cross information pamphlets.

Especially tragic were cases when a prisoner received news that his wife at home was expecting a child or had already had a child by another man. What was there to be done in cases like this? A distant divorce? Certainly there was no compassionate leave from our circumstances! There were more than enough occasions when one had to think about one's own fate and also about one's friends fate and talk it over with them.

At this point I judge it is appropriate to mention again the many POW letters that my parents collected and kept very conscientiously. Judge when reading through these letters I realise how much I left out, how it was impossible to communicate some of the most important things that were worrying me and what the real conditions were like (Notes in brackets are to help the reader understand what would have been obvious to the members of my family). For example, my parents knew nothing of my three escapes.

On 27th December 1941 I wrote to my father (Christmas 1941 began in solitary confinement in Bowmanville, after my second attempted escape that ended in Montreal):

'Because I have been busy with other things, it was not possible for me to write before the end of the month. In the meantime the whole world has joined in on the war, but we are still confident. I spent Christmas with Father Philipp!
- Your Uli!"

The only hint I was able to write about an event as important as my escape on a goods train to Montreal was my reference to *'other things.'* The reference to *'Father Philipp'* is soldier's expression for solitary confinement, *der Teng.* Whether, at home, they were able to 'read between the lines' I didn't know; or if, perhaps, our *Abwehr* (military intelligence) had been reading the American newspapers at home and knew what I'd been up to I don't know. After all, my escape to the United States across the Niagara border had been well publicised in the U.S. and Canadian press. Whether my parents had been informed through official sources that their son had been courageous twice when escaping I didn't know. Or, for that matter, if they would soon know that yet again I had been out but had been recaptured? There were no means of knowing. Certainly there was no point in trying to send them a detailed report in my POW mail because it would just have been censored.

On 6th January 1942 I wrote to my mother whilst still in *der Teng*:

'This year I began in a special way, that's why I now send you my best wishes to the beginning of the year.
Last year I had to think an hour different from you (English time) and this year I already thought of you at 5 pm, (central Canadian time) and hoped you were also drinking one to my health! Yes, and the next time I will drink with you, you can rely on that. For the time being I have a lot of time for writing letters (Solitary). It's a pity that I only have a few to write, otherwise I would have something to help pass my time away. But that's also very nice, one has to go through that also. I haven't heard from you since father's letter of 30th November. It is time that I heard from you again, otherwise I will soon have to believe

that you have given me up since the United States joined the war. But you don't need worry Muttel, your 'Unkraut' (stubborn little weed) will not be destroyed!

I have just read the book Pompei and Herculaneum. One could find some interest in going on a journey after reading a book like that. You certainly are in agreement with me when I invite you from this funny place, to go for a short ride with me after the war is over. Therefore, should my DKW Meisterklasse still exist, then please take care of it! Your Uz!"

In the letter there is a sort of *gallows humour* and more than enough hints about taking journeys, but there is also confidence. Confidence that I would get out of that situation, either through the ending of the war or through another, more successful, escape.

On 3rd March I wrote to my sister, Trude, for her 20th birthday:

'If you want to do something for me, just write me a letter. You must have experiences that you could share with me. I have also gone through some quite interesting times which would prove you can rely on me (the escapes). I am also experiencing a lot here (that was after my third attempted escape which ended in Watertown, written whilst in solitary confinement in Bowmanville), but I am not as fortunate as you are, in that I am living through things which I am not allowed to write about. You will have to have patience until I am back with you again. Trude, now I send special birthday wishes from me: take all your youthful strength and help Muttel to get over these times, even though you might not feel like it!

Your Uz

The worries about the family members at home were a burden! One should not forget that at that time my mother was all alone at home. Father was serving as a *Hauptmann der Reserve* in Moravia (CSSR), and Trude, the older of my sisters, was a *Nachrichtenhelferin* (assistant communications operator) with the Army. My mother was not only in charge of the *Volksschule* (elementary school) in Heutingsheim, but also had to give hours of private lessons and played the organ for and was in charge of the church choir. Then there were the household chores and our youngest sister, Helga, who had to be taken care of as well.

I wrote a letter on the subject of being 'tied' to another person, postmarked 12th May (I say *'postmarked'* for the simple reason that the censor had blacked out the date as it was shortly before we were transferred from Bowmanville to Gravenhurst). First I comment on the end of my youth friendship and then I continue (to my mother):

'...You can be calm over my inner reasoning. I am really glad that after the war I have no ties in this direction. Already after having been taken prisoner in England I had resolved that I wouldn't write to any girls. I only wrote to Gretl because I'd promised to. Now I don't have to worry in that direction any more.

To give you some reason for my direction all I can say is that I am not the type that, immediately after this war and the monotony of the imprisonment, wants to settle down to a tranquil family life. Although I see there in also the fulfilment of life, but I would like to browse through other aspects of life first, to develop myself in my occupation. That I would rather do without any firm connections or ties.

Now I have already filled a letter again with this subject, it's a pity that I cannot let my thoughts run free. But please do me the favour and ponder no longer over this subject.

The heartiest greetings,

Your Uz'

So that's how I wanted to get over things. Free and without any ties and, naturally, after we had won the war. Above all I wanted to be free then. There the pilot in me came through and the ultimate freedom, the freedom of the sky. Of course I didn't want to restrict my present nor my future ambitions by ruling anything out, but freedom would be the first and most essential ingredient.

Similar thoughts were also in another letter of the 3rd August 1941. I wrote:

'Lieber Vater,

Yesterday was your birthday, and I could only wish a happy birthday in my thoughts. During such difficult times, such as now, our small personal fate has to step back and I believe we can all bear it easier if we accept that if, in the end, things are not going as one wants them to go, fate will decide.

On 27th October (the day I was shot down) I had threequarters of a year behind me and it was also a Sunday. If I had imagined at the time - that I would be a prisoner so long - I don't know how I would have been able to bear such thoughts. But one hopes, as the months go by, that in the next month our hopes will be fulfilled. But I am also slowly coming to believe that this part of our life is not completely lost, but that can be judged later in life.

Now, it is still summer and before the winter breaks a lot can still happen. During this we still let ourselves bake in the sun and are pleased about it as long as possible. I hope that a letter from you will soon be coming! Hearty greetings to you all from your Uz!'

That was from Camp W, after the beginning of the war against Russia. Nine months later I made the following comments:

3rd May 1942:

'Liebe Muttel,

Yesterday was your birthday and certainly you knew I would congratulate you in my thoughts... perhaps it was because I didn't have my spectacles on (a reference to some people's apparent inability to concentrate when they can't see properly), but you shouldn't worry so much. Your Uz finds his way through life, you can rely on that (with or without spectacles)!

Otherwise I was pleased with the photos of you and Trude... you ask me whether I am still having problems with my kidneys. At the moment I am as healthy as back in those days in Creglingen when I was going back and forth between the football field and swimming in the river. I have my thoughts fully under my control, so that they cannot challenge me any more...'

Yes, in the meantime we had been imprisoned for another year and had learnt more... especially patience... I knew only too well how one's fate was being formed by others. World history, this *'great time,'* was governing our lives.

When, nowadays, reading about *'this great time,'* many questions arise which would exceed the medium of this book. But, having said that, one has to consider that we prisoners of war could only live through these times. Times when our conviction, because of our isolation, remained untouched. Having fought for great goals, amongst mine being a united Europe, we had been incarcerated. But who amongst us 'young idealists' had the opportunity, during our school days and trade training, to travel beyond the boundaries of our *Vaterland* before the outbreak of war. A journey to France, not to mention England was, for various reasons, almost impossible before 1939. Financial limitations as well as administrative problems when crossing borders were hard to overcome without very special circumstances: this being a hangover for us Germans from the First World War. One of my student teachers at school, *Studienrat* Wöbbelmann, had always maintained that the best thing in the world to have would be a British passport. "With that," he would say, "you could go anywhere!"

The German press was so well controlled that we accepted whatever they wrote with very few exceptions. Those who, today, claim that they sounded a warning at the time should not forget how many of these 'followers!' there were. I don't understand the compunction which many Germans seem to have today to suggest that what happened in the thirties was the result of the ill-advised efforts of a few people. It was the will of the majority or it couldn't have happened. Circumstances conspired to produce as set of circumstances and we who are alive today must shoulder the responsibility. In Germany we call them *Wendehälse* (wrynecks) - those twisting their necks and saying, "I told you so!"

The summer of 1942 was much more pleasant in the climate of Gravenhurst than it had been at Lake Superior (Camp W) in the middle of nowhere.

21st June 1942:

'We now have proper summer and I am doing a lot of sports. Mainly I am knocking myself around with sandbags, punch balls and other boxing equipment. My requirement in intellectual nourishment is presently very low. It's definitely not my ideal to become a book worm...'

30th June 1942 (to my father):

'...We are playing a lot of fistball here! Over the last Saturday-Sunday we had a tournament. I, as 'backman', represented the colours of Canada (Air Force) - against Libya, (Army and Navy). Besides that we won the second prize - the cakes!
Your Uz.'

30th September 1942:

'In a similar way to last year, the summer is coming to a close. However, this camp is further south than Camp W was and the warm days should last a little longer, enabling us to do our sports outdoors. But slowly I will start with the winter schedule.'

24th October 1942:

'Now, the so called Indian summer is also over and the miserable weather is starting. As far as sports are concerned there's nothing going on any more. Until winter finally comes we are going to have to return to our books again...three lines censored...The comrades in Russia must be preparing themselves as well!...'

That's how we experienced the summer of 1942 on the banks of Lake Muskoka. What worried me during my imprisonment was again whether I was the type who could manage to live through these times?

5th June 1942 (to my mother):

'...You are asking for recognition of your letter writing efforts. I can say, over and over again, that mail is the most beautiful thing for me and in the last few weeks I have never had to wait longer than 7 days and the next letter came. If only it were the same for you . It is not my fault that it isn't, I am writing as much as I am allowed to. When Uncle Karl thinks I have become more serious, then that is correct. But that is not bad at all and you don't need to believe that I have lost my humour. When I come home, whenever that might be, you'll be surprised. Although I don't know yet in what position I will be put, one thing is certain, I will pull my share whatever is expected of me.
Do you know, when you have gone through what we are going through laughing, one is forced to continue 'ice cold' and that hardens one. Raging, grumbling and suffering are things that you cannot show, you have to have yourself under full control. It is all a matter of education, which does a strong human good. Because I know for sure, I will fulfil my duties as in the past, as if I were still at it with the enemy, that is no burden!
Your Uz.'

Also the *physical* well being is mentioned in a letter:

16th July 1942:

'Liebe Muttel,

I have received your parcel with Christmas biscuits, smoked sausage, smoked ham and chocolates - the small 'brezeln' (pretzels) were especially welcome! About 8 days ago, I received three letters (dated 24th March, 3rd May and 18th May). Now I am glad that I have waited with my letter writing, because now I can respond to your thoughts. The parcel took an awfully long time before it arrived and the sausage and the smoked ham looked terrible. But after we cut the outer mouldy layer away, there was still enough left for us to have a tasty meal in our room.
Here in this camp we are presently nine men in one room (it must have been before the partition walls were installed). There are four members of the army from Libya, one submariner and four airmen. From the composition of this room you can see that we are being kept quite well up to date.
You see you don't need to waste any thoughts in that direction, we are well informed and can wait!...'

What a vital function the letters had! It is worth considering what an important subject communication of all sorts was to help maintain a balanced state of mind. Letters were basically the only form of communication across the enemy world which surrounded us. Brief exchanges with someone who was sympathetic to our problems, someone to whom we were of worth. How much worse must it have been for poor *Kapitänleutnant* Hans Rahmlow, captain of the U 570 - surrendered virtually undamaged in August 1941 - not only imprisoned by the enemy and cut off from his family, but also ostracised within his own peer group.[1] Almost unnoticed he was transferred from Bowmanville to Gravenhurst long after we had been transferred. Because he lived on our floor, the topmost, we saw him every day. He had been allocated a small single room at the end of the corridor, towards the roof terrace where he even had to take his meals. The orderly would knock and it would be opened; then, without saying a word, his tray was handed to him. Afterwards he put the tray back outside the door in the corridor. That's what *Ächtung* (proscription) was like. He went for his rounds everyday, but always alone. How could someone stand that the whole time - in the end for years?

After the war he was to be tried before a German Court Martial - that was the decision reached by a court of honour consisting of *U-Boot* officers at Grizedale Hall (Camp 1) in England. Up to that time he would remain *Geächtet* (banished), nobody was allowed to talk to him. Even the orderlies were pitiless. It was sad comment that his most vociferous critics of the mysterious seizing of his U-Boat were his own crew. Again and again we debated the question in our room: what would we have done in his situation? The same as his first officer, *Oberleutnant sur See* Berndt? (see also [1]). The Canadian guards, who were well informed of his situation, did nothing to ease his situation. It was clear that here international solidarity ruled.

I lost track of Rahmlow due to other events that were to follow. Later, well into 1943, I heard he was still going through this terrible isolation at Gravenhurst. After that he was transferred to Camp Grand Ligne, and lived there in a single room in the same isolation. Much later I was to discover that he had returned to Germany the same as all the others and then died at home.

When comparing our problems with this man and what he had experienced our worries could hardly be taken seriously. It was remarkable what a human being was able to bear but, nonetheless, with some of them it was getting critical in the summer of 1942. It wasn't until the first parole walks, and then later when the farm was bought, that change was affected. The fact that we, the officers, in accordance with the Geneva Convention, were not allowed to do any type of work was not always a blessing. In the Non Commissioned Officer's and the enlisted men's camps, farm and forestry work was becoming available at this time. Such work brought a change to the otherwise humdrum life in camp and helped distract the mind.

29th July 1942:

'...at the moment I have a slight cold, caught during my boxing training. But I am doing my best, so that I can be well again by next Sunday. In fact I want to take part in our sports festival and box in the light-heavyweight class. Joking tongues have given me the good advice that I should have a portrait painted before the match, so that I can at least keep my face in the portrait. But it certainly won't be that bad, although a three round fight can be very demanding. Anyway, by the time this letter gets to you it'll be too late to keep your fingers crossed. Yesterday I received books from Mrs Stephan and from father. If this continues I will soon be able to open a library here.

Actually I do very little reading, but should we be here for another winter then I'll have time enough..."

17th August 1942 (to my mother):

'...My throat did not get better in time for our sports festival and I lost the fight by a few points. Nevertheless, I am glad that I stood through the three times three minutes, because I believe there is no other sport that is so demanding in such a short time. About eight days later a proper angina began again and I had to wait a few more days for the ulcer to open. But now it is all over and done with. Before too long I'll be doing my sport again.
While I was lying in bed, the parcel arrived with my uniform jacket and the other contents. That was relatively fast. Now I will have to write to Father...'

17th August 1942 (to my father):

'...A few days ago I received your letter of 21st June... In it you mention the performance of my previous Squadron... I hope there are still enough 'alten Hasen' ('old rabbits')...You want me to write more about your books! You are right, I have received all those that you had announced would be coming. I have read very few of them, but you know the next winter will bring more time for reading... By the way, give yourself a treat and go and visit a doctor by the name of Dr. Schön when you are in Konstanz (Constance). You two will certainly have a lot to tell each other! I completely forgot your birthday because of feverish preparations for the boxing match...'

Father had then been in Konstanz for quite some time. Slowly, I could read from his letters which, even prior to my being shot down, had been written in an *enclosed* style for the *Feldpost* - a kind of subtle code which we understood. He had advanced to be *Kompaniechef* (Company Commander) of a mounted training company. This was exactly to his liking and he enjoyed it very much. There he could ride and jump with the military horses as much as he wanted. This was a relationship he had begun in the First World War. My hint to Dr Schön was for the simple reason that his son, *Hauptmann* Werner Schön, of the *Afrikakorps*, had also arrived at Gravenhurst as a POW and was one of my friends.

23rd August 1942 (to my mother):

*'In the meantime I have received your parcel with the uniform jacket
and the other contents. (Experience showed that one had to confirm
the receipt of important items twice, one never knew whether a letter
had got lost.)... When my trousers arrive here safely then next winter
can come, I am ready.*
*Muttel, now I have to apologise that I didn't write birthday letters to
father and Helga. I was just not in the right mood. You mentioned
once that I should write a letter occasionally when I was in such a
mood. I believe I wrote the letters, but now and then I must also write
letters I can be sure will get to you (the censor was unlikely to pass
a really black letter.) That you have received letters from me pleases
me for the simple reason that you not only have something in your
hands that proves that I still exist, but also because it is completely
different writing a letter in response to a letter from just writing.
(...three lines were ruled out with thick black...) Heartiest greetings!
Your Uz.'*

20th September 1942.

'Dear all,

*Today it is Hinnerk's birthday. I am ashamed I hadn't written earlier.
But I can assure you that my birthday (the 14th) was also very nice
this year, as nice as is possible here. The comrades had prepared a
birthday table, which, if you'd done it at home you would have had
to have gone to great efforts. But you can hold on to that, it will be
a festival once I am back at home again to celebrate. By the way, I
just remember that Major Robitzsch was also present at my birthday,
and it dawns on me that you didn't know that he was also here and is
sharing the same fate. Another classmate from Stuttgart (Walter
Maurer) is also here, I ran into him without knowing he was here.
In fact you can't imagine what a colourful mixture of human fates are
gathered here. Pleasing, however, is the fact that only few show
mental suffering under the existing circumstances. I have, I believe,
now overcome the hardest time period here. Having managed to go
through the past experiences, I think it can now continue as long as
is necessary, and I don't believe that anything here can seriously put
me in question! Uli!*

20th September 1942 (to my father):

'...Soon I will have reached the quarter century mark. If I were to count the years of 'life', then I would only reach twenty-two, but the two years here must also be counted. Perhaps they count in some things not just singly. They aren't nice, no matter how you look at it. The time here can only be evaluated in its effects at a later time. I hope that the hardship of this school of life, contains some values. These hopes I will continue to support.
Now to your letter of 9th July. One can be really proud of Trude for her volunteering (she had volunteered to go to Riga). I am pleased with her, but also I hope that I will later be able to enjoy some nice times with my sister when she has gathered her own experiences in life.
You are right, when you say that I did not get to my foreign language studies this summer. I will not force myself to do this during the coming winter and ignore the sports. Should, however, no sports be possible, then I will have to change horses, although I know from experience that then the so-called 'balance' would no longer exist. Let's hope for the winter sports!
Heartiest greetings.
Your Uz'

Very religious readers of these letters of mine might think that life in the POW camp could have been easier if one had put more trust in God. But, although brought up in the Christian belief, there were limits. There was the experience during the *Kriegsschule* (military school), when I was very disappointed by the Catholic clergy in the *Kasernenabendstunde* (barracks evening hour) following the death of a comrade (Fischer - see 'Spitfire On My Tail' p.69 -): This comrade and I had seriously discussed the issue of life after death. When he then had a fatal flying accident the clergy said his opinion was that this had to happen and that there would be no place in heaven for a heretic like Fischer! Thereafter the whole class boycotted him (no mean action for young cadets in a military institute). Besides that I had experienced, again and again, in those places where I grew up and went to school, the real *humanity* taught during religious instruction and practised in the clergy's households. Christianity and its Ten Commandments give me the direction, however, I always ran into conflict with God's earthly representatives. I therefore did not find myself putting my fate in the hands of faith during my imprisonment.

Important things were taking place in the camp that one couldn't write about. Here is another letter about the daily routine:

29th October 1942.

'Liebe Muttel,

Yes, the long awaited trousers finally arrived and brought other pleasures at the same time. The cakes and the sausages again found great recognition! Now at least I need no longer worry about this parcel; however, the last one, in which my gymnastic shoes have been promised, has not arrived yet.
This time everything arrived in perfect condition, and I must express my greatest thanks to you. Today I can send you a photograph that was taken here. In the photograph you can see to my right Hauptmann Eberhard Wildermuth from Cannstatt and the second person from the right is Hinnerk Waller. Should this photograph arrive by Christmas, then I hope it will give you some confidence in the present times and also that it conveys some pleasure from me.
Two days ago, two years of imprisonment came to an end. When can I tell you everything that I have gone through? For the time being be quiet, I have as much patience as you have! For the time being it is important to get the transition days behind me. It won't be until winter that ice hockey will bring us sporting possibilities again. Without sport one gets into a mood in which one could eat oneself.
Therefore happier Christmas...'

The photograph mentioned earlier was a postcard photograph that took its time being printed under Canadian control and was now released for mailing home to Germany. On the reverse side of the postcard was written:

'Liebe Muttel,

This photograph was taken in May. You should still be able to recognise me, although my face is a little lop-sided. I'd had a boxing match the day before. "Do kaascht nix macha!" (Written in Swabian dialect -'There's nothing you can do about that!') Otherwise I am still the same old person.

At this time my father had already been transferred from Konstanz to Mülhausen in Alsace, but of course I didn't know of this until after the usual mail delay. Forwarding of mail within Germany was still functioning well, although the circumstances were difficult due to the war. This can be seen even today, with the addresses having been changed by the postman. My asking again in the above letter *'When I can I tell you everything?'* had been prompted by more events within the camp. Amongst other events the *Fesselungsaktion* (the shackling) was beginning in the camp.

But before this, extracts from a further letter:

28th November 1942

'...Today, more than ever before in this damned time, I impose almost all of my hopes on you. Other than the ties to our country, all I have left is you as an anchorage... In fact the worst thing for me here, imprisoned, is not the lack of freedom of movement, but the fact that one does not live one's own life. It is lived for oneself through circumstances which one can in no way influence. This does not mean that these times are getting me down...

These lines were written in connection with the experience of the *Fesselungsaktion*, at which time even our POW mail service was tampered with as a form of retaliation. More detail of this, and its consequences, follows in the next chapter.

Notes on Chapter Ten

[1] Hans Rahmlow was the Commander of U 570 and even whilst in a camp in England he had been ostracised, outlawed by German *Kriegsmarine* and *Hilfsmarine* officers, because he had surrendered his boat when it was, apparently, hardly damaged. This had had serious consequences for all of the German submarines and navy personnel. A court of honour, consisting of submarine officers, had been convened in England and it was decided that for the duration of the war nobody in the camp would talk to Rahmlow. It was also decided that immediately after the war, he should be put in front of a Court Martial at home. His first officer, who was similarly outlawed, *Oberleutnant zur See Berndt* (*'zur See'* distinguished him as a navy officer),

made a desperate escape attempt while they were in England. He was recaptured but tried again and again ever more recklessly until he was finally shot. In this way Berndt made certain that the accusation of cowardice in the face of the enemy was erased. Berndt is buried in the little English village of Hawkshead, in Cumbria.

CHAPTER ELEVEN

SHACKLES AND TUNNELS

Although I was finished, or so I thought, as far as escape attempts were concerned, I couldn't refrain from assisting in the construction of a tunnel when I was given the opportunity. The whole operation had been planned in conjunction with the camp leadership which was then working well. Wüstefeldt, together with *Major* Müller, was responsible for the escape authorization. The occupants of Manni Manhart and Reini Pfundtner's room, where *Hauptmann* Baudler was the *Stubeältester,* were responsible for the execution of the plan. This room became known as the centre of escape activities and was, therefore, assured of very special attention from the Canadian guards.

There were more and more escapers arriving in the camp and it was a pity that the name 'escaper' was also used for a special group who were generally known as *Die Ausbrechern* (those who break out - escapers). It was a fairly large group who kept themselves busy with escape plans and preparations. However, they did in such a manner that made it very obvious and visible for all camp inmates; but mostly they were only keeping themselves busy making plans and preparations. Their main aim was to overcome the obstacle of the fence with the least risk and for this a tunnel was the ideal solution.

The plans for the escape that might then follow were very thorough. They were experts in making false documents and had the most fabulous ideas of escape routes that could be taken and the most adventurous diplomatic tricks. The astonishing thing was that in most cases the plans were never realised, the risk, the fence and the *outside* were, an insurmountable barrier for them. I don't wish to sound disparaging of their efforts but this type of *Ausbrecher* was to be held responsible for the word slowly getting a bad taste to it. However, whilst all this feverish activity went on under the watchful eye of the Canadian *Frettchen*, others were quietly planning and working.

Walter Manhart, a great sportsman and seasoned escaper, was continually searching for an opportunity to tunnel, although the layer of soil was very thin. Under the classroom on the ground floor he found a large hollow space beneath the floor-boards. There was a chance it might work, if it were dug at an angle away from the main building, the layer of soil looked deep enough to support a tunnel. At the end of the planned route, where it reached

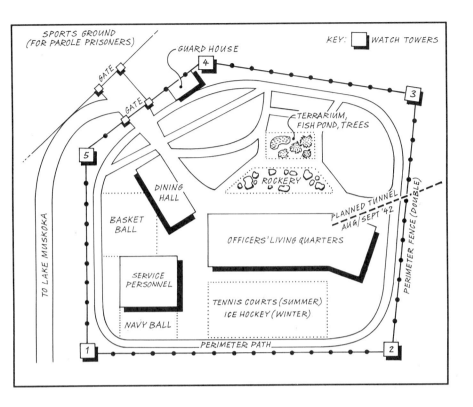

the fence, there was a gap in the vertical control rods which would allow a tunnel approximately sixty centimetres wide to pass. One would have to watch the rods weren't damaged in the course of the tunnel digging activities, but it might be possible. The direction had one great disadvantage - the distance! On one occasion, when it was possible to clandestinely take measurements during shot putting, a proposed tunnel length of forty-seven metres was the result. With a roof height in the tunnel of a bare forty centimetres it would naturally yield a tremendous amount of soil and there was the first major problem - disposal.

Such a quantity of soil, in a camp as small as Gravenhurst, could never be spread out on the ground without being discovered. But there was another possibility: the Canadian buildings, especially the newer ones, mostly had double-skinned walls for insulation and the air gap could be filled. However, from the beginning of operations, nobody could speculate accurately about the volume of soil that could be introduced in this way before the downward pressure burst the walls out at the bottom. Nothing could be calculated in advance; that's why a start had to be made as soon as possible. The first penetration was carefully scheduled for a time when no lessons were being held. Tools were no problem, in the meantime enough had been stolen, found in camp or had been smuggled in from Bowmanville. The floor-boards were not sawn, but were loosened length wise and then prepared so they could be easily lifted when the need arose.

The complete tunnel team consisted of twenty men, who, in the event of success, were authorised to 'go' in a predetermined sequence. Leader of the operation was *Major* Müller and principal *engineers* were Manni Manhart and Reini Pfundtner. It didn't take long before *Hauptmann* Eberhard Wildermuth and I also belonged to the *Tiefbau* (underground construction company). During the day work was conducted in two shifts. There was no intention to hurry the digging - the latest target completion date for the project was the spring of 1943. A very clear policy of caution against speed was introduced and it was resolved that should the project be completed earlier than predicted, some comrades would be able to get out during the winter. Then, however, the tunnel would be carefully closed and the next group would not be let out before spring. Although I was sceptical about such operations where so many were involved and about which to a much lesser extent, the whole camp was aware, I was glad to be able to assist. Wouldn't it be wonderful, at least once, to be able to get out without great risk and be able to take all the clothing and equipment which otherwise was always governed by the crossing of the fence?

The first shift went into the tunnel at nine a.m., and worked until shortly before lunch. At two p.m. the second shift entered the tunnel underneath the floor and worked until about five-thirty. It had taken a while to reach this rhythm but, once established, it worked very well. The first shift always entered the tunnel shortly before the first lesson began in the classroom. The entrance was in front of the podium on the floor. Sometimes, when there was a delay because of the Canadian *Frettchen* or something else, the lessons were interrupted as four or five men climbed down into the tunnel and the floor-boards were carefully closed again. For the class it was always an interesting show, and the classes being held were the perfect cover up for this operation.

Soon it was discovered that the earth that had been dug out could best be transported away in linen bags of approximately three kilograms in weight. Because the transportation and the emptying on the surface was a very frequent operation it had to be done very quickly, but also securely. This could only be done once a day. It worked like this: upon the signal for the first sitting to gather for lunch, the lessons in the classroom were also stopped and the floor opened ready. As the mob came pouring out from all

A group photo with a purpose: Manni Manhart is deliberately standing off to the left so he could later cut his head and shoulders from the photograph to use in false identifaction papers. Fourth from the left Dr Huppert, E. Becker, Döring, 'Fritz' Oeser and second from the right R. Theopold.

the classrooms and from the other three floors on their way to the dining hall the assigned *Erd* (short for *Erdarbeiter* - earth workers) stepped into action. Sacks filled with earth were handed up out of the hollow space under the floor. Behind the podium was an opening to the staircase and a disused lift. The sacks were passed there, flying hand to hand. In the open lift shaft the defunct lift car hung half-way up and the floor and roof of it were fitted with flaps by us. These were opened and then the sacks just 'flew' all the way to up to the roof void. That went really quickly as our hungry comrades came down the stairs and ran along the corridor to the dining hall. The sacks flew from hand to hand as if they were fire buckets; first over the podium, then through the wall and then up the disused lift shaft to the top. There, all the earth was emptied into the walls.

Of course our own *Posten* (guards) had to be on the alert during this operation. They immediately gave warning when the Canadian *Frettchen* appeared or indicated that caution was necessary. The most important rule was: no earth to be spilled! One hint of digging and the Canadians would be immediately on their guard and would not rest until they found the source.

Every day was a day of action, but it all went well for several weeks. Even I pushed my own doubts aside and became an enthusiastic mole. In the beginning I worked at the 'face,' lying, as one had to, with a sort of coal shovel to stab into the earth in front and auger it out. The resulting spoil was then shovelled away backwards and behind the 'faceman' lay another miner who then filled the sacks. A third member of the team then piled these close to the tunnel entrance, from where they could be whisked away. After a short stretch had been dug out a very accurately prefabricated wooden prop-frame was hammered into position. If hard spots or stones were found amongst the earth then one had to use hammer and chisel to make one's way forward, inch by inch. For myself this work which, in the beginning was rostered every two to three days, was only viable as long as I, with my legs stretched out, was not more than two or three metres away from the entrance. Beyond that I started to feel something which must have been claustrophobia. I tried hard to keep up with the same amount of digging, but Manni was not satisfied - in my shift I didn't bring enough out. It was found that the shorter men, like Pfundtner, Wildermuth and Manhart (even although he had wider shoulders), were the better diggers. That was alright with me, there were enough other tasks that had to be done!

Manni was so enthusiastic he volunteered to work extra shifts. We quickly agreed to this, because he, with the strength of a bear, could shift more, much more earth than anyone else. However, once the tunnel reached the length of approximately ten metres the shortage of oxygen also struck him. Others before had already complained of a shortage of breath and the candle that was burning at the face kept going out. One day we reached the point where Manni could hardly crawl back to the entrance, he was almost unconscious for lack of oxygen; this was a new problem for us. Neither in Swanwick nor in the tunnel at Bowmanville had we ever experienced this, but soon it was clear why: those two tunnels had been shorter and in England we'd had the tunnel collapse on us, though this had not only brought danger with it, but also oxygen.

Of course the resourceful POW found a solution: an air pipe had to be laid to the very face of the tunnel and a blower would be needed for this. Electricity should also provide the necessary light for working, and while we were at it we needed something to save us from having to push the earth back with our hands. We would lay small railway tracks on the floor of the tunnel. That was going to delay us in our digging efforts, but at least the time was used in a productive manner. Disused electric wiring was soon found in the old building in sufficient lengths and light fixtures were soon acquired, giving us light and power underground.

The construction of small carts, for transporting the earth, represented no problem either. In the camp we had many personnel who built clocks as a hobby. They were capable of making complete pendulum clocks of wood, and they ran exactly to the minute. Housing, cog wheels, the thicker of the spindles, and the hands were all carved out from wood. The thinner spindles, the weights, the chains and the pendulum, had to be made of metal and for this there was always scrap to recycle. For these craftsmen a carriage with four wheels carved out of wood was no problem at all - they made two while they were at it. At each end of the cart we attached a strong string which enabled us to pull it in both directions along the wooden tracks in the tunnel. It was a proper toy cart, but for older boys!

It seemed the blower was to become an insurmountable problem, but before we gave up the craftsmen again came to the rescue. They'd had their eyes on the ventilator in the upper half of the kitchen window. The fan was rotated by the electric motor that was built onto it, and was used to extract the steam and vapours from the kitchen. The removal, construction and testing of this blower in our tunnel had to wait until a wooden replica in the exact colours of the kitchen ventilator had been made. The wooden fan was so well made in its shape and colour that one could hardly see the difference between it and the original one. Once completed the ventilator was taken out of the window and replaced by the replica. The replica was so good, that the normal flow of air out of the kitchen would get the wooden propeller turning at a reasonable speed.

Once acquired, the fan was mounted onto a board and covered with a casing made out of torn up newspaper and flour glue. On one side the ventilator sucked the air in and on the other side the opening had been reduced to the size of a milk tin. This construction blew air with enough force into the pipe which was constructed from more of the multi-purpose milk cans. Before taking the blower underground, its constructors had tested it so well that it could be put into service without delay as soon as it had been connected to the tin can ducting which had been installed in advance.

From then on it was possible to work properly in the tunnel. Manni had already tried digging again after the electric light had replaced the candle light and thus reduced the oxygen demand, but again he ran a great risk. An official work prohibition had to be levied by the team leader before he would take a break. But once the blower system had been installed there was no holding him.

The longer the tunnel got, the more depressing the work got. I tried occasionally to help out at the face, but the further down the tunnel I got the more anxious I became. To understand this one has to imagine how it feels when one tries to move in a tunnel that is just wide enough for the average pair of shoulders and so low one had difficulties when trying to turn over on one's back without getting stuck; and that some thirty metres in! It was a dank, dirty, dark place which terrified me. Perhaps this had something to do with my upbringing in the open Schwabian mountains, I don't know, all I was certain of was that the face of the tunnel was something I didn't look forward to.

How solid the supports were always remained a question. One thing we were afraid of, because the ground above us was not too thick, was a small cave-in which would leave a tell-tale depression in the ground above. That we could be buried under the collapse was of secondary consideration! We were also afraid that one day the Canadians could drive across our tunnel with a delivery vehicle. The path to the house was very close to our tunnel, but week after week everything went very well, or nearly everything. One time, in a room on the ground floor, one of the cardboard walls burst out and tunnel earth appeared, but this was very quickly repaired before the *Frettchen* noticed anything. This, however, served to illustrate that we had reached the maximum pressure of earth this wall would hold and that up in the attic the earth had to be tipped into other parts of the walls.   The tunnel had reached an impressive length of thirty-five metres, when one morning immediately after breakfast, a group of Canadians appeared in the camp. The Duty Officer, the Intelligence Officer *unser Pferdedieb*, the Sergeant Major and many *Frettchen*. They all marched straight to the entrance of the main building - which was most unusual - and even interrupted the class that was being held in the tunnel entrance room to open, with obvious purpose, the boards that covered up the tunnel entrance. Tragic as this was for us it could have been worse. A lucky coincidence was that this morning the digging team had not yet entered the tunnel, but was little enough recompense. The tunnel, all the exhausting work, all the ingenious ideas was *futsch und kaputt* (gone and wrecked) in one stroke. What was it Churchill had to say about *'blood, toil, tears and sweat'?*

How the Canadians had managed to locate the tunnel we never discovered. The wildest rumours of betrayal and carelessness were making their rounds, but nobody could prove their assumptions (see further comment later). Curiously though, there were no bad consequences or reprisals. The Canadians regarded the tunnel to be too dangerous to enter and only pressed on it from the top until it collapsed, filled the resulting depression with earth and poured concrete into the entrance cavity.

It was sad, but at the time both the attention of the German and the Canadian camp leadership was occupied by a threat to shackle prisoners taken in France. The situation had arisen during the Dieppe raid in which the Canadian divisions had played a significant part. At first we were able to read in the Canadian newspapers how approximately six thousand Canadian soldiers had, on 19th August 1942, been landed at Dieppe as a rehearsal for the actual invasion of France. The landing had been a bloody debacle with a high loss of life, but was also, in part, a triumph for the Allies. They were able to capture the newest German *Würzburg* radar equipment from a coastal radar station, situated above Pourville near Dieppe. The German soldiers who were operating the secret equipment were overrun by Canadian soldiers from the South Saskatchewan Regiment and were taken as prisoners, together with all the dismantled parts of the *Würzburg*, back to England on board the boats.[1]

Again it was obvious what importance the Allies gave the radar and radio communications technology. With the seizing of *U-Booten* (U-Boats) they were able to eavesdrop on the complete coded radio communication system of the fleet, including their supply boats. Now they also wanted to know how advanced the German radar was. This was of great importance for the air raids that were being stepped up over Germany. What a comparison to the earlier lack of initiative regarding *Funk* (radio) in the *Luftwaffe*.

The Canadian losses at Dieppe were dreadful. Of the six thousand soldiers that had gone ashore, approximately two thousand two hundred were either wounded or taken prisoner and one thousand two hundred had been killed. Some one hundred and twenty-eight Canadian Officers were amongst the prisoners. Against this the German had lost three hundred killed or missing and a further two hundred wounded. For Mr Churchill the operation had been a "success," he said, because of the knowledge that had been gained, in spite of the high losses.

We in our camp, in far-away Canada, never thought that these events, which we had been able to read about without any form of censor, could have any effect on our camp life; but they did. How it evolved can only really be put together from fragments of the whole picture because the censor soon began to clamp down hard. As far as we could ascertain the story was that amongst the dead and the wounded that were left back on the beaches of Dieppe, a German soldier was found who had been shackled hand and foot. He was, apparently, fished out of the sea in this condition. Another German soldier who was, at the same time, seriously wounded, was found similarly shackled. Then, amongst the Canadian documents that had been left back on the beach, a British order was found in which the shackling instruction was found. The reason was stated as being a precaution to prevent prisoners from destroying their own personal identification documents.

With this discovery the whole situation escalated and we began to feel the effects remotely in Canada. Hitler was so incensed that he intervened personally and ordered the shackling of all Canadians that had been taken prisoner in the course of the operation. The British Ministry of War published a counter-order to the 'shackling order', but because of numerous reported contradictions, reprisals followed on both sides in September of 1942. Thus began the *Fesselungkrieg* (shackling war) and for us this was no light matter.

The situation began to calm down a little, but then, at the beginning of October on the Channel Island of Sercol (Sark), a similar incident occurred. A German *Arbeitskommando* (work detail) consisting of one NCO and four enlisted men was surprised by a British commando raid. In this case the Germans were again shackled and were to be led to the beach but, apparently, when they resisted, the NCO and one man were killed and one other man was injured by shots and bayonet. One *Pionier* (Pioneer) managed to escape and reported the incident. Again Hitler intervened, and again the Canadian prisoners from Dieppe were shackled; Churchill responded with his reprisals and the Canadian Press added to it all "The Huns are guilty!" From this minute on, the Canadian newspapers were so censored that we only knew fragments of what was going on in Europe. But in the Canadian camps action was started, most probably on orders from England. It was threatened that two thousand German Army POWs were to be shackled in Canada until the shackling of the Canadians in Germany came to an end. Something at least came from this - for the first time we began to feel that we weren't completely forgotten. For a time we came back into the spotlight but what then?

It wasn't until much later that we found out that in Bowmanville really serious confrontations had taken place, the so-called Battle of Bowmanville. There, the complete camp refused to be shackled and the Canadians had to call in an active battalion of front line troops to support the Veteran Guards. For three days the camp was stormed as the shackling of the army officers was enforced. At first the soldiers that stormed one house after another were armed with clubs and truncheons. But, after a Canadian captain had been taken prisoner inside the camp, the first shots were fired from the watchtowers. During this *Oberfähnrich der Marine* König was shot through the thigh. On the third day the Canadian soldiers were armed with bayonets and enforced the shackling in Bowmanville. During these hand to hand fights, sad to say, the Austrian *Luftwaffe Oberleutnant* von Troha lost an eye.

In Gravenhurst everything went completely differently and in our view more equitably. Around sixty army officers were to be shackled in our camp.

The lists of names were handed to *Oberstleutnant* Meythaler and *Major* Wüstefeldt and the shackling was ordered. When the Canadians then entered the camp, to put on the handcuffs, there were suddenly no army officers to be found any more. All officers in camp wore either *Luftwaffe* or *Kriegsmarine* uniforms. The Canadians were less than amused and it took almost a week for them to filter out and handcuff a limited number of *DAK* officers. Then, overnight, (the original order was for day and night cuffing) the handcuffs were removed using the sharp corners of the beds or simply by prying them apart. They were of variable quality, some were made of really hard steel and gave us great problems, but eventually every set of cuffs was removed and went straight into the red hot stove. The next day the Canadians could take a look at the mess, it was a pleasure to return the melted parts to them.

Both sides gained from their experiences during this time and it obviously could not continue. The Canadians then decided that the shackling should take place in the camp within a specially designated square that was marked with a rope. This square was then surrounded by the Veteran Guards who were armed with bayonets. The cuffing was limited to specific times and no longer overnight. Daily between ten a.m. and twelve noon and then again from two p.m. till four p.m. the nominated officers were handcuffed. For us the whole affair began to take on the air of an amusing distraction, although we obviously appreciated the serious side to it. We all shared the irksome duty and volunteers from the *Luftwaffe* and *Kriegsmarine* all did their share of sitting it out in the rope square. That didn't bother the Canadians at all, the main thing for them was that at the predetermined time sixty officers were there to be handcuffed. However we weren't quite ready to accept the routine unchallenged.

During the night, when the handcuffs weren't in use, some of our *experts* took a very close look at them and, amongst the *Fremdenlegionären* (foreign legionaries) we had an expert toolmaker who manufactured perfect skeleton keys. As time went on we were then able to unlock all the various types of handcuffs. And then came our day to act: the volunteers reported to the roped-off square, the Canadians handcuffed them and locked the cuffs with their keys. The handcuffed officers then moved around restlessly within the well guarded roped off square. This was partly to distract the guards and partly to cover their activity in the middle of the square. After half an hour the first handcuffs flew out of the square and landed on the ground. There we had previously assigned *runners* waiting who snatched the cuffs up and ran to the rooms. In the rooms other comrades waited with their stoves glowing a nice cherry red. It only took a few minutes from dropping the cuffs into the improvised blast-furnaces before they were reduced to melted and useless lumps of steel. Hardly had the first handcuffs flown out of the square when the next ones followed.

In the beginning we were not able to unlock all the handcuffs, although the Canadians were astonished and helpless at the sudden action. Within the Canadian police organisation, the Provincial Police and the Royal Canadian Mounted Police (RCMP), there was no standard type of handcuff. In the beginning our keys didn't fit all the *shackles*, as we called them, therefore many of the shackled volunteers had to bear the whole two hours. But as soon as samples of every type were available so the keys were made and in comparatively little time we had keys for them all.

The Canadians weren't at all enthusiastic about the whole operation, that was obvious from their demeanour. It could clearly be seen that they were just acting out the orders from above. Only twice did we run into critical situations, one occasion being when one of the tower guards became irritated by our pranks. As one of our runners was making off to the canteen with several sets of cuffs the incensed guard took his rifle and shot several rounds into the canteen. Fortunately the only casualty we had was a sausage that was fatally wounded. The cuffs were melted as usual. Another time was when the Canadians tried to lead off the culprits they had caught unlocking their handcuffs and an ugly scene began to develop. Those prisoners who still had the cuffs on one hand were forced down some steps in the garden at bayonet point. One of the *Entfesselten* (the unlocked ones) felt threatened by the bayonet of one of the Veteran Guards and hissed at him, "Don't touch me!" The Guard not only answered, "I'll show you!", but also stabbed his bayonet into the bottoms of two or three comrades who were passing. The injuries were restricted to the less precious parts of their rear ends and our doctors were glad that they once again had something they could stitch up. On the Canadian side it was clearly depressing for our guards, it was obvious that here was something that they had never before experienced in their lives as soldiers

Already, on the first day of the *Fesselaktion* (shackling action), it was impossible to handcuff all the volunteers who reported for the afternoon session, too many sets of cuffs had been destroyed during the morning. As a matter of urgency more and more handcuffs were brought from Toronto, Montreal and Ottawa. But again and again they were unlocked, removed and thrown into the waiting stoves. When the Canadians then positioned guards beside some of the stoves to prevent them from being heated to red heat, we readied stoves in other locations or the handcuffs went the same way that the earth from the tunnel had gone... into the depths of the double walls, but

Gravenhurst. Back row - from the left: Döring, Schwochau (our opera singer), Erich Böhle, 'Doc' Wagner, Waller, Stix. Front row; B. Malischweski, Strehl, Wildermuth, unknown Luftwaffe Leutnant, R. Theopold.

definitely out of the reach of the guards. At the height of the operation, the Canadians needed one hundred replacement sets of cuffs a day, just for our camp. How many were being required for the NCO and enlisted men's camps and, of course in Bowmanville, we never found out. The operation didn't quite last seven weeks in the end, principally because of the lack of serviceable handcuffs left in Canada.

By the end of November the crisis was over. The Police Headquarters was no longer prepared to deliver further handcuffs to Gravenhurst. Apparently their attitude was, "The stupid soldiers don't even know how to use handcuffs!" We heard from our *Frettchen* that they were as glad as we were that the whole operation was over. In Bowmanville, after *'the battle'*, the operation continued until 12th December 1942. By that time the Swiss Protective Power had managed to negotiate a solution that was acceptable for Germany, Canada and England. For the POWs at Gravenhurst the whole action had been a mental boost: 'common sense and clear thinking' had won over confrontation and we were proud of it. Besides that, it was a nice feeling to know that the highest echelons of command at home and within the Allies were doing something for the prisoners of war. We hadn't been written off completely - yet!

It has to be noted here that the all-in-all sporting and fair execution of this whole matter was only possible because the number of German and Allied prisoners were both still fairly well balanced in our favour. Later, when no reprisals were to be expected on Allied prisoners (at the end of hostilities), we were to be treated very differently! The Geneva Convention, we were to discover, was only of secondary importance once one side had the whip hand. Even though, during this *Fesselaktion*, the Red Cross and the Protective Powers had been successful with their activities, that was to change as the war came to an end.

Notes on Chapter Eleven.

[1] Another and probably more important mission was also undertaken by a British radar engineer. He was taken to the German Freya and Würzburg sites to evaluate the equipment and above all see if they had discovered the cavity magnetron valve - the core of the very advanced British system. In order to do this he had to have extensive knowledge of the British system and was, therefore, escorted by two soldiers whose job was to kill him if capture looked inevitable. Happily all three made it back - see the book 'Green Beach.'

CHAPTER TWELVE

THE SNOW TUNNEL

Once it became known, through newspapers and the American Time magazine, what injuries had been inflicted at Bowmanville and in other enlisted men's camps as a result of the *Fesselungsaktion*, pure rage spread at Gravenhurst. What was there to be done? As if it were a hint from heaven, snow fell at night through the weekend 6/7th December, almost a full two metres! At first it was impossible to leave the building and the Canadians had to hold the roll call in the dining room but we were not willing to accept this winter hindrance and immediately detailed *Schaufelkommandos* (snow clearing commands). The Canadians provided us with sufficient large metal shovels and we got to work.

The Canadians pushed a path from the guard house to the main house with a snowplough during which time we not only shovelled *die Runde*, our rounds track, free of snow but also dug out a path diagonally across the skating rink to the fence in the direction of the lake. There the blizzard had blown an exceptionally high snow drift between the fences. Whilst looking at this an idea suddenly dawned on Eberhard Wildermuth and after taking a closer look at the situation he returned to our room and announced: "That is just right for a snow tunnel! We'll be out this evening!"

Even in Canada the weather could be unpredictable, changing a lot in a short time. We didn't know, therefore, how long this deep snow would last, things had to happen quickly if they were to happen at all. When Eberhard and I took another, closer, look at the snow drift, it was clear to us that a snow tunnel could be made! Penetration of the fence was possible too because Wildermuth was in possession of a short piece of a hack-saw blade, about ten centimetres long, which he had found sometime during the summer. Most probably any other person would have thrown that piece of scrap away, it was just lying on the ground somewhere in the garden, but not the 'Boss' as we called him.

We called him 'Boss' because, although the smallest in the room, he would sometimes squabble with 'Babyface' Rudolf Theopold, who was the tallest and also the youngest. Sometimes this was in fun, but also sometimes seriously and, at times, it would become really venomous. There was not only difference in rank, Wildermuth was a *Hauptmann* and Theopold was a

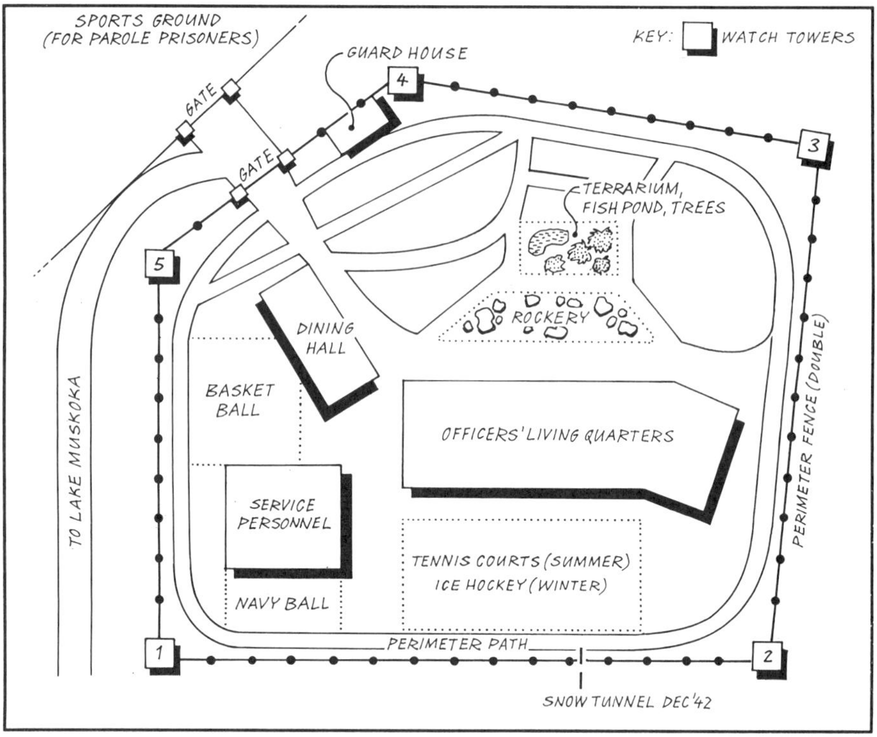
SPORTS GROUND
(FOR PAROLE PRISONERS)
KEY: WATCH TOWERS
GUARD HOUSE
GATE
GATE
TERRARIUM,
FISH POND, TREES
ROCKERY
DINING
HALL
BASKET
BALL
OFFICERS' LIVING QUARTERS
SERVICE
PERSONNEL
TENNIS COURTS (SUMMER)
ICE HOCKEY (WINTER)
NAVY BALL
TO LAKE MUSKOKA
PERIMETER FENCE (DOUBLE)
PERIMETER PATH
SNOW TUNNEL DEC '42
1
2
3
4
5

The Snow Tunnel

young *Leutnant*, but also the substantial difference in their flying experience which counted in a POW camp! Mostly, when the squabble ended in a friendly atmosphere, Theopold would say, "Never mind Eberhard, you're the boss anyway! Here in the room and everywhere else too!" If it ended less humorously, then he would add, "Don't be so disappointed that you're so small!"

I had laughed at the 'Boss' when he found that short piece of blade, especially because he said, "Perhaps I'll saw through the inner fence with this!" Now he had the chance: *die Runde*, in accordance with the Canadians security instructions, was approximately two metres away from the fence. From this snow corridor, which was originally so high that the tops of our heads were just visible when we walked along the path, we were going to dig a short tunnel - almost an extension of the path coming from the main building - to the thick mesh fence. At ground level this would be invisible and 'Boss' would then get to work with his piece of blade, cutting through the wires one after the other, until the hole was about sixty by sixty centimetres.

No sooner said than done! First, a short side corridor was dug with the snow shovels and then the tunnel was quickly dug to the fence in the deep snow. When Eberhard then went into action with his short piece of saw blade, hopes rose that this action might be successful. We closed the tunnel behind Eberhard with white cloths and snow and he sawed away diligently, hour after hour - wire after wire.

My task was now to quickly inform other would-be escapers of the opportunity, but not to be too hasty. First, of course, we had to request permission from the camp leadership for the attempt and they gave immediate sanction to the enterprise. Our reasoning was that although the chances of getting far in winter, especially with the amount of snow there was about, was not at all good the time had come where we had to prove to our guards that they hadn't suppressed all our courage. At first I informed those people who had participated in the digging of the tunnel that had been discovered. They had documents and clothing prepared and would be in the best position to make the most of this opportunity. Amongst these were, of course, Walter Manhart, Reini Pfundtner, Hinnerk Waller and Hannes Strehl, an old friend who had already made several courageous escape attempts.

It was inevitable, with such feverish activity, that knowledge of the snow tunnel would spread like wildfire through the camp and it needed the discipline of the *Ältestenrat* to control the applications for participation. By lunch time, it had been decided that no more than six would leave that evening, at intervals and always in pairs. First would be Steinhilper and Wildermuth, then Manhart with Pfundtner, followed by Waller and Strehl; each pair ten minutes behind the other. That allowed sufficient time for each pair to clear the fence area before the next would follow. I had enough reasons to be put in the 'pole position' by 'Boss': first of all because I was bigger than the others and if the tunnel which would have to continue between and beyond the fences was large enough for me the others could easily follow. Secondly, I had 'front line' experience of barbed wire and the use of a normal pair of cutters from my second escape.

During the Sunday afternoon we realized that perhaps we might not make it. The reason for this was that the blade was getting blunter and blunter and there was no replacement available in the camp. Doubts started as to whether the saw blade would hold out. That meant a change of plan: it would not be this evening we would be leaving, it would be the next evening after dusk. There were another two metres between the fences that had to be dug by myself before the outer coils of barbed wire could be attacked. And this all had to happen without the snow over me collapsing. It was when pondering this problem it occurred to me to get two cardboard bread boxes from the kitchen; the Canadians used these to deliver the bread to the camp. They were approximately sixty centimetres by sixty centimetres square and about one metre high. By putting two in tandem and connecting them together, they would provide a temporary support that should hold for about twenty four hours.

We spent the rest of the Sunday evening hoping the *Frettchen* wouldn't discover the tunnel. We had to put the cardboard bread boxes in position and then, to close the tunnel at the *Runde* end for the night, we packed snow into the opening. The Canadians patrols were easy to follow in that weather, they had no other choice but to use the paths we had shovelled free of snow. This made it easier for us and we could work a simple routine at the tunnel entrance. One just had to wait until the *Frettchen* had passed by, then work diligently until they appeared again on the straight stretch along the fence, in front of the main building. Their round of four hundred metres was easy to calculate, they needed about five minutes as a rule. That gave Wildermuth enough time to creep into the tunnel, put the cardboard box into position, or get other equipment. Of course the opening was packed with snow every time before they came around again.

The postponement until Monday also had other advantages, for one thing it gave more time to prepare documents and clothing for this type of escape. I decided, for myself, not to overdress for the crawl through the tunnel and the wire cutting. I would pack enough warm clothing and underwear for Boss Wildermuth and myself in a sack which I would pull along behind me on a rope. Once through we would pull the remainder of our kit through before we made off. The *Ältestenrat* really had their hands full, more and more people wanted to get out, but they remained firm. The risk of being discovered was too great when too many got out at one time. It was decided that after the first six had got out there would be a pause for an hour, then the escape could continue. That was the decision and that's how it stayed.

Only one modification was announced, Siegfried Schmidt, known as 'Body' because he was very proud of his well trained physique, would also 'go'. He wouldn't actually escape, he intended to hide in the camp to make it appear as though he too was on the loose. When the hunt had died down and the Canadians had got used to the idea he was gone, he would then try to get out. He didn't know how he was going to do that, but it certainly was an interesting thought; to escape at a time when nobody would be searching for you too intensely.

All night long we worried about our tunnel, especially when it began to rain. Already, when creeping into the tunnel, 'Boss' had to be careful because the snow had sunk so far that both towers could now again see to the end of the straight stretches of the fence. Our activities were no longer so well hidden by the high sides of the path through the snow. To cover our activities we gathered two small groups either side of the tunnel entrance and they milled about to cover the activity. The hole was soon sealed again and Eberhard reported from inside that the cardboard was soaking wet, but it was still high and wide enough. But the saw blade was getting blunter and blunter and it was almost dusk before he finally reported that the hole in the inner wire mesh fence was completed. However, as he started digging outwards between the two fences it could be seen that the snow was beginning to sink as he dug below.

Again, the new situation required new tactics. It was, as planned, to be my task to dig the two metres to the outer barbed wire while also having to cut the outer fence. But there was less and less snow cover for that. It was thawing rapidly and more cardboard boxes could not be taken in through the hole in the mesh wire fence to support the tunnel between the fences, because the hole in the wire was too small. There really was no solution. The 'Boss' had sawed like a madman, but nobody had thought it would take so long. Even the weather seemed to be against us. The new measures agreed were that if the snow over me collapsed while I was creeping through, or while I was cutting the barbed wire, then snowball teams assembled close to the two immediately adjacent towers would go into action. Not only would they throw snow at each other, but would also, by *accident* of course, throw snowballs at the windows of the towers to obstruct the view.

Around six o'clock it was dark and the spot where the tunnel ceiling had sunk lay in the shadow of perimeter lighting when I opened the tunnel. Creeping to the first mesh wire fence was damned tight and I didn't know if the clothing sack would go through. Behind me, also sealed in the tunnel, Wildermuth waited ready: "Eberhard, pass the sack up to the front!" I said, and here we hit our first snag, the height of the cardboard boxes was insufficient for me to pull the sack behind me and that meant it wouldn't go through the opening in the fence! Everything had been so carefully planned and there we were, already stuck! I crawled back again and told Eberhard it was no use, we'd have to go back to the living quarters for a rethink.

With the willing help of our colleagues we quickly put on some of the more important warm clothes, the last being a civilian overcoat. I asked Eberhard if he wanted to follow with the emptier sack or whether he too wanted to wear the warmer clothing. One thing was certain - we were not going to give up. It was a difficult situation, one in which one had to make one's own decisions and now a much greater element of risk lay ahead but in our view there was only one course, whatever the consequences.

Again I crept forward in the tunnel and dug out the snow between the fences. Hardly had I passed through the opening in the first fence when I became aware that the overcoat was badly snagged on the ends of the wires. Every time that I had to move or turn the fence shook and it seemed to get lighter above me. Nevertheless I made it to the barbed wire coils and started cutting. I realised that a tightly strung wire was easier to cut than a loosely rolled section. On a taught wire I could apply the jaws of the cutters and worry them back and forth until the hardened strands parted. But with the loose wire it was a case of working it with cutters and hands. But at least this time I'd had a chance to try pieces of wire in the camp and it held no surprises.

By then I was lying in the open and there were more strands than we had expected; again and again our progress was barred by more wire and again and again I was caught on a barb or a cut end and had to turn to release myself. As I did this I was shocked at what I saw, it looked as if the tunnel between the fences had almost collapsed and I was sure it must be visible from the towers by then! Our comrades had realised this and, especially to my left near the closest tower, a wild snowball fight was taking place. I wondered whether I would make it, let alone if anyone else would follow. What a tragedy!

It seemed to take ages to make progress and every second we expected the alarm to sound. I was in the open and in the perimeter lights but slowly, oh so slowly, I managed to crawl along clear of the wire. Three metres, two, one and I was out of the bright arc-lights and I gently slid down a slope on my belly, easily done in the snow. Should I wait for Wildermuth? I didn't want to take the risk, the guards would be sounding the alarm any minute, the collapse of the tunnel between the fences was too obvious. There would hardly be a chance to make a break for it in the deep slushy snow once the hunt was on. I had to move off towards the lights of Gravenhurst and, perhaps, wait there.

Astonishingly there was still no alarm to be heard as I loped away from the camp. I stopped to think again, should I perhaps still wait for Eberhard? I thought I might but first of all it was more important to get out of the wet snow because it was easy to follow my tracks all the way from the camp perimeter should the alarm be raised. Having reached a road to the town, I looked back and unbuttoned my coat to straighten out my clothing underneath. I was sorry to see everything was wet, from the inside because of profuse sweating and on the outside from the wet snow. I didn't wait too long, there were still no signs of Wildermuth. Besides, I soon felt the cold when I stood around and the need to get my limbs moving. It was not until then I realised that the weather had changed again. The sky had cleared and the first stars could be seen in the winter sky. The cloud cover had gone and this naturally heralded a bitterly cold night.

Approaching the town I found it deserted, most probably because of the bad weather. Cautiously, following the streets that were laid out in rectangles, I finally reached the main road at the other end of town. I assumed that this must be the road leading to Washago and from there to Orilla, Barrie and later to Toronto. That's where I wanted to reach, if possible, and go into hiding; perhaps find a job as a dish-washer or something similar. When necessary, I would use the story I had concocted about being a released *Red Spaniard,* a refugee of the Spanish Civil War seeking political asylum. We had read in the newspapers that the US Army, in the course of their invasion of North Africa, had discovered an internees camp. The prisoners had previously been *Reds* in the civil war and had been released by the Americans. According to the reports they were initially brought to America and my false documents were based on this information.

I took my time but there was no sign of anyone else, so I struck out on the march to Washago alone. It was terribly arduous, the roads hadn't been cleared of snow, but there must have been a lot of traffic because there were numerous tracks in the slush. The mixture of snow and slush was knee-deep and every time a lorry passed by, and there were only heavy lorries on the road, I barely managed to reach the surrounding woods. There I would wait, chest heaving from the exertion and lungs raw from the freezing air, until the tail lights disappeared and I could continue on my way. Because the road was almost completely straight, I could see lorries in time, whether they were coming towards me or from behind, but it was an exhausting process.

I quickly came to the conclusion that I couldn't sustain the effort which walking and avoiding the traffic required. I had to risk stopping one of the lorries and taking a ride. The chance of being recognised and being reported by the lorry driver was necessary, a calculated risk. The next lorry approached from the rear, splashing its way through the freezing mush, I waved it down and it stopped immediately. The door was opened for me from inside and I climbed into the warm oily atmosphere. I immediately started telling my story, that I had arrived in Halifax, on a goods train, reached North Bay and was now trying to make my way to Toronto. The driver, in his thick overalls, didn't really want to know too much, and I soon stopped my act. He had a load of timber and took me to the other side of Orilla. I estimated that we must have made some forty kilometres in the hour we had driven.

There he stopped for the night: "Don't you want to stay with me?" he asked. I declined, although he said that he was going to spend the night in a guest house that belonged to friends. It was surprising how well I understood him and he got along well with my English. I replied that I wanted to try my luck for a while more and try and get closer to Toronto. He was surprised and answered: "In such hellish weather!?" I shrugged and gave him a friendly goodbye wave and was on my way again.

I wasn't quite prepared to take the risk of appearing in public yet. I really wasn't very far away from the camp perimeter if the alarm was raised. I had to get on if I could but hardly had I left the warmth of the driver's cab, than I realised how cold it had turned in the mean time. It was a perfectly clear night and so light I was even able to read the time on my Eaton's pocket watch; it was already eight o'clock. In camp I had exchanged something for this all-steel one dollar watch, I needed a robust time keeper for my travels. Almost all of my clothing and equipment that had been confiscated after my last escape had been returned to me by the Canadians except for my good wrist-watch. It had been a Christmas present from home in 1941 and, because I had lost the glass, I'd always kept it in my shaving kit. This steel watch was perfect for my requirements and it even had luminous figures and hands.

Again the road was straight and led through a forest that lined the road on both sides. But now the slush quickly became ice with deep frozen ruts which made walking difficult and dangerous. Apparently driving had also become impossible because no more vehicles appeared. My driver must have known it was time to stop for the night, he knew the state of the roads and how conditions would probably develop.

After I had tortured myself for an hour in my attempts to make headway, my clothing started to freeze stiff. Luckily I had no problem with the direction in which I had to go, whenever a signpost came into view it showed: Barrie, Newmarket and, almost every time, Toronto. I had no doubts that this was the right road to follow. Should I perhaps look for some kind of shelter I wondered, but what? An old hut of some nature would be the best, a sort of log cabin alongside the road would be ideal. Then I might stand some chance of drying my clothes and taking something to eat. Although I had left my sack behind I had managed to stuff sufficient edible supplies into my pockets.

Even given the terrible conditions again I wasn't getting too depressed, but there were no huts, no matter how much I looked about me and explored the side tracks that had been cleared of snow. It was slowly getting closer to ten o'clock and I soon had to reach a decision. It was necessary to approach an inhabited house; my assumption was that anybody who knocked at a door after about ten would probably be treated with the gravest suspicion. It was, therefore, not too difficult for me, when I saw light through the trees to the left, to give myself the little mental shove that was required. I had to take the risk! My clothes had frozen so stiff that I could hardly move in them and soon the effects of the cold and hard going would begin to tell on me.

First of all I had to pass the house, which was approximately two hundred metres to my left away from the road in the forest. Through the trees I could just make out that there were several lights. When I tried to go diagonally through the forest, I soon had to give up, it was impossible. The snow was not only deep, but when my legs went through the hard crust on top it was damned near impossible to get them out again. I stood there for a while and tried to reason it out. The people who lived there must have got there somehow! Then I remembered that when I had almost passed the lights there had been a track leading back in the direction of the lights but at a very sharp angle to the road. Dragging myself out of the deep snow in the wood I backtracked and found what I was looking for.

The track had been well used and was all deep frozen ruts. My heart was pounding as I went forward, not just from the effort in the wood but from fear of what might happen. At the house there was a light up on a very tall pole and a corner room of the house was also lit up. Although my steps seemed, at least to me, to make a hell of a racket in the cold night air nobody heard me approaching. Unnoticed, I was able to continue from the corner of the house to the right where there was a rear door that was again in the dark. In passing the window I saw three people, they were still having a meal; a man, a woman and a younger man about twenty years old, most probably their son, I thought. As I stood at the door, I pondered again - should I not rather look for an open stable door in which I could spend the night unidentified? But then a dog inside the house started barking and I had no other choice than to knock, I couldn't find a bell. The door opened and the man turned on a light over the door and looked at me most astonished. I immediately began with my story but he was still suspicious, however, he let me continue into the room so that I didn't need to repeat my story for the others. He listened patiently, but was definitely suspicious.

Finally he spoke, "You have any papers?" "Oh yes," I replied, and immediately pulled out my identity card and other documents at the same time, all proving, in my eyes, my story. I had decided on the christian name of Otto, that fitted well to Alsace, to Strassburg where I was allegedly born. As surname, this time I had Paul on my documents. My name therefore was Otto Paul. I had thought long about this name, I wanted it to be easily understood in English and it should fit into German and also French so it would fit the Alsace story. In Watertown my name had been Paul Sumser. Nevertheless, I was of the opinion that should the expected search begin for Otto Paul there would be no direct connection with my previous identity.

He didn't study the documents for long, he actually seemed surprised that I was able to produce such good documents so quickly. I explained, "We're in the middle of war and one should always have such documents ready." Apparently that was enough to convince him and he became more hospitable, offering food which I gratefully accepted. Would I like something to drink also? I was mainly just thirsty, very thirsty, but there was nothing else I could do other than to sit down and not only drink a lot of their warm tea but also eat some excellent bread and smoked ham. The farmer's wife (apparently I had landed in a farmhouse) even wanted to fry something for me, but I thanked her and refused. Then of course I had to tell my story.

Again, as in the past, the more often you tell your story the better it gets over to the listener. Yes, I was born in the Alsace region of France, near Strassburg. When the civil war broke out in Spain, I volunteered to fight for the *Red* side, less for idealistic reasons, rather more because it was hard to find work at that time. It was 1937 when I volunteered. At that time I was still very young, Franco had won the civil war, and we just managed to escape via Barcelona to North Africa, where we were then interned. We were there for a long time until the Americans finally came and released us. I said I was lucky and managed to get a boat from Oran which took me all the way to Halifax. A most adventurous story, but it went down well. Because it took a long time for me tell my story, it had reached bedtime for my hosts.

I was instructed to go with upstairs with the 'farmhand', not the son as I had assumed, and sleep in a room up there. The woman, I estimated her age to be around forty-five, gave the lad the necessary bed linen and we went up the stairs. He was friendly and very helpful. I didn't want special treatment at all but he immediately took the bed linen from the better bed, on which he normally slept and remade it with my linen. There was nothing I could do, that's how he wanted it done, saying I must certainly be very tired, considering everything I had gone through! During the winter months his work wasn't as hard and he would sleep on the field bed, which was also in the same room. One could hardly imagine how my conscience was bothering me. How badly had I lied to these honest people, and now this good treatment that I was being given but I had no other choice.

In the room under the sloping roof there were all kinds of junk standing around, but it was just as warm as downstairs in the living room. I started to get undressed and now my friend was astonished at the amount of clothing

I was wearing: "You've a lot of clothes on!" he commented innocently. "Yes," I agreed, "It's very cold outside, and when you're tramping along the roads you never know what's coming next." That was about the sum total of our conversation. I distributed my wet clothing as well as I could over all the junk, hoping that it would dry by the next morning.

Considering my situation I didn't stay awake for long. Even after the tension of the escape and the anxiety of being a fugitive again I slept through the whole night and even had to be woken up in the morning! The friendly young man shook me awake, he had already got dressed and told me it was breakfast time. As quickly as I could I got up and dressed. As I pulled my layers of clothing on I realised I had too much and gave my new friend a good set of green tricot pyjamas. They hadn't dried completely overnight, and were really in excess of my requirements. The previous evening, in the rush, I'd put on two pairs of pyjamas over my underwear. At first he didn't want to take the gift, but then he decided he'd accept them as a reminder of my stay.

Downstairs Mr and Mrs 'Farmer' were already waiting at the breakfast table, on which nothing was missing. For breakfast we ate ham and eggs followed by pancakes with maple syrup and the choice of either coffee or tea to drink. The radio, which looked very similar to our *Volksempfänger* (a basic radio mass-produced in Germany), was producing music that nobody listened to and, thank goodness, there were no 'news flashes' about a breakout from Gravenhurst. Even so, every now and then my conscience bothered me, how was I able to lie to these friendly hosts of mine. But then came the eight o'clock news, at the end of which my heart almost stopped and the pancake stuck in my throat.

"Yesterday evening, seven German officers, all Air Force, broke out of the Prisoner of War Camp at Gravenhurst. Five have already been caught, but two are still being looked for: Lieutenant Siegfried Schmidt, 24, five feet nine inches tall, weighs 165 pounds. He has blonde curly hair, parted on the right side, blue eyes, normal nose, average chin, full lips, good build and good teeth. He speaks some English. Still missing, also Lieutenant Otto Steinhilper, 22, five feet ten inches tall, fair complexion, clean shaven, with a turned nose (the Canadians had even corrected their description after my nose had been hit in that boxing fight), round chin. He is of medium build, weighs 176 pounds and speaks only German. The type of clothing he is wearing is not known. Steinhilper has fair hair, brown eyes, fine mouth, normal teeth and a scar on the left forefinger."

An exact description of Sigi and myself! It was a miracle that I didn't suffocate on that pancake but I managed to get it to sink down. I had looked at my left hand forefinger that moment the scar was mentioned in the radio, that was pure insanity, but perhaps nobody noticed. Then I had to digest the information I'd heard, they had all apparently managed to get out but all, except for Sigi and I, had already been caught. But then I didn't know if *'Body'* Schmidt had actually got out or if he was just executing his plan to feign escape and then get away later. All this and then such a good personal description of myself while I was sitting at someone's breakfast table... it was some kind of madness and it really took some control to appear normal.

I acted as if I liked the maple syrup very much and said, "This honey is excellent!" and was my salvation, although everybody had heard what had been broadcast over the radio, they were more interested in demonstrating their pride in their syrup, "This is Canadian Maple Syrup!" came the answer and then followed a lengthy description of how it was collected and processed. I was relieved to be able to sit and listen as they told me that the juice was obtained by cutting a groove in the bark of the sugar maple, letting it trickle into a bucket or similar. After thickening, it was then the product that we had on the table in front of us. It was clear I had weathered the first potential disaster, but could things go well with a report like this one on the radio?

I noticed how everybody around the table pestered me with questions now, although the conversation was on many completely different subjects. As I answered I tried to think at the same time, trying to judge what was in my favour. At least one point in the description wasn't correct, '...speaks only German!' That might help assuage some people's doubts.

The farmer couldn't cope with this new situation, he seemed doubtful and concerned. He said he would be driving to Barrie with the station-wagon immediately after breakfast, he had some shopping to take care of. He offered to take me that far and from there I should see that I made my own way. Nevertheless, he wanted to see my identification documents again. This time he took a very close look at them and even gave them to his wife to have a look at but she seemed suitably impressed, there was even an Immigration Certificate from Halifax amongst the documents. Thank goodness they didn't question the name Otto, which I had one time at a roll call used for fun, after somebody else had just escaped. At the time I never thought that this name would stick for ever, even when the Canadians had checked all other personal details so carefully before they included them in the search report. Had I known this, I would never have decided on the name of 'Otto' Paul!

Without a word my documents were given back to me and, immediately afterwards, we left for Barrie. As the farmer, the farmhand and I sat in the front of the small lorry, I wasn't at all sure that he wasn't going to drive straight to the Police with me, but what could I do? Perhaps he had suspected something, but he let me get out when we reached the first houses at the outskirts of Barrie. I thanked him for his help and hospitality and he drove a further fifty metres or so down the road and turned off to the right. It was possible he sympathised with me but had seen through it all, I couldn't worry about that. My way led straight through the middle of the medium sized town of Barrie.

Because there were several turnoffs within the town, and with them the possibility of ending up going somewhere other than my goal, I decided to wait until I got to the other side of the town before I tried my luck for a lift. In town the slush was at such a level that I could just walk through it, but I knew that once I left it would again reach a level which would make progress impossibly difficult. I made my way unchallenged through the town and got to a point on a slight rise where there didn't seem to be any more turnings and I was sure any ride would take me where I wanted to go. Still trudging along near some big square buildings I was ready to try my luck with cars and lorries. The first car I waved down, a black Ford V8, stopped immediately. A tall man got out, all dressed in black, and asked, "Want a ride?" "Yes!" I eagerly replied, "I'm heading for Toronto!" I waited for a positive answer but all he did was to walk over to me and tug my trouser legs up to look at my boots. I was wearing my Elk boots with the thick crepe soles and very high uppers that had been returned to me by the Canadians after my escape to Watertown. I had strengthened them by inserting leather insoles so that they wouldn't bend so easily and before I escaped I had used copious amounts of dubbin on them to waterproof them. He didn't say anything for a moment, just took out a piece of paper, looked at my boots again and grinned, "You'll get a ride," he said, "but not this way, back the other way... back to the Police Station!"

'Verdammt nochmal!' ('I'll be damned!') I said to myself. Again, such a stupid situation. It was not until that moment that I saw what was written on the side of the black car. There in stark lettering was 'Provincial Police' - I'd stopped a bloody Police car! Trying to run away in this situation would have been stupid, all now depended on how good my identification documents were! This time I wanted to deny everything to the very last, to take advantage of every chance I was given. I was therefore going to deny my true identity as long as possible.

I was to find out later that the description that had been given to all Police contained additional information that the escaped Steinhilper was most probably wearing a pair of 'half-high' boots made of Elks leather. The policeman told me to get into the car and drove back to the RCMP station in Barrie and turned me over to them. I immediately got my identification documents out again and asked whether they could help me find my way to Toronto. But the two Mounties weren't at all impressed, my driver was again raising my trouser legs and pointed to his piece of paper and my shoes. 'Well I'll be damned,' I thought, did the Canadians only return my Elk leather boots to me so that they could identify me? In the face of all this I still didn't let myself be intimidated and told my story over and over again, each time going into more detail; how I'd fought in the Spanish Civil War as an Alsatian; how we had been evacuated to North Africa at the last minute to escape the wrath of General Franco; and how we'd been interned there and finally released when the Americans invaded Oran. I appealed to them to have a little understanding for my situation and not put me in a prison again.

Nevertheless they put me in a cell for the time being, located behind the office, and got me out again and again for questioning. Sometimes I had a feeling that my efforts were achieving small results, but again and again one of the policemen kept saying: "Look at his damned poker-face!" At first the word 'poker-face' had no meaning for me and I asked them directly what they meant. They explained to me that when playing the card game poker, one always had to watch out that one didn't let one's opponents know which cards one had through the look on one's face. That was, in the view of the policeman, exactly the type of face that I was pulling! I protested against such accusations and, as a result, they began speaking French with me as far as they were capable and also asked whether I spoke Spanish (many North Americans speak a little Spanish).

They seemed to be suitably astonished how well my foreign language ability fitted to my story. Again I was sent back into the cell and they had a new idea. The interrogation had now been going for a good two hours, on and off, and the clock was showing eleven o'clock when they brought me back into the office. There I was confronted with a man, who introduced himself very politely. He had very good manners and explained he was the headmaster of a girl's high school where he taught German and French. Again I told my story, how I'd had grown up in the Alsace and because of the poor economical situation there I'd joined the International Brigade in Spain. I was getting better and better every time I told my story. He interrupted me occasionally, and asked me to tell my story in German or French, he was also fairly fluent in Spanish, and after a little over an hour he evaluated my language capabilities, the results of which he told the Police: my German was better than my French (although I'd deliberately been searching for words whenever I was talking German to him), but also that my knowledge of Spanish was in accordance with my story. He had come to the conclusion that my knowledge of the three languages was consistant with the story I was telling.

Shortly after that, with a very polite comment that his wife was waiting with their midday meal, the well educated professor of foreign languages said goodbye and left. For my policemen, of course, the result was of no help at all. They were more uncertain than ever, and started debating whether they should release me. At that moment the officer of the Provincial Police returned for his midday break and he had no doubts: I was the man that was being searched for, Otto Steinhilper, and back I went to the cell.

I was left to ruminate on my misfortune for a while until one of the two policemen came and explained that I wouldn't have to wait too long for a decision any more. They had just received a telephone call from the Camp at Gravenhurst, the Sergeant Major was already on his way and would arrive in about an hour. He was, they told me, positive he could identify the fugitive and I had no doubts it was true. They said, I suppose to help me, that my true identity would soon be known - or at least they would know who I wasn't. If I wasn't this escaped German flyer then, they assured me, they would release me immediately.

I wondered if what they was saying was true or just another ruse to see how I reacted. Was the Sergeant Major indeed coming - that was something I really needed to know. "Yes," both Mounties reassured me, "he's arriving soon." I heaved a sigh and really resigned myself to the fact that I was 'in the bag' again. There was no point in stretching it out, the Sergeant Major knew me too well and I suppose I did not want to grant him that triumph. "Well," I said..."if that's the case, I admit, that I am Ulrich Steinhilper!"

Actually I'd expected the two would now get mad at me for having continuously lied to them, but it was exactly the opposite. They almost fell around my neck and were of the opinion that I'd had played my role as 'poker-face' very well, but now they were glad I'd admitted my identity to them. I'd seen this kind of relief before and in the camp we'd begun to wonder if the police actually got a monetary award for capturing us escapees because their exuberance when it was confirmed we were who they thought we were was always wonderful to behold. Like at Niagara Falls, on my first escape, one of the two policemen went to a nearby cafe and brought me some coffee and two large pieces of cake which I didn't have to eat in the cell, but together with them in their office. Amongst my identification documents that I'd shown to them there were also my genuine dollars which I'd had since Fort Henry. I wanted to pay for the coffee and the cake with these, but they refused saying I was now their guest! I didn't feel like celebrating too much.

The Sergeant Major arrived and pulled a very sour face when he heard that I had already admitted my identity. He formally took custody of me with his signature and did at least grin when he was able to take custody of my identification documents and my dollars, he knew how valuable they were to me. Shortly after that I found myself on the way back to Camp 20 Gravenhurst. We departed from Barrie at around two o'clock, arriving in *der Teng* at Gravenhurst about an hour later. There they were all gathered: Hinnerk, Hannes Strehl, Manni, Reini Pfundtner and also Eberhard Wildermuth. With a loud 'Hallo', they welcomed me through the door of the detention block. There were six cells in that long corridor and now they were all occupied. We had all forfeited freedom, the false documents and that little money we'd had without being able to make full use of it all, but the atmosphere here in this shed was not bad at all!

I, personally, never ever mentioned having spent the night on that farm during subsequent questioning, nor did I tell any of my colleagues about it. Therefore, even later in the newspapers, there was no mention of where or how I had spent the night. The farmer, no doubt, must have felt he had his reasons for not saying a word!

CHAPTER THIRTEEN

THE EXCHANGE COMMISSION VISITS THE CAMP

In the new, almost unused, punishment cells I was quickly informed of the fates of my comrades. Hinnerk and Strehl were discovered within the camp grounds, shortly after having crept through the fence, and were very badly treated by the furious veteran guards. In the course of this they were beaten and repeatedly hit with rifle butts, mainly on their heads, but also all over their bodies. All the camp inmates had to watch this through the fences and started a loud protest. Nevertheless, the raging soldiers apparently released the safety catches on their rifles and pointed them at our two comrades and from all accounts seemed ready to pull the triggers they were so incensed. It seemed it was only the volume of protest from so many witnesses which made them secure their weapons and be satisfied with the beating. Strehl and Hinnerk had to live through some very tense minutes.

They shouted their story loudly down the corridor so I could hear it. We had been imprisoned, with bureaucratic efficiency, in the sequence of our recapturing. At the far end were Hinnerk and Hannes Strehl, then came Eberhard Wildermuth, Manhart and Pfundtner, who was closest to me in the neighbouring cell. Nothing was said about 'Body' Schmidt for obvious reasons and as the Canadians weren't allowing us the usual exercise, the prescribed walks of an hour every morning and afternoon, there was nowhere we could talk without unwanted ears hearing what was said. Naturally we protested against this treatment and were given a rather weak excuse as to why we couldn't be allowed out. We wanted to resolve this, to establish contact with our comrades within the camp and through them with each other. We had already, through the well tried and tested method of secreting messages in food brought out from the kitchen, established that a commission of the Swiss Red Cross had announced their impending visit to the camp. We also, through the kitchen, returned details of our escapes and our capture through the leftovers. Hannes Strehl and Hinnerk reported on how their injuries were treated in the same night by the Canadian doctor and that Strehl had a quite severe head wound.

That we were all in *der Teng* didn't make us at all sad, the whole action in the middle of winter had mainly served to show the Canadians that they had by no means managed to break our courage or spirit. Wildermuth recalled the happenings from memory in a letter to me dated 1st May 1988 - almost fifty years after it had happened:

'...On the next evening we then, in groups of two at a time, got out every ten minutes and you were the first, because you had to cut the outer fence...

I was, at first, immediately behind you but then in the metre deep snow and the darkness we lost each other, still within the immediate vicinity of the Canadian camp. It was 40 degrees below zero and it was a clear starlit night.

I walked to Washago, managed to board a goods (freight) train where I lay flat on the roof. In the meantime the camp had given the alarm for the area around the camp. The train was searched at the water tower and I was discovered (thank goodness, otherwise I might have frozen to death). The locomotive driver had stopped the train so that the coach I was on was on the middle of a bridge. From both sides I could see the guards walking along the roofs towards me. I jumped down from the roof, over a railing on the bridge onto a white patch of snow and was surprised that nobody followed me.

Later I was to find out that this was the first night that this river had frozen over. I hid myself from the searchlights behind a storage shack that was built on poles on the river embankment, broke through the ice, but managed to pull myself back up one of these poles. I then moved over to the guardhouse which gave me protection from the searchlights and waited there, behind the guard, who didn't notice me, to see what how the situation would develop. There I was then discovered by the search dogs and recaptured.

'Body' Schmidt also wanted to disappear during this escape action, but wanted to stay within the camp, until all search activities had been terminated. To change his appearance, he even got Doctor Heitsch to operate, putting a piece of ice hockey puck into his chin...'

Overleaf follow reports from the Montreal Gazette, Toronto Daily Star and the Montreal Daily Star which reveal how the Canadian press viewed the escape. We were only occasionally able to read articles like this once we were back in camp, they only reached us when the Canadian censor happened to overlook the particular item. Those articles reproduced in this book mostly originate from Canadian Newspaper archives researched post-war.

DEAL TURIN KNOCK-OUT BLOW

Jap Warship Sunk, 3 Set Afire By U.S. Planes

HUNT LAST TWO OF SEVEN ESCAPED NAZIS

SEVEN NAZIS TRY BREAK
FIVE BACK IN FEW HOURS
SIXTH SUSPECT IS HELD

Flee as Fire Distracts Guards
—Search Centres in
Toronto

WEAR WHITE SUITS

Police this afternoon were sure that five of seven German prisoners who escaped from an internment camp in the Gravenhurst area were captured and believe that a sixth may now be in custody.

Having participated in the capture of two previous prisoners, Provincial Cor stable Walter Robinson at noon in I arrie was "flagged" by a man on the street who asked him for a lift. The officer drove him straight to headquarters. The man is still being questioned, as police say his stories do not tally and he had forged papers in his possession.

"It seems as if he may be Otto Steinhilper, the Nazi air force lieutenant who who away," an official said.

The seventh missing Nazi is Siegfried Schmidt, age 24.

Camouflaging themselves with home-made white suits, cut from sheeting, the seven strolled away shortly after dark Tuesday night. Two were caught after they reached the camp's outer enclosure, two more were definitely caught at Barrie and another at Washago.

Those already recaptured are: Albert Waller, 24; Hans Strehl, 22; Aberhard Wildermutch, 23; Rheinhart Pfundter, 24; Walter Mahnart, 24.

WATCH
For These
Nazis

SIEGFRIED SCHMIDT: aged 24, rank unknown, 165 pounds, long, curly hair, five feet, nine inches tall, blue eyes, round nose, full lips, speaks a little English.

Meanwhile, a New England-wide police alert was ordered by the F.B.I. as they sought two Germans who escaped from an internment camp near Sherbrooke, Que., Sunday night. The fugitives were described as Franz Gripsch, 21, and Martin Lorenz, 30, both merchant seamen, and wearing regulation internment overalls.

According to guards at the prison camp, the seven men dressed themselves in the white sheeting and manoeuvred themselves beyond the wire fences. They started to walk away. One of the guards noticed them and gave the alarm. He ran after them and captured two. The other five started to run. "The guard might have fired at them, but he obeyed a corporal who told him not to," it was said.

After a struggle, the guard, aided by a comrade, subdued the five prisoners.

The Nazis escaped when attention of the guards—many of them new men at the camp—had been diverted by a fire which broke out in one of the cabins. "I don5t know how the fire started, but it looked as if they had it all figured out in advance," a guard said.

Including the seven who escaped Tuesday, a total of 102 Axis prisoners of war have escaped in Canada since the war began. Four were shot resisting capture. One man, Sub Lieut. Baron Franz von Werra, escaped to the U.S. before that country entered the war and from there made his way back to Germany via Peru. Later he was reported by German sources as killed in action. All the others but four of this week's

OTTO STEINHILPER: air force lieutenant, aged 22, five feet, 10 inches, 176 pounds, fair, clean, shaven, brown eyes, scar on left forefinger, speaks German only.

escapees have been recaptured.

The largest mass escape occurred on April 18, 1941, from a camp near Peninsula, in northwestern Ontario, when 28 men tunnelled their way out of the internment camp. Two were shot to death resisting capture. Two others were shot resisting capture in other escape attempts. Von Werra is the only prisoner to date to make a permanent escape.

All six of us sat for quite a while in *der Teng*, our sentences this time being extended because we were continually protesting against not being allowed to take the authorised walks every day. When it was reported to us from the camp that the Swiss Commission had arrived, our dissatisfaction became acute, almost reaching boiling point. What a damned cheek! A blatant breach of the Geneva Convention and this at a time when a neutral Commission was present in the camp. This wasn't the only contravention either: it was also the first time we were not given any books. Everything looked as if we were going to have to fight again for normal conditions.

Just One Nazi Still at Large

Six Escapees Now Back in Custody

SOME WELL EQUIPPED

GRAVENHURST, Ont., Dec 9 (C.P.) — Otto Steinhilper, 22, an escaped German prisoner-of-war was recaptured near Barrie, Ont. this afternoon. He was one of seven men who escaped from a prison camp near here last night. Five others had previously been recaptured.

There is a possibility Steinhilper may be Ulrich Steinhilper, who had made three previous escapes from prison camps. Once he crossed the Niagara river on a locomotive and then came back to Canada on the same train without realizing he had been in the United States. He was recaptured and again escaped to be captured at Windsor Station, Montreal, where he hid under a railway coach by tying himself to the rods. On a third escape from an Ontario camp he was soon discovered.

The only Nazi now at large is Siegerd Schmidt, 24, who can speak English. Steinhilper could not.

Albert Waller, 24, and Hans Strehl, 22, were captured last night after getting past the first enclosure at the camp. Two other officers were caught at Barrie, 40 miles south of here, after riding into town on the snowplough of a train.

The fifth, Aberhard Willdermuth, 23, was caught early today at Washago, 18 miles south of here. He was seen in a coal chute by the night operator at the Canadian National Railways station, who turned in an alarm.

Registration Cards Held

The Germans captured at Barrie were Reinhard Pfundter, 21, and Walter Manhardt, 24, who were chased through the town and caught on a highway by Provincial Constable Walter Robinson. Manhardt is believed to be the same prisoner who escaped from a camp at Bowmanville, Ont. Dec 30, 1941, and was recaptured Jan. 2 by a United States border patrol near Ogdensburg, N.Y.

Police said both Pfundter and Manhardt were carrying registration cards and false identification cards, as well as concentrated food and German-English dictionaries. They told police they wanted to go to Halifax and get on a ship to return to Germany.

Two Make Slight Error

BARRIE, Ont., Dec 9 (C.P.) Two Germans who escaped from a prison camp near Gravenhurst were recaptured because they accepted an invitation of two police officers to ride in their car.

Dr. Harold Smith of Barrie was the first to spot the two prisoners. He had received a call to a village six miles south of here and police asked him to be on the look-out for the two men. He saw two hitch-hikers on the highway and telephoned police.

Constable Walter Robinson of the Ontario Provincial Police and Constable Colin Stewart of the Barrie force took up the search in Robinson's car.

They came up with the hiking pair two miles from here and asked "Want a lift." The escaped prisoners accepted the invitation, got in the car and were placed under arrest.

The two were Reinhard Pfundter and Walter Manhardt, who had been shot down over Britain in 1940.

Pfundter said that he had been substitute centre ice player on the German hockey team in the 1936 Olympic Games and had played against the Canadians.

They now have been taken back to Gravenhurst. The car which came here to take them back to the camp picked up another escapee on the way. He was Aberhard Willdermuth, who was arrested at Washago.

Appeasement Charge Denied

Korean Woman Barred From I.P.R. Conference

A representative of a Korean political faction, claiming Institute of Pacific Relations representatives meeting here are considering appeasement for Japan, has been barred from the conference, an official said today.

Representing Kilsoo K. Haan, head of the Korean National Front, with headquarters in Washington, a young Korean woman attempted to take a seat at the secret discussions but "she was politely told that Korea's interests were already ably taken care of by Younghill Kang," head of the Free Korean movement and a member of the Board of Economic Warfare in Washington.

With a gust of laughter, a member of the I.P.R. Secretariat dismissed the appeasement charges, saying "far from appeasement this conference has blood in its eye as far as Japan is concerned. I think this was shown in our significant gesture in inviting the head of the most important Korean political group."

(Korea was represented at the conference for the first time in I.P.R. history; in this, the first time that Japan has not been represented.)

The official pointed out, however, that I.P.R. discussions, while participated in by important Government experts from various United Nations interested in the Pacific area, were not "anybody's law" but rather "helpful background sometimes used by various

U.S. Air Force Hits Japs Hard

Warship Sunk, Three Others Left in Flames

WASHINGTON, Dec. 9—(U.P.) —A Japanese warship was sunk and three others were left in flames by an American dive bomber and torpedo planes attack in the Solomons last week, the Navy announced today.

The attack occurred last Thursday (island time), and it frustrated another enemy drive on Guadalcanal, the Navy disclosed.

In addition to ships hit, 10 float-type Japanese planes were shot down by American fighters.

The fact that the attack had been made was announced last Saturday by the Navy, but results were not known at the time.

The American air-striking group intercepted an enemy force of about 10 cruisers and destroyers approximately 150 miles northwest of Guadalcanal and headed for that island.

The Navy said that the enemy suffered the following damage:

A cruiser hit by two 1000-pound bombs.

Another cruiser hit by a 1000-pound bomb.

A destroyer or cruiser hit by two torpedoes.

Another destroyer or cruiser possibly hit by two torpedoes.

"On the next day, aerial reconnaissance showed that one of these vessels had sunk, but it was not disclosed which one. Three other enemy ships were sighted in flames, still in the vicinity of the previous day's action.

American losses were a dive bomber, a torpedo plane and a fighter.

The Navy said that ground fighting on Guadalcanal on Tuesday again involved patrol activity, with heavy artillery fire supporting the American operations. The American patrols maintained contact with the Japanese to the westward of US positions on the island.

Buna Expedition Routed

GEN. MACARTHUR'S HEADQUARTERS, Australia, Dec. 9— (B.U.P.) — Allied heavy bombers on the New Guinea front blasted almost at its source a seventh Japanese naval attempt to reinforce the dwindling enemy garrison at Buna, it was announced today.

Medium bombers at the same time went back to Lae, main Japanese fighter base on New Guinea, and gave it another battering.

Today's Allied communique said Japanese planes had violated the rules of war, since Nov. 27, by repeated attacks on field hospitals and dressing stations.

In ground fighting, Americans despite heavy cross fire repulsed

The Gazette

MONTREAL, THURSDAY, DECEMBER 10, 1942.—TWENTY PAGES

7 GERMANS ESCAPE CAMP; 6 CAPTURED

Prisoners Make Break from Internment Camp Near Gravenhurst

1 STILL AT LARGE

Two of Men Captured a Few Minutes After Break; Some Had Made Previous Escapes

Gravenhurst, Ont., December 9—.—Six German air force officers who escaped from a prisoner-of-war camp near here last night were ither back in camp or on their way back tonight while police throughout Ontario kept a close watch for the seventh man who articipated in the break—second argest from a prison camp in Canda since the war began.

The man still at large is Siegfried chmidt, 24, and searching police elieve he may be in the neighbor ood of Washago, 13 miles south of ere, where one of the seven—berhard Willdermuth—was pick d up last night.

Two of the men were captured by a guard a few minutes after the break from the prison camp; two others were arrested during the night on the highway two miles south of nearby Barrie while a sixth was picked up on the outskirts of Barrie at noon today.

The sixth to be recaptured was Otto or Ulrich Steinhilper who figured in three previous escapes. Posing as a French merchant seaman and a veteran of the International Brigade in the Spanish war, he was questioned by police at Barrie for three or four hours before he admitted his identity.

Albert Waller, 24, and Hans Strehl, 22, were captured at 7:30 o'clock last night just after the seven made their escape wearing home-made suits of white sheeting as camouflage. Reinhardt Pfundler and Walter Manhardt were the two arrested during the night at Barrie, being taken into custody when they accepted the offer of a ride from Constable Walter Robinson of the Ontario Provincial Police and Constable Colin Stewart of the Barrie police force.

Constable Robinson also figured in Steinhilper's arrest. The escaped prisoner stopped him and asked him for a ride. The constable took him into the car and drove to headquarters.

Steinhilper's story to the police was that he was born near Strasbourg in Alsace Lorraine and had been interned at Oran, gaining his freedom when United States forces invaded French North Africa. He carried a false registration card and what purported to be an immigration certificate issued at Halifax describing him as a friendly alien with experience as a merchant seaman, farmhand and lumberjack and recommending him for employment in these occupations.

Dr. Harold Smith of Barrie assisted in the capture of Manhardt and Pfundtner—the latter saying later that he was a member of the German hockey team which played in the Olympic games in 1936 and that he had played against the Canadians. Dr. Smith answered a call to Stroud, six miles south of Barrie, and having been asked by police to watch for the escaped prisoners, notified them that he had seen two hitch-hikers on the highway. The two were picked up by Constables Robinson and Stewart.

Provincial Constable Thomas Watson, assisted by guards, captured Willdermuth, who dived into a snowbank in a futile effort to elude his pursuers.

SEVERAL ATTEMPTS.

On one of Steinhilper's previous escapes he crossed the Niagara river on a locomotive and came to Canada on the same train without knowing he had been in the United States. After being recaptured he escaped again at Windsor station. In Montreal, where he hid under a railway coach by tying himself to the rods. On his third escape attempt he was captured shortly after he left the camp.

Pfundter had been in one previous escape, from a camp near Bowmanville, while Manhardt said he had previously escaped three times.

Including the seven in the break from the camp near here, 102 Axis prisoners-of-war have escaped from prison camps in Canada since the war began. The largest mass escape was from the prison camp near Peninsula in northwestern Ontario where 28 men tunnelled their way to freedom April 18, 1941. Two of them were shot to death resisting capture.

Only one man, Sub.-Lt. Baron Franz von Werra, has so far made a permanent escape. He reached the United States, before that nation entered the war, and made his way from there back to Germany via Peru. Later he was reported by German sources to have been killed in action.

Reini Pfundtner, although by no means the duty senior, was, because of his knowledge of American English, marked as our spokesman. In this new role he asked the guards if he could speak to the Duty Officer who was in charge of the guards in the punishment block. He did this several times that day and continued over the next few days.

The guard commander didn't appear but we had hints through the veteran guards of his opinion. It didn't apparently seem to make any impression at all that Hinnerk Waller and Strehl demanded to see the Commission because of their injuries, nor did the protest concerning the books and the exercise evoke any obvious reaction. The feedback we got was that his view was that we should be glad the guards hadn't shot Strehl and Waller! Still he didn't come and we knew from our exchange of messages in the food that the Commission was still in camp. What should we do? Soon they would be gone and it would be too late! Together we decided to raise hell in our cells. We would demolish the wooden bunks, the wooden corner table and the cell

163

stool and with the pieces of wood we would start beating on the cell doors. All agreed, we waited for the command from *Hauptmann* Wildermuth as the senior officer.

The command, *"Rabbatz!"* ("Raise hell!"), echoed through the cells and we all started venting days if not years of frustration and anger on the cell furniture. With good physical condition from the boxing training I tore the boards out of the wooden bunk, smashed the three-legged stool into pieces and the corner table was debris in minutes. Several times, during our terrible racket, the guards appeared at the 'peep-holes' - the observation flaps in the cell doors - and threatened us with their rifles. It didn't impress us at all and I almost hit one in the face with the boards from the bunk I was so mad by then: *Rabbatz ist Rabbatz!* was my motto! - a riot is a riot, no half measures!

Then the Duty Officer actually appeared, upon which Wildermuth gave *den Krawall einzustellen* (the command to stop rioting - a cease-fire). The Canadian officer promised to take our protest forward to the Camp Commander, including our request to speak with the Swiss Commission. Should we continue with our acts of violence, he warned, he would not hesitate to issue orders to start shooting into the cells. With this, we were satisfied for the time being. The guards came into our cells and cleared away the debris. Afterwards, my cell looked very bare, not one piece of furniture was left over, two blankets was all I had. There were no mattresses in the arrest cells anyway and I had no other choice than to sleep on one blanket on the bare metal floor and use the other to cover myself. The Canadians, after the hole Manni Manhart had cut in the floor of his cell in Bowmanville, had put metal floors in the cells which rose some forty centimetres up the wall all around.

When I enquired how my comrades were doing, they laughed at me: I had done my work too thoroughly! None of them had demolished their furnishings *and* their bunk! I was quite annoyed after that, surely a riot was a riot, not something you did with one eye on the future. The rest of the time in *der Teng* I slept on the cold steel floor as a punishment and I developed a sort of rheumatism in the shoulder and in the hip which had been damaged during my parachute jump. It was to stay with me for a long time. The rest of my comrades gave me very little support when I protested to the Canadians. None of the others had destroyed their bunks and they pulled my leg because it really was because of my own stupidity. The Canadians, for their part, sarcastically asked: 'Who was it who had destroyed my bunk?'

Once we had returned to life in the camp, we were immediately interested in hearing what had happened to 'Body'. He had, in fact, carried out his plan of 'passive escaping' and lived in his hide-out under the roof for quite a while. The story of how the hard rubber wedge, which had been cut out of an ice hockey puck, was surgically inserted into his chin is still, even today, told in various versions: in one it is said that he was excessively inebriated and another claimed he had been rendered unconscious by a punch on the chin or head. Hannes Strehl, who lives in Munich now, knew the actual detail:

'After 'Body' had made up his mind that he wanted his face changed Doctor Heitsch stepped into action. More against his will than with enthusiasm, he made himself the required scalpel out of an appropriate piece of steel and stole some ampules and hypodermic needles from the Canadian doctor to use as a local anaesthetic.

The operation took place in the evening and lasted too long. Because it is possible the 'Body' had also prepared himself with alcohol and for that, or some other reason, the injections didn't work. Nevertheless the operation was conducted with the patient being fully conscious. I was present the whole time because, at the time I was the translator for medical matters.

Suddenly it was roll-call time and we had to interrupt the operation until after the counting and hid 'Body', for the time being, in the attic."

The truth is that this *foreign object* was not accepted by Sigi's chin. He let a beard grow over the suppurating wound and for quite some time he had a slightly raised temperature. After five months, during which he had not been present at the roll-calls but had otherwise been moving around occasionally in the camp, he was discovered. He hadn't been able to make the planned breakout but had he been able he must have had a better chance than we would have. It had been an interesting and innovative plan if nothing else.

How the whole affair surrounding the surgical operation and all its attendant problems became known to the Canadians remains a mystery to this day. Coupled with the unexplained discovery of the tunnel one might speculate about an informer in our company, who can say for sure. Sadly to say, for Doctor Heitsch, the results were not comfortable. For his medical 'misdeed', the Canadians put him *der Teng* along with Sigi.

The Exchange Commission did not visit us in the arrest cells as promised and we *Arrestanten* (arrested ones) were never given clear and decisive confirmation that they weren't coming. We were continually kept waiting until information, in the form of a tiny roll of paper in an apple, reached us. Sadly we read the truth: the first medical Exchange Commission, consisting of two Swiss, two Canadian and one English Military Doctor, had left. Actually this could be understood by us and, in the end, accepted. The job of a Commission, like that one, was already difficult enough. It was this action which was known in the First World War as *Austausch* - exchange or substitution. It really did involve an exchange, under special circumstances (usually medical), man for man from the two nations that were fighting. Should such a Commission also have worried about escapers? The aim of the scheme was to get as many of their badly wounded back. Men who, through their injuries, were clearly not going to play a further combative role. It was a very humanitarian scheme which was aimed at not imposing on seriously wounded men the further hardship of imprisonment. Because of this philosophy each side was very careful not to exchange anyone who might subsequently return to active service. This was especially important where men who'd had an exceptionally high standard of training, for example aircrew, were concerned.

Of course it was also known, from earlier wars and previous exchange activities, that amongst the genuine seriously injured and sick there were always the pretenders. With all the available medical expertise and the strictest measures, it was known by both sides that some *patients* just weren't genuine. How difficult it is, under normal circumstances, to make a clear distinction between genuine and feigned illnesses. There were no scruples amongst the *Simulanten* (pretenders) on both sides, they knew only too well it was an exchange, a man for a man, and perhaps squared their conscience by thinking that without them going one way perhaps a genuine case couldn't come in return. Certainly in our case the difference in numbers of prisoners, German against Allied, was so disproportionate, even with the new influx from the African campaign, that without some *Simulanten* getting through only a small number of the genuine Allied cases would get home. Even their own camp doctors were reluctant to intervene to prevent this from happening because if they didn't go along with it, they would be stuck with the *Simulanten* tying up time they could better spend with their genuine cases.

There was one case where one of our officers had qualified for an exchange, but at the same time was a heavy smoker. He knowingly inhaled the smoke although this aggravated his condition and swallowed almost poisonous substances which damaged stomach and system to such an extent that, soon after being exchanged, he died in Germany. For our own German camp doctors, exchanges were not an easy subject.

Perhaps when reading this introduction to the problems surrounding *des Austausches von Kriegsgefangenen* (exchange of Prisoners of War), it is, perhaps, not surprising that the Commission was not at all willing to also get involved in the fate of escapers who were being punished for their doings; that is presuming they were actually told at all. But what new and thought provoking knowledge this was. We never found out exactly how many were to be exchanged in Canada but we could reckon from our camp, towards the middle of 1943, about ten officers were to be exchanged, their names had already been listed.

Although amongst them were some very tragic cases: pilots who, whilst bailing out of a burning aircraft, had suffered appallingly, such severe burns to their faces that, due to the lack of eyelids, they hadn't been able to close their eyes to sleep since that day. Hands so hideously distorted by the heat that they could hardly do anything for themselves. They were the obviously genuine cases but one had to wonder if, amongst the others, there might not be a less than genuine case. It must surely be a better proposition, we began to think, than a risky escape attempt. What had happened to Hinnerk Waller and Strehl had given us much food for thought. What would their fate have been if they hadn't been apprehended within sight of their comrades?

There were people who, with intelligence and ingenuity, got to work. One of the POW officers, due to his good knowledge of English, worked his way into the right position in camp. He had the chance to go to Toronto for a medical check in a hospital. Whilst there he managed to exchange his x-ray negatives of his stomach ulcer for negatives of another prisoner who had, in the meantime, died of cancer. He managed to get exchanged. Hesitation over such fraud was never considered because actually all those who were really suffering had no problems getting on the exchange lists because of the ratio of prisoners on the two sides. In any case, when we returned to the camp after Christmas, several escapers had already completed the transition from inveterate escaper to dedicated patient. They had begun their preparations for a long term simulation of illness. Although the exchange was still only a plan that was proposed to be conducted from Canada we knew, through the 'grapevine', that those severely wounded prisoners that had remained in England a year and a half before had arrived in Germany. Some of the names quoted as being exchanged included some who had been involved in the early escape attempts in England and we were forced to consider that *Simulieren* (simulating) brought more success than escaping.

Manni, Reini Pfundtner, Hinnerk and myself, discussed whether we should also switch over, but came to the conclusion that an illness which could lead to being exchanged would not be viewed credibly when it concerned people that had up to four escape attempts 'under their belts'. Although we didn't get to see the Commission whilst in *der Teng* our *Rabatz* did lead to the reintroduction of our exercise and we were given reading material and at

Christmas we were allowed write letters. I had exceptional difficulties doing this because I had to write lying or sitting on the metal floor.

During the exercise period we watched part of the ceremony for the burial of *Major* Bach. Naturally we weren't involved but we all stood and said a silent farewell to this gallant soldier.

Back inside the detention barracks I wrote home:

4th day of Advent 1942 (to my mother):

'A few days ago I received your letter dated 10th September (quick delivery.)... I also believe there are not many mothers who could write such letters in your situation. Just in these times, I am especially glad with every piece of 'home' that gets through to me. I don't think I could find more 'Heimat'(homeland) than in your letters anywhere else. Throughout many an hour, 'Muttel', I have thought over what great value the family has in the life of a human being. There I envy those who come from farms or other secure backgrounds. But at the same time, I have also set myself a target together with all of you. Shouldn't we later, with united efforts, be able to buy some property that could then be the Steinhilper family castle?
Maybe I am looking at it far too idealistically, but I believe that I do have your support... Those are my Christmas and New Year's thoughts. They bring me so close to you that I can almost hear Helga (my younger sister) chattering and almost see our Christmas tree! I'll be celebrating differently, but I hope you will be pleased and that will also make me happy! To you and Helga, a lot of pleasure!
Your Uz!'

It was difficult that Christmas in the punishment block. Writing letters was about the most pleasant task.

Still from *der Teng:*

5th January 1943.

Liebe Muttel,

Now I am in possession of all of your September letters. If only I could answer as I wanted. But where could I find the space on this small sheet of paper?... 'Muttel', again and again I admire your efforts. (It is astonishing the efforts that were made and sustained by our women during the war years.) I hope that you really are in the best of health as you wrote me you were! - For myself I can say that I am full of life's power. Although I sometimes feel I am spending the best years of my life here, they are not completely lost. I am building up, as best as I can, and believe that I will be able to benefit from this later. I believe that the present times are a very good school for life, and I don't believe that fate will confront me with such difficult tasks again. With this attitude I will also go into a later marriage. Today it is clear to me that a kind-hearted fate had prevented a firm liaison. Problems that I had pushed aside at the beginning of my exchange of letters have now found a natural solution.

It was good that 'Vatel' has now written to my unit (concerning my promotion). I am not afraid of the future! I will find satisfaction on my way through life! I am already looking forward with pleasure to the task, which later a 'free' person will be given by fate. This person will be, this I firmly believe, more experienced, be harder and have more steadiness, than the person thrown out of time in 1940.

Heartiest greetings,
Your Uz.'

Such dramatic words can perhaps be understood when one considers that they are something akin to 'whistling in the dark', helping to blow away the fear, the fear of actual life. After all I was only twenty-four years old, had had set backs with all my escape attempts and couldn't even discuss it with those who were in the midst of the 'proper life' - reality - not even in letters.

CHAPTER FOURTEEN

WUNDERZANGE - MIRACULOUS CUTTERS

After detention we were released back to camp and, having served our time, we returned to our comrades in the room. Although we had just tried, failed and paid the penalty, the discussions immediately returned to the vexed subject of escaping. It was being compared more and more with the *Austausch*, the exchange system. Here was new information, possibly a different direction, food for thought. It was good that Wildermuth and I had gone through the escape and confinement together, it had given us time to exercise our minds on this subject.

Approximately six weeks after we had been released from *der Teng*, the protest of our German camp leadership, who had seen firsthand how Waller and Strehl had been treated by the guards, brought a partial success. Official Swiss representatives came to the camp and interviewed both Hinnerk Waller and Hannes Strehl. Their injuries had, in the meantime, almost completely healed, but they used the opportunity assertively, making it clear how badly they'd been treated, stressing this brutality had occurred after they'd raised their hands in surrender. At first the Swiss didn't want to commit their report to paper in its full detail; a sign, we thought, which indicated such reports reached home. However, Hannes Strehl could prove by showing the wound on the back of his head how they had been beaten during their recapture. Both men insisted on a true and brutally complete report being submitted without 'sanitising' the facts. The report was duly submitted and we wondered what the outcome might be.

While this was going on I was beginning a kind of friendship with the camp shoemaker, Karl. Before the war he had served in the Foreign Legion and, because of the laws of the Third *Reich* on serving with foreign powers, he was called up to serve in one of the *Strafbataillon* (punishment battalions). He was one of the few survivors of the *Bataillon 900*, which had fought in the desert war in Africa. These soldiers, with special status similar to that of convicts, could only obtain an assignment to other more normal units through exceptionally heroic deeds, and with this the hope of reaching more humane conditions.

Karl had originally learned the trade of the toolmaker but had, during his Foreign Legion service, undertaken many and various tasks. He'd travelled widely with them too, to North Africa and also to Indochina (later Vietnam). He had reinforced the soles in my Elk boots in which I escaped and was sorry to hear it might have been those very boots which had given me away. For me he was a most interesting talker and I often went to sit with him in his shoemaker's workshop where he repaired shoes so well you might have thought it had always been his trade. Of course, in return for his tales of former French imperial power, I had to give him a report of my short escape and my recapture in Barrie in full detail. Our conversations were therefore never one-sided. He had many interests, especially flying, and wanted to know all about the *Luftkampf* (air-battle) over England.

He, for his part, had a lot to tell about the members of *Battaillon 900* and their deeds. How they, for example, stayed in holes in the earth and let tanks pass over their head while they attached magnetic mines to the bottom of the tank. The bottom plates being probably the most vulnerable, this usually resulted in the destruction of the tank. It was daring deeds like this that helped them to win the *freedom* of life as a *normal soldier*, to get out of the *Strafbataillon*. We were both sorry that it was the former Foreign Legion soldiers, the ones who already had the most experience in the desert war, who were the ones that in many cases were unnecessarily *verheizt* (wasted) by being abused in the punishment units.

As early as March of 1943 he hinted he was going to make a pair of cutters with which one could cut the *most beautiful fence in all of Canada* - the thick wire fence around the camp. He never said more, he just worked for himself, without informing or consulting anyone else. During the autumn just passed he had been most successful making the keys for the handcuffs, but that also took place under conditions of great security; the time he'd spent in the Foreign Legion had made him very distrustful. Only one other person had been taken into his confidence, *Obergefreiter* Gutberlet, also known as the *Zerstörer* (destroyer). He'd acquired this title because on the football field he was the most feared full back in camp. Otherwise Gutberlet was *die gute Seele* (good spirit) in our kitchen. He always knew when he could give a room or an individual special service, either by request or just on his own initiative. When, occasionally, our *Stubenältaster*, Peter Döring, had had a bad day, the *Zerstörer* would suddenly appear after breakfast and deposit a *spare* can of delicious bean coffee on our shelf. Although this can contained enough to make two litres of coffee, Peter would manage to drink it all in the course of the day. We were later to discover Gutberlet had helped to organise the necessary materials for these cutters but neither he nor Karl ever boasted about their beautiful finished product.

Meanwhile normal camp life continued. On 14th January 1943 I wrote:

'...Slowly but surely one has got used to the length of time that letters are taking. So much so that one can, without blushing, talk of exchanging thoughts over a time span of six months. It is only in conjunction with episodes that are immediately involved in the progress of the war that one realises with what long pauses these letters are being exchanged...'

On 21st February 1943:

'... Sometimes one is astonished, how the human being learns to adapt to other circumstances of life, as long as one retains the will-power and the belief in the future. I now have so much experience in this that I believe I can safely say: "For myself, this situation could be extended for a while, without me suffering bodily or mentally! Slowly one has, above all, learnt to overcome time in such a manner that one, most astonished, asks: "What! That was a week, a month, or even a year ago!" - In the beginning this wasn't the case!
Vatel, should it be possible for you, then please send some photographs occasionally. I can't even imagine how Helga (my younger sister) has grown! Over the past days I have been doing quite a lot of skating. The rink is, however, very small! But the books have also taken my attention...'

I only want to quote extracts from some of the letters, quoting them in full would be too much. I feel that the feelings recorded within them report more accurately on the conditions and my frame of mind than anything else I could write now. It is, however, difficult to choose. I sent about three letters and four cards a month, almost all of which are still in my possession. Some cards were also sent to addresses outside the closer family circle; some were censored, or even totally withdrawn and a very few were lost. As a rule I wrote as moderately as I could - I wanted my post to reach the recipient, especially in the case of my parents and my sister, and I wanted mainly to brighten them up with my correspondence. However, this was a very heavy mental burden; many times there were other problems which kept me busy but about which it was pointless to try to write. The censor's thick black pen waited poised to remove anything controversial.

26th March 1943:

'... It must also be spring with you, while we had the first frost-free morning this morning. Around noon we have been having a terribly slushy snow over the past days. This winter we had a lot of snow... presently I am doing a lot of piano practice. Since I started with the Schule der Gelaeufigkeit (School of Fluency - I imagine this is the name of a practice book of music for the pianist with which my mother would probably been familiar) I have noticed improvements. As a target I also set myself your ability on the piano (my mother was a piano teacher) and look forward to what you say about my playing one day.
That my Staffel (former squadron) is still remembering you is, indeed, a pleasant gesture. Please don't lose that contact and convey my best kindest regards. Although I doubt very much that there are any old comrades left there, you can inform the Gruppe that they can be assured that I am here in alter Frische! (the same old freshness). Most of all I would be interested to know what happened to Bert Göbel...(He used to be roommate at Luftkriegschule but unbeknown to me he'd aready lost his life in Russia on 25th June 1942.)'

Now comes something exceptional: because, in Canada, it was not permissable to write from one camp to another (it was possible in other countries), I was especially pleased that *Unser Kurt*, who cared for us in Fort Henry, had written by means of internee mail to my mother hence my letter:

5th April 1943:

'Please give my regards to Kurt Ohrt: I still remember that one time we wanted to go to the mountains to do some skiing. He can carry on with his 'dry' training course. For your information, he is a very faithful person who had been fireman/stoker on a merchant navy ship. He repaired my socks, ironed my trousers and almost cared for me as well as you did. Should it be possible for you to spare a parcel for him, then rather to him than to me! Here things are being curtailed continually, for clothing I now have to depend completely on you. I repeat: 1 pair of trousers, 2 shirts, shoes, gymnastic shoes... Should this letter reach you in a short time, then I definitely need a pair of shorts as well; white or Air Force grey are permitted. Should my request reach you too late, then I'll just have to make do with what I

have. Nevertheless, send what you can. On the whole, I would like to know, for the sake of clarity, whether it is difficult for you to get all these items or not? Because we live here completely locked up, I have no idea whether my requests exceed your means in the present times. When necessary, I can do without or with less. Otherwise, April weather!
Herzliche Grüsse (heartiest greetings),
Dein Uz (Your Ulrich).'

This letter also emphasises how stilted and unnatural our correspondence was. I was not able to make mention of the third escape attempt which had ended up in the civilian internees camp. What would they think of all of this at home - a fireman/stoker from a merchant navy boat had *cared* for me?

In the letter of 10th May 1943, there was a very vague hint that I had put my escape experiences to paper.

'... Because there is a gap in our relationship I am starting to write down the most important facts already for you at home. Wait until you can get to read it all! - Here the buds are just beginning to open...'

Recording the first three escape attempts (I couldn't manage the fourth one at the time) kept me very busy. First I wrote as I had learnt at school, a concept which I later corrected as I developed a style. Then everything was written down finally in very narrow but neat handwriting - forty two lines per sheet approximately two hundred and fifty pages. After I had finished writing I filed it neatly in a folder to keep it for my parents at home, but many comrades were interested in my writings. The staff officers, especially, were so interested in this reading matter that I often had difficulties in trying to get the folder back again. The last one who insisted on reading my journal was our *Kriegspfarrer* (war vicar) Frense. It was due to his interest that I was lucky that the folder was not stolen like many other souvenirs.

Because it was generally known that I had successfully overcome the fence four times I was every now and then given a Canadian or an American dollar by various comrades who were sure they would never attempt an escape. Also, through Karl, the shoemaker, I occasionally received dollars donated by the NCOs and enlisted men. In many cases this money originated from trading with the Canadian guards who, as time went by, no longer strictly obeyed their rules (trading was strictly forbidden). They wanted to buy highly prized souvenirs such as the *Flugzeugfuehrerabzeichen* (the pilot's

Wings), or the *Eiserne Kreuze* (Iron Cross). Later, when *Schnaps* was being distilled in most of the camps, this also became a most important trading item. I kept this money in one of the bookshelves in our room, which contained mainly school books, because we were never safe from being searched. Such searches were very thorough, but we assumed the *Frettchen* would not go through each book page by page.

Other than the lessons which I was attending, mainly in technical subjects, and writing down my experiences, I also had another hobby. I was successful in arriving through experimentation at a recipe for making dough for genuine *schwäbische Spätzle* (a noodle-type speciality of the south German Schwabians). I then made *Spätzle* for special occasions, such as birthdays, and would serve them in our room. On such occasions, the kitchen would deliver the normal roast with gravy to be complemented with our *Spätzle*. The cooking was a welcome change for the room mates and the invited guests. For such cooking experiments we had an unused kitchen in our old house with an old coal stove.

Our *Nordländer* (northerner) Peter Döring was very quick to pull my leg when I announced that I would make a *Zwiebelkuchen*, an onion cake; he couldn't imagine what it was. "You can leave it if you don't like it," was my answer, but it was a challenge. As in old times, when I'd helped my mother, I got to work: first a stool was turned upside down and a clean cloth was hung between the three legs. Next curdled milk was poured into the cloth so that the fluid drained away leaving the curds. Onions were available in large quantities from the kitchen and I only had to cut them into small pieces and lightly cook them. Even the dough for the bottom of the cake was a success, neither were the traditional small pieces of ham to top it missing. Not until I was confident I had full control of the coal burning oven did I push the baking pan into the oven. Very soon a delicious aroma pervaded the whole house and I had a problem explaining to the numerous visitors what was going on and to prevent them from prematurely tasting my work.

Soon Döring was convinced: it was something similar to the north German *Schinkenkuchen* (ham cake). After this success we wanted to go for the whole thing: we decided to hold a Swabian celebration with *Zwiebelkuchen und neuem Wine* (onion cake and new wine). The wine was no problem at all, my country upbringing was paying dividends! We had already bought ripe apples in the canteen and borrowed the meat mincer from the kitchen to passed our apples through. After that the mash was then suspended in another cloth between the legs of the stool. After the juice had all dripped out the apple mash was packed into a pillow case and wrung out by a pair of strong hands. The juice we had extracted was then transferred to gallon bottles which had originally been used to deliver vinegar to the kitchen. All we then had to do was to wait for the juice to ferment. We didn't need any fermentation traps for the corks, that would have been too obvious. One of the Canadians' strictest rules was no alcoholic beverages to be made in the camps. Later, however, there wasn't a camp in Canada in which *Schnaps* wasn't being distilled.

It was a logical progression to extend our *Apfelmost* (cider) production methods to real wine. Grapes could be bought almost all the year round at a very reasonable price in the canteen. We chose to use the blue grapes because this gave a nice pink juice. The fermenting procedure naturally dictated when we could have our *Swabian* celebration but soon enough our *nouveau* was ready. It was to be on a Wednesday evening and I started preparing the curd, the onions and the dough the day before. We had invited several guests to come to our room. Altogether we had three gallon bottles filled with our fermented grape juice, our wine. There were also approximately twelve litres of new Rosé wine standing on the bookshelves ready for our celebration.

The Wednesday itself was a very busy one with a lot of lessons going on. About eleven o'clock in the morning Wildermuth and I were just tackling some tricky mathematical tasks when Peter Döring burst into our classroom in a rage. He was so angry that for a few moments he was incoherent, almost hysterical. He finally took a deep breath and the story began to boil out of him. "*Die Kanaker*[1] have searched our room! They held me as they did it! Everything has been stolen! - they've taken the wine, and Uli's collection of newspaper clippings has been confiscated and they've found all the money in the books!" We sat him down and asked questions as the impact of what he'd said began to sink in. Again an exercise book full of newspaper clippings had been stolen, the guards valued these as souvenirs, especially because of the personal notes that had been added. Loss of the money was a very bitter blow and above all the wine as well. The clever *Frettchen* had, every now and then, peeked through the door and saw us with our fermenting wine but they'd just winked and not reported it. We now wondered whether the fellows had just waited until that good *Stoff* (stuff) had fermented properly then come and taken it all?

Our Camp Adjutant protested immediately, but all the rules were against us. With a bitter-sweet look on my face I nevertheless pushed the fragrant onion cake into the oven, the wine was replaced by beer which we'd quickly managed to drum up from our sympathetic comrades. But how we grumbled that evening - grumbled about those crafty Canadians! It didn't actually take all that long before we really did serve onion cake with new wine! But this time, however, we were at pains to hide it so *die verdammte Frettchen* knew nothing about it. But it was the loss of the newspaper clippings that was the worst for me. I had already planned to use them for illustrating my journal and now they were all gone again. At the time I couldn't imagine that after the war there would be such excellent newspaper archives available so at the time it was a complete and irrevocable loss. I soon recovered from the loss of the money, the trading with the Canadians was going well and they were paying more and more with genuine dollars, but the loss of the cuttings weighed heavily.

It was Karl who calmed me down most, he literally radiated confidence. The construction of his cutters had, in the meantime, progressed quite well. He explained to me how he'd disassembled some of the hinged metal leg-braces from some of the folding tables in the dining room. They were required to make double lever arms. He was now busy selecting those knives from the cutlery, the steel of which could be shaped by forging when red hot, then hardened again by quenching. To achieve this he had, however, already used up eighty knives and our comrades in the kitchen were already quarrelling with him because the Canadians refused to provide replacements as our loss of cutlery was too high!

Actually the cutters were an obligation, rather than a wish of mine to attempt an escape again. Should the *Wunderzange* (miracle cutters) turn out to be as good as *Werkzeugmacher* (toolmaker) Karl was saying, then I would have a double obligation to escape: first because it was my duty as an officer and, second, by way of expressing my personal thanks to Karl. He'd said he would let others use them in time but that I would have *first refusal*. I wasn't sure it was an obligation I wanted.

However, when looking at this possibility I really began to think seriously about another escape. This time I could, for the first time, take advantage of the warmer part of the year, the summer. Once I was out I could then sleep out free and at one with nature, hiding and feeding in the woods. Berries would be available in the woods in unlimited quantities and, perhaps, I could catch a fish occasionally. In any case I would take the necessary line and a hook with me. Fishing hooks were being made in the camp and fishing was being tried during the bathing sessions in the lake.

Not only fish were being caught. Eberhard Wildermuth swam one time long enough under water to bring back a whole bucketful of fresh water mussels to the camp. Again I was asked to play the role of the cook but at least the whole room helped to scrub the mussels. The brew, with vinegar, onions and seasoning, I had to invent from what I remembered and to improvise what I couldn't. At the meal that followed I let the *Norddeutschen*,

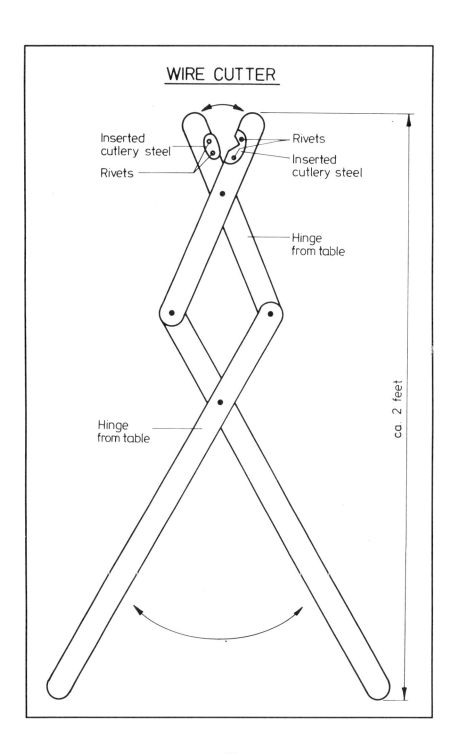

WIRE CUTTER

Inserted
cutlery steel

Rivets

Rivets

Inserted
cutlery steel

Hinge
from table

Hinge
from table

ca. 2 feet

178

the northeners, have the first go. Everyone enjoyed the special feast which was not, this time, ruined by the attention of *die Frettchen*.

Although I was now beginning the preparations for another escape in earnest, I wrote a letter with *educational* value to Fräulein Trude Steinhilper, *Stabshelferin, Feldpostnummer 40148, Wilna*. In full length:

'Liebe Trude,

Hardly had my card, in which I complained that I hadn't heard from you for a long time, gone with the mail than I received your letter of 8th April 1943. I enjoyed it very much. I hope that you also receive mail from me in response because hardly a month passes in which I don't write to you. I was pleased to hear that you, in addition to your official duty, also find time to further your education. You are now almost at that age I was, seemingly ages ago, when this terrible life started. At that time my mind was just beginning to have more sensible thoughts, just like you are now having, when all of a sudden everything changed. Certainly I would have concentrated on this valuable life if I'd have been at home during these harten Kampf (hard times), and would have matured and gathered my experiences. But just now, under these circumstances, one seeks to find the sense of this life and the solutions to the present situation, rather than climb the walls. Out of those experiences that I have gained here, I would like to give the good advice to seek a healthy balance between efficient performance and pleasure. Both are indispensable in life, but both depend on each other. True and sincere pleasure and diversion are only then possible when one has achieved something.
You wrote that yourself!
Your Uz.'

A little concern is included; concern about the young, good looking sister, far away in enemy country, who had to serve amongst the soldiers. Later I was to hear that during these difficult times she had more independence than could have been expected under normal circumstances.

In this letter there is also mention again of the *harte Kampf* (hard times - a challenge), a certain sign that I was again prepared to escape very soon, to go into a dangerous enterprise. Every time it required a greater and lengthier effort to prepare myself for it. More difficult in some ways than getting ready for a combat flight over enemy territory. One had to make the decision to give up this peaceful, calm, comfortable and safe life in camp and to exchange it with the danger of going through the fence. It didn't get easier with experience, it just got tougher. Every escape had brought new knowledge and with it greater fears. I'd seen what the guards had done to Hinnerk Waller and Hannes Strehl and I knew what they'd threatened to do to me. But it had to be done, it was a question of duty.

The *Wunderzange*, when finished, were a masterpiece of engineering art. The illustration will help in explaining the construction but, essentially, locksmith/shoemaker Karl had only used two braces from folding tables, but he'd put these together in such a manner that the ratio and the efficiency of the levers were multiplied twice. In the actual jaws he had inserted the carefully selected knife blade steel. He had annealed and forged, all together, over one hundred table knives in the kitchen oven until the small piece had the right curved shape and was tempered perfectly. Throughout all this work his shoemaker's rasps had been of no real help, too soft to shape the high-carbon steel. Instead he'd searched in camp and along the shores of the lake for hard stones which he then split. These split stones then served at first to grind the levers out of the table braces and then also to grind the recesses for the steel inserts. After that he also ground the steel inserts using the split stones. These had to be inserted and removed again and again until they finally had the right cutting curve. Only then, after long experiments, did they cut silently through the thick wire mesh like a hot knife through butter. These first trials naturally took place in the workshop, there was little chance of a live test on the fence.

The hardened steel inserts were secured, each with two rivets. That meant that Karl had to drill four small holes in the recesses of the jaws. Just this drilling work took over two weeks to complete; the method of drilling was almost Stone Age: A thin wooden rod was rotated by a taut string in a bow, like the ancient method of making fire, and fine sand was introduced into the hole to be drilled. The thin rods would brake, the string would part, but the patience of our *Werkzeugmacher* wouldn't falter.

By the end of June the cutters were completed and oiled and I entrusted them to Rudi Baudler, Manni and Pfundtner. They knew of a very safe hiding place; when they lowered the window in their room all the way down a gap appeared at the side of the window frame, deep enough to accommodate the cutters which were some sixty centimetres long. They could be laid on their side, completely hidden, but also accessible from the outside, if necessary, because it was on the ground floor. I informed the *Ältestenrat* of the existence of the cutters but not of their hiding place or any other details of the escape. We said more information would follow as soon as the date for the escape was set and the detailed plans finished.

This was erring very much on the safe side. We didn't know what or who was to blame, but more and more events inside the camp were being *discovered* by die *Frettchen* who seemed to be developing an uncanny knack of uncovering projects in very sudden but extremely accurately aimed searches. I have mentioned before the possibility of a *mole* being in place, but we had no proof. Much speculation was made over the source but it could as easily have been a matter of carelessness or boasting on someone's part. We could only protect ourselves, to a certain extent, by using the time-honoured principals *of need to know,* confining those who knew anything to an absolute minimum. In that way we hoped to reduce *die Frettchen's* good luck.

Notes on Chapter Fourteen.

[1] *Kanaker* - There is no direct translation of this word into English because it is in itself slang. The use of slang has changed over the years but a close equivalent of the time would have *Wog* or *Wogs.*

Note: When the war was lost, in 1945, Camp Gravenhurst registered one *Überläufer* - a defector or turncoat. This *Luftwaffenhauptmann* was taken into Canadian protective custody so as to experience a better fate than he could have expected at the hands of his colleagues. I was never able to find out what happened to him. None of us knew whether he was already transferring *'Nachrichten'* (*news* reports) in 1943.

CHAPTER FIFTEEN

A GREAT RISK IN BROAD DAYLIGHT

The explanation of the escape plan was difficult. However, it was well prepared and everything was ready. This time I wanted to try my luck as a Canadian, equipped with a magnificently reproduced Identity Card. My home state was to be Alberta, where there were many residents of German origin who spoke worse English than I did. Furnished with a letter of recommendation from the vicar of my home village, I wanted to find work as a farmhand or casual labourer in Eastern Canada. The identification documents were again prepared by willing experts in the camp who, in the meantime, not only had better examples to copy, but also had better pens and inks at their disposal. During one of the *Ehrenwort* walks one of the comrades had found a genuine Canadian identity card, which now served as a pattern.

Because I needed about one hundred and twenty helpers and confidants for my ambitious scheme it was necessary to write down the complete plan and sequence of events on paper. Also the names of those who were to be involved were listed on another sheet. *Major* Müller, the head of *der Ausbrecherkommittee*, could present all of this to *die Ältestenrat* for their authorisation. This time I really needed their very extensive involvement because of the size of the project and the number of people it would involve.

In the midst of this very tense period I wrote to my mother:

4th July 1943.

'Liebe Muttel,

Yesterday I received your letter of 19th April and several days earlier the one from your birthday (2nd May). Vatel wrote also on 2nd May; his letter arrived yesterday. My receipt of letters is therefore again satisfactory. Vatel wrote how he had been passed over (for promotion). I know what that means for him, but I know he will calmly live with this. In his occupation I think it is of less importance to find recognition from above than to have the trust and admiration of one's subordinates. Vatel will be able to get pleasure and incentive from his virtues, they are a reliable source.

You are of the opinion that our family is not having luck. You are certainly right but, measured against other German families, our fate is easy to live with. We still have hopes for a future, even you and Vatel, the main thing is that we stick together later on.

I got a letter from Trude, which I was very pleased with. She seems to be getting down to the roots of life and is laying herself a healthy set of directives. Vatel was of the opinion that I should congratulate her personally next year. He should know better than I, but I am sensible enough to have more patience than that if necessary. The consequences of this war are too serious not to demand the ultimate in strength and endurance from the victors...'

Such normal letters had to be written home even though inside I was bubbling with excitement and longed for an honest conversation with somebody, just to let them know how I felt at that moment. Was it worth the risk? Dead at the fence or worse, shot and crippled for life. Or even later to be shot *'on the run'* like Martin Müller or half beaten to death while being recaptured like Hannes Strehl? It wasn't a pleasant prospect and it would have made so much of a difference to be able to talk things over in detail with someone close. My comrades were close but because they had shared similar experiences it wouldn't have been same, to bare one's soul to them - we knew each other too well anyway. The only solution was to take one's own counsel, to arrange it all with yourself.

During the second week of June the news was read to us, as usual, during our midday meal. Also, as usual, these news sessions contained the *Wehrmachtsbericht*, the armed forces report, which we had received via the home-made short wave receiver. Surprising for all was the list of names that was also read out to all the officers that were present in the dinning room. Those nominated were requested, on behalf of the camp leadership, to gather after lunch in the large upper classroom. They all came and the room was full to the brim. This particular classroom was in the attic and was, therefore, as safe as it could be against unwanted listeners; unlike our mess hut where one could never be sure if the Canadians were listening.

Without much preamble *Major* Müller explained that I was going to attempt an escape that afternoon, the sequence of which I would detail immediately afterwards. He also announced that all those present had an important role to play and asked if they were willing to do so. Unanimous agreement followed and I then gave them my written plan in full detail. In short: Manni was to cut a hole for me in the strong mesh fence adjacent to the basketball field. It was mentioned that a new pair of wire cutters, which of course were not shown in public, were to be the key to this bold plan. The signal for me to creep through the fence would, as usual, come from *Hauptmann* Baudler. A small group, Manni, Baudler, Pfundtner and I would then slowly mingle with the spectators of the game of basketball at the fence side of the field.

It was arranged with Manni that after I had gone through the fence he would immediately start repairing the fence by dropping the triangular section, which was to remain attached at the top, back into place. This would be secured with thick, insulated electric wire which had been coloured grey. Here the perspective of the guards in the towers has to be considered. From their position the mesh fence was a grey wall, however, they would recognize me as soon as I had passed through this wall.

It was also arranged that the cutters were to be brought from the ground level window frame at the very last moment, and that they were to be hidden there immediately after the hole had been cut, even before the fence was repaired. Manni was very keen to get hold of these cutters and it had been arranged with Karl that Manni was not only responsible for safely hiding them after my escape but it was solely his right to decide what these cutters were to be used for afterwards.[1]

The whole thing was to take place in broad daylight that afternoon and whilst between the fences I would be completely exposed to the rifles of the guards from both towers. To cover this exigency, excellent diversion manoeuvres had been planned adjacent to both towers. One group planned to be busy with the watering hose close to the left tower, where they were to work in such a clumsy manner that they would even spray water - by accident of course - into the open window of the tower. In front of the right tower was our boxing ring and it would be most unusual if the tower guards attention wasn't distracted by the KO blow that was planned for that very moment.

I had organised myself a good pair of khaki coloured trousers from the *Afrikaner* and also a shirt. Tailoring a typical Canadian military type cap to wear on my head was no problem at all. As I didn't want to rely solely on myself once I had penetrated the inner fences and had to make my way to the third barrier - the coils of barbed wire - which was further out, I decided to ask two football teams, including spectators, for their support. They were to stage a football game on the field which lay outside the camp. Although they would be there on parole and were forbidden to attempt an escape, we thought it wouldn't be infringing the rules if they enthusiastically supported a match.

'The most beautiful fence in Canada.' The hole was to be cut just left of where the white spot appears. Guard Tower 1 can be seen in the background.

After the complete plan had been read and the numerous helpers had been assigned, I asked them again for their voluntary agreement to my plan. There wasn't a man among them that didn't spontaneously say, "Yes!" and declare their readiness to fulfil their assigned tasks. We all left the classroom and hardly an hour later they were all in their positions: the lawn watering group, the basketball players with spectators, the boxers with their spectators, the men outside the gates; two football teams including their spectators and last but not least, the small group at the fence.

While I was waiting at the back door of our building for the sign to go I could feel my heart beating. I was more excited than I had been in

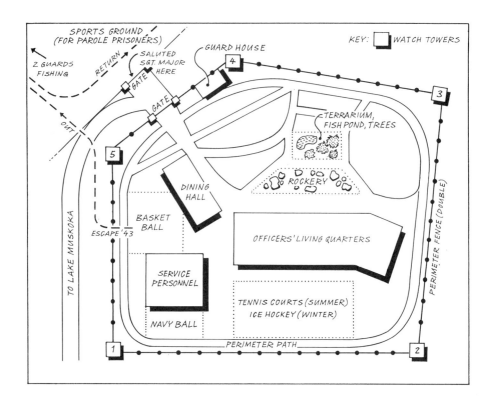

Coquelles, sitting in the cockpit of 'Yellow 2' as she rocked on her undercarriage while Peter, my mechanic, wound the eclipse starter for the engine before a flight over England. There was also a deep grinding dread of what might result - the same as the stomach-churning anxiety which came in the latter days of the Battle of Britain - when you knew, statistically, *'your number was up'*. But I was committed, there was no turning back.

After a casual signal from Baudler, I dawdled past the posts of the basketball field... the spectators were standing tighter together than usual... and I was soon in the midst of my group... Manni was there and whispered: "It's open and large enough!" - Baudler again raised his hand giving the signal, Manni pulled the cut out patch of wire mesh upwards like a small doorway and Reini Pfundtner offered me my bag by the shoulder straps through the opening... and I realised I was already through! The first stage had gone like well-oiled clockwork. I hoped it would continue as easily!

Glancing to the left I realised how well I was presented to the guard tower (see photograph). They surely only had to look to see me and my only hope

A 'Fistball' game in progress. The hole was cut where the white dot has been placed.

of survival was that they might hesitate to shoot at a comrade in khaki, or would they? At that moment I could also see that the jet of water was already splashing against the window of the tower so I dragged myself forward as quickly as I could, this time unencumbered by layer upon layer of winter clothing. There was no more time left now to make further observations, it was pointless - I'd soon know if they saw me, that was for sure!

My position had been chosen after much deliberation. At the outer entanglement, the coils of wire were only one metre and twenty centimetres high and the wire was very loosely laid. I easily managed to wedge strands open with a piece of wood and after quickly tossing my bag through, followed it on the next heartbeat. Although this had been practised before in camp, I tripped and fell on the ground outside the fence, losing my cap. My heart stopped and I must have gone awfully pale as I saw the guard to my left cast a short glance over his shoulder in my direction. I simply greeted him with a grin and a casual wave and against all odds it worked. He immediately turned his attention back to the clumsy lawn watering group and started grumbling at them that they should be more careful with the water.

The worst was now behind me. On the outside of the fence I followed the guards' path along, behind the right tower adjacent to the boxing ring and saw this guard still had his eyes fixed on the victim of the KO blow. The 'unconscious' boxer still lay in ring and was being treated. I could see this all clearly from outside the fence, which reminded me that they could also see me. Nonetheless, a feeling of success was slowly arising in me but it was not long-lived.

Again my mind wandered back to the preparations for flights over the Channel and southern England. There was always that funny feeling before and during the take off: Will you return? Will you be successful today? It is quiet in the headphones and you wonder when the crackling will start... the mix-up in the radio messages? The warnings of attack and the cries for help! Then you'd be in the midst of the fighting, no longer able to think of the danger, of success, of failure, or even the excessive strain on man and machine - only to react; your experience and skill the only factor in your survival. The machines were no longer present but the rest of it was the same - sudden, unexpected and not always as planned!

With casual strides I walked past the football goals and continued towards the lake shores, heading for a rocky spot in the third fence where large rocks formed part of the boundary of the camp. There, over these rocks, the barbed wire had been strung very carelessly. I had earlier very carefully chosen this spot where I wanted to climb over the fence as it was out of sight of the guard towers. Up until then everything had gone as planned, the comrades on the *Ehrenwort* football field, players and spectators hardly took any notice of me. I had already reached the lower end, behind the corner flag, when a completely new situation arose. Exactly at that spot where I wanted to climb over the barbed wire and the rocks sat two Veteran Guards fishing!

My steps were getting slower and slower as I got closer to this new situation, but nothing changed. The two guards were there fishing and there they would stay for quite some time I imagined. There was no other way out, other than the unpleasant choice to turn around and not only go back, behind the goal, but also to change direction so as to get through between the field boundary lines and the open patch in front of the camp gate; making my way through with, I hoped, sheer audacity.

No such luck! Between the football field and the gate was where there were always a few unarmed Canadian guards and others watching the game. I had already seen when I had passed by the first time that of all people my special friend, the Sergeant Major, was standing there amongst the spectators. Nothing could help me - my route lay between the gate and the football field, there was no way I could avoid this without giving up. There was still the slimmest of chances, after all I was wearing a sort of Canadian uniform, but perhaps my *Brotbeutel*, my bread bag, looked a little suspicious. Nothing like that was ever carried by the Veteran Guards. I couldn't quietly drop it, inside was everything of importance; documents, identity card, fishing equipment, emergency rations and a sort of mosquito net.

At the same time as I took the corner around the flag, a ball went out of play but not for a corner kick. I stopped the ball and kicked it towards the person that was to throw it in again. He recognized me, and almost dropped the ball in surprise. It was clear to me now, all eyes of both the players and the spectators were now turned in my direction. Among these were, of course, those of the Sergeant Major. But what could I do? I continued behind the rows of spectators and saw the Sergeant Major was standing further back, closer to the guards at the camp gate. I had no other choice but to continue and with a sharp military salute I walked by. Automatically he returned my salute.

I'd hardly gone another thirty metres, not daring to look back, when uproar started behind me. It wasn't until then that I turned around and saw how the Sergeant was waving me back as I increased the speed of my steps. Then it came, his hard barking voice as he realised something was wrong, "Haalt! Stop him!" Had he now registered who I was rather than just someone doing something they shouldn't? That was all unimportant now... only another forty metres... to the left... forwards!... There was the last fence strung nice and tight... I'd just have to force my way through the barbed wire with the strength and dulling of pain which comes with full fight-flight response... Already I was running as fast as I could... running in a zigzag always a zigzag... changing direction like a rabbit in case they started shooting!

As fast as I ran it seemed to take ages before I got to the fence, and still there hadn't been any shots behind me. While I threw myself between two tightly strung wires, my shirt and trousers were ripped to shreds. Immediately after the fence came the bushes and I was able to hide from the followers who were now hot on my heels. How fast I tore the rags of my uniform from my body, nobody knew how severe the punishment would be if I was caught in an enemy uniform. Beneath the tatters of the khaki uniform I had my civillian clothes and was glad to leave the rags behind me. My bag was still with me and that was the most important thing. The alarm siren began its baleful wail and I also heard jeeps as they left the camp at speed. Running again in a wide curve through the bushes I reached the camp approach road. A quick look to left and right and I was already on the other side - the side on which the town of Gravenhurst also lay. Nothing else mattered but to get away...! 'Away from here...!' was my dominating thought. Not until I was able to mingle among civilian citizens, would I be relatively safe from being shot on the spot.

On the other side of the road I ran until I was exhausted. Climbing breathlessly over a small wall I suddenly realised I was amidst stone crosses - I'd landed in Gravenhurst cemetery. For the time being I was so exhausted I just lay on the ground between the graves, gasping for breath. What should I do now? The woods I was heading for were about three hundred metres away. To reach those I would again have to go left and forwards where I hoped to be able to cross the camp approach road without any troubles. Then I would have to cross a wide highway which we assumed would immediately be well guarded and blocked off after any escape alarms. For the time being though I'd just stay lying on the ground in the cemetery, nobody would be looking for me there.

There remained very little time to think things over, the situation required immediate and spontaneous action! There was dog barking in the distance behind me and there was more than one canine voice in the chorus. I listened carefully - they were on the right track, at first in the bushes and then working their way closer to where I was. I couldn't lie there any longer. What special irony there would be in being recaptured in the cemetery?

Very cautiously I stood up. Carefully easing myself back across the wall and the hedge I kept a careful lookout. I was dragging my bag behind me in the tall grass and the weeds and it was good that I did it. To our mutual surprise a Canadian guard suddenly stepped out in front of me from behind a hedge. I had no other choice than to let my bag sink into the weeds. He was immediately suspicious but I had the presence of mind to try to bluff my way through again, "I am just looking for some strawberries, but it looks like there are none here, maybe I'd better get across the highway, there is nothing to be found here," I said. He looked relieved and accepted my story and added, "Better be very careful, a German prisoner has just escaped and there are soldiers with guns around, they are looking for him!" He actually let me continue and I found myself in the most frustrating situation. I'd dropped my valuable bag some ten metres behind me and couldn't proceed until I'd recovered it. The guard went back behind the hedge and I frantically backtracked looking for the bag. This was madness! I searched and searched for many valuable seconds and with every one of those seconds the barking was getting closer and closer but I just simply couldn't find the damned bag!

Somehow that guard must have thought twice. He came back again, and with definite purpose he approached, "You'd better come with me," he said, "I want to know who you are." Once more I felt that terrible draining inside which told me it was over. I had no choice other than to calmly follow his instructions, anything else would have been suicide! This time he had approached me with his machine pistol levelled at me and his finger on the trigger. It didn't take long before more troops, dogs and jeeps approached from the rear. The Sergeant Major was, of course, amongst the first to be on the spot. This time it wasn't going to take long before I found myself in *der Teng!* For all such incidents, especially such unexpected incidents, the arrest cells were always ready to accept guests.

My complete escape, from the fence until I was locked up again, didn't last longer than three hours. But what a three hours! The rapid final preparations, the execution of the plan, the capture and sentence - all equivalent to the success! On the other hand: how often had we flown our fighters over England without firing a single shot? Our presence was enough to provide a deterrent many a time and at other times a diversion for other activities. Now in this case our guards would be forced to recognise that we were still very active! They wouldn't be able to relax. But was it worth the price?

I hadn't been locked up for an hour when who should appear? None other than the Sergeant Major with my bag and contents. Triumphantly he held my, *'Oh, so excellent documents,'* under my nose. "This won't help you very much this time!" he said sarcastically. But I was certain that at least they hadn't found the cutters or how I'd got out. Then the questioning started again: how had I got out this time they wanted to know? With this it was clear to me that Manni had successfully managed to repair the fence quickly and camouflaged the repair well. A small comfort, with all this rotten luck again!

In *der Teng*, I received books, writing paper and postcards within a few days and soon I wrote a normal letter again:

20th July 1943.

'Liebe Muttel,

The day before yesterday I received your letter of 30th May. This must certainly be one of the fastest ones in our correspondence... Just for me you must be doing an amount of petitioning. Here I am, 25 years old, and still hanging on to you, just as if one were still going to school. But, Muttel, nowadays I know to acknowledge this, rather than in those days gone by where everything appeared to be a matter of course... I just remembered that I have not thanked you for the parcel which I received 14 days ago (just before the aforementioned escape). It contained Brezeln, sausage, biscuits, liver pate and anchovy-paste. Everything was wonderful, Muttel! I have to repeat: be sure to keep something for yourself! I don't have to starve here! We all enjoyed everything you sent! On the 9th July we celebrated two birthdays in our room! - I hope that the clothing reaches me just as well...'

How much I would have liked to write in this letter that I had just undertaken my fifth escape and was once again sitting in detention. How terribly boring it was there because there was nobody for the next four weeks with whom I could have a decent conversation. This time I was all alone in *der Teng*, and the guards really let me feel their displeasure particularly since they still didn't know how I had got out of the camp. I wasn't going to say a word on this matter and, therefore, they exchanged no unnecessary words with me.

Those four weeks were damned boring and when I look at my letters, which were written with such painstaking and time-consuming care they looked like they'd been printed, I am reminded of the very boring times when I had to sit it out, hour after hour, day after day, week after week.

A postcard dated 27th July:

'Mein Liebe Muttel,

Today I received your letter of 25th May. One could easily read how proud you must be of the work you are doing (as headmistress). I am pleased with you when, from your words, I can gather that you are still capable of giving your best. If only I could once again work together with you all!... Yes, you must definitely do something good for Kurt Ohrt (our helper at Fort Henry). I will always keep him in the best of memory. At home we want to meet again...'

With very small print, when time was no constraint, one could put a lot down on a postcard!

2nd August 1943 (date of my father's 51st birthday - still in *der Teng*):

'Lieber Vatel,

And again a birthday passes by! For your new year in life, all the best. What we understand from this we need not put in words... It is astonishing how young you have kept. Always when I look at your photos I have to admire that. Your sporting activities during your youth must have contributed towards this. I have also, therefore, given myself the goal, to do as much sport as I can get to... You write about books that you have read. I have also read quite a lot since I have been here. During the last winter, in a small working group, we even took a try at Kant (a German philosopher). Nevertheless, the extract of knowledge remains, in relation to all that has been discovered and is worth knowing, still very limited...Presently it is very hot and sweltering here. The thunderstorms are very fierce, but too short to provide some cooling down. The climate here is even more a continental climate than what we are used to at home. These are, however, all manner of things of minor importance. For us the sun never goes down.
For to-day: all the best!
Dein Uz.

Around 10th August the results of the fifth escape were coming to an end, the arrest was over and it had all slowly been digested. But already, new tasks were throwing their shadows. I was especially glad that there had been no repercussions from having worn a *Canadian* uniform; the rags had, of course, been found in the bushes.

Notes on Chapter Fifteen.

1944 Manni Manhart conducted his last and successful escape with the assistance of these cutters.

CHAPTER SIXTEEN

POW EXCHANGE

INFORMATION FOR THE HOME COUNTRY

Back in the room, at the end of the four weeks, the best news that I received was that a group of twelve *'medical exchange candidates'* had finally been selected by the Commission of doctors. The exchange was on a one to one ratio for Allied prisoners in Germany. Like ours, they would be drawn from those unable to fight any more, badly injured or incurably ill officers, non-commissioned officers and enlisted men. The exchange was scheduled for the coming summer, at the latest during the autumn. Apparently a Swedish boat, the *Gripsholm*, was travelling regularly between North American ports and Lisbon in neutral Portugal. From there the exchange was conducted through Portugal, Spain and then, with the help of Vichy-France, to Germany (and vice versa).

Many of my comrades in the camp had very busily been writing down everything that they had heard about the shooting of aircrew after they had made an emergency landing, or had come down by parachute in England (hard though it may be to believe such things happened, even in the early days of the war). Franz von Werra had transferred important information to Germany as early as 1941, but in his case it mainly concerned the interrogation methods used by the British and the living conditions in their POW camps. Because he had escaped upon arrival in Canada, virtually on the spur of the moment, he had not really been thoroughly prepared. We had heard of his reports from comrades who were taken prisoner later in the war and, also, how important this type of information was for preparing those who would follow us through interrogation. It also had an important impact on the treatment that the Allied prisoners were to get in Germany.

Our room was directly involved in the collecting and collating of information. At the very beginning of our imprisonment in Canada, Peter Döring had ordered himself a Remington portable typewriter from Eaton's catalogue. In the early days we'd been able to order things like that and actually received them. Later, such items were regarded as *luxuries* and we were not allowed to order them. The most likely reason for the ban was that a letter of recommendation for some escapers had been written using one of

*The Swedish boat 'Gripsholm' which, initially, transported mail and parcels.
Later it was used on the exchange of seriously ill prisoners.*

these typewriters. The purchase of such a machine was not only a question of whether it was allowed but was also a significant financial burden; with our low POW wage it meant years of instalments until it was paid for.

Now Döring had the only private typewriter in the camp, and it was used under the supervision of the *'legal advisers'* to write down everything we thought could be useful to prevent further abuse when being taken prisoner, especially during the interrogation that always followed. In the meantime there were more and more American and English aircraft being shot down over Germany. Because of the outcome of the handcuffing in connection with the Dieppe Raid it was realised that the German leadership was not going to accept any abuse of us POW's without appropriate measures being enforced against Allied prisoners.[2]

It can also be assumed that with the very large number of Allied personnel prisoners in Germany there must also have been far more injured and ill. Therefore, when taking into account the total of just seven hundred POW officers from the *Wehrmacht, das Heer, die Kriegsarine and die Luftwaffe* in Canada, we were sure our leadership was in a strong bargaining position.

Among those Allied aircrew were also known to be *'important'* people; among the R.A.F. and U.S. Air Force (USAF) personnel in camps there were many whose parents and relatives had a strong political influence. It was therefore very important that Germany was informed of incidents that were in extreme contravention of the Geneva Convention.

Our comrades who had received legal training or who were practising lawyers pre-war laid down the rules which qualified an incident to be recorded. That it was necessary for there to have been at least one witness was the first stipulation. Only such cases were recorded when, besides the victim, there was at least one witness. If the victim had been killed in an incident, then it was only recorded on paper when there were at least two witnesses whose names and addresses were known.

It was dreadful, the things that were being reported. I assisted by actually typing some of the statements and so gained a fairly intimate knowledge of many of the cases. We began by writing down the details of bad treatment and, on occasions, even the shooting of some aircrew in England; mostly, apparently, conducted by the civilian Home Guard. This seemed mainly confined to the period of the Battle of Britain and was almost exclusively confined to personnel who'd been shot down. It seemed, in a lot of the cases, to have been a reaction motivated by extreme anxiety because of the air attacks, perpetrated by these *'Damned Hunns'*! Later reports, from the years 1941, 1942 and 1943 were even worse, particularly what was reported by some of the *Kriegsmarine* personnel who had been captured in the Mediterranean. The name of the Allied naval base at Gibraltar figured in many accounts of terrible beatings, particularly from *U-Boot* crews.

I cannot and will not write down everything that was recounted in our room, sometimes in great excitement and anger. It is certainly not my ambition that this book should reopen old wounds or to revive old enmity But perhaps, in order to appeal for more humanity and to ensure such things do not occur in the future it is worth mentioning briefly. I will say that the number of victims - enlisted men, non commissioned officers and officers - who were captured in various theatres during the Second World War and subsequently died was far greater than the majority might imagine. They lost their lives through cruelty, neglect or such mistreatment during interrogation that they ultimately died. Such incidents perpetrated by the Germans have now been well recorded and documented but that, of course, is the prerogative of the victors; they write the history. Very few of the cases which involved the abuse of prisoners in Allied hands have ever been investigated, nor will they be now. But it would be terribly naive of anyone to think this kind of cruelty was only practised by one side.

Very quickly word spread in the camp of the important work our legal advisers were doing and more and more prisoners were pressing to make their statements. Especially bad reports came from the enlisted men and the non-commissioned officers who were there as our service crew. Slowly they lost their distrust and their reports were also included in the official reports. But the few we had in camp only represented a small proportion of the O/R (other ranks) personnel in Allied hands. How many more accounts were there to be told in the O/R camps?

From all the reports we now heard it was, apparently, generally close to my experiences during my own interrogations in England; the officers were better prepared for the clever methods that were employed. Also from what we heard one could draw a clear conclusion: those prisoners that began to talk in the hopes they could improve their treatment were to find they were mistaken. The interrogators were like terriers with a bone; once given a taste of it they would sink their teeth in and not let go. The best advice seemed to be: the more decisive the person to be interrogated was about saying absolutely nothing, the shorter the interrogation was likely to be. But the conviction that you are prepared to risk your life, rather than divulge information has to show through. Anyone who started to talk when the first threat was voiced or who started to weaken would find no mercy whatsoever. Once they noticed they'd made the slightest impression they were relentless.

In all the cases brought forward to the attention of the Legal Commission, the rule of witnesses was strictly adhered to. But, nevertheless, more material was gathered than could be registered. The certified reports were first written down using the small Remington typewriter. Then our *Heimkehrer* (home goers) - those to be repatriated - declared to a man their willingness to take these reports back to Germany. The complete contents, approximately thirty pages, were typed again this time onto both sides of linen handkerchiefs. The typed pieces of linen were then sewn into the lining of the *Heimkehrers* uniform and wherever else they could be hidden.

The written records were doubly secured: each of the volunteers was given approximately three pages, which he not only took along on the linen but also learned the contents by heart. Of paramount importance were the names and addresses of the witnesses. It was not a very pleasant experience, having to listen to these terrible reports over and over again when the *Heimkehrers* came and recited the portion of the report they were carrying home. If the hidden reports were found, either in the camp or en route, there was no need to worry that the carriers were going to be subject to reprisals. The duplicates on paper were to be kept in the camp and, if necessary, the reports could be given to the next Exchange Commission that came. It was not only the task of these international commissions to safeguard the conditions in the camp but to help prevent any kind of abuse.

Of all the assembled information I think the cruellest things which stuck in my memory were those involving the *U-boot* crews. There were reported cases where, after their boats had been crippled, they had managed to jump overboard or if the boat had been sunk they came up via *Tauchretter*, the escape apparatus. On the surface they swam defencelessly in the cold water but were nevertheless targets for the machine gunners on the enemy ships. This reduced their numbers or eliminated them completely. Those who had managed to survive were then rescued and lived to face interrogation.

The methods of interrogation were especially brutal. There were reports of being blindfold whilst being beaten and in some accounts we were reminded more of medieval times or the Spanish Inquisition rather than a twentieth century conflict. Setting aside these reports it must be said that these incidents were the exception to the rule. The capture and interrogation of the vast majority of the POWs was conducted in an almost chivalrous atmosphere. As I have stated, there is little or no point in going into this matter any further, there is nothing to be gained, but I feel it is necessary to remind us all that there were very many people, on all sides, who achieved their goals in the war by cruelty and inhumane methods.

Whilst we carried out this unpleasant and rather demanding task, life went on as normal. I wrote to my father on 15th August 1943:

> *'...At first some requests. In a few days a working group here in the camp wants to start studying the material relevant to three terms in the Technical High School. I will be taking part in this and need very urgently the following items: drawing instruments, a good slide rule, logarithmic tables and either die Hütte book 1 and book 2 or from Duppel: Taschenbuch des Maschinenbaus (pocket book of machine construction) (2 books). Should you have problems in obtaining these items, then contact the V.D.I. (Association of German Engineers). As you can see, I have set myself a lot of work, but the more time that is filled out with this the better you can get over these times. It should also do me good to thoroughly refresh my knowledge of mathematics. I keep on looking at your photo...how young you have kept! For the first time I see your equestrian badge. I will certainly have to work hard later on to catch up with that. With your tuition it should be possible, what do you say? Now I hope that this letter passes the censor quickly and that I should soon be able to use the requested items.'*

Occasionally we wrote indirectly to the censor like this. Whether it helped or not I don't know. From this letter it can be clearly seen that I then intended to turn my attention to studying seriously, not necessarily preparing for a civilian occupation but to fill out the time.

Der Reichsminister der Luftfahrt
und Oberbefehlshaber der Luftwaffe

Luftwaffenpersonalamt
Az.Verl.10 Nr. 1391 (Chef-Abt.IIB)

(In der Antwort bitte vorstehendes Geschäftszeichen,
Datum und kurzen Inhalt angeben)

Berlin W 8, den //.Juni 1943
Leipziger Straße 7
Tel.-Adr.: Reichsluft Berlin
Fernsprecher: Ortsverkehr: 52 00 24, 21 92 41, 12 00 47
Fernverkehr: 21 80 11
Hausapparat: 2156

Betr.: Hauptmann Ulrich S t e i n h i l p e r

Herrn
Wilhelm Steinhilper

Heutingsheim Kr.Ludwigsburg
Württemberg

Sehr geehrter Herr Steinhilper!

   Es ist dem Luftwaffenpersonalamt eine besondere Freude, Ihnen mitteilen zu können, daß der Herr Reichsmarschall Ihren z.Z. in englischer Kriegsgefangenschaft befindlichen Sohn, den Hauptmann Ulrich S t e i n h i l p e r , mit Wirkung vom 1. Juni 1943 zu diesem Dienstgrad befördert hat.

   Anliegend erhalten Sie 2 beglaubigte Auszüge der betreffenden Personalveränderung. Damit die Bezüge Ihres Sohnes schnellstens in der nunmehr zustehenden Höhe überwiesen werden können, senden Sie zweckmäßigerweise eine Ausfertigung an die Ihnen sicherlich bekannte Anschrift der die Gebührnisse zahlenden Dienststelle. Die 2. Ausfertigung ist für Sie selbst bestimmt, darf aber nicht Ihrem Sohn zugesandt werden. Die englischen Stellen werden von hier aus auf dem amtlichen Wege benachrichtigt.

2 Anlagen

                                    Heil Hitler!
                                    I.A.

The official confirmation of my promotion to Hauptmann which was sent to my parents. As can be seen from it the date was 19th June 1943 and the promotion effective 1st June 1943. However news didn't filter through to me until 23rd August 1943 (see letter overleaf).

This letter contained important news:

24th August 1943.

'Liebe Muttel,

Yesterday I received two letters from you, dated 21st and 23rd June. My promotion was a success! It would be wonderful if we got the official notification here too but that, here, is a law unto itself. There are comrades here that have been waiting in vain for years so that they could at last get a few cents more (a Hauptmann was paid four Canadian Dollars more than an Oberleutnant). These mills grind very slowly. I would be grateful if you could, from your side, try and contact the International Red Cross, then we will have done as much as we can from our side. The promotion exceeds all these little matters. I am glad our home country is still standing true to us, just as we are remaining true to our country. It was again a clear signal that we are not yet forgotten and later on will be set tasks again, just like all the others luckier than us. However this promotion also says things like: "If you were at home now...! Or also: "How long have you been there...?"

The notification of my promotion was sent to my father's home address, not to where he was stationed at Mühlhausen. That is why it was my mother who informed me of my promotion to *Hauptmann* effective 1st June 1943. How pleased I was with this promotion can be read in the letter. It was confirmation for me that we had not been forgotten.

The following letter gives a good impression of normal life in camp: Sunday 19th September 1943:

'Liebe Muttel,

We celebrated birthdays (the 25th and the 14th - mine), my Stubenatester Döring made a nice speech, I almost thought that you and father were standing in front of me, that's how well he knows you from my accounts. I did not get round to writing a letter on this day. We celebrated every minute of free time that I had available on Tuesday. Don't laugh about 'free time' - I have reached the point here in camp where every minute is filled. My head is spinning with all this mechanics and mathematics. Actually I didn't see my task during this war in cosines and tangents, but the days here are not wasted and they are passing faster than ever.

...In the aftermath I have also toasted your silver wedding. I hope you didn't forget the pleasure just because of work. I have now take up a lot of your valuable time, so that you can hardly rest. How well it worked with the accordion, I hope it reaches me safely.'

My father had a brother who worked for Hohner in Trossingen. Although it was wartime, he was allowed to buy an accordion for me. Later on it did actually arrive safely in Canada. Because of my other activities I was never able to perfect my abilities on it, although it had a piano keyboard. As in earlier days when I was with my squadron in 1939/40, I had tried to play the accordion but I had the same problems as I experienced as a POW, I just couldn't seem to cope with the stops for the basses. During this time of almost regular letter and parcel exchanging there was an humorous incident in one of the neighbouring rooms: the room senior there, Dr Huppert, had

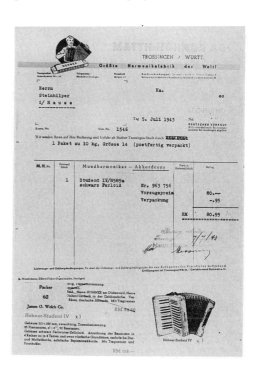

The original reciept for the accordion.

asked his wife in Germany to send some of the well known hair lotion, *Mampe halb und halb* (which is actually a sweet liquor like Bay Rum but not for human consumption). He actually wanted another liquor in the bottle for drinking and passed this message to his wife. When the parcel arrived with what seemed to be the correct contents, Huppert was especially proud of his clever wife. In front of all his room-mates he raised the bottle to enjoy the first swallow, but *Au Weia!* (Oh dear!) it was horrible. To set the scene for future supplies, his wife had actually left hair lotion in the bottle in the first parcel to fool the inspectors. When the next parcel arrived with a similar bottle, our room neighbour first of all rubbed some of the bottles contents into his hair, and I will never forget how he yelled! It was heard through the thin wooden walls: *"Verdammte Scheisse!"* ("Oh shit!") he cursed. This was not the way Dr Huppert usually expressed himself, but this time this yell was most appropriate. The bottle did contain the liquor he had asked for but before it could finally be tasted and enjoyed he had to wash his head thoroughly.

Amongst the *Heinkehrer* (the home goers) who were given a farewell ceremony from Camp Gravenhurst in August 1943, was the pilot *Hauptmann* Karl-Ernst Wilke. When he was shot down he had suffered severe burns, especially to his face. Although I had little contact with him before the exchange action, I did ask him to sew a small piece of linen into his uniform bearing a personal note from me to my parents. On the small piece of a handkerchief was typed:

'Hptm. Wilhelm St., Mühlhausen/Elsass, Hermann Cossmannstr. 18. My five escape attempts so far all in vain, due to lack of money. Acquisition of Canadian or U.S. $ through Adolf Bay (my uncle) or official sources. False documents (possibly Swiss passport) get from official source or Adolf's documents. Send to me in accordance with arrangement. Consult Stephan Cannstatt. Mark the mail with green cross.'

It was astonishing that one was able to type on both sides of this material and it lasted so well. On the reverse:

Frau A. Döring, Berlin-Karlshorst
Auguste Viktoria 2
Tel. 501212 oder 502060
(Döring is room-mate)

[ND Uncle Adolf was my mother's brother who, in 1910, returned to Germany from the USA by way of Japan and Russia. Herr Stephan in Stuttgart, Bad Cannstatt, was an acquaintance who I knew had casual connections in Switzerland (see 'Spitfire On My Tail'). Relatives of this family in the USA had sent parcels with presents to me in several camps. had arranged with Wilke that he would tell them that if dollars could be obtained, these should be concealed in glued-up walnut shells. Documents if they could be obtained, should be in the same parcel and be bound into the cover of a book. The parcel, for identification by me, was to be marked with a green cross on the outside wrapping.]

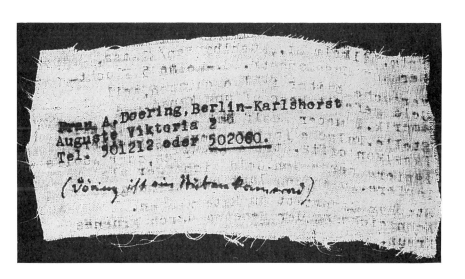

Hptm.Wilhelm St.,Muehlhausen/Elsass,
Hermann Cossmannstr.18.-Meine 5 Flucht-
versuche bisher fehlgeschlagen,weil
Geld gefehlt.Beschaffung kanad.und
amerik.$ ueber Adolf bei oder offiziell
Stelle.Falsche Papiere,(evtl.Schweizer
Pass)von offiz.Stelle besorgen,oder Adolfs
Papiere hersenden.Geld wichtiger als
Papiere.Zusendung laut Verabredung.
Stephan Cannstatt zu Rate ziehen.
Kennzeichnung der Sendung durch gruenes
Kreuz.

Frau A.Deering,Berlin-Karlshorst
Auguste Viktoria 2
Tel.501212 oder 502060.

(Döring ist ein Würtenkommand)

My original typed pieces of material which went back to Germany with Karl-Ernst Wilke and which were kept by my parents along with my letters and cards from the camps.

203

<u>A b s c h r i f t</u>

Lager Lechfeld, den 28.10.43

Sehr verehrter Herr Steinhilper!

Vor wenigen Tagen aus der Gefangenschaft heimgekehrt, beginne ich
mit meiner Korrespondenz an die Angehörigen vieler meiner Kameraden
der letzten 2-3 Jahr mit Ihnen, da Ihr Sohn mir beiliegende Nachricht
besonders an's Herz gelegt hat, als ich mich am 15.8. vom Lager ver-
abschiedete. Ich habe sie soeben gerade aus der Uniform wieder herausge-
trennt.

Natürlich habe ich viele herzliche Grüße zu bestellen und kann von
mir aus hinzufügen, daß Ihr Sohn äußerst gesund und frisch, ein ausge-
zeichneter Sportler ist, der mich im vorigen Jahr sogar im Tennis hoch
geschlagen hat. Vor allem aber verdienen all' seine bisherigen Fluchtversuche höchste Anerkennung, und wenn sie - wie bei fast allen Anderen -
scheiterten, so ist das nur den unerhört großen Schwierigkeiten politischer
und geographischer Art zuzuschreiben.

Ich selbst war Augenzeuge seiner letzten Flucht Anfang Juli:
Am hellichten Tage wurden die Posten durch ein lebhaftes Korbball- und
Medizinball- Spiel sowie durch das Spritzen mit einem Gartenschlauch
(in an sich ganz alberner Art) so beschäftigt und abgelenkt, daß der
stabile Zaun von Oblt. Manhardt (auch ein "Ober-Ausbrecher") mit der
Zange durchgeschnitten werden konnte. Ihr Junge kroch hindurch und ging,
verkleidet als Tommy, an den Posten grüßenderweise vorbei, - eine Leistung,
die bei uns allen wegen seiner Kaltblütigkeit und des Schneids, mit dem
er sie ausführte, große Achtung hervorgerufen hatte. - Leider kannten sich
aber offenbar die Kanadier unter einander zu gut, als daß ihnen das
fremde Gesicht nicht verdächtig erschienen wäre, oder seine Ehrenbezeu-
gung war zu deutsch - militärisch gewesen, - jedenfalls wurde er nach
kurzer Zeit ergriffen und mußte wieder einmal 4 Wochen absitzen.

Ich würde mich für Ihren Sohn sehr freuen, wenn es Ihnen möglich wäre,
sehr verehrter Herr Steinhilper, ihm die gewünschten Papiere, und vor
allem das Geld, zu besorgen. Auch jede fehlgeschlagene, aber gut geplante
und schneidig durchgeführte Flucht steigert die Achtung vor dem deutschen
Soldaten und auch den Geist innerhalb des Lagers.

Indem ich Ihnen jederzeit zu weiterer Auskunft zur Verfügung stehe,
bin ich

mit Deutschem Gruß

Ihr Karl-Ernst Wilke

*Wilke's original letter to my father, also retained by my parents.
Naturally it wasn't until I finally got home that I was able to
appreciate the effort that had been made by comrades like Wilke.*

That had not been easy for him; it is hard to imagine how many such orders the first *Heimkehrer* were given when they left for home. It was not until after the war that I discovered not only the piece of cloth, but also Wilke's personal letter amongst all the letters that my parents had kept:

Lager Lechfeld,
28th October 1943.

'Dear Mr Steinhilper,

Having just returned home from imprisonment a few days ago, I will begin with my correspondence to the relatives of many of my comrades over the last two to three years by writing to you. When I left the camp on 15th August your son had urged me to take the attached news (the piece of cloth) and forward it to you. I have just separated it out of my uniform lining where it had been hidden.

Of course I was asked to convey many hearty greetings to you and can on my behalf add to this that your son is in the best of health, an excellent sportsman who beat me last year in our tennis competition. Above all his escape attempts deserve recognition. When they, as happened to almost all the others, failed it was due to extreme difficulties of a political and geographic nature that have to be overcome.

I myself was witness of his last attempted escape at the beginning of July: in broad daylight, the attention of the guards was distracted by lively basketball and medicine ball games and by spraying water on the lawn (in a very clumsy manner). They were kept busy so that the very strong fence could be cut by Oberleutnant Manhart (also an 'Oberausbrecher' - leading escaper) with a special pair of cutters. Your son crept through the opening and then, dressed as a Tommy, passed the guards, saluting as he went. An accomplishment which, because of the manner in which he conducted it with courage and calm, was greatly respected by all of us. Sorry to say the Canadians must have immediately recognised his face as not being one of them, or was his saluting too German? - too military! Anyway, after a short while he was recaptured and had, once again, to spend four weeks in detention.

I would be pleased for your son if it were possible for you, dear Mr Steinhilper, to obtain the documents he is asking for. Even every unsuccessful but well planned and courageously conducted escape

attempt improves the respect for the German soldier and also supports
the morale in the camp.
In that I am always willing to answer any further questions that you
might have, I remain with the Deutschem Gruss (the German salute),
yours sincerely,
Karl-Ernst Wilke.'

It was a pity that after the war I never managed to see Wilke again, not even later when the Canadian meetings were held. How much would I have liked to thank him.

Even today, after so many years, I am slightly jealous of the assistance extended to the numerous Allied aircrew who managed to escape through the occupied countries. For us from the moment of escape we were in 'enemy country' with little or no hope of outside help. It was really only Peter Krug who managed to obtain help and even that didn't get him home. Of course, in Europe, this wasn't conducted without terrible cost to those who helped and to some of those who escaped. The shooting by the *Gestapo* of the fifty officers from *Stalagluft III* in an attempt to deter other escapers was an utter disgrace, a deed of complete barbarity. Today it is still part of what we Germans carry as our collective conscience.

Following his receipt of Wilkie's letter, my father had no other choice but to ask for private help. Official help or support from German Government offices was never forthcoming to my parents nor to myself. Following are a few postcards and letters, which have to be read completely independently from the following chapter:

Postcard, 29th September 1943:

'Lieber Vater,

Yesterday your letter of 12th July, today the one from 26th July. The
matter with the accordion worked very well. Muttel wrote to me on
your achievements. You drive throughout the whole night and then you
start the morning riding your horse. Just like me in my Leutnant
years! Instead I now sometimes start the day with a 5000 metre run
before morning roll call. You shouldn't expect too much of yourself.
Heartiest greetings,
Your Uz.'

10th October 1943:

'Lieber Vater,

The 'Indianersommer' is, this year, bringing us a few sunny autumn days, however, we already have Eisblumen (ice flowers) on our windows in the morning and one can slowly pack away the short trousers; soon the first snow will fall. The only variety in our life is brought to us by nature, otherwise everything remains the same. Even we ourselves have become 'uniform'. One notices only here and there that some things are being suppressed and are resting, but one also knows exactly that one day this will awake again. Sometime this day will come! Then we will lose this rigidity and will begin to live.
I am especially pleased with your confidence. I have now been here for so long without any contact with home that I can't make out a clear picture any more from the news that is available for us. Of course, our faith remains as strong as ever, however, one would like to feel that we are with you. Otherwise it is too difficult to bear this state of inactivity!
...You will have to keep on writing a lot to me! Heartiest greetings, Your Uz!'

Our reports reached home via the medical exchange personnel without any problems for the carriers. What official reaction they triggered off on the German side, I could not ascertain.

In the camp there was a noticeable improvement with learning material, sporting activities and walks. The renting of the farm became possible and one can only speculate that this may have resulted from protests at the very highest levels. Some reports did reach the German Press in those days and our government may have issued a statement, I don't know.

Notes on Chapter Sixteen

[1] In recent years I have had reports of two such incidents recounted to me by people who apparently witnessed the immediate aftermath. PJO.

[2] - According to my information there were, by the end of the war in 1945, at least 16 000 Allied officers from aircrew were in German prisoner of war camps. No small figure and one which always offered 'leverage'.

CHAPTER SEVENTEEN

A PACKAGE WITH SPECIAL CONTENTS

- THE SECRET CODE -

Apart from our mail and packages from home we were also receiving an increased number of packages and letters from the USA, together with gifts and parcels from the German colony Blumenau in Brazil. With these came a plentiful supply of real bean coffee. One day, in 1943, I received a package about the size of a postcard and some five centimetres thick. From the outside it looked strange, the handwriting was neither that of my parents nor anyone else from whom I regularly received mail. It was written in a somewhat childish hand, I judged, with both my address and that of the sender upon it. I wondered if this was, perhaps, a gift from a schoolgirl or similar as, once in a while, we were sent such touching greetings to encourage us. I went about opening the package with real anticipation but found the contents odd. Who could have been so thoughtless? Inside was an almost rotten razor, including blades, shaving soap and brush. We had then been prisoners for almost three years so who, for heaven's sake, would think we still lacked shaving equipment? The rest of the contents showed little more imagination; some commercially baked cookies, broken and inedible, and a round tin box which certainly didn't look new! Inside I found some soft centred candy that was also almost rotten. Having thrown away the cookies, I was about to follow suit with the candy but then felt a little guilty. After all, this had come from home and who knew how long they'd been saving this from their normal food ration. I therefore encouraged my room-mates who were present to enjoy them and started to hand the tin around. They didn't taste too bad, the filling was a kind of sweet jelly. On biting into a second one, I discovered a sort of soft kernel, about three millimetres thick, which I couldn't bite. Thinking that the filling was rotten, I was just about to spit it out when I thought, 'Even a prisoner shouldn't behave that badly.' I took the little piece carefully between thumb and forefinger and looked at the fibrous formation before finally throwing it away into our waste basket. Fortunately, my room-mate, Wildermuth, saw it and recognised it for what it was. Apparently, during his army training, he had been on a course in which this kind of transmission of information had been explained.

Completely to my surprise he filled a round wash-basin with water and put in the brown kernel. With great care he unfolded the little lump and after some minutes a very thin foil was floating in the water. It was about A4 size and, after careful drying, writing was legible on both sides.

Printed on the front was the speech Göring had made after losing Stalingrad. In there we found confirmation of how critical the situation in Germany was becoming; up until then we'd not believed the reports in the local Canadian press. On the reverse was something quite unbelievable which, to me, illustrated much more than the speech how critical things were at home. There we could see the heading:

Sendet Feindnachrichten
(send reports about the enemy).

There then followed an exact description of a letter code which could be used within our POW letters home and would not be affected by the use of the prescribed special paper which was impervious to secret inks. We knew that our submarine officers actually went into action having been taught a secret letter code so they could communicate if they were taken prisoner. This code, however, was well known within the camp and probably equally well known to the censors and the intelligence officers.

These vague memories came back when, in 1985, I started to write the first lines for the book, 'Ten Minutes to Buffalo'. Now I started researching as well as using my memory. I had all of my letters home which my parents had saved and somewhere in the recesses of my long-term memory was something about code words. *Stern* (star), I thought was one; wasn't the other *Hasenkopf* (rabbit's head)? I tried to remember the instructions and again there was a vague memory of printing the alphabet below with numbers ranging from one to three.

Of course when I finally returned home I'd asked my father and mother whether they had been informed that I had been given a secret code with which I was sending home secret messages. They hadn't, but father remembered that at some stage he had been asked by someone from a completely unknown army headquarters in Torgau to submit certain letters from me for checking. However such things, in the aftermath of the war, were less than important for the family so the question fell into abeyence.

In 1986 I began researching the stack of inherited mail which my parents had left together with all the other documents, papers and photographs which related to my story. They were to be my main source of information because, in the meantime, my father had died and my mother had emigrated to America. At the age of eighty eight she went to live with my sister, Helga, who was seventeen years my junior. There wasn't anyone to question so I began to digest the mass of documentary material in my possession. I soon found two letters from Torgau dated 19th July 1944 and 18th August 1944, both marked *Eilt sehr!* (most urgent) and *'Streng vertraulich'* (strictly confidential). The letters were instructions to my parents to forward any mail from me in which the word *Stern* appeared; so I'd been right, *Stern* was the key to the code!

The first letter, dated 19th July 1944 reads:

Disguised text in letters of Hptm. der Luftwaffe Ulrich Steinhilper, Kgf. number POW 18 310 Camp 20, Canada.

The High Command Wehrmacht/Abt. POWs (IIIe) has been informed that the above German prisoner, in order to protect against any censorship, has been, since 1.1.44, transmitting latent reports which contain news about the treatment and living conditions of our POWs in the camps. As the Oberkommado der Wehrmacht Aby. Allgemeins Kriegsgefangenenwesen (the department of the military high command which dealt with matters concerning German POWs abroad) is interested in these reports you are asked to, as soon as possible, send in all letters received since 1st January 1944, from the above German POW, so we can check the contents. After this checking has been done all the letters will be returned to you. However, may we assure you that you need not be disturbed in anyway by these circumstances. At the same time, however, we are informing you that you should not talk to any third parties at all about this subject as it is highly confidential. This is to protect the POWs who, if you should talk, might suffer as a consequence.

Signed.

The second letter appears to have accompanied the return of my mail:

Torgau, 18th August 1944.

Subject - the same.

Enclosures (my letters) 6.

We return to you four original letters and two postcards, which after taking notes, are being returned to you.
Should you, in the meantime, have received further mail, containing the password **STERN**, it will be of a certain importance. Such mail, in the interest of the POW, should be sent to Oberkommado der Wehrmacht/Abt. Kriegsgef. as quickly as possible until you are informed to do otherwise.
This also applies to all letters and postcards you have received for about one to two months previous to the current mail which you have already sent. We inform you that it is in the interest of the respective Prisoners of War that you do this as quickly as possible and do it confidentially.

Signed.

From then on, I went painstakingly back through my mail from February 1944 (at which time my letters home stopped completely because of circumstances which I will detail later). It was, therefore, clear that any letters which contained coded messages would have been written after the package and code had been received in 1943 so I extended my research back to January 1943 because I couldn't remember exactly when the package and contents had arrived. I soon found a letter to my father dated 24th November 1943 in which I asked for a book about *Sternkunde und Physik* (Astronomy and Physics) by Pohl.

It then occurred to me how earnestly my parents have would searched Germany for the rather unusual book I'd asked for. They wrote to me, of course, letting me know that this was the case and I was rather disappointed, assuming they had not been informed of the existence of the code and were still trying to find the book which I didn't want anyway. I had assumed they had been informed and as such was using the title *Sternkunde*. My parents were convinced that this book was most important for my POW studies in mechanical engineering and were genuinely sorry they could not obtain a copy. Also, up until the time they were informed of the significance of my letters, they were probably also wondering about my writing style. What a collection of strange words I'd started to use and my grammar, to my teacher parents, must have become an abomination! I'd had to use every trick I could muster to provide the correct words to convey the necessary message!

For me, nearly fifty years later, it meant looking at this letter of 24th November 1943 and the more I looked the more I could see this letter had to contain a coded text. Not only the password *STERN* was an indication of that, but also the strangely halting and cramped style. Clearly there was the address then the usual salutation, *'Lieber Vatel'*, there then followed unusually small print to get a maximum number of words onto the permitted twenty-four lines. It was obvious that in this letter there had been a long coded text.

Such letters, I remember, sometimes took me up to two weeks to write. After all, the contents of the POW letter still had to show some reasonable sense whilst still fulfilling its new primary purpose. Such exacting and demanding work would have its limit and often I was so completely fed up that I'd almost throw it all into the corner and called it quits. But to turn to the actual letter and examine the contents: How strange is the beginning: *Nun ist drausen Winterzeit.* (Now is outside wintertime). *Ja! So ist das! Damit hat mein 4tes Jahr in Gefangenschaft nun angefangen.* (Yes! So it is! With that my fourth year in captivity now has started). Whoever read that certainly must have had doubts as to whether or not I had been hit on the head or something. There was no doubt this was a coded letter and with the help of this, in 1986, I tried hard to reconstruct the code.

It took me a long time but the longer I thought about it the deeper my mind searched my long-term memory. It is probably one of the most remarkable facilities of the human mind and everyone will have experienced the results of such deep searches; days and sometimes weeks after a question has been posed the answer will come to the conscious mind as if from nowhere. This is how I reconstructed the code, from dribs and drabs of information that were gradually dragged out of the deepest recesses of my memory. At the oddest times a snippit of information would flash into mind and I'd be off to jot it down before the significance was lost. In this way the matrix was brought together and the secret code revealed.

To help follow the description it will be necessary to refer to the next three illustrations. The first is a copy of the letter with a full transcript overlaid. The second is typed transcript of parts of the letter together with the numerical breakdown. The third shows the complete breakdown.

H	A	S	E	N	K	O	P	F	B	C	D	G	I	L	M	Q	R	T	U	V	W	X	Y	Z
1	1	1	1	1	1	1	1	1	2	2	2	2	2	2	2	2	3	3	3	3	3	3	3	3
1	1	2	2	2	3	3	3	1	1	1	2	2	2	3	3	3	1	1	1	2	2	2	3	3
1	2	3	1	2	3	1	2	3	1	2	3	1	2	3	1	2	3	1	2	3	1	2	3	1

Wortlängenschlüssel:

Bis 3 Buchstaben = 1
Bis 6 Buchstaben = 2
Über 6 Buchstaben = 3

Lieber Vater!
Nun ist draussen Winterzeit.Ja!So ist das!Damit hat mein 4tes Jahr in Gefangenschaft nun angefangen.Wie diese unaufhaltsame Lebensuhr weiterläuft!
Was man zu Hause in diesem Zeitraum tun können hätte!Dieser Verlust ist auf
die Dauer ja kaum wieder wett zu machen.Doch das ist Nebensache,wenn man
seinen persönlichen Vorteil dem der Gemeinschaft unterstellt.Von mir kann
ich sagen,daß es wie bis heute auch weiter gehen wird. - Sag mal!Musst Du
in diesen Tagen viel Dienst verrichten?Mittels Post ist erfüllt von Bewund-
erung für Deine nie müde werdende,ausdauernde Arbeit.Es ist nur zu hoffen,
daß Dein Tun Dir rechte Freude macht und dadurch das harte Los der ewigen
Sorgen dämpft.Ich kann mir vorstellen,wie leidvoll es in solchen Tagen der
nie aufhörenden Not Dir manchmal ums Herz ist. - Besonders heute würde ich
mit Dir gerne die grosse Zeit teilen.Das Schicksal der ganzen,vor Europa
liegenden Geschichte wird dieser Tage von Euch allein in hartem Kampf zur
Entscheidung gezwungen.Dabei nicht Zuschauer sein und mitzuhelfen muss Euch
in diesen harten Zeitläuften als der beste Lohn für Euer Tun dienen. - Wie
bitter ist das,wenn wir unsere Menschenleben dabei dahineilen sehen und gar-
nichts mit zum Wohle unsres geliebten Vaterlandes beitragen.Das ist aber un-
abänderlich und wir ertragen das weiterhin mit alter Ausdauer. - Ja!und nun
hab ich für den Unterricht,der bei uns im Winter im Lehr - Plan erscheint
noch mit Dir Einiges zu regeln.Bitte schicke!!Sternkunde= und Physik -
Buch von Pohl.Ich brauche dies notwendig.Es ist sicher noch erhältlich.
Notfalls sende Anforderungen an die Vereinigung der Ingenieure in Berlin
(Hauptgeschäftsstelle).Es ist ja so gut,dass mein Brief Dir heute wieder
vor Augen führt,wie notwendig im Augenblick die Wissenschaft uns zu sein
hat.Man verschwendet sonst den ganzen Tag nutzlos mit Grübeleien,die den
Kopf schwer machen und das Leben

The password was *STERN*, which meant each letter containing the word *STERN* was coded. It was recommended that, after a certain length of time, both the password and the code word be changed. For this the coded text within the letter was to be used.

The code word was *HASENKOPF* (rabbit's head). These letters were lifted from the alphabet and written on one line, followed by the remaining letters of the alphabet (leaving out the letter 'j', which could be confused with 'i'), as shown at the top of illustration 1. Under this line of letters three lines of numbers were to be written. Beginning at the left:

Line 1: the number '1' nine times; number '2' nine times; number '3' to the end of the alphabet.

Line 2: the number '1' three times; number '2' three times; number '3' three times; repeated to the end of the alphabet.

Line 3: the numbers '1', '2', '3', repeated to the end of the alphabet.

Now below each letter in the alphabet it was possible to read downwards the three numbers which formed the three digit code for each letter and with this it is possible to code text into a normal letter.

The length of each word written in the letter indicated the digits to be used ie: a word of up to three letters = '1'; up to six letters = '2'; more than six letters = '3'. Three words gave the three digits required to represent a letter of the aphabet. For example, reference to the first illustration will show that the first word is *'Nun'*. This, therefore, would represent the number 1 (because it was a three letter word). Similarly the second word *'ist'* is also three, the next word, however, is over six and corresponds to the number 3. The first three digit code is therefore 1 1 3. Reference back to the alphabet table shows that to be equal to 'S'. As we continue, progressively T, A, N, D... and so on are decoded. The full text is shown in illustration 3. Using this information we were able to encode messages for transmission.

```
1 3 1 1 2 1 2 3 1   2 2 3   1 2 1 1 1 3 1 1 1 1 2 2 1 1
1 1 1 2 1 3 3 1 2   3 2 1   2 2 2 1 1 3 3 1 2 1 2 2 2 2
3 1 2 2 3 1 3 1 1   1 2 1   1 2 2 3 2 1 3 2 1 1 2 1 1 2
S T A N D O R T E   M I T   E I N S A Z F A E H I G E N

2 3 3 1 2 2 1 1 1 2 1 1
2 2 1 2 3 1 1 2 2 1 2 2
3 1 3 1 3 1 2 1 2 3 1 2
L W V E R B A E N D E N

2 1 3 3 1 1 2   2 1 1 2 1 2   2 1   1 1 2 2
1 3 1 2 3 3 1   2 1 2 1 2 3   2 2   2 3 2 1
1 1 1 1 1 1 3   1 2 2 3 1 3   2 2   2 3 3 3
B O T W O O D   G A N D E R   I N   N F L D

2 2 1 2 1   2 1 3   2 1 2 3 2 1 3 3 1   1 1 1 2 2 3 2 1 1
2 2 1 1 2   1 1 2   1 1 3 1 3 3 1 1 1   1 1 2 2 1 1 3 2 2
1 3 2 2 1   1 2 3   3 2 3 1 1 1 2 1 1   3 1 1 3 1 2 3 2 1
G L A C E   B A Y   D A R T M O U T H   S H E L B U R N E

3 1 2 2 1 3 3 1   2 1   1 1 3 1   1 2 1 3 2 1
2 1 3 3 3 1 1 1   2 2   2 3 1 1   1 1 3 1 2 1
3 2 3 1 1 2 1 1   2 2   2 1 3 2   3 2 1 1 2 2
Y A R M O U T H   I N   N O V A   S C O T I A
```

After digesting these instructions the members of our room studied in complete secret for a long time and experimented until we fully understood it. Then, having reached an understanding of the system, we had a final careful discussion again, limited only to those within our room. The question was whether this kind of espionage was permitted for POWs within the Geneva Convention or if, in entering into such clandestine subtefuge, we would lay ourselves open to the most severe penalties for spying. We decided to inform no one, not even *die Ältestenrat*, of our decision that I should go ahead and try to use the code. We would take the matter upon our own heads. This would not only ensure security but also keep to a minimum those laid open for penalty should we be caught.

When looking at some of the other illustrations it will become clear that once we really got going we were reporting some very *'hot news'*. The *Luftnachrichtenoffizier, Oberleutnant* Niehoff, soon recognised how much information the Canadian newspapers contained. Even in the smaller Canadian newspapers there were several pages in which small articles reported on who had got married, who'd had a child born, what religion they were, who was going to which school, to what training, etc. etc. In our German newspapers there was actually nothing comparable, we had lists of births, deaths and marriages but not in the same personal detail.

Very early on, Niehoff specialised in collecting these small reports as a hobby and stored them in a drawer, not really hidden at all. From these he began to formulate a file in which he cross-referenced all names of military personnel. Apparently in the end it contained in excess of fourteen thousand names of personnel of the Royal Air Force and the Royal Canadian Air Force. By his diligent research he knew, for instance, when they had entered the Air Force, when they had qualified for their Wings or when they had passed their test as navigator, wireless operator, bomb aimer and even when they were flying their first sorties. Later reports on these people would follow their careers in detail giving information on their unit, the kind of missions they were flying, their decorations and when they were awarded and many other things which were contained in these very small reports and announcements. It was all there if you knew where to look, many times as much as we could handle.

The newspapers we had access to inside the camp had been carefully censored, especially any information relating to reports on escapes. However, it didn't seem to occur to anyone to take out those innocuous pages which were only of local interest; those pages containing the social news. After all they were, apparently, only harmless things reported there. About furlough, about engagements, marriages and, sometimes, sad things such as who had been killed, when and where. However, when followed over the months and, eventually, years they contained a wealth of information. How and where crews were trained, how many flying crews were trained in Canada. Much of this information was not obvious in the articles and it took a dedicated specialist like Niehoff to *'read between the lines'*. In the end his local knowledge was truly encyclopedic.

In 1988 I was going through more of my letters and, naturally, I spotted the word *STERN*. Dated 20th July 1943 to my mother, I was once more asking for something else:

> *'Until this letter reaches you, shouldn't I get richer by one more star (Stern), father should ask.'*

I was asking in this strange way whether they had, in the meantime at home, heard if I'd been given *another star*. This is a reference to promotion; as an *Oberleutnant* I would have one star on my braided shoulder straps and two stylised eagles on the collar patches of my uniform. As *Hauptmann* I would have two stars and three eagles. I wasn't particularly interested in promotion, after all what was there to command? But many of my comrades had received notice of promotion, sometimes years late, and as a consequence they'd lost pay and privileges. It was also important to write it in this clandestine way because if the question of promotion was put clearly, the Canadian censor sometimes inked it out. Because in the content of the letter mentioned above came the word 'star' (*'STERN'*), and it also had this strange formulation of words I thought this letter was also coded. I looked at it for a long, long time but couldn't read anything from it, other than the obvious text. Did this mean I'd stopped the coded letters for a while? Or was the decoding and reconstruction faulty? Having tried my best I abandoned the task.

In 1989, when I began research for this, the last book, I found the letter again and couldn't resist trying once more, but to no avail. In the meantime I'd found a letter dated 26th September 1943, it contained the message: *REDE GÖRING ERHALTEN SCHIKT IN KONSERVEN AUDIO NVI MCI EAL ROERE FUER KWH UND ERTZ NETZ TRAFO FELT WARTEN* (Have received speech Göring. Send in tinned foods radio NRI MCI EAL valves for KWH and ERTZ ENV. Net transformer missing. Warten). Warten was used in morse code at the end of a message. As already mentioned, our radio builders made even the most difficult parts themselves, but there was always a shortage of valves and they were indispensible. So I used my first coded letter to order some as well as to confirm that we had the code. The valve did, by the way, reach us safely in Canada in January 1944, packed in a tin of blood sausage. This parcel again came from *'strange hands'*. The most important thing though was that it became clear that this was the first confirmation to Germany that we'd received the code, hence the reference to Göring's speech. Now that I'd found this letter it was clear to me exactly during which time period I had to research my letters. The earlier letter and my unwitting use of the word *'Stern'* had been a *'red herring'* and I'd just wasted a lot of time trying to decode a message that wasn't there!

Then came the letter of 17th October 1943 to my sister which I wrote in longhand, rather than the small print I usually used to maximise the space available. I pondered for quite a while as to whether an experienced censor would start questioning the style of letter because the address line was separated, the sentences were in funny sequence and the selection of words was often abominable! I therefore decided, this time, to include the address (by this I mean the initial salutation) line into the coding and then the whole letter was written in longhand. We, in the room, had discussed these variations for quite a while and had come to the conclusion that the *experts* in Germany should be in such a position to immediately recognise all the essentials of a coded letter.

That the contents of the coded message should, in this case, be of a more personal nature was agreed because it was still the duty of the soldier to escape and we saw no reason why we shouldn't ask for support in these enterprises. At this time we still didn't know whether our news, which we'd sent through the first group of comrades who had been medically repatriated by exchange, had got through to home. The message was then:

'MIR FUENF FLUCHTVERSUCHE MISLUNGEN FEHLTE CANAD GELD ADRESE PAPIRE HELFT MIR UND HPTM WILDERMUTH MIT OBIGEM.' ('My five escapes failed. Had no Canadian money, address, documents. Help me and Hauptmann Wildermuth with above.')

We'd had to decide how we could best clearly identify Wildermuth for ID documents. We decided to use Hptm not because of his rank, but because it was shorter than his Christian name, Eberhard. Length of text was always the problem, the message was very restricted because of the twenty-four lines letter length. But in a way it was also a relief. Besides this brain-numbing exercise I was also diligently studying material science, physics, mathematics and statistics, etc, for the *Physicum*, the physics curriculum. Had I been responsible for encoding much longer messages I think it might have proved too much.

As it was we managed to transfer information on a regular basis and the text gleaned from my letter dated 8th November 1943, was certainly of great importance for the *U-Boot* campaign. From talking to recently captured *U-Boot* officers it was clearer than ever that the Allies were now able to decipher both the letter code used by the captured *U-Boot* officers and also the radio traffic of the *U-Boote*. Certainly the Allies had collected and collated much information from these sources particularly in respect of the damage inflicted by bombing and depth-charging. We encoded:

'SCHLUESSEL DES BDU MIT SICHERHEIT DEM FEINDE BEKANT ZENSIRT POST AN UNS BEZUG BOMBENWIRKUNG FEIND WERTET AUS.' ('Key to the code of the officer commanding U-Boats certainly known to the enemy. Censor letters to us referring to effect of bombing. Enemy evaluates.')

Whether or not this was read at home, believed and appropriate action initiated can no longer be ascertained. Looking back it is doubtful, the office in Torgau most probably woke up too late. It wasn't until my father received a letter dated 18th August 1944 that they asked him to send all 'Stern' letters to them. I'd sent our message on 8th November 1943 and it was postmarked 10th November. At that time the average delivery time for a letter was two months. Our warning could have been known in Germany in February of 1944 and one wonders what the results might have been. There is one small comfort, as much as perhaps our information was not swiftly decoded and used it is also now clear that the intelligence officers in Ottawa did not use their knowledge of the *U-Boot* officers' code to their full advantage. So, essentially, the two cancelled each other out.

On 24th November I wrote to my father and encoded information on the Atlantic protection flights. This was information that Niehoff had gradually assembled by his cross-referencing of information in the papers. We gathered it from Niehoff without actually briefing him on the letter code. It had information on the bases from where the Allies were guarding the Atlantic with flying units. This was transmitted as:

'STANDORTE MIT EINSATZFÄHIGEN LW VERBÄNDEN' ('Towns with operational air force units') *'BOTWOOD GANDER IN NFLD GLACE BAY DARTMOUTH IN NOVA SCOTIA.'* ('Botwood and Gander in Newfoundland, Glace Bay and Dartmouth in Nova Scotia.')

My last coded letter was dated 7th December 1943. I tried to decipher this one for a long time with all kinds of sequences of numerals but because of the lines that the censor had blacked out, it was not clear whether this letter contained the word *'Stern'* or not. Only the short word *wenn*, written with a dash above the *n*, revealed that this letter might be coded. Many times when I was badly in need of a three letter word (which gives a 1), I would use this trick. In the old German style of writing it was common practice in words where one letter was duplicated, one could write it only once with a dash above it. i.e. *Sommer* (summer) could be written as *Somer* with a dash above the *m*. *wen* with a dash above the *n* was clearly *wenn*. I searched and searched again... started with the longer piece of text with the word *Heilig-Abend* (Christmas Eve). With the text split into three there were only three possibilities to maintain the rhythm. However none of these made any sense!

In October 1988 my wife and I spent our holiday in West Canada, touring British Columbia with a mobile home. Upon our return home, we again tried to decipher this censored letter.

Before this holiday, the row of letters I had decoded but could not enterpret were confusing, it really made no sense at all! They were:

..INCERUPERTBELLABELLAUCLUELETTOF..

Long after our return from our Canadian holiday, in June 1989, I tried again from the start of the letter. Quite quickly I found: *LW VERBAENDE IN..* (Air Force units in) before the censor's ink blacked out the rest. It was clear that this was definitely a coded letter, so I looked at this jumble of letters again. What was hidden there? Together Lore and I pored over the map from our trip to British Columbia and suddenly the answer leapt out at us. All that had been missing under the censor's ink were two letters, P & R. That gave us: *PR...INCE RUPERT BELLA BELLA UCLUELET TOFINO COAL HARBOR PATRICIA BAY I....* and then the text is lost again under censor's ink. Emerging after the ink was: *SPORT COMMAND IN GOOSE BAY BEI HAMILTON LABRADOR.* So in total we had: *Air force units in... Prince Rupert, Bella Bella, Ucluelet, Tofino, Coal Harbour, Patricia Bay I... support command in Goose Bay near Hamilton, Labrador.*

Although these locations are on the Pacific coast of Canada there was no reason why the German intelligence officers should not have passed this information on to their Japanese counterparts. But again we will never know if this happened.

The POW letters, after December 7th 1943, do not contain any more coded messages. The reason for this will be revealed in the next chapter. I remember very distinctly that, because I might be leaving the camp, I didn't want to have the code lost. With great care I looked within the camp for a man who could continue my work with the code. I can only remember that, of my room mates, nobody wanted to continue, probably because they were very much aware how demanding it had been. But who did then continue I, sadly, can no longer remember.

CHAPTER EIGHTEEN

WORRYING ABOUT GERMANY

The speech given by Göring after losing the Battle of Stalingrad was very touching. From this I drew two conclusions: first, in my home country I was apparently recognised as a reliable soldier. It seemed evident that in either political or military offices someone was well informed of my attempted escapes and had singled me out as recipient of the code. Second was the perception that instead of helping me, my assistance was being sought, the assistance of a prisoner of war! From all this I could only conclude that the conditions in Germany were far worse than any of us had assumed.

Although the Canadian newspapers and American magazines such as *Time*, *Life* and *Look*, which we regularly read in camp, were continually reporting on Russian victories, the Allied successes in North Africa and the Japanese retreat in the Pacific, we couldn't believe it all. We had to bear in mind that at the time when we had been actively involved in the fighting on the various fronts (and fairly represented within the camps we had all the various arms of *die Wehrmacht*) the news as reported by foreign newspapers was always of Allied victory. Of course there were casualties of the various battles, but often casualties of a campaign that had been won. How, for instance, the debacle of Dieppe could have been reported as a *'success'* was beyond us. We preferred to believe our own *Wehrmachtsbericht* (Armed Forces Report) which we listened to on our own radios. But we weren't so naive as to believe that completely either, we were experienced soldiers and we could read between the lines. 'Tactical withdrawals' and planned retreats to 'straighten the line' were euphemisms, we knew, for reversals in the field but we couldn't believe it was all going one way.

The 'parcel with special contents' really made me pause and give thought to the conditions at home. A few weeks before we had given the most important news to our sick comrades who were being repatriated, relying on them to pass it on uncensored when they got home. This saved me from having to code all my letters, a task that would have been impossible without letting half the camp into the code as I would have needed assistance in coding everything. As it was I also wrote normal letters in parallel to my coded ones.

A postcard dated 27th October 1943:

'Liebe Muttel,

Once again I have been having a very good time. Last week the accordion arrived and the day before yesterday the parcel with Gesälz (Swabian for jam, otherwise known as marmalade) and the biscuits. Nothing was broken and everything arrived in perfect condition. That was a good idea of yours and we all enjoyed it, it tasted very good. Your ears must have been ringing yesterday evening, the praises of my room-mates knew no end. At the same time the accordion was used for the first time. Thanking you very much!
Your Uz. '

It was fortunate that at the time we had absolutely no idea of the terrible conditions being suffered by our captured comrades at the hands of the Russians[1]. The victories were being reported in the Allied Press, but no mention was being made of the thousands of German soldiers who were being captured and taken to Russian prisoner of war camps. Today I am glad that at the time I knew nothing about it, who knows what I and other prisoners might have done in their despair.

Postcard dated 9th November 1943 to my sister. [In the address the *Feldpost* (Field Post) number had been altered twice and then there was written: *Stabshelferin* (staff assistant), Ostland Lazarett (Wilna)]:

'Liebe Trude,

Thankyou very much for your letter from August. Actually you could write more often to me! You should have just that little bit of time for me. How much do you think I would write if I had more space available? You just cannot imagine what mail from home means for us. Everything interests me, even with the smallest fraction of news you can give me great pleasure. I have now been sitting here for over three years and know less and less of how things are with you and what you are all doing! Have yourself a happy Christmas and success for the coming New Year.
Best greetings from your brother,
Uz. '

When writing to my sister, I would occasionally let the bad sentiments come through, however, when writing to my parents I would always be more confident. On Christmas Eve 1943 I wrote two postcards, one to my father, the other to my younger sister.

'Lieber Vatel,

This evening we will all be thinking back to the many nice celebrations that we had over the past years. Most probably our greatest pleasure will be, when we think of it, how these festive hours are lying ahead of us in great abundance (in the future). The present situation can certainly not last longer than our separation has already existed. Thereafter the most beautiful times for us will begin. We all believe in a higher justice. Greetings,
Your Uli.'

'Liebe Helga,

Santa Claus will be coming today! By the time you hold this card in your small fingers everything will already be over and you will be looking forward to the next Christmas Eve. Perhaps I will be at home by then, perhaps later.
Nevertheless! That Christmas, when your Uli is at home again, is the one that you should really look forward to, then you will have to tell me what presents you want me to give you. There is so much that I have to catch up with. Until that time comes, be a nice girl to your mother!
Many greetings,
Your Uli.'

As an address I wrote: To *die Kleine Fräulein* (little Miss), Helga Steinhilper, Heutingsheim, although I knew perfectly well my mother would have to read the card to her. With this I was sure that I was providing both of them with a pleasure. Was it possible to read between the lines of the card?

In the meantime I had started another *crazy* scheme. Actually I'd thought about whether I should write about this segment of my life as a prisoner, or if I should just be glad when I got out of the *insanity* safe and sound and forget it. For several reasons I decided to write about the whole affair: first of all, one should, at some time in life, record those events that one had, in

Gravenhurst, the fence in the background. Left to right: Hptm. Neumann, Hptm. Fiebig, Obltn. Machui, Kptltn. Schulte, Maj. Wüstefeldt, Obltn. zur See. Albrecht, Kptltn. Stamer (U-35), Kptltn. Schilling (U-33), Maj. Keil, Obltn. Hennings.

earlier times, regarded as being approved and appropriate. This is because, inevitably with the benefit of hindsight, one will tend to view those events differently in the future[2]. In this there may lie the only possible way to prevent other people from doing the same thing, irrespective of their reason for doing so. Maybe my complete report contains some information which could be of great assistance for doctors and nurses who are working with the psychologically ill, genuine and otherwise.

When I look back today, after so many years, to the time around 1944 and 1945 and also read the report I wrote of my life between the ages of twenty-two and twenty-six I get clear pointers: from my school-days up to the war, on to the day I was shot down and then to the dangers of escaping - there I definitely do not wish I'd done things any other way. But this new scheme which I was contemplating was, once I had experienced it, something I would never do again. It was to take me to my limit of endurance and to the edge of insanity. Even so many years later this is the most difficult part of my whole story to write.

A view of the camp, probably taken from the 'The Rockery'.

My second reason for writing the journal was that I didn't know if my parents would ever know what I'd done in terms of escapes and the hardships I'd endured. I didn't want them to think I'd just had a soft time in a comfortable camp, sitting out the war and waiting to go home. Besides which I really didn't know if I'd survive this last attempt I was about to make to get home. Because I wanted a true and accurate account I wrote it all down, divided the sheaves of paper into two lots and glued them into the lining of a suitcase I'd bought from Eaton's. This I entrusted to my colleagues for safe keeping before I began the last phase of my imprisonment.

At this time various ice hockey teams had been formed in Camp Gravenhurst. They competed in various leagues and at varying levels, conducting their games on a points system. Because we were *Technikstudenten* (technical students) we filled our days with studies,

The T+ Ice Hockey Team. Front row, second from left, Reini Pfundtner.
First from right, myself, third from right Eberhart Wildermuth.

however there were many sport enthusiasts amongst us and we decided to form a *Techniker* hockey team which we called *T+*. This had the advantage that both our training games and also our point scoring games were arranged to fit into our study schedules. In our *Techniker* team we played with nine men and because I had already played in the upper league where Pfundtner and Manhart were the crack shots, I was elected team captain. Thanks to eager training and a tremendous amount of ambition it was not too long before the *Techniker* team played in the upper league. During the winter of 1943/44 we were allowed to build, on an *Ehrenwort* basis, a new and larger hockey field on the sports ground outside the camp fence. It was a tremendous improvement compared with the small field on the tennis court inside the camp on which we had played before. To get to the outer hockey field the Canadians had to open the main gate and let us pass through, but counted the team members and the number of spectators. After the match was over we returned to the camp through the same procedure.

During the preceding winter, I'd had such a heavy collision during a game that after I got up I started playing towards the wrong goal and had to be taken off. At the time Dr Eitze, our German doctor in the camp, happened to be among the spectators and immediately took me from the ice and put me to bed for a couple of days. I was suffering from concussion, mainly because we were playing with only partial protection for the body and no head protection whatsoever. We, the *Techniker*, fought with more enthusiasm than with the necessary technical expertise, but never lacked in toughness when it was required. Wildermuth was quick as a flash in defence and Hannes Strehl, the Bavarian, was also with us in $T+$.

With fighting spirit we managed to reach second position in the upper league during winter 1943/44 and shortly before Christmas 1943 another of the hard games took place. I was the middle forward and in the second third of the game, while moving at full speed after a shot at the goal, I was pole-axed as a hockey stick hit me full in the face. Was this time for another concussion? Time to start playing in the wrong direction again? The spectators all saw the accident happen as did the Canadians who had come in numbers to watch this important game. Blood immediately started flowing from my nose and forehead and it really did hurt like hell! I was in real pain but resolved to stay on the ice to make my point. I wanted it to be obvious for everybody that I had been hit on the head and was badly injured. I'd given it some thought and although I hadn't planned the circumstances which had offered me the opening I knew a *'gift horse'* when I saw one. To my mind it was possible to create a mental disturbance of some kind as an effect of this terrible and public injury.

The game was interrupted and, covered in blood, I was stretchered away, back through the main gate to the medical centre. After very careful questioning and a close examination by Dr Eitze I was released to my room. This time I was not concussed - that was his diagnosis. That night I slept very badly, my nose was swollen and I was in some considerable pain. In one respect I had actually been lucky, the hockey stick had hit my nose on the other side from where I had been hit while boxing. This way my nose was, to an extent, brought back in the other direction. For the whole night I tossed and turned in my bunk, full of thoughts: Was this perhaps a one-time opportunity for a man who had already made five attempts to escape (and would therefore make a very suspect subject for exchange) to aim at *des Austausches von Kriegsgefangenen* (exchange of prisoners of war), to become one of the *Simulanten?* Who, at the time when I was really concussed and started playing against the wrong goal, would really know whether this was genuine or if I was only pretending? Who could, therefore, say with certainty whether or not my brain had been affected? Especially now that I had suffered another and more graphic accident. The Canadians had been shocked at the amount of blood I had lost from the injuries in my face, even the guards made comments as I was carried past. When the clock was approaching two o'clock in the morning I made my decision. Waking Wildermuth I said, "Eberhard, don't be surprised about things to come but I am going to start acting insane!" He wondered if he'd properly woken, shook his head and looked at me in the dull light of the room. Then I left him to begin what was, without doubt, to become the worst phase of my life.

Dressed only in my pyjamas I left the room, barefoot, and walked down the stone stairs to the back door. There I stood and, for a short while, looked at the pane of glass in it. I did not need to think it over much longer, I'd already reached a final and clear decision while I was still lying in bed! Drawing back my right arm I punched my balled fist into the glass with all the force I could muster. The glass broke and my arm went through, pushing the sleeve of my pyjama jacket up my arm and peeling back a large flap of skin which hung loose like the tongue of a boot. Blood began to well out of the torn flesh and I began to feel the pain of what I'd done, but it wasn't enough. I started picking up some of the glass splinters, I wanted to look really *military* (a reference to the duelling scars still common in Germany, at that time, with students). I started scratching my temples and my cheeks on both sides with the glass shards, closing my eyes and gritting my teeth to take the self-inflicted pain. Now bleeding heavily from my injured arm and from the cuts on my face and head, I waded barefoot through the snow and ice leaving a red trail behind me. Upon reaching the gate I gripped the wire and started shaking it desperately and shouting alternately in German and English: *"Ich habe von der Gefangenschaft die Schnauze voll, ich will nach Hause!* I'm fed up! I can't stand being a prisoner, I want to go home! *Ich will nach Hause!"* The guards, including the Sergeant on duty, were as astonished at my ravings as I was myself. As soon as I began to act out my part so much anger, sadness and frustration came boiling out it must have been very convincing. They took me into their warm guardroom, stopped the worst of bleeding and cleaned the blood from my face and arms as best they could. They even gave me warm socks to wear as I sat there muttering almost incoherently, "*Bitte ich will nach Hause!* ("Please, I want to go home!") Already the first encouraging comments were coming as I listened to their excited chatter, "...isn't that the fellow, the one who had the accident during the hockey this afternoon?" It was working, not bad at all! But beyond this, all they did was to take me to the camp medical centre and there I immediately asked for Dr Eitze.

First of all he was rather sour when I explained to him what I was planning. Perhaps he was beginning to question his first diagnosis? Maybe I had suffered concussion after all. Anyway, at that time of the night he wasn't willing to discuss my plans any further. His opinion was that before any irreversible decisions were made I should have a good night's sleep.

The next day the discussion with Dr Eitze continued, he had already spoken to *Oberstleutnant* Meythaler who, of course, had already heard what had happened; my 'case' was already the talk of the camp. Dr Eitze said it was his and *Oberstleutnant* Meyerthaler's view that it would be foolish of me to follow through with this nonsense. Their view was that nobody would believe that I'd gone mad. Nevertheless I had my arguments which I brought forward: had there not been cases during the First World War where particularly those who were hungry for freedom had become ill with 'camp disease' (going *wire-happy* in Allied parlance), a sort of mild mental disorder? Surely I could at least try it - couldn't I? Last but not least, I argued that the opportunity I had would not, in respect of the two well documented accidents, occur that conveniently again. Wasn't it mainly only a risk to myself that I was running? Who wanted to lay down the regulations that I had to follow? Nothing impressed Dr Eitze, perhaps he was only trying to stretch things out, to give me enough time to think it over. Or enough time for himself to counter my arguments.

His overview of the situation wasn't encouraging. He said the way I was presenting myself wouldn't convince anybody that I had such an illness; my physical condition was far too good for something like that. If I was to do it at all, the well trained sportsman, Steinhilper, would have to lose weight, would have to look pale and walk around in a weakened condition. That's how we parted: for the time being I would take a 'break', lose weight and continue with sport and the lessons we were having. After all, he said, even the Canadians would not forget these incidents that fast. In the meantime the journeys of the *Gripsholm*, the ship which operated the exchanges under the guidance of the protecting power, were becoming a more and more regular affair. The periods between the exchanges were now somewhere in the region of every six to eight weeks and because our German doctors were involved in the preparations, they were able to estimate when the next exchange journey was due. Of course I couldn't write home about things like this and that's why a normal letter to my sister was posted on 30th December 1943.

'Liebe Trude,

Tomorrow is the last day of the year. We look back and look ahead. Behind us is most probably the hardest war year that we (the Germans) have had. We here felt very little of this and we had to strengthen our hearts so that we could cope with the continual reports of the enemies' victories. Can you imagine how humble our position is here in the camp? But we put our trust in all of you at home and are well aware of who is leading Germany today or perhaps better said, who is leading Europe.[2]
You should know better than we do everything that has been prepared this year. We can only hope for the best. The new year will show it. One thing is certain and that is that by now even the last German should know: it is a case of 'to be or not to be' for our VATERLAND! Knowing this we go into the year '44 and each and everyone of us has to contribute his part, so that our folk can earn the position they deserve. In this respect, all those of us here can do is to prepare so that our work, after the great victory, is of more value. Each of us here is trying to define precisely what is going to be his future responsibility and learn for this... That is why I am now again attending school, just the same as seven years ago: arithmetic, technical drawing, raw materials, physics etc. are my daily pastimes. I have already learnt quite a lot about languages in the past so I am not concentrating on those too much. Music, which I had been studying quite intensively, is now also more in the background. Athletically I am very fit and want to retain that as well as I can. During the winter months we play ice hockey, a very pleasant and exciting game which, by the way, should you have the opportunity and the time, you should attend a match.
The most difficult side of our existence here is the monotony. Can you imagine how you would have felt back in your school days if you had been imprisoned for just three months in your school, meeting

nobody else other than your own classmates. Really boring, what do
you say! But it can be tolerated. Even the coming year is nothing that
we can't survive!
Heartiest greetings,
Your UZ.'

A letter in full length which expresses precisely my inner feelings of the time. It is astonishing what can be put to paper in only twenty-four lines, especially when the printed letters were written with indian ink and a crude steel nibbed pen.

25th January 1944:

'Lieber Vatel,

After a long time, I once again received a letter from you... It's a shame, again, we can't talk to each other about those things that are really concerning us. However we still want to continue to understand each other.
Sometimes here in this place, you tend to reach an attitude where you just don't want to write, simply because our problems appear to be of everyday nature and so unimportant that one feels as if one were just 'thrashing phrases' (getting the last out of them - 'beating them to death') when one tries to draw comparisons with your situation. You are all making and experiencing living history day by day, whereas we are having to exert ourselves so as to escape the continuous monotony, but then we envy you and fall back into our monotony.
Mother asked, in her recent letter, what do we do all day long. Should I write about that and should I write about all the food they are serving us in the mess hall? Writing something of this nature is against my convictions because my letters should, in a way, convey to you what is of importance to us in our present situation.
Whatever happens or doesn't happen here, we will put up with it because, in our hearts, we have our thoughts directed towards the future. Where would we end up if, in our present life, we only tried to reach a state of satisfaction; even if it were only very limited! Therefore: (1) We are still far from moping. (2) As far as I am concerned, every POW camp could be a Folksfest (carnival) ground: it wouldn't make any difference, I still wouldn't want to be in it!
As you see, this subject is not pleasant and is therefore avoided

because it upsets me too much and you will get a false picture of our situation. Our letters should contain what we need to further our mutual understanding. I'd rather repeat myself, than have to force myself to write something different.
I think that I have made myself clearly understood?
Heartiest greetings,
Your Uz.'

14th February 1944 a postcard:

Lieber Vater,

The day before yesterday I received your letter of 10.11.43. I was especially pleased with this letter, because now I know that you really know how our life is over here... Now that those comrades who only six months ago were still amongst us are with you. It is, for us here, an unbelievable fairy tale! I hope that it gives you a certain amount of reassurance!
Heartiest greetings,
Your Uli'

How long had I waited for this good news? Now at last my father could write and make it clear to me that he was 'informed'. He didn't mention it directly that he had met *Hauptmann* Wilke, however, for me it was immediately clear that he had spoken with him and was now well informed of our Canadian imprisonment and all my attempts to escape.

Dated 28th February 1944, the last postcard for a long, long time:

Liebe Muttel,

(Sunday evening.) Outside it is alternately raining and snowing. This morning and afternoon I spent my time at my drawing board and now I am going to fill the evening with some greetings and will let my thoughts travel with them, but only in thought. I had better suppress my feelings today. The weather is depressing me too much. But that will, at some time, be better again and then the good German sun will shine again. Yes, we have so much patience and can stick it through.
Heartiest greetings.
Your Uli!'

My condition was getting more and more unbearable. I was starving, had lost some weight, and was most probably looking pale, more because of my bad mood than anything else. The worst thing of the whole situation was that I was feeling weaker and weaker. My strength was no longer sufficient to play hockey and more and more comrades asked what was actually wrong with me. Dr Eitze was still advising me to drop my plan, and I myself was beginning to doubt whether I would be able to continue with this slow torture of losing weight and slowly getting weaker. The question occurred to me whether the loss of physical strength also weakened the will to end up in *ein Irrenhaus* (the loony-bin). Not being able to participate in the sporting activities anymore was already unbearable but then, when I felt that having to suffer hunger also influenced my participation in the lessons, I was at a point where I almost began to question what I was doing.

Slowly Dr. Eitze showed more understanding, but he was of the opinion that the next journey of the *Gripsholm* was too soon, my condition had to be worse! I discussed with Wildermuth whether there was any sense in me missing some of the lessons? I just stayed on my bed, but then my conscience bothered me and I returned to the classroom. Of course *Hauptmann* Kahlenberger, the leader of our training course, was somewhat surprised with my inconsistency, but I couldn't really let anybody else into my secret. This continued for about two months, at which time I was suddenly, and without any warning at all, overwhelmed by the whole sorry mess. It was at about eleven in the morning and we were sitting in the large classroom, one with a long row of windows. *Hauptmann* Kahlenberger was lecturing in the mechanics of the distribution of tractive stress and pressure in a bridge. I could hardly follow, my head was empty as a result of hunger and I had a terrible headache again. I whispered to Wildermuth, "Eberhard, don't be surprised about anything anymore!" There was no other way ahead for me! For the others it was very easy, continually giving me good advice, especially that it was no longer possible to continue but I had come so far, it was time to 'turn the screw'.

I got up, screaming: *"Diese Lastverteilung halte ich nicht mehr aus! - Ich will nach Hause!"* ("I can't take any more of this distribution of forces! I want to go home!") I believe the good *Hauptmann* Kahlenberger's heart almost stopped when I suddenly got up on the tables, walked over the next row and ran towards the windows, diving straight through one of the large panes of glass. Splinters flew in all directions, but I had managed to push the pane of glass away from my eyes with the palms of my hands and my lower arms![3] Once through the window I fell about two metres and landed in a shower of splintered glass on the ground. I'd managed to get away without serious injury and immediately got to my feet and ran full tilt against the wire mesh fence, hitting it at approximately the same spot where we'd built the snow tunnel the previous winter. Just as though I was performing a heavy body check in ice hockey, I hit the fence and again began to shout; *"Ich will nach Hause! Ich will nach Hause!..."* This continued until my comrades, who had quickly followed me but by a more sensible exit route, took hold of me, tried to calm me down and carried me back into the building.

Earlier on I had thought up this spectacular event, thinking this is how a genuine victim of *Lagerkoller* 'camp disease' should look. I'd resolved that from then on nobody was going to interfere! Absolutely no one was going to change my mind, no matter if it were the commanders of the camp or the doctors, no-one! The Canadians received the report from the guards on the two adjacent towers and also from other sources. My dive out of the window had made a great impression, but then it was supposed to! Before I realised what had happened, I found myself in a small pavilion outside the actual camp and next door to the detention barracks. There I was laid on a bed and a Veteran Guard, with fixed bayonet, was positioned beside the bed eyeing me with great suspicion. This change of situation appeared to be encouraging. At least I no longer needed to act for my camp comrades.

Notes on Chapter Eighteen.

[1] The war in the east, as is now being appreciated, was total war beyond belief. The hardships, the terrible losses, and the inhuman treatment of prisoners on all sides were to be the hallmarks of this theatre. Many of the German POWs were not released until the fifties and only one in six captured at Stalingrad ever saw Germany again. In some ways I counted my blessings.

[2] Reviewing my letters today I have to say that the word 'incorrigible' springs to mind. Of course today, with the not insubstantial benefit of hindsight, we know what *Nationalsozialistische* leaders had as plans and what they already had on their conscience. Naturally I now look at many things more realistically. However, at the time when 'holding out' and loyalty to one's *Vaterland* were the orders of the day, this frame of mind gave many something to hold onto in the POW camps. This is why, again, I stress the importance of quoting, wherever possible, the way things were and not how we'd like to remember them.

[3] Later some of my fellow students apparently wondered whether I'd learnt that in a firefighter training course or similar.

CHAPTER NINETEEN

INTO A DIFFERENT WORLD

When the Canadian doctor appeared he was surprised that I had hardly any injuries. The cuts and scratches that had resulted from my first contact with glass in the back door of the sleeping quarters had healed, leaving hardly any scars. This time only the flaps of skin on my right arm had been torn open again and needed a few stitches. Other than that, miraculously, I had no really serious injuries from my spectacular dive through the window. What surprised me was that he put no questions to me that could be connected to *'mental disturbance'*. I wondered if he was a general practitioner, rather than a *'head shrinker.'*

It wasn't until later that evening that the Intelligence Officer, our *Pferdedieb* (horse thief), came to see me. It really surprised me to see him there, but before too long there were to be more surprises for me. Very reluctantly, and obviously uncomfortably, he started talking and, at first, apologised for his coming so late. He explained that not only he, but also the Commandant, had been on the telephone to Ottawa several times and that had been terribly time-consuming. 'Why Ottawa?' I wondered. 'Why are they seeking such high level advice? Was that a good sign or not?' No doubt all would be revealed in time.

He very carefully questioned me by way of a circuitous route, slowly getting closer to the heart of the matter. 'Who had been following me in the camp? Was I just running away for the fun of it? Or was somebody seriously threatening my life? Initially I really didn't understand what he was getting at, his knowledge of German was really very poor, it would have been better if the Canadian Commandant had come to question me. I said that to him quite bluntly, but our *Profi* (slang for *professional*) interpreter didn't want that and glanced around at the guard who was present, somewhat dismayed. Very quickly we came to an agreement in his very basic German, and the Veteran Guard was asked to take up position outside the door of the pavilion. That done, we soon reverted to English which suited us both better.

This helped clear things up quickly: there had been incidents in other POW camps where German soldiers had been condemned and then executed by their own comrades. Had my numerous *'desperate'* escape attempts been demanded by a Court of Honour like Oberleutnant Berndt in England?

Der zäheste unter den Ausbrecherkönigen war der Jagd-
flieger Ulrich Steinhilper. Nach vier Fluchtversuchen faßte er den gefähr-
lichen Plan, über die Irrenanstalt in die Heimat zu entkommen. Um
die Kanadier von seiner „Krankheit" zu überzeugen, sprang er aus
einem Fenster im oberen Stock des Gefangenengebäudes.

The small pavillion in which I was temporarily held.
The row of doors to the right gave access to the detention cells.

Wasn't *Kapitänleutnant* Rahmlow, the commander of U-570 also in the same camp and hadn't he also been condemned? Didn't I know this was causing Colonel Bradshaw, the Camp Commandant, a great deal of worry? It finally hit me like a bolt from the blue, I'd never thought they would make this assumption. No wonder I'd been whisked out of the camp so quickly! That's why they'd spent so much time in conversation with Ottawa! I really should have thought this possibility out myself, but I had simply concentrated on developing my *'illness'*.

After Tschramshenkow left, I was, at first, rather perplexed. The guard, who seemed rather downcast about his having been ejected whilst *Pferdedieb* and I spoke, tried to start a conversation but that was the last thing I wanted at that moment. 'How the devil can I make it clear to them that I am mentally ill?' I wondered, 'not condemned, or willing to *change sides?'* (another reason why someone might want to spend some time outside the camp). I thought this over for a very long time before I came to any firm conclusion. It was, by then, way past midnight and the guards had been changed every two hours. I had resolved that there was no other choice but to demonstrate my *Lagerkoller* (camp disease) again, to firmly underscore the

237

case that I was ill!

The guard sat beside me on a chair, his rifle with bayonet between his knees, his head dropping as he began to doze. I got up, only dressed in my pyjamas, and pushed the guard, complete with rifle and chair over backwards with some force. There was a loud crash as he hit the floor and tried to regain his feet. I stood in front of him shouting at the top of my voice, "You're not going to stop me! I want to go home! I am going home! *Ich will nach Hause!*" The guard struggled to his feet as I began trying to bend the small bars in the window of the door outwards so I could jump through. But it wasn't the window or the bars that gave way under my assault - the complete door burst out of the frame and fell down the small flight of wooden steps with me on top of it. I landed on a mixture of wood and glass splinters.

The guard was galvanised into action, now fully awake and a little frightened by this German *'madman'*, and shouted even louder than I for help. Other guards came running over to help subdue me and the Duty Sergeant had me taken to the gate guard-house. The Canadian doctor was called again to bandage my injuries; this time I'd done more of a job of it. I had contusions on the head as well as many bleeding abrasions on my head and arms; and this time the wound on my forearm, that had been sown up before, was wide open again, so wide that it couldn't simply be sown up. It required the careful use of ointments and bandages to attempt to pull the wound together. I managed in time to remind the doctor of my allergy to iodine before that added to my problems. With that I was bedded down in the guard house and slept fitfully.

Next morning a council was held between the Canadian and the German leaderships of the camp at which the doctors were also present. The decision reached was that for the time being I was to be accommodated in a special room in the German camp medical centre. However the Canadians stipulated that the big window in that room had to be covered up with a blanket and I was to be tied to the iron bed with ropes; two of my comrades were to be assigned to watch me, day and night!

I was the one who objected most to this proposed treatment and it didn't take long to convince *Oberstleutnant* Meythaler, in short bursts of conversation, that it wasn't the way ahead. He came to speak to me, eyeball to eyeball as it were, wanting to know whether my performance was genuine or if it was just an elaborate hoax. I told him the truth and we agreed that I should try, as quickly as possible, to get out of the camp and get into *ein Irrenhaus* (a loony-bin). I had already got my ticket as far as he was concerned, he didn't want that kind of *'theatre'* in the camp at all. It would be far too disturbing for the other prisoners and might, of course, give other people ideas.

Dr Eitze did not come to see me, a clear sign that he was not in agreement with my behaviour. But what difference did that make? It was becoming clearer and clearer to me that for something unusual like this, I just had to pull on my own. I was prepared to be even rougher with myself if the circumstances required it, but I promised myself I would stop at anything that was really life-threatening - if possible.

As agreed with Meythaler, the guards were only provided from the comrades who were from my room and those from the medical centre. This meant that the guards were there more to guard me against the Canadians than to prevent me from jumping out of the blanket covered window. There was a smaller ante-room in which the appointed *'guards'* slept at night as I tried to rest tied to my bunk. Vater, Theopold, Wildermuth and Döring, from the room, and Strehl and Büsgen from the medical centre all took their turns, uncomplaining, on this guard duty.

It was quite a commitment of personnel and after two days, with still no signs of a transfer to a mental clinic, I questioned the German doctor on duty. He was one from the *DAK (Deutsche Afrika Korps)* and probably because of their participation in the tough desert war he was more down to earth. "What must I do to finally get out of this camp?" I asked, "Isn't it a bloody waste of time for everybody concerned? The extra room, the blanket covered window and the continuous guarding!" He agreed and quick as a flash just said, "Attack the doctor! The next time the Canadian doctor visits, physically assault him. You'll see," he said, "you go for him and it'll all go *'ruck-zuck!* (wham-bam!)"

I was both stunned by this simplicity and appalled at the prospect. Why had I never thought of that? Really, I had *carte blanche* to do what I wanted. Once I had embarked upon this course they couldn't put me in the punishment block any more. They would have to react differently, but the prospect of assaulting someone who seemed genuinely concerned for my well-being was difficult to address.

Usually the Canadian camp doctor didn't visit the camp medical centre every day; but now I was a patient he seemed to feel obliged to visit daily. Every day he appeared; and every day he had more flimsy questions; and every day Tschramchenkow translated those questions and my answers terribly. The new action was planned for the next day. As soon as the door to my ante-room was opened I would try to *'go for the throat'*. To prevent actual harm coming to the doctor, but to keep up appearances, it would fall to my guards, Wildermuth and Döring - the two with the strongest nerves -

to try and hold me back. So that the grappling looked genuine, Döring, the larger of my two guards, was to give me a good blow on my left eye so that I would arrive at the Mental Hospital with a black eye. This, when combined with my existing cuts and scars, would add authenticity to my appearance. What surprised me most was that he was immediately prepared to do this for me when I asked. He volunteered! It was time for the play-acting to end!

I remember the date and time precisely: it was 15th March 1944 at eleven o'clock. The door to my room opened and, as if it had been rehearsed, the first person to enter was the Canadian doctor - wearing a captain's uniform - it couldn't have been more perfect. With a diabolical scream I leapt at him with outstretched arms, my hands clawing for his neck, screaming insanely, *"Ich weiß was Sie wollen, Sie wollen mich in den Arrest bringen... Sie wollen mich in den Keller bringen... sie wollen mich sieben Meter unter den Boden bringen... sieben Meter und noch viel tiefer... Sie wollen mich nicht einsperren... Sie wollen mich umbringen!..."* ("I know what you want, you want to take me to the detention barracks... You want to take me to the cellar... You want to get me seven metres down under the ground... seven metres and a lot deeper... You don't want to lock me up... You want to kill me!...") I kept up this avalanche of hysteria for much longer but there is little profit in recording it all. Suffice to say I had learnt it well for this incident and would use it for other delicate situations, sometimes louder, sometimes quieter.

The reaction would have won praise in a theatre. Naturally the doctor was shocked, but reacted quickly, like he was a boxer, swaying back from the waist so my initial assault fell short of target. But then came the punishment! Wildermuth, also a boxer, hit me on the run and threw me to the ground. Our German doctor was right with him and helped bear me down. Döring stepped in right on cue and aimed a very precise punch, only the one, at my left eyebrow. I felt the impact, but no real pain and thought, 'Thank you, Peter, that's going to be visible for quite some time!' Apparently stunned by the blow I was tied to the bed again, I'd only been untied for the visit. All the *'specialists'*, the doctors and Tschramchenkow, retreated to the ante-room and I remained with my guards, Döring and Wildermuth. As the door was hastily closed we could hardly suppress our laughter. It couldn't have been better for a film.

After a short discussion outside, Dr Gress returned and made it clear to me my transfer would take place that day. He said the Canadian doctor was actually glad there was no other choice. How and exactly when I was to be moved, whether by rail or in an ambulance, hadn't been decided, but most probably it would be that afternoon. Was I glad to hear it and, to be perfectly honest, so were my room mates. The extra guard duty had been a chore, but they'd done it without complaint for my sake and I was grateful. Soon after the decision had been announced Dr Eitze appeared, asking if he could have a confidential chat with me, just the two of us. There were no Canadians in sight so it was agreed and he came to sit with me.

He thought for a while and spoke to me, obviously choosing his words carefully. "My dear Steinhilper, I actually like you quite a lot," he began, "but you don't seem to be aware of what you are now letting yourself in for. As well as I know you, I'm sure you're not going to give up, either you're going to get home or you'll really go bats!" Again he thought for a moment then looked at me really seriously. "Promise me," he asked, "promise me that you're not going to do this for more than six weeks at the most, or better just four weeks. Within this time the *Gripsholm* should be sailing again. Don't do it longer. You can always start over again, you're now already on the right track and nobody will easily get you off it."

Initially the conversation was embarrassing, but then I was able to explain why I had staged the events in the way I had. He didn't take it too seriously, and quickly gave me some advice in the short time that was left. Whilst we were still in conversation it was confirmed I would be leaving the camp that same afternoon. I was to be accompanied by a Canadian doctor, a psychiatrist, and an armed sergeant. The Germans were instructed to tell me that before leaving and while *en route*, I would be given sedative injections.

Dr Eitze was, in the short time that was left, able to tell me that psychiatric disorders were not his field of medicine but that he'd naturally had some instruction and passing experience. He'd thought it over and decided my *'illness'* would most probably best fit into the category of manic-depressive. To help this diagnosis he first advised me that I should continue to lose weight for as long as I could bear to refuse food. My already erratic eating habits should also, for proper effect, be interrupted with sudden, apparently irrational, refusals to eat certain items or certain colours of vegetables. It would also fit the diagnosis, he said, if one day I would be in high spirits, and then suddenly very low and depressed. He also reminded me of what had been on my mind all along. "With five escapes behind you, these people are going to want a lot of convincing. Maybe this will need very special efforts from you," he suggested. "What do you mean?" I asked. He looked at me gravely. "You saw how effective your assault of the doctor was this morning! Wherever you land up prepare the same difficulties for the personnel there once in a while. Or, alternatively, when your mental and physical condition allows it, stage a fit of real raving madness. From what I heard about this morning," he joked, "there's not much more left for you to learn!"

Encouragingly for me, he added that hardly any mental illnesses have the same symptoms and sequence of development. The diagnosis is, therefore, very difficult, even for a specialist. Again and again he repeated his warning, "Don't do it for longer than four weeks, and if the *Gripsholm* sails without you, see to it you get back to this camp." I thanked him for his advice, I could see it ran against the grain for him to advise me to stage further attacks on personnel, it was inevitable that people would be hurt and, naturally, he couldn't condone that; I was grateful for his help. Although he'd been less than enthusiastic about my idea in the beginning he'd come to recognise that I was determined and so had given what support he could. I was to rue the day I didn't heed his warning.

Very soon afterwards a young Canadian military psychiatrist from outside the camp arrived with his sergeant. The doctor was in uniform and his sergeant was clearly a front line soldier, not one of the older Veteran Guards, and looked like he'd been specially selected for the task. One look at him told me there was nothing but endless pain in store for me if I were to try any *'funny business'* with him. In the presence of Dr Eitze I was given the first injection and felt its effect slowly and insidiously creep into my brain. I couldn't recall much of the journey because the whole time I remained in the half dream state. I was aware that we'd driven to the station in Gravenhurst and, after that, when we had changed trains in Toronto, then travelled onward in a reserved compartment. Every now and then the psychiatrist leafed through a green folder. I do remember thinking it probably contained a catalogue of my sins! Every now and then the doctor exchanged a few words with the sergeant; he mentioned the five attempts to escape and even the demolition of my cell, they certainly had logged every detail! It hadn't occurred to me that the protest *'riot'* in the my cell would also be indicative of a violent and unpredictable nature. Smiling to myself in the woolly effects of the sedative I watched the countryside flash by, any further coherent thought was impossible.

Before we changed trains in Toronto, I imagine for safety's sake, I was given an extra injection, the effects of which lasted until we arrived. I remember, very vaguely, being driven up to the front of a brick building sometime after nightfall. The car stopped at the front steps and I discovered later I had arrived at the Westminster Hospital in London, Ontario. Next morning I woke up in a small room and was addressed in German. At first this made me very suspicious, I hadn't during the whole course of my *'illness'* spoken German to anyone other than our German doctors. The loss of my knowledge of English was something I had planned for the future and

The main building of the hospital, very little changed from the day I arrived.

The white door was the direct access into C Ward.

apparently, as one of the symptoms, it fitted the prognosis anyway. Soon the voice struck a chord in my still fuggy mind and I calmed down. It was *Oberleutnant* Weigel, asking if I remembered him from Bowmanville, and indeed I did. Almost whispering, he told me how he had tried to take his life. All an *'act'*, he confided, just like the *'serious depressions'* that had followed. *'For his own protection,'* he had been brought to the hospital and had, apparently, been waiting for months for his transfer. 'Months!' That was a jolt for me but as he went on, absolutely certain that it would take place, he virtually radiated a most infectious confidence which offset the initial shock of having to think about months of waiting. My initial concern was for security and thought he was being a bit too free with his conversation, what if the room was bugged? "Are you sure these walls don't have ears?" I asked. "No, Steinhilper, things aren't that delicate any more. Once you've reached this place you just have to watch they don't put you back in the camp. After that they have no other choice, they can't do anything other than transfer you home."

After these secret conversations, it soon became apparent that it wouldn't be anything like as simple as that. A nurse called Jenny was responsible for distributing the medicine, bed linen and clothing, also for the administration and had nominated Weigel as official interpreter. As his first task in his new role he had to explain to me that I had to give up my uniform and all my private belongings, especially my shaving kit. Instead, I was to wear institution clothing, the same as Weigel was already wearing. I would be issued, I was told, with a white night-gown and underwear and, after that, I would be taken to Ward C. This was situated one floor lower down and I was told I was going there because I was, compared with other Germans there, marked as a *'bad boy,'* (*gewalttätig* - outrageous - was the word Weigel translated for me, although I understood the English well enough). While saying this she, Nurse Jenny, was thumbing through the green folder which had apparently been given to her for inspection. It wasn't until later that I found out that *'bad boy'* was a special classification there.

In the C ward, I was told, they would first spend quite some time just observing me and evaluating my case. This was, apparently, so that they could reach an accurate diagnosis and then decide what was going to happen to me. Even for Weigel, who claimed to know all the methods in use there, this news was not very encouraging. After this flood of information we were left alone again for a short while and I asked him, should he be transferred before me, if he could, perhaps, inform my parents of my circumstances. They would, I explained, be worried when all of a sudden, no more post was coming from me. Weigel not only promised this, he was good for his word (see the section at the end of this chapter).

Immediately after this last chat the young psychiatrist, who had accompanied me the day before, appeared. This time his uniform was covered by a white doctor's coat and in the company of an orderly (that's what I learned the 'keepers' were called) he took me to the next floor using the lift. The orderly, in his clean white suit, was a rather sobering sight, just another new thing to get used to. When we reached the lower floor, we had to wait outside the lift door for a few minutes for the Director of the hospital, it gave me a chance to take a look around. The first impression was dreadful. There were people swarming around everywhere, all in blue clothing, and so many of them! They all looked exactly alike. All dressed in what we would have called *'blauen Anton'* (blue Anton - coarse blue material, bib and brace working trousers - denims). Under the braces they all wore grey work shirts with a blue jacket over that. There were so many and they all looked alike, it was an unnerving sight. The way they moved around, like bees or wood ants, they just ebbed and flowed like the tide. Some stood along the walls in the corridors, some stood leaning against bunk-beds, some had their hands folded, others were kind of dry-washing them in a ceaseless motion and others were gesticulating wildly. Mouths chattering, giggling, occasionally shouting and others stolidly dumb. One thing was common to all of them I could see, their eyes were empty, expressionless. I had never seen anything like it nor would I have believed it existed unless I'd seen it myself. Not only old people, but many young faces were amongst them too. 'What sort of adventure had I now committed myself to,' I wondered?

Before the Director came a young and very good looking nurse came and led us through a very heavy door. This iron door closed immediately behind us with a solid thump which chilled my soul; something inside me said this was a prison from which there would be no escape. A glance at the inside of the door revealed no facia to blend in with the decor, but a solid functional armoured door. We were in C Ward, the department for 'bad boys', we had reached the place for the dangerous ones. Again later, I found out that all unclassified newcomers were brought into this ward upon arrival. Before I could look around any more Dr Rogier arrived. He was introduced to my accompanying doctor as the Director, the Chief of the Sanatorium, and they immediately got into a lively conversation. Naturally interested, but trying to feign indifference, I understood the conversation very well. My companion from yesterday wanted to give some short explanations concerning the green folder, after which he then wanted to say goodbye. Dr Rogier nodded animatedly at the explanations and added that he had further Germans in custody there. That, he said, was nothing to do with me, however. I would not come into contact with them. I was, he said with particular emphasis, a *'special case.'* That was actually directed towards the nurses and the orderlies, three had already gathered around me and nodded their understanding of his comment.

I had to laugh inwardly, I'd already been in contact with one German, Weigel, but none of them was going to tell Dr Rogier that. 'Here was a man,' I thought, 'who exerts total control over his staff, or at least thinks he does.' This was his realm and he didn't brook strangers intruding, he couldn't say goodbye fast enough to the doctor who had brought me. Then he turned to me and spoke in English. When I didn't apparently understand he easily switched to extremely good German, another surprise. "*Hauptmann* Steinhilper, you are now in a mental hospital; you will not be treated here; you will only be kept here until we know what is going to happen with you! I speak some German, during the last war I was in a German prisoner of war camp in Silesia, I believe you call it *Schlesien*." So there was my next surprise, the Director was an ex-soldier and POW. What else would be revealed I wondered?

Letters from Oberleutnant Weigal and others:

Postmarked *Jagdfliegerheim Bad Wiessee*, 20.6.44 to my father:

(n.b. *Jagdfliegerheim* - Fighter pilot's convalescence home).

Bad Wiessee, 19 June 1944

Dear Mr Steinhilper!

I am writing to you today on request of your son with whom I was, just recently, in Canada. All is well with him and now he wants to return home, if possible with the next exchange. In advance I would like to ask you to read this letter first for yourself, and then, with appropriate changes, inform your wife.

I myself was part of an exchange in May. I managed to cheat my way through after an attempted suicide and depression. I played this role for four months and spent the time in a mental hospital. It stands to reason that, beyond yourself, Mr Steinhilper, nobody else should get to know of these matters. I oblige you to make no mention of this to anyone and also that my name not be mentioned in any letters. Absolutely nothing! Also, if you should be in contact with the families of other prisoners, make no mention of my name. This is most important for the well being of your son as you will read in the following.

Earlier on I was together with your son in Camp 30 and then met him again in March in that mental hospital. In the meantime he had been in a different camp. Your son has now decided to play the role of someone with a nervous illness, which he is doing very well. His aim is to get home with the next exchange. In the mental hospital we helped each other and talked a lot about the whole affair. I had started much earlier and have now been exchanged. Your son didn't manage to get included in this exchange but will most probably be included in the next one. On the whole, his condition is actually quite good and there is no need for you to worry. There will be no after-effects to be worried about. I carried it through for a little more than four months and have suffered no lasting harm.

For you it is now going to be a little difficult because there will be no post coming from your son. Writing letters to you doesn't fit his illness. You will have to put up with that and look forward to the day when your son can soon return home, that is with the next exchange. It is obvious that in letters to your son nothing whatsoever of these affairs be mentioned. You must write exactly the same way as you had been writing to him in the past and nothing else. Of course you can, in your letters, express your concern over the fact that you are not hearing from him, but your concern has only to be pretended, because you really do not need to be concerned. Your son knows very well that I have informed you and through this he knows that your concerns are not genuine.

It would be advisable that you contact the Red Cross and inquire about the well being of your son because you haven't been hearing from him. Also you should contact the Oberkommando der Wehrmacht (O.K.W.) Prisoner of War section as well. However, you must remember nobody other than you and I know of the true circumstances and nobody needs to know more so as not to endanger your son's venture.

All I reported to O.K.W. was that your son is seriously ill and we have to leave them in this belief. You know that your son is ill and you are concerned. Ask about his health and similar but don't feel upset over the answers you will be getting because you know it's not genuine, it's only pretence! Should you ever receive a letter from your son, then don't be upset, the letter will be written as if it came from a mentally ill person.

Mr Steinhilper, other than your wife you shouldn't inform ANYBODY else about these matters. Talk about it as if everything were in order and you were receiving regular letters from your son as in the past. It may not help but you must, if you want your son home soon, play the game. Anything else is completely out of the question. That's what your son is expecting from you and you must not let him down. There is no sense in you trying to get him to change his mind. First of all it would bring absolutely no results and beyond that your son would never forgive his parents and would feel as if he had been betrayed. He is playing this role so that he can get home and that you can really look forward to, irrespective of the terrible time that you now have to experience together with your son.

When the next exchange can be expected, I do not know, negotiations are continuously going on. I just want to repeat: other than you and your wife, nobody else needs to know of these matters, no relatives or friends - nobody. That's what your son is expecting - you have to act as if everything was in order. Only your inquiries to the Red Cross and the O.K.W. should reflect your great concern about the whereabouts of your son, but only because you haven't heard from him and you KNOW he his ill with his nerves. However, I repeat, never mention my name! Continue to write to your son as in the past, HOWEVER, no mention or references to his condition. You can express your concern in your letters but never, ever, mention the exchange of soldiers or anything similar. Your son knows perfectly well that I will inform you and therefore you don't need to write about that or make any mention of it.

Make absolutely no mention of me, theoretically I am still seriously ill. Should the Canadians over there read my name in the course of their censoring, they'd know perfectly well I was only pretending, and this would then worsen the situation for your son and everyone else.

Presently I am experiencing four weeks holiday here in the Jagdfliegerheim in Wiessee and am having a good time. Mr Steinhilper, I will always be willing to assist you wherever and whenever I can and will be willing to answer all questions that might arise. Now don't write to your son immediately, rather think it all over. I will be here until 12th July. Oberleutnant Weigel, Jagdfliegerheim Bad Wiessee - Tegernsee (136). My home address is: Stettin, Werderstrasse 7. In that I convey the heartiest greetings from your son to you and your spouse. I remain, with best wishes,

Your Kurt Heinz Weigel.

What comradeship! The amount of sympathetic understanding that this letter contains is unbelievable. Apparently my parents must have followed the instructions contained in Weigel's letter precisely. Proof for this was in a reply from the *Deutschen Rotes Kreuz* (German Red Cross) dated 5.7.44:

File number S.W.II v. Li/Wi
Subject Hauptmann Ulrich Steinhilper
Reference Your letter of 24.6.44.

We are sorry to say that the postal connection with the prisoners of war in Canada is very irregular. Ignoring the fact that there are times, every now and then, when absolutely no post comes from Canada, it can also happen that some families are receiving post on a very regular basis and others hear absolutely nothing from the prisoners. What causes these fluctuations is difficult to say.

Nevertheless the German Red Cross sees no cause for serious concern regarding your family member because many other relatives of prisoners of war complain of having heard nothing from Canada.

The German Red Cross, together with the Oberkommando der Wehrmacht, is continually working on an improvement of the post connection.

Heil Hitler!

Signed: The Special Representative.

A further answer from the Red Cross Headquarters Staff:

Berlin SW 61,
5.9.1944
File Number: SW II v. Li/Bck
Subject: Hauptmann Ulrich Steinhilper, Service No. 18310,
Camp 20, Canada.
Reference: Letter this Office dated 4.7.44.

Mrs Paula Steinhilper,
Heutingsheim, County Ludwigsburg/Wttbg.

To the request submitted on 4.7.44 to the International Committee of the Red Cross at Geneva, concerning the whereabouts of your son, the reply was received to-day.

The International Committee informs you that your son is suffering from depression but is, however, in good physical health and is being appropriately treated.

Heil Hitler! Signed: The Special Representative.

The good comrade Oberleutnant Weigel even wrote two more letters to my father:

Wiessee, 4.7.44

Dear Mr Steinhilper!

I am sorry that I was not able to inform you in time because I spent a few days in the mountains. How did you enjoy Tetzlacht's visit? I am very concerned that he most probably told you a lot of unnecessary nonsense.

That man, irrespective of what he did in order to be exchanged, is far from being normal and I did not regard him as being a very useful person.*

It was a pity that during your short stop at Munich recently you couldn't take a short diversion down here. I will be here until and including 9.7., in case an opportunity should come up again. According to reports from Berlin I will most probably be back in south Germany, giving us the chance to arrange a meeting sometime in the future.

I ask you to give my kindest regards to your wife.

With best greetings,

your Weigel.

Last letter from Weigel:

Kitzingen, 3.9.44

Dear Mr Steinhilper!

Sorry that our meeting at that time was not possible. I am now in the greater area of Stuttgart, however only for a few days. It is yet still possible, that I will stay close. As soon as I know precisely, I will let you know. Could you please let me know if and what kind of news you have received from your son. I have heard that a further exchange has been planned for the very near future and hope for the best. Most probably by way of Sweden this time.

With best greetings,

your Weigel.

As was discovered later, there had been a previous exchange that had taken place before September 1944, in fact in May. Prior to that time it was not a lack of good will on either side that held up the exchanges being organised. It was that the political climate had not been *'ripe'* to begin the exchanges. After all, the basic premise of these exchanges was just plain humanity - and what have politics or politicians ever had to do with that?[1]

A further letter that reached my parents also referred to the earlier exchange that took place in May of 1944. *Oberleutnant* Schnabel, whose report on Gravenhurst I had already quoted earlier, wrote to my parents:

Zwickau, 3.8.44

Dear Family Steinhilper,

Because of illness, I was exchanged from a Canadian prisoner of war camp in May of this year, and am now here to receive treatment.

For a long time and up to 13th March 1944 I was in Camp 20. On behalf of your son, Hauptmann Ulrich Steinhilper, and the Camp Commander of Camp 20, Oberstleutnant Meythaler, I have the following good news for you: your son is in the best of health and is mentally in as good condition as in the past. He is only trying to reach home as soon as possible by PRETENDING that he has a mental illness. This is, of course, a very difficult operation, but as previous cases have proved, not impossible. I do not want to give you unnecessary hopes, because really nobody knows when the next exchange of sick and injured prisoners of war can be arranged. However it is the only possible way to get home from Canada before the war is over.

This matter has now been going on since March 1944, shortly before I left the camp. Since this time you have most probably been receiving unfavourable news from your son. This is not the truth! This was all part of his plan and will continue for quite a while to come. I was able to convince myself of the completely healthy condition of your son, because from September 1943 to March 1944 I sat beside him in the Technical Work Group and worked together with him every day.

I would be pleased to answer any questions that you might have, as far as I am in a position to do so.

With the German greeting,
I greet you,
your Heïnz Schnabel.

Later, because the first months after the war overshadowed everything, I never really found much time to talk to my parents about this period, what thoughts they'd had at that time when they must have been exposed to quite confusing and contradicting sources of information. First of all there had come the weird stylistic change in my letters (because of the code), then the news and request to support my escape which they received through Wilke and then the varying reports of my sudden illness through Weigel, Tetzlacht and Schnabel.

I never really discovered what happened to Schnabel after his return to Germany. In the same exchange group was our first Camp Commander at Camp W, *Oberstleutnant* Hasso von Wedel, *der letzte Ritter*. His badly shot up leg got worse and worse as the years passed in the Canadian camps. As with so many of them I never saw either of them again. I was told von Wedel might have fallen in the final fights for Berlin in 1945 and that wouldn't have surprised me at all, he would have stood his ground.

Getting back to Germany via the exchanges did not ensure that fate would write good news into people's 'books of life.' *Austausch-Kamerad* (exchange comrade) *Hauptmann* Weigel was killed in 1945. *Oberleutnant* Buhr of Soltau, was also exchanged out of Gravenhurst after he had tortured himself over a long period of time and then pretended to be deaf. He was repatriated, but was murdered by foreign labourers towards the end of the war. There are so many others with whom I lost contact and do not know their fates.

Hauptmann Weigel - It was not until 1988, that I found out what had happened to Kurt-Heinz Weigel. The photograph overleaf was taken in 1943 at the airfield at Tailfingen in County Böblingen. From this photo it was clear that Kurt Weigel had been assigned to the night fighters. From this I researched the War Diary of NJG 6 (Night Fighter Wing 6): The entry dated 5.3.45 reads:

'Approximately 600 combat planes flew past heading for Chemnitz. The IV. Group was employed from Kitzingen and Gerolshofen.

Successes: None.

Losses: At approximately 21.58 a Ju 88 of the VI.Group, was destroyed after having touched ground: Hauptmann Weigel, Feldwebel Milord, Feldwebel Antoni, Unteroffizier Graf, all dead.

So was to end was the life of a loyal comrade.

Tailfingen Sept/Oct 1944: NJG 6. Left to right: Ltn. Swoboda, Hptm. Böhner, Hptm Weigal, Ltn. Artus.

Notes on Chapter Nineteen

[1] (1) I didn't know Mr Tetzlacht, he must also have been an inmate in the Westminster Hospital before he was exchanged, but before I got there.

(2) At this time my father was serving with the *Feldjägern* (Military Police) and was mostly on railway patrols accompanying trains.

CHAPTER TWENTY

PITIFUL PEOPLE

After the introduction by Dr Rogier and the explanations in German, the pretty nurse began to remove the bandages on my right arm. It looked terrible: there was pus everywhere and it was so inflamed that the positions of the stitches could only be guessed. Dr Rogier gave some instructions and disappeared.

The young lady in the smart white nurse's uniform diligently took care of my wounds. Right from the beginning she called me 'Steenie' and seemed to have a deep understanding and a real interest in my fate. It was heart-warming to have someone who seemed to care, but it was a double edged sword, it also played havoc with my conscience. First of all she arranged that I was issued with pyjamas, the sleeves of the night gowns were so tight they couldn't be easily fitted over the new bandages. For this I was taken into the orderlies' *Glaskasten* (glass cage), their office, and while I changed clothing they looked at my body. That certainly evoked a reaction: "Look at him!" they said, "That's a real trained Nazi if ever I saw one. Look at his muscles! If he ever goes wild we're in trouble!" they said, full of concern. Although I had been abusing my body and not exercising for some time I was still young and the muscle tone acquired from boxing and ice hockey had not completely gone. I would have liked to have debated the use of the word *Nazi*, but it was hardly the time or place.

During all this I sat on the floor looking aggressive and unapproachable and beside me, on her knees, was this young and pretty girl tending to my wounds. As she worked she was continually whispering to herself about my bad injuries, that I was so far away from home, and that I was certainly homesick. One good thing with the whole treatment so far was that I hadn't seen any of the dreaded iodine. I was acutely allergic to this common antiseptic and there must have been a note to this effect in my papers. The other orderlies called my happy little nurse 'Sunny' when Dr Rogier wasn't around and when Chief Nurse Victoria wasn't casting her shadow over the ward. It was immediately apparent that they too enjoyed her company, she really was a ray of sunshine in that lightless place.

I was to have more contact with Nurse Victoria later, but in the meantime, I overheard Chief Orderly Opel, when he was instructing a young colleague, mention Victoria: "She's very *'imperial'*," he said, "and you won't get any cooperation from her *at all!*" He emphasized *'at all'* by sarcastically mimicking very round and obvious English, what I imagine he thought was *'King's English.'* Indicating, I suppose, that Chief Nurse Victoria was very right and proper. *'Cooperation'*, I was later to discover, meant a cover-up among the staff to keep something from the attention of Dr Rogier.

Having finished tending my cuts and suppurating wound, Sunny left and the realities of life began for me. While she was still bandaging me, I'd had a look around. I was in a long room, devoid of decoration. On the one side was a long row of barred windows and on the other side about six grey cell doors. At the head of the room was a small, fully glazed, nursing station, suitable for two orderlies - their *Glaskasten*; a round-the-clock vigil was mounted there. Opposite the cells were four beds, side by side, then there were two recesses in the wall with single beds in them, separated by hip-high walls, painted in a light green.

When entering the room I had seen that one of the beds was empty and I wanted to head for it. But then one of the orderlies held me tight by the arm and before I realised what was happening he'd opened one of the cells and I was inside with the door banging shut behind me. On the floor lay a sort of mattress with a leather-like plastic covering, but other than that... nothing. The door opened again quickly and a few oranges were rolled into the cell. I was hungry and thirsty, I'd had nothing to eat since we'd left the camp, but wasn't that perhaps a trick? "They wanted to observe me!" that's what they'd said. For this I saw the little peep-hole in the cell door, small and round like an eye itself, set in the middle of a small hatch that could be opened to hand things into the cell.

Before reaching for the oranges, I looked around. Bare walls! Why was it we'd always joked about padded cells, *Gummizellen* (rubber rooms)? There I was, surrounded by stone-hard concrete against which I could, if I'd really wanted to, beat my skull to pulp. At the back of the cell, opposite the door and unreachable from the floor, was a window with iron bars through which some light filtered. I estimated it would be at ground level on the outside. Otherwise nothing - absolutely nothing! I don't know what I'd expected, but here was the stark reality.

I noticed that the peep-hole was occupied, again and again, by the curious. 'Let them look,' I thought. I started to peel the first orange and eat its contents while I tore the peel into little pieces and then, playing like a small child, laid the pieces out on the cold tiled floor in the form of letters. Then I took the next one, peeled it only half-way because I was so thirsty and then sucked the juice out. With this I felt I had instinctively reacted quite well.

Later on I was to learn that those patients who were suffering worse trauma when being brought to this place completely forgot their upbringing, their good manners, and they would eat the oranges like apples, with peel and all. That, I was to learn, was the purpose of C Ward: the cases were taken there 'fresh', still in shock and at a good stage to be observed. Many of them had, as a result of their mental derangement, completely lost any vestige of civilised behaviour and acted like animals.

Why, on the first day, no midday meal was served I never found out, but otherwise they took good care of me. They came into my cell, led me to the toilet and allowed me to drink water there. It was a normal WC, two cubicals without doors where I could relieve myself while an orderly watched. In the ante-room there was an open shower and a wash-basin, but I didn't think too much voluntary hygiene would fit my case so I just obediently went with the orderlies.

After a boring afternoon, with the only outlook the limited view through the peep-hole, I waited for a meal. In the evening a portion of stew came which I, being ravenously hungry, gobbled down. Only wearing my pyjamas, not even with the small comfort of a blanket, I settled down on the mattress. I couldn't sleep and thought of what Weigel had told me. What use was that to me? I was a *'bad boy,'* the worst category possible in that place! Would there ever be an exchange of someone like me? Was there be a better way of being included in an exchange? After what seemed an eternity I must have fallen asleep, waking early the next morning.

During my nocturnal deliberations I planned to bring some 'life' into these premises! If I had learned one thing it was that the assault on the Canadian doctor had certainly acted as a catalyst in the progress of my case. Alone in that cell, in the dark of night, I had come to the inevitable conclusion that things needed speeding up again. The cell doors weren't sound proof and I could hear the breakfast trays were being brought to the cell doors on a trolley. One by one they were being given to the inmates and the doors secured again. I heard the bolt slam home on the cell next to mine and then the short movement of the trolley and the rattle of a tray. I was ready. The door opened a little and I saw an orderly new to me, he wore spectacles high on his nose and, as if he were a waiter, he was balancing a tray at shoulder height. He tried to put the tray down through the barely open door, wanting to reach it through the gap and place it on the floor. I exploded in my loudest-parade ground German, *"Ich will nicht in den Arrest... ich will nicht eingesperrt sein... ich will raus!"* ("I don't want to be in detention... I don't want to be locked up...I want to be freed!") With *'raus!'* as my action word I pushed the tray upwards into his face... He was overwhelmed, staggering backwards as his glasses disintegrated. I hadn't dared expect what came next.

The orderly made it to a small button on the wall beside the cell door. I had pushed my way out of my cell but only to hear several alarm bells were ringing. I was bemused for a moment and the orderly was on me before I knew what was happening, my arms painfully locked with grips which demonstrated his good training. I was virtually immobilised before I realised what had happened and surrounded by numerous white-clad figures. One of them pulled my arm upwards behind my back, causing me to bow my body backwards while another began to drive his elbow into my taught stomach. Even my well trained muscles couldn't help me as blow after blow was driven into my abdomen. I wanted to stage a really raging fit and there was no room to show any kind of pain.

In those terrible moments I remember thinking, 'They're going to beat me to death!' and that brought the strength of fear to me and I was able to carry on. With every ounce of their strength they beat me brutally! All manner of blows drove painfully into my stomach, my back, my neck and my kidneys. From all sides the storm of violence swept over me as I jerked convulsively from the terrible impacts. Inside my head I was yelling, 'Stop it... stop it, for God's sake stop it!' but outwardly I gave no indication. Not a word passed my lips. I was resolved that if they killed me, then that's how it would be! Finally it stopped.

I was on the ground. Had I fallen to the ground, or had they beaten me down? I didn't know or really care, I just hurt so badly. An exceptionally burly orderly kept trampling me with his big feet as I lay on the ground for quite a while. From somewhere far away beyond the awful hurting I could hear his voice, "There you have it you bastard! You damned Nazi!" Only half conscious they threw me onto a metal cot that had been quickly pushed into the cell. It just had the metal springing but no mattress and I lay on this as they shackled me hand and foot. After a while I began to regain full consciousness and tried to move a bit. It was agony. As far as I could tell they'd done a very professional job on me. They'd hit about everything that would cause me the maximum pain, but they hadn't caused any real physical injuries at all.

While I remained in C Ward I saw many other cases brought in and saw this kind of treatment, 'education' as the orderlies called it, meted out by them. Aversion therapy, I suppose they'd call it now. I didn't know to what extent the doctors condoned this kind of treatment but they certainly knew about it, as will be illustrated later. It became clearer and clearer that this kind of severe beating was a result of the orderlies being afraid themselves. It was their primitive way of teaching new patients that violence against them would be met with severe punishment. Destroying my orderlies' spectacles was, in this respect, a very serious misdeed and led to brutal reprisals as my aching body could attest. I was quick to appreciate that the arrangements in C Ward were structured to deal with the most violent of patients effectively. Every time the alarm bells sounded, the door to the neighbouring Lower B Ward would open immediately and the orderlies on duty there instantly came to the assistance of their colleagues in C ward.

After this experience I'd had enough of rampaging, the orderlies' 'education' had certainly decided me on that. Together with the midday tray came Sunny and with her some sympathy and light. She was clearly fully briefed on my case and tried to talk me out of my plans. "You must stop fighting, Steenie," she suggested, "You're a good looking boy and shouldn't behave like that..." I listened as she talked and it became clear why she'd come. My right arm had obviously been bleeding again and the blood had soaked through the bandages; I hadn't really noticed. With infinite care she removed the bandages; I couldn't look at it any longer. As a result of my fight, the complete suture had been torn apart and the whole flap of skin had been pushed aside, revealing a really horrible mess below it. Sunny decided that stitching it up again was out of question so, as well as she could, she replaced the flap of skin in the right position, applied some ointment, and bandaged me up again. "And now Steenie," she said, her smile touching my heavy heart, "you're to be a very good boy." With that she left and the cell darkened again. What a pity I couldn't tell her why I was doing all of this, why I *had* to do it.

The following night was dreadful. I can hardly imagine how I managed to stick it out. How could one kill time, chained to an unyielding steel bed and without even anyone to talk to. The only prospect being more self-starvation, losing more weight, staging more fits, and then being beaten up again. It would have been so easy to have given in then, in the dark loneliness of that terrible place. But I stuck it out. I kept myself busy, at first, with other 'stupid' ideas I'd had. One of them was that every morning, after breakfast, I wiped my porridge bowl clean with my pyjama jacket. When my beard became too stubbly, I decided to use my porridge as a shaving cream and asked if I could have a shave. After that I was allowed to shave, but under close supervision, twice a week. This brought me the name *'Master Shaver'* with which they teased me for several weeks. Another one of my *crazy* ideas was to hold my breakfast bread roll against my ear, to find out if it ticked. This gave the orderlies a good laugh, but all of these incidents added to the fact that I was soon regarded as being *'genuine'*.

Except for my raging fits, which I staged every few weeks, sometimes in the daytime, sometimes at night, life, incredibly, was becoming routine. In the course of these episodes of violence I always took great care that no more spectacles were broken. The beatings I received in return were still hard enough, but nowhere near as tough as the first. As time went on, I learnt that it was better to grumble at beds, doors or windows and attack them if need be. The orderlies could then hold me back before I really got violent and nobody got hurt. One day, I don't know how long after I'd arrived in C Ward, Dr Rogier came and, in my presence, gave the orderlies new instructions in English. The International Red Cross, he said, had issued new instructions. Accordingly, the POWs were no longer to receive *'education'* but from then on they were to be given sedative injections.

Whether that was healthier or not I didn't know, but in any case it was a good deal more pleasant for me. After a raging fit they hardly beat me, they only twisted my arm up my back and held me in the *Schwitzkasten* (sweatbox) until a nurse with the injection came. And that was it - usually after about twelve hours I awoke, lying on my leather mattress in my cell, wondering what had happened. At first I was surprised that while I was unconscious they fitted a stout leather strap around my waist which had two loops in it to hold my wrists. I always woke up manacled in this manner and I wondered why they did it if I was unconscious. In time I realised it was for my own safety, not theirs.

Life went on and every Thursday we had a shower, under strict supervision, and we even got to use the soap. At the same time we were issued a complete set of freshly washed clothes, including pyjamas. We were weighed at the same time and our weight was recorded neatly on a list, week after week. From that I could follow that I was losing weight quite steadily. Every morning and afternoon a nurse came with a white tray, on which there was always the same medicine for the long term customers: a small glass filled with a light purple-coloured liquid (bromide). "Your cocktail," she would call it. At first I tried to do the same as Ray, Harry and Kean, the other long term customers, not to swallow it, but to spit it out as soon as the nurse turned her back. Soon, however, I noticed that if I did take it the effects were good, I suffered less hunger and could sleep better.

The long term customers names were those I learned first. Then gradually, during periods where I was quieter, I was allowed to join them, lying on one of the beds in the area opposite the cells. There were five of them altogether: first there was Ray, who always had to lie directly in front of the orderlies' *Glaskasten*. Earlier in life he had been an American Air Force Lieutenant but was now, at twenty-four, completely *'off side'* as the orderlies put it. But not always, sometimes he ate his meals very normally, and was talking sensibly to everybody; then, abruptly he'd change, tearing his clothing into rags and would even continue his terrible fits when heavily shackled to his bed. Then they had to feed him by hand and keep him constantly under observation, that's why his bed was at the very front of the room.

At other times Ray would rub his own excrement all over his body and the cell. When this happened there was no solution other than to put him in a cell and turn a hose on him. He'd be kept there until he stopped doing it then he'd be taken back to his own cell. One time I watched him, he was writing on the cell wall using his fingers and his own excrement. 'That's life!' was all he wrote. It was so odd, he was good looking and had the build of an athlete and at times could be so normal, but at other times I could only wonder at what happened inside his head. Especially tragic was what happened when he was in a good condition and his mother was informed that she could come and visit him. Most times the cyclical nature of his illness was quicker than her. I remember one time when this had happened and they'd tried to prevent her visit, but she had already arrived after a long journey from the USA. She was a very elegant looking woman who wore a hat, we could see her through the window as she insisted on seeing her son! She must have been a person of some importance because Chief Nurse Victoria, who was always present when high ranking visitors came, and Mr Opel the Chief Orderly, appeared in the doorway to Lower B Ward and tried to get her to change her mind. I followed everything with interest because, during incidents like this, you never knew what you could learn. I lay around close at hand, ostensibly uninterested in the proceedings, but at the same time wide awake.

We knew that Ray had already embarked upon another 'bender' and as his mother entered the ward Ray was already roaring at the top of his voice, attempting to tear his clothes from his body and smear himself with excrement - all at the same time! She tried to talk to him affectionately, hoping the familiar sound of her voice would bring about a change, but there was no reaction, no sign of recognition... all efforts of the nurses and orderlies were in vain!... Ray was completely out of his head again. After only a few minutes his mother had seen enough and was led sobbing from the ward. While she stayed outside, releasing her grief for her son, Ray was shackled to his bed again until the storm passed and for a short while he would pass for normal again.

In the next bed lay Lieutenant Geoffrey Kean, as he introduced himself. He originated, as was the case with most of the inmates in the lower floor, from the First World War. He was approximately forty-five years old, smoked like a chimney and, when the orderlies allowed him, he adopted a role as my self-appointed protector. Geoffrey always spoke in a friendly manner with me, sometimes throwing in the few pieces of German he knew. He would even take my side against the orderlies if they were beating me too hard. In my presence the orderlies always spoke very openly about *'education'*. My *'forgetting'* my English was paying off, when they were talking close to other inmates, they were very careful of what they were saying, but in front of me they were very free.

There seemed to be a measure of disagreement among the orderlies on the subject of *'education'*. The big orderly, the one who had trampled around on me when I first rebelled, held some kind of position of authority and was able to insist on his point of view. Just at the moment when the *'bugger's'* resistance was weakening, that was the time to exert more force and keep on beating them as hard as could be. It was then, in his view, that the *'buggers'* would feel it and the *'education'* would be most effective. Not all the orderlies dismissed us with the same derisory term as the big fellow and not all of them were in agreement with the supposed efficacy of *'education.'*

A further hated *'educational'* measure or *'therapy'* was in a white tiled room, located immediately beside C Ward. In there were located several bath-tubs and the patients from C Ward and Lower B Ward were put in these, mostly upon instructions from the doctors. Sometimes they were left there for hours. I was spared this particular aspect of the curriculum, but apparently the water was always cold because those being *'treated'* in the bath-tubs always moaned bitterly that they were freezing. Just the question being asked, whether they wanted "to have a bath", meant that they should mend their ways. Often a fist that had been raised would drop impotently to the side or a shouting voice would drop to a whisper. Sometimes, when they had given me a good beating, Geoff could get so worked up over it he would start attacking the orderlies himself. For his trouble he was also beaten, then either found himself in a cell or in the bath tub again. When he lost control because he was so angry he would spring at the orderlies as if he were a cat. Although he was very tall he was also still very agile and supple.

Harry's illness also originated from the First World War. He was always talking about the big battles and then asking me many times if it was true that I was a German officer, whether I was really a Captain? Even in this case I felt sorry that I couldn't answer his questions. Very disappointed and shaking his head he would then always walk away from me, turning to the orderlies who then had to explain to me about his special number. Some of the orderlies spoke quite a surprising amount of German and that not too badly. Many of them had been soldiers, mostly in the NCO ranks, in the last war. Some had fought in France and had been members of the occupation army in the Rheinland. That's where they had learnt most of their German, and they could put it to use with me, particularly in explaining about Harry's special number.

Harry was very proud that he could still memorise the serial number of his service rifle. He was continually trying to find allies who would confirm for him that he didn't really belong here amongst all these *'crazy'* people. A man like him, he would say, that still knew the number of his rifle shouldn't be in there. But Harry could also, quite unpredictably, explode in a riot of violence, flaying about and injuring the unwary. Geoffrey Kean was of the same opinion as Harry although his *'sanity'* was demonstrated in a different way. He received, and read, his newspaper every day. Kean was too proud to participate in the daily floor-polishing activity, preferring to retire to study his paper as only befitted an officer and gentleman. Again the logic was that anyone who was so well read and informed on current affairs could not, *per se*, be *crazy*.

Harry only participated occasionally in floor polishing but I, however, immediately pounced upon the biggest broom with enthusiasm as soon as I was let out of the cell for the first time. I recognised that this was an excellent opportunity to get some movement for my body and to keep my muscles in better tone, although I was still going hungry. Every morning, with exception of Sundays, floor-polishing equipment was issued, next door in B. The *'bumpers'* were only part-made of iron, not like the solid heavy ones at home. Most of the examples in the clinic were made of wood, up to thirty centimetres wide, seventy-five centimetres long, and up to twenty-five centimetres high. They had strong bristles at the bottom, and were pushed by means of wooden shafts almost two metres long. Most service personnel world-wide would have used similar equipment to polish their barracks or similar during their basic training. This kind of equipment disappeared later with the advent of electric floor polishers.

For the floor polishing the steel door to Lower B was opened fully and through this a distance of about thirty metres was created between the two wards. The first time I guided a floor-polisher I experienced, with fascination, how up to fifty people could be simultaneously kept in constant motion. Every morning for two hours I joined in and was immediately carried around in the tide, lost in the mob. If I came late because I had to be fed or had to change clothes, there was always the possibility of a dispute concerning *'my floor-polisher.'* Perhaps it was already being pushed by someone else and that person wouldn't want to give it up. Sometimes I would be reasonable, other times a fight could be the result. The causes for disputes could be very different but the results were, for all participants, equally hard.

Those involved in any affray were *'subdued'*, another euphemism for a damned good beating which would be more or less violent depending on the grouping of the orderlies. I always ended up in a cell, the Canadians mostly landed in the bath-tub.

It was an unforgettable sight: all these men with their monotonous movements, almost devotedly pushing the *'bumpers'* through the room. All dressed in the same blue hospital clothing, going back and forth. It was remarkably seldom that collisions occurred, but when they did they could be the cause of small, and sometimes larger, fights. The orderlies, however, knew their men and were quick to intervene. That saved them trouble as well as preventing the situation escalating. They weren't at all interested in beating people for the sake of it and often complained of strains and sprains collected whilst sorting out the squabbling inmates.

For myself the floor-polishing was a wonderful diversion. Not only did it give me the opportunity to get some very necessary exercise, it also helped to integrate me into the whole, to make a *'genuine'* patient out of me. For the orderlies it was hard to believe that a German officer would push the *'bumpers'* day in and day out unless he was really ill. The orderlies talked about it freely, even when I was lying very close to them on the day beds. This was especially the case later on, after I had spent quite some time in C, comments could be heard as to why, of all people, this *'poor fellow'* hadn't been exchanged. I frequently heard it said, that the *'smart boys'* from upstairs had already travelled home (*'smart boys'* was the expression used for our *Simulanten* - those who were faking their illnesses, including the Canadians).

'Upstairs' was, down in C Ward, a very important word. As soon as newcomers, mostly young soldiers from the overseas battle grounds, had improved and were beginning to behave like more normal human beings, it was hinted to them that they might soon be ready for *'upstairs'*. Ready to be sent through that armoured door and up those stairs, up to Upper B Ward where I'd been briefly upon arrival, where most of the Germans were being held.

One time I heard them talking about me and a small knot of panic rose in my throat. "He is smarter than any of them - pushing the polisher, he keeps fit - better than any of them". Fortunately the author of this keen observation was a young orderly whose word wasn't yet of great importance.

Again to pass the time and to do something creative I rolled cigarettes for both Harry and Geoff. Each of the inmates there was issued a ration of tobacco and cigarette papers and after I'd seen that even Ray and Jimmy, who were the most muddled up of all the patients, could roll their own cigarettes on good days I decided to try. To do this, I sat down on the floor and started rolling, ten cigarettes, sometimes as many as twenty at a sitting and I quickly improved my skill. Put the tobacco in neat and tidy, lick the paper, tamp the tobacco even once more, then roll the cigarette until the paper sticks. Before too long my cigarettes were the favourites in the whole room, not only among the patients, but also amongst the orderlies. They'd call me over and show me the tobacco and papers and slowly and carefully ask me to roll the cigarettes. "You roll us cigarettes? You take t-o-b-a-c-c-o and roll c-i-g-a-r-e-t-t-e-s?" Proffering the materials they'd look at me and I'd dutifully look confused and then at the tobacco and papers with the dawn of realisation slowly coming over me. Then I'd take the *'makings'* and get to work and the orderlies would roundly praise my work. I'd soon reached the point where my products were so nice and round they almost looked as if they'd come out of a packet. However the smokers were, in one respect, still completely dependent: the patients had no lighters or matches, and if they didn't chain-smoke, they had to ask the orderlies for a light every time they wanted to smoke.

Sometimes I rolled large quantities of cigarettes and piled them in small heaps on the floor, pausing from time to time to talk to myself. I had observed many times that almost all the inmates talked to themselves. Why shouldn't I do the same? This wasn't only for effect either, I also did it to keep my brain active and to exert control over it. First of all I started by repeating the multiplication tables up to ten. I quietly spoke my litany: *"Neun mal neun ist einundachtzig, acht mal neun ist zweiundsiebzig,"* forwards and backwards until it was child's play for me. It started getting difficult when I started tables using higher numbers... *"Zwölf mal zwölf ist hundertvierundvierzig..."* Most people can usually deal easily with the lower multiplications, but as the number gets larger and the multiplier increases in size it can begin to tax the mind. When I'd managed to memorise the tables for eleven to nineteen, both forwards and backwards, I began multiplying larger numbers. At first I helped myself by scratching the results on the stone floor with a little pebble I'd found. Later I did it only in my head because once I was caught by surprise by one of the orderlies, who immediately exclaimed, "He's calculating!" Actually this wasn't really that terrible for me, many of the patients had extreme deficiencies in one direction, but were exceptional in others.

That was the worst thing of all in this bloody C Ward! There was never ever a minute in which you could be sure you weren't under observation. When I kept some of my porridge one day, so as to cover up the peep-hole in my cell, it didn't take five minutes before an orderly came and cleaned it.

It was natural that I made mistakes and it largely went unnoticed because, even amongst the professional observers, there was no one who seemed to be absolutely sure of what he was doing. There were far too many variations in mental illness for a definitive set of symptoms, and this was especially noticeable with the newcomers. Nevertheless, the less suspicion that fell on me that I was, perhaps, trying to be *'smart'*, the better it was. Every time I thought I'd made a mistake, I would follow it up a few days later with an impressive fit of rage. This was always a very strenuous affair but with it I was sure I always cleared away all doubts.

I not only kept my mind busy with numbers. Every day I thought up a four line rhyme like, for example, the following:

Der Sonntag ist jetz rum, (Sunday has now passed again,)
Die Wärten gucken wieder dumm, (The orderlies are glum,)
macht gar nichts, es geht weiter, (it doesn't matter, nothing's wrong,)
muß sehn, wie blieb ich heiter. (I have to stay happy, for so long.)

Just like this, I thought up a new verse every day, which I then repeated on the next day and continued with another verse. Sometimes I felt lazy and just repeated the one from the day before. There also came times when my thinking up of verses dominated my time and my calculating was left out. This was, nevertheless, very demanding for my memory. I don't recall how many verses I had to repeat by the end of my time in C Ward, but it must have been somewhere over fifty!

Besides Ray, Geoffrey and Harry there were also three other *'long-term customers'* in C Ward. At the far end there was Alex, the Russian. Why he was here, I never really understood. He wore the same sanatorium clothes, and was very similar to Charlie, an American. Both lived within their self-imposed barriers, both always wore a collar and tie, both were over fifty years of age and, with their small tables in their cells, they acted ostensibly quite normally. They read their newspaper and fetched their own meals from the orderlies themselves. Alex was always talking to himself in Russian and was never aggressive. Only when I came crawling along the floor, in preparation for a surprise attack against the back door which was beside his corner, did he shout loudly for help. He was afraid that my attack would be directed against his realm, his private little world. He always smoked using a silver cigarette-holder, rolled his own cigarettes and may have had a better tobacco than us because he always refused to smoke the ones I'd rolled.

Charlie wasn't on my list of cigarette customers either. He was so well-off that he had special Navy Cut cigarettes brought into the hospital.

Sometimes he was even given permission for a short visit outside and before he returned from such excursions, he would deliberately walk along the outside of the windows of C Ward. If we didn't notice him *'at liberty'*, then he would knock at Kean's window. Charlie hated women. When it overcame him he would suddenly let loose on anything and everything he connected with women. Apparently, in the course of his divorce, he must have got into such a traumatic state with his own woman, his wife, that he landed there in the mental hospital, and she was most probably paying for it, albeit maybe with his money. If anyone touched on that subject he could start screaming and shouting to such an extent that nothing or nobody could stop him. Sometimes, during the warmer weather, advance warning was received of such a fit and he was immediately served *'cocktails'*. Sometimes this big strong man suddenly turned so bad that he had to go into a cell, but he was never put in the bath-tub. I assumed that Alex the Russian and Charlie were private patients. They were the exceptions, because including Jimmy, the other *'long-term customer,'* all the other newcomers were soldiers.

Jimmy was a case almost as sad as Ray. He was twenty-two years old and seemed to have been totally normal prior to his training for the Canadian Army when something seemed to have happened to him. He came from Alberta, and was claimed to be of German origin, or so I'd heard. Jimmy didn't dress himself or eat of his own accord, he had to be spoon-fed. It was a very sad picture, every morning after waking he would just stand in his long white night gown with an empty look in his face. The orderly, trying to raise his spirits, would give him a sock which he then just waved around in circles, like a propeller, that's all he did... nothing else. He had to be washed, dressed and fed and would sometimes, during his meals, become really stubborn. Then the orderlies would get mad with him but there was no point in beating him for *'education'*, there was nobody there to hurt.

Kean took great care of Jimmy as well, he took all the lame ducks under his wing; he even helped feed Jimmy. Even I, on my *'good days',* would occasionally feed Jimmy, he was just a sad, empty shell. One time, however, my good will almost ended with negative results. On that particular day he wasn't at all helpful. Whilst feeding him beetroot I tried to persuade him to eat and, at first, he gave me a bad look. Then suddenly he tore the spoon out of my hand and pushed it into my face, he almost got me right in the eye. As with everything that happened, this was reported to Dr. Rogier and for a time I was not allowed to do the feeding. Jimmy didn't vary in temperament as much as Ray did. When he became stubborn, he would turn in a gentle way, and everyone learned to read the signs. Ray's problem, on the other hand, was more black and white, he was either passive or really on a bender.

There were hardly any signs of improvement to be seen in him and about three months after my arrival he was transferred to an American hospital, probably upon request of his mother.

Younger patients began to arrive in steadily increasing numbers. In all cases where it was suspected they could be violent, they were first put in C Ward. For this the back door, which was at ground level, was always opened. A vehicle pulled up, not always an ambulance, and the lads were accompanied in. Sometimes they were unconscious and were carried in on a stretcher. If a cell was empty, the newcomers were always accommodated in one for initial observation. If there wasn't a cell empty, then a bed was simply pushed in between our beds in the open ward (by then I was only locked in one of the cells during my bad times). After a few days, almost without exception, they were all transferred to Upper B Ward.

One time an American Air Force Captain, a pilot, was brought in on a stretcher. He was put in a cell with a mattress but no bed, the same as I had been. Hardly had he regained consciousness later that night than he woke the whole ward shouting: "Turkey is your target boys... tak, tak, tak, Turkey is your target boys... tak, tak, tak, take off the land... off the air... off the sea!" This continued without interruption day and night. Loud enough to penetrate through the cell door and when the orderlies, during the daytime, opened the cell door for the poor fellow, one could see him, squatting down in the corner on the cell floor rhythmically accompanying his litany by slapping his hands on the floor either side of him: "... tak, tak, tak. Turkey is your target boys... tak, tak, tak, Turkey is your target boys... tak, tak, tak..."

Where did this man get the strength from? For days he refused all kind of nourishment. Once in a while he would grab a large cup from the food tray and run with it to the toilets and then literally poured the water down his throat. One time, when returning, he suddenly smashed the big cup into the face of the orderly who had been accompanying him. An alarm was too late to help the orderly and almost too late to control the tall American. He developed unbelievable strength and it took ages before they had him on the floor, but they managed it in the end. As though on cue my big *'friend'*, the senior orderly, arrived to demonstrate, "... how to deal with another one of these buggers!" Before the other orderlies could stop him he was bashing the American's head against the stone floor long enough for a trickle of blood to start seeping from his ear and begin to stain the floor.

Then they stood around the unconscious body wondering what to do next. They quickly telephoned for a nurse and as luck would have it for them it was Sunny. She knelt on the floor beside him and took care of the mess the orderlies had made. She stayed there long enough for the captain to recover. He didn't even realise he had been on the rampage. He just asked for more water and peacefully returned to his cell.

I was really worried about him, but this *'education'* hadn't apparently done him any harm; something of a miracle in my judgement. Next morning, when the doctors did their rounds he didn't say a word and a few days later, even this patient was transferred to Upper B Ward. Another young officer, a Canadian Air Force lieutenant, arrived at about the same time. He hadn't been there more than two hours before I knew he was feigning illness. Actually I couldn't have cared less, but the way this lad reacted at night was completely stupid to my now practised eye. Dressed in a sheet, like a ghost, he ran down the corridor and jumped from bed to bed, including mine and I certainly wasn't accepting that nonsense a second night. The night-watch slept quite soundly behind their glass window and I was able to get hold of the young lieutenant: "I'm a German prisoner of war and you certainly know why I am here," I said. During the daytime he had been observing me quite closely, just as I had been watching him. "You're a Canadian officer and I know why you are here! You're a shirker! If you ever jump over my bed again I tell you boy, you've had it!" I'd said this clearly in my best English. In his case I was very certain that I need not fear being betrayed. He never jumped over my bed again and avoided me whenever he could. Before long he was transferred to Upper B Ward but wherever and whenever we came into contact he avoided me like the plague.

Summer had come again, why wasn't the damned *Gripsholm* sailing again? Since July they had even opened the back door every afternoon for a few hours and we were allowed out into a very well secured yard. This had now gone on much, much longer than I ever thought it would and still there was no end in sight. Dr Eitze's warning of only remaining in the hospital for four weeks had long been passed.

CHAPTER TWENTY-ONE

...UND GOTT LENKT! (...AND GOD DECIDES!)

A Canadian General came to inspect the sanatorium. His explicit wish was to see C Ward and the cells. He even had the doors unlocked and opened, including my door. I sat in the cell and took the opportunity to mumble a few confused words at the General. He seemed suitably impressed. When walking away he asked what was going to happen to me, and what did I hear? It was as if from an angel's tongue I heard Dr Rogier's reply, "We'll send him home. A Swedish boat is soon going to take him home to Germany for treatment there." What was that? I couldn't believe my ears! 'We'll be sending him home, a Swedish boat is soon going to take him home to Germany for treatment there.' Swedish boat! Home to Germany! I could have shouted from the roof tops, I could have entered upon a rampage of joy, but I had to contain myself, I obviously didn't want to *'give the game away'* at that late stage and, secondly, I was far too weak for any histrionics. Week after week I had maintained the same weight loss of two kilograms and was by then terribly thin. Again and again I had refused all kind of nourishment or had stated, irrationally, that I didn't eat a particular colour of vegetable because they weren't good for me. I was also being given laxatives because I had hardly anything to evacuate in my bowels. I had arrived there weighing a lean eighty-two kilograms (180 lbs) and had reduced to less than fifty-eight kilograms (128 lbs). Nevertheless I continued with my self-imposed hunger strike; I had to force them to exchange me, it couldn't all go to waste!

It had been so hard, so terribly hard to take the deprivation, the beatings and to be isolated from contact with normal human beings. But at last it looked as though it would all be worth it. From then on I began to get impatient. Damn it! Why wasn't the bloody *Gripsholm* sailing again? He'd said she would *'soon'* be sailing! Even though I'd come this far I couldn't endure it here for ever, all alone in C Ward! What had Dr Eitze said? 'Don't do it for more than six weeks, or better only four.' I'd then been there for over three months! And always alone, nobody else to exchange a normal word with, and nothing to read. There was only the radio from which I could occasionally here the news, and this was only possible when I was lying on the floor outside the orderlies' armoured glass office. And the news that was to be heard there, from Italy and Russia, it was enough to drive one to despair. Last, but not least, I had heard of the successful landing of the Allies in Normandy. Did this have something to do with the *Gripsholm* not coming? Was the war nearly over? Surely not.

Since the middle of June, whenever the weather permitted, we were allowed out in the fresh air in the backyard which was fenced in and behind the row of cells. I mostly laid on the ground at a spot close to the wall where there was no grass growing. In the dry dirt there I could write down the large numbers that I was multiplying and whenever one of the orderlies came by to see what I was doing, I could just simply wipe them away. One day, while working on my *'blackboard'* I found a glass splinter in the earth. I wanted to take advantage of this opportunity because my body was then so weak I was no longer capable of staging really violent fits. With this shard of glass I saw an opportunity of help in a different way. I resolved I would immediately cut the veins in my wrist. It was easier said than done. I could feel my pulse and that was the spot to aim for but there is a natural defence mechanism that has to be overcome. I gritted my teeth and tried to cut my way in but I couldn't get any blood to flow... in my undernourished state everything was stringy and tough, no soft flesh to cut through. Still working on the left wrist, I tried at two other spots, but again without success. Perhaps it was the wrong side? I tried it on my right wrist... again I tried it where I could feel my pulse... I tried it twice at different spots... but then one of the orderlies discovered me. He'd come too early, but the effect was almost the same. That little trickle of blood coming out of both wrists was almost enough to cause a major alarm. 'Not bad,' I thought, that way I got all the *'benefits'* without really having to do anything really life threatening. I was acutely aware that any major loss of body fluids in my weakened state might kill me through shock.

I was bandaged by Sunny who tried to console me. "Poor Steenie," she said, "now he doesn't even know what it's all about. Keep your chin up, you'll soon be going home!" So she knew about it too! I should be going home! Where was the bloody *Gripsholm* then?![1] The elation I felt at hearing that news was short-lived. Annoyingly, I was excluded from going out into the fresh air for several days, that's about all I'd won for my *'suicide'* attempt. There seemed to be no other immediate action. It appeared to take no end of time before the nurses, the orderlies and Dr. Rogier started to worry about me. The first measure decided upon was to stop giving me the bromide. It was apparently assumed that my loss of weight was one affect of the bromide treatment. "That suits me!" I thought but I was wrong, it didn't suit me at all. I started getting withdrawal symptoms, I felt the hunger far more and, at night, I could hardly sleep. Before, whilst taking the medication, I had been able to doze away quite nicely, even during the daytime, but now the nights were interminably long. What could I do?

First I resolved to start eating better, this would help improve my strength, both physical and mental. But even if I forced myself, I just didn't seem to have the ability to take the food down any more[2]. At times I was very hungry but when food was presented I couldn't get it down. I was becoming more and more desperate and more and more confused; and just to add to it all I got a parcel. Never before, while in the hospital, and never after did I receive any kind of mail. In front of all the other patients and two curious orderlies, they tossed the parcel to me in the middle of the ward. I glanced at the wrapping and saw to my horror that there, plain as day, was a green cross, the very warning I'd asked Wilke to put on a parcel containing money and documents.

What did this mean? Were they trying to set a last trap for me? Or was it something else? "Go on! Open it!" the orderlies called, starting to get impatient. I had no other choice than to publicly open the parcel, there were no corners in C Ward where you could have some privacy. I only hoped everything had been concealed with a view to an inspection before it was passed to me. I did it the way I guessed it was expected of me, I tore the wrapping off in bits and pieces. It looked as though the parcel was intact, that it hadn't been inspected on its way to the hospital. But what did the green cross denote? There was some cake from my mother, some chocolate and a pair of shorts in there. The shorts were immediately taken away from me and while the orderlies were busy with them I opened the last inner-most box: it contained WALNUTS! How could I get around that now? With great enthusiasm I distributed everything that was edible amongst the other patients, mainly to give myself time to think. I quickly cracked open two nuts on the floor and then carefully selected another handful, those I suspected had been glued up again.

All of a sudden something surprising happened, "Look at him!" shouted one of the orderlies, "He goes for the nuts! He gets the nuts first! " he laughed, "He really is not only crazy he is 'nuts'!" The orderlies were shouting to each other and slapping their thighs. The whole ward erupted in laughter with everyone calling back and forth, "He's nuts! He's nuts!" They had all gathered and were sitting on my bed so that they could have a better view of what was going on.

The opportunity was good, I gathered up my nuts and scuttled to the toilet, while the others were still helpless with laughter in the ward. Alone in the toilets I cracked the first suspicious nut open with my bare hands... and there it was! A $ 20 US bill, folded up inside the nut. There was still some time left, I could still hear them laughing as I climbed up behind the showers. There I'd seen a clamp with which the water pipe was secured to the wall. This clamp was ideal for hiding my neatly folded dollar bill in security. Besides which the showers were where the weekly change of clothing was always conducted. I could, therefore, when in need, always conveniently reach my hidden treasure. Back in the toilet I cracked all the other nuts I had brought, but none had anything by way of special contents. There hadn't been a book in the parcel so I concluded there was no need for me to look for any false documents. I wouldn't be needing them anyway, I consoled myself, I was soon to be travelling home complete with the blessing of the Canadian government!

Many times the next day, the story of the nuts and *'the nut'* was told and even brought forth a satisfactory smile on Dr Rogier's face - this time they were certainly sending home a genuine case, not one of the *'smart boys.'* This excitement was short-lived. Dr Rogier said to me in his broken German, "Tomorrow, Captain, you will be receiving a visitor, a Swiss from the Red Cross will be coming tomorrow!" That was all I needed. Then, just at the point when all seemed to have been convinced, could this possibly compromise my scheme? Would this Swiss see me for what I was? Was he coming to tell me I couldn't go home? After the loneliness and deprivation of the months in C Ward it was easy to be paranoid. During the night before the impending visit I was terribly restless. I asked several times for water and, once it passed through my system, I trotted to and fro to the toilets. I didn't even take part in the polishing, but just sat on the floor rolling cigarettes and mumbled away to myself.

It was late morning when my visitor arrived. Dr Rogier had set the time of the visit so that he could accompany the Red Cross delegate and immediately upon entering the ward he pointed in my direction. I had already rolled quite a heap of cigarettes, mumbling to myself and was not at all pleased when someone, speaking in a very friendly tone, addressed me in German. I stopped my cigarette production and stood up, staring at the friendly visitor in horror, *"Ich weiß was Sie wollen,"* I began, *"Sie wollen mich in den Arrest bringen... Sie wollen mich in den Keller bringen... sie wollen mich sieben Meter unter den Boden bringen... sieben Meter und noch viel tiefer... Sie wollen mich nicht einsperren... Sie wollen mich umbringen!..."* (I know what you want, etc... my well-practised litany). I could recite this senseless sermon automatically, almost all of my *'fits'* had been accompanied by my screaming these words.

Nobody could possibly have realised how much I would have liked to talk to this man completely normally, to ask him whether he had any news from my parents. Whether, given the present stage of the war, there was any chance of being exchanged? Who knew the truth there in that place, who knew whether they weren't all lying? Were they, perhaps, just putting me off? Obviously appalled by my verbal assault, he stepped back a little and left C Ward almost as fast as Ray's mother had on her last visit there. In departing I heard him say to Dr Rogier "I can't stand anything like that, let alone watch it!" The danger had passed but inside I was still in turmoil. If it was so certain I was to be exchanged, why did a representative from the Red Cross, a Swiss at that, come and visit me?

Without the twice-daily bromide *'cocktails'* the days were passing even slower, they turned to weeks, and although I was getting some food down I was still losing weight. What was wrong with me? Hadn't Dr Eitze said, "Don't do it longer than six weeks or better only four"? I had now been there for over four months, nineteen long weeks, something like one hundred and forty long, painful days. It was then the end of July and I'd arrived there on 15th March.

One Sunday, 6th August 1944, I wanted to eat a proper meal. Once again I was feeling very bad, both physically and mentally. I had then really begun to ask myself if I was normal any more. The question had also arisen in my mind that if I wasn't, would I realise it? For over four and a half months I had not exchanged a word with a normal human being (apart from my brief statement to the young lieutenant), I was still doing my arithmetic and reciting my *'poems'*, but was I really still normal? When I was sitting on the floor during the midday meal, my plate beside me, I watched my hand shaking to such an extent that I hardly managed to get the half-full spoon to my mouth and it really came home to me that I'd have to think again.

What was the sense of it all, if I returned home as a human wreck and I had to admit I was more than halfway there, what use would I be? Would I ever be able to recover? I didn't know. At the last weighing session on the previous Thursday my weight loss had reduced, but I barely scaled fifty-four kilos (119 lbs). No, I had to do something about it, something that would possibly get me to the other Germans in Upper B Ward. Once I got there, I could then, in the course of conversations, find out how things really stood with my condition! If necessary, I could speed things up again by reverting to my unstable behaviour.

How long altogether had they been talking of exchanging me?! Two months? Maybe more, and still nothing official had taken place. The news on the radio was continually reporting Allied victories in France, one could really begin to doubt whether they were still thinking of exchanging at all.

The thoughts were immediately put into action. The decision had to be made and the next day, Monday, Dr Rogier always led the visit. As he approached me I spoke to him immediately, I'd thought everything over very carefully. I was well aware that all patients I had observed had their rational moments from time to time. For the first time, and in good English I said, "I am a German officer. I am a prisoner of war. It isn't right to keep me in a mental hospital just because I had an accident in an ice hockey game. You should send me to a prisoner of war camp."

I don't know what I expected but Dr Rogier's face didn't betray any shock, however his expression slowly changed to an enigmatic smile. It said to me he was thinking, *'Something's not right here.'* At last he spoke, "I'm just so glad that you, Captain Steinhilper, just at this very moment are getting better. However," he sighed, "we cannot immediately send you to a POW camp. First we have to make sure you are really well. But tomorrow, you will go to another ward. There you will find some more Germans." Actually I should have been satisfied with this, it was exactly what I'd hoped to achieve. But what was that sudden twinkle in his eyes? Why that wry smile? And why had he emphasized 'just at this very moment'?

That Monday afternoon the weather was beautiful so we were allowed out in the fresh air. Because our afternoons out were always announced in advance, I was able to make my preparations. Several days before a change of policy had begun to allow a few selected patients from Upper B to use the same lawn which had been fenced in for us, the C Ward patients. I'd overheard the orderlies saying the 'German boys' were to be among those selected B patients. Because there was a presumption against contact between the B and C patients the times were arranged so that we wouldn't mix. That was fine for me, it saved the temptation to talk, but it also gave me a way of keeping my twenty dollar bill. As soon as the midday meal was over, I went to the toilet and, because I was behaving well at that time, I was able to go unattended. Reaching up to the pipe bracket I was able to recover my carefully folded note and put it into the breast pocket of my grey shirt, which would be well hidden under the blue jacket.

For the half hour that passed before we were let out, the note was safe enough. Hardly had I reached the fresh air when I sat down in my dark corner and started playing with the earth. This time I didn't do any calculations, I was watching the orderly until he was being kept busy by something else. I then quickly transferred the folded note into a dry hiding place under a clamp that was securing the rain-water downpipe to the wall. Should I not be able to get there again for some reason, it would be easy to describe the spot to someone else. This successful operation calmed my

The back of C Ward with the door through which, in good weather, even the 'Bad Boys' were allowed out in the fresh air; within a fenced in compound. Behind the row of windows with the iron bars are where the cells were. The rain water pipe the dark rear corner furthest from the camera is where, for four weeks in autumn of 1944, I hid a folded up $20 note and did my 'maths'. This part of the hospital was virtually the same, in 1987, as it had been in 1945.

nerves which had been in turmoil over the almost imperceptible twinkle I'd seen in Dr Rogier's eyes. What the hell did he mean? - *'...just at this very moment'*

Next morning I was given breakfast in C Ward and then most excitedly climbed up the stairs. At the top there was an immediate turn to the left into a corridor, halfway along which was a room without any doors. There, Mr. Opel the Chief Orderly, introduced me to *Major von Casimir*. I knew him from Bowmanville, however, I naturally had no idea what he was doing there. In accordance with his *'role'*, he didn't even glance my way. Then there were an *Oberfeldwebel* Hein, a pilot, and an *Obersteward, Herr* Gehrke, from a passenger ship. Because I was having a *'good day,'* I greeted each of the Germans, only if they acknowledged Mr Opel's introduction and didn't just stare into the distance. Then I was told that I could stay and Mr Opel left. The dust had hardly settled when von Casimir, 'the Major' as the Canadians referred to him, spoke up like a shot from a pistol, "Oh boy,

Steinhilper, we didn't think we'd see you again! We all thought you'd travel direct from C Ward! And now you've actually come to us. Now, tomorrow morning, four will be leaving from this ward. You and three sailors of the *Handelsmarine!* They were informed yesterday..."

There was no need for him to continue, I knew everything then. His voice faded into the background as I realised what he didn't. That strange twinkle in Dr Rogier's eyes, those few words I'd been turning over in my mind, *'... at this particular time.'* The reality of it broke over me like a huge wave. I didn't want to think it, to realise it was true, but I couldn't escape it. Although my name was on the list it would probably be removed because of my 'improvement'. "VERDAMMTE SCHEISS!" ("Bloody shit!") I cursed, four and half bloody months! Four and a half bloody months of isolation and purgatory and I miss out by one bloody day! Typically for me, again at the very last moment, bad luck dogs me! 'Why me?' I thought, 'Why is it always bloody well me?' In my weakened state I could have broken down and wept, what I'd suffered to have it all fall about my ears again!

Both Casimir and Hein were, at first, confused. They could see the agony which tore through me, but what was wrong? "What else do you want?" they asked, "Certainly your name is on the list, we've read it there!" I calmed down for a moment. Could I still hope? The answer to that was before my eyes before the hour was over. The list had been amended, Steinhilper was crossed off and another sailor was to travel in my place - two were *'genuine'* and two were *Simulanten*, or so I was told.

That didn't interest me any more. I was just able to witness how Hans Hein quickly hid his tablets under his tongue and I turned to him for help. Already, before the *'round'* during which the nurse distributed the medicine for all patients, Hein had shown me his collection of strong brown tablets, which he had been *'taking'* twice a day! He'd collected them all and hid them away. "Oh boy, Hans," I said, "that's just what I need right now! How many can I take at once?" When Hein had started taking these tablets he had noticed that they were narcotising him quite quickly. "Take four for a start!" he suggested. I took them gratefully and then quickly disappeared into the big dormitory, which was absolutely full of patients. I couldn't have cared less how much extra work the orderlies were going to have with me. In fact not much, I was unconscious in no time. In the middle of the night, Tuesday to Wednesday, 8th/9th August, I woke from my drug-induced sleep and went to the washroom. It was all much easier than it was in C Ward. There I took another four tablets from the supply Hein had given me. Then I fell asleep again on the floor underneath somebody else's bed.

Later in the afternoon I regained consciousness and had to come to terms with the reality of it all: on 7th August 1944, after nearly five months of C Ward I had opened my mouth one day too soon. That very morning I would have begun my journey home, the culmination of everything I'd suffered for. If only I could have kept on in the old style for another two days. If only, if only, if only! If only I'd known Canadian locos didn't travel in the USA, if only I hadn't worn white socks under a train in Montreal, if only we hadn't stopped the only bloody policeman in Watertown who'd seen our escape notice, if only I hadn't worn my Elk boots, if only two guards hadn't decided to go fishing! If only, if only, if only...! And now they had deleted me from the list, somebody else had travelled instead of me that very morning.

At least I had slept very well and when I returned to the room in which my bed waited, Von Casimir and Hans Hein both tried to comfort me. They'd had to stay back as well, they said. Everything hadn't been lost yet, the *Gripsholm* would be sailing again. That was easily said, what did they know about what I had gone through and what I'd done in C Ward? It didn't help, I just had to be patient, I had to recover and behave in a manner typical of Upper B Ward. It was time to take a good look at my new surroundings and the people with whom I would now live.

On the other side of the department there was a similar dormitory. In there were three more German *Handelsmarine* sailors who had also been left behind. The ship's boy, Freddy, who was approximately eighteen years old, was clearly among the *Simulanten*. Another sailor, who'd had a bad case of syphilis, felt a prickling in his head and would, in time, get worse. Then there was a *Schwäbische Landsman* (fellow countryman, or in this case countyman of mine), Seifried. He was *'Hans Dampf in allen Gassen'* (literally Hans Steam in all the gases - Jack of all trades). He, to help convince people of his *'illness'*, had developed the trick of being able to foam at the mouth on request. Like myself, he had observed the other patients talking to themselves and followed suit. This actually wasn't too hard for him because his own *pidgin English* was virtually incomprehensible to everyone else. He was well liked by everyone, German and Canadians alike and because he'd been there so long, he'd worked himself into all aspects of hospital life. He helped to distribute the medicine and was especially busy sorting the washing as Nurse Jenny's assistant.

She had a most important function in that ward; she controlled almost everything, from the washing and the issue of clothing to the patients, to the dispensing of medicines and the allocation of hypodermic syringes. This was of the greatest importance for her because she was addicted to morphine! We heard all this from Seifried who, virtually since his arrival, had been conducting an illicit but very passionate love affair with her. This had mainly been conducted in the store rooms for washing and medicines, which could be locked from the inside. Jenny was giving herself the injections in secret, but even the orderlies exchanged knowing looks when Jenny had that special light in her eyes. Later on I was to find out that the orderlies didn't dare to report this to the Head Nurse or even the Director because these *'gentlemen'* were deep in her debt in other respects. They had their own *'sidelines'* of which Jenny was fully cognizant.

Apparently soon after the affair had started, Jenny had admitted to Seifried that she was an addict. Seifried, being the helpful soul he was, soon offered to help and Jenny taught him to give her the injections which helped her; it had never been easy for her to self-inject. For us Germans, this affair meant we were gradually getting to know everything Jenny knew about us and about matters that concerned us as a group. At first Seifried said he'd hardly dared ask, but as time went on she unwittingly became our secret ally.

There was no way that Upper B could be compared with C. In B there were only two orderlies during the day, who not only had to keep an eye on the two rooms in which we Germans were, but also to look after the Canadians on the floor. This was the larger part of their work as there were approximately sixty Canadian patients who slept in two large dormitories. Compared with Lower B, where the patients were just herded into bunk beds, the single beds and good facilities were a luxury. Either side of our dormitories were, alternately, toilets and wash-rooms. These were always open and could be used at any time, day or night and without supervision.

Before too long I realised what I was lacking was exercise, but in the ward all tasks requiring some physical effort were spoken for. Just as Seifried was employed in the washing and medicine administration, there were other long-term patients who were responsible for window cleaning, for the polishing and for the cleaning of the ablutions. There wasn't a task open to me by which I could exercise and yet still show no enterprise. I therefore wandered aimlessly around, but it did give me time to observe some of the other patients.

I have already mentioned young Freddy, the clever little ship's boy with whom I soon established a friendship. While there in the mental hospital he had learnt how to knot carpets and was always on the look out for other little paying tasks and jobs. He, unlike the adults, wasn't receiving any pay. Even the *Handelsmarine* sailors were paid a sort of pocket money, but he had to depend on what he could earn from the other patients and from nurses and the orderlies, so that he could also do some buying in the canteen. I would have willingly diverted some money from my POW account, but I didn't want to *'advance'* too far too fast into *'normality'*. To go shopping, or even to demonstrate the ability to administer my own money would, I thought, show my hand too much. Perhaps it was better, in this situation, to be as apathetic as possible, taking my cue from fellow patients.

There were marked differences in people's *'ability'* but nobody seemed to be watching too closely. Maybe it was easily dismissed by the unpredictable nature of mental illness. Hans Hein, for instance, bought himself cigarettes, while von Casimir remained apathetic and lethargic. He was simulating chronic depression. Hein was acting somewhat similar to myself, but had not demonstrated any acts of violence since entering the hospital and maybe that was best all round. The orderlies were particularly afraid of him, he was roughly six feet two inches and built like a tank. That was why he was prescribed the strong sedatives which he always cleverly managed to hide under his tongue. Who knows what would have happened to him if he had ever swallowed them all!

Gehrke, who was also in our room, suffered with a persecution complex, he was really a sad sight! Everywhere and everything presented a threat to him; nor could he conceive of a positive outcome of anything. If we were talking about our secret plans he would wag his finger, saying: "Definitely don't do that! That'll go wrong! That's what the Canadians are waiting for! You'll see!" However, if we wanted to know what he could suggest as an alternative he was always silent and withdrew into himself. He was genuinely ill and it was a shame to have to watch how his continuous anxieties gnawed away at him.

'Why hadn't the Canadians sent him home?' was a question we often asked. Either they thought a man like that wouldn't survive long within the perfectionist codes of the *Dritte Reich* (Third Reich), or maybe they thought, compared with us, his behaviour was normal? The Canadian psychiatrist had a difficult job with him too. Sometimes Gehrke knew too little English to be able to talk, or he just simply didn't want to talk; other times he was in tiptop shape, clean, washed and shaved and fairly bright, just as if he was getting ready to go out. As far as secrets were concerned, one was one hundred percent safe with Gehrke. He wouldn't tell anybody anything.

We were not so sure about the man whose syphilis they were trying to cure through a fever treatment. Why was he, compared with the other Germans, being given such an expensive therapy we wondered? We were never able to find out, simply being left to puzzle about it. However, we did discover that before he was given this treatment he was asked to give his consent. He was taken away for long intervals to another part of this spacious hospital complex for treatment. When he returned he was always lying in a coffin-like container which was still steaming. He had told us, and also

Seifried had reported it to us, that in this *'coffin'* he was warmed up to high temperatures - over forty degrees celsius (104 F) - the theory being that this would help the body overcome this insidious infection. Although he lived in the other room, the carriage with the coffin was usually pushed into our room to cool off.

Ship's boy, Freddy, had taken over the daily task of cleaning the wash rooms and the showers. It wasn't very attractive employment for him as there was no pay. I soon saw my chance and willingly took on the cleaning. First of all the rows of white basins on the one side and the showers on the other side had to be thoroughly washed. They were in a good condition and really very easy to clean. This first gave me something to do and secondly began to offer the exercise I craved. It got better when I discovered I could lock the doors from the inside and then do my gymnastics unobserved as well. At first the orderlies wouldn't allow it, but when I refused to do the work unless the doors were locked, they let me, dismissing it as a cranky foible. So that nobody could watch me while I was in there, I stuffed toilet paper into the key holes for the duration of my cleaning. The cleaning, combined with my gymnastics, allowed me to pass two hours of my time every morning.

Even in this ward time passed very slowly, but everything was much better than down in C. Anything was better than C Ward! We were even allowed to read and there were books, magazines and even newspapers available. Von Casimir and Hein read in public but I, however, didn't want to go that far. When I wanted to read I would go and lie under one of the empty beds in the big dormitory. From there I just had to watch when black shoes with white trouser legs turned up. For the most part I was successful in avoiding being observed.

Once, at the time all other patients were having their meal (only we Germans were served our meals on trays in our rooms) I was lying under a bed reading. Before I realised what was happening, white trousers and black shoes were approaching from both sides. I had just enough time to push my newspaper up between the mattress and the springs and then lay still. Two orderlies sat down on the bed above me and one remained standing, they hadn't noticed I was lying underneath and I could hear everything they said. Soon it became clear to me what the subject was. The man that was standing was Mr. Opel, the Chief. He was in overall supervision of Upper and Lower B as well as C Ward. The two orderlies were from that floor, Upper B: "Damn it! You must be more careful!" he said to the two in hushed tones. There then followed a discussion through which I could ascertain what the row was about.

The orderlies were responsible for receiving the *'difficult cases'* when they arrived at the hospital. These people were sometimes unconscious or only partly conscious and were then *'taken care of'* by those two orderlies. They helped them undress, just as when I'd arrived, and saw to it that they were provided with hospital clothing. They were then taken downstairs to C Ward to wake up in one of the cells. Part of their responsibility was not only for the uniforms of the patients, but also for their valuables and this included their wallets. For this Nurse Jenny had wardrobes and also lockers where personal items of value could be placed under lock and key. "It's damned well happened twice in a short time now!" said Mr Opel, "Patients have woken up and their money is missing. Yesterday one of the newcomers wanted to buy cigarettes in the canteen and he knew he'd had forty-four dollars when he came in!"

It transpired that because the money had already been split up and distributed among those staff involved in the racket it couldn't be recovered. All that could be done was to ask the patient whether he realised why he was there? Didn't he realise his mind might be playing tricks on him? Upon hearing this the patient had turned angry and started beating around, really raving mad. Although he had been taken to a cell, he still complained to Dr. Rogier, who now wanted an explanation from him, the Chief Orderly, and from Nurse Jenny. "I'll take care of her," said Mr Opel, "but in the future you'd better be more careful!" My heart nearly stopped, I hardly dared to breathe! If they'd have caught me, what chance would I have had of surviving then? They didn't notice me and parted, agreeing that they would continue to split any money between the three of them, but only when they were totally sure a patient was completely *'out of his head,'* and, in future, they'd not empty the wallet completely. I thought it was rather sad that these poor people were robbed in this way, but there was absolutely nothing I could do about it without *'showing my hand'* and possibly putting myself at risk. No wonder Nurse Jenny didn't have to worry about them disclosing anything about her own *'problem'.*

A true chamber of horrors was located between the wash-room and the staircase. Every now and then the door was open and I could take a look into it. There stood something that looked like the electric chair used in the USA for executions. A type of hood hung over the arm rest; it had a copper headband and leather straps to secure it. There were also bands to secure the arms and the legs. Naturally I turned to Seifried for information on this diabolical instrument and he was, as usual, well informed. The chair was used for giving electric shock treatment, although the use of this method of treatment was, apparently, still very much experimental.

Shock treatment was only used on patients after permission had been obtained from their relatives. Seifried said that there had already been some incredible cures using this new apparatus. "My God!" I thought, "If they ever had the idea of putting me in that chair..." My resolution was clear; I would immediately report that I was one of the *Simulaten*, but on the other hand, would they believe that now? Would I end up in the same position as the poor patients being robbed; would they suggest that I was bound to think I was only pretending - that would be all part of my disorder, part of why I was there! The thought worried me a great deal until Seifried calmed us down. He was certain this therapy was not to be used on prisoners of war and internees, but it still hovered there in the background like some awful spectre.

On one occasion I had the opportunity to observe the results of this electric shock therapy. The patient, Frankie, was a slim young man, hardly eighteen years of age and had been diagnosed as chronically depressed. Other patients, mostly young soldiers, who recovered very quickly and were soon ready to be on their way out to freedom again, used to spoil Frankie whenever they could. He let them treat him like a grown up doll. If they offered him a cigarette, he would sometimes shake his head, sometimes take a cigarette and not light it and occasionally he would have the cigarette lit up; then he would smoke it quite normally. With chocolate it was the same, sometimes he would eat it, other times he would simply refuse it. They tried to fulfil every wish he had in an attempt to cheer him up because he was always so sad and apathetic. Many, many times he didn't want to go along for his meals and they would either carry him over their shoulders or he would even ride like a child on the shoulders of another patient to the dining room.

One day his parents appeared in the ward and one could see them in deep discussion with Dr. Rogier and another specialist. There the decision was reached: Frankie was to receive, in small doses and over a period of time, several electric shocks. It was really odd, having to watch what developed day after day. Initially, after the first shock treatment, he was really happy and the whole ward was celebrating for Frankie. He was jovial and on top of the world! A few days later, the same old Frankie returned, almost worse than before. There was nothing, absolutely nothing, that interested him, he was a really sad sight. As the therapy progressed he was up for a few days and then crashed back into the blackness of his depression. After some time he was completely apathetic, refused all kind of food and had to be taken to the intensive care ward. Seifried told us that he died there soon afterwards.

We heard from Jenny that, because of the invasion of the Allies in France, there were difficulties in conducting the exchanges through Lisbon but efforts were being made to have the *Gripsholm* sail to Sweden. Christmas came and it was one of the unhappiest I had experienced; bad news from the war fronts: major reversals in France, Russia and Italy and also, in the Pacific, the Americans were recapturing one island after the other back from Japan. And there we impotently sat, in our room in the *Irrenhaus* (loony-bin) while our country slowly bled to death. A splendid turkey meal was served on Christmas day 1944, but we didn't enjoy it.

The volume of information that we were receiving at that time was improving, even if what we learned was not to our liking. There were two patients who seemed to have a real soft spot for us German POWs and spent time with us, giving us all the information we wanted on the war to date. Tom had come from the war in North Africa and was in the hospital because one night he'd taken it into his head to shoot the two other soldiers who shared a tent with him. 'The voice of God' had apparently ordered him to do it. In our conversations with Tom he appeared to be normal, but if we touched the subject of why he'd shot his two comrades he became excited and very affronted. "Not killed!" he would shout, "Not killed! - I helped them to get to God! They are now in heaven and relieved of all earthly sufferings! - Don't you understand? - I dealt explicitly with God's command! - I heard his voice clearly!"

This was the only subject which would bring about such excited behaviour. Besides that he acted apparently normally for most of the time and was more than willing to help us as much as he could. For instance, he was continually going through all the newspapers looking for news of the *Gripsholm*, or any other kind of news that could have something to do with the exchange of prisoners of war. The orderlies hinted that a case like Tom wouldn't stand much chance of ever being released into normal society again.

The way in which the other patient, Peter, helped was completely different. He was tall, like a tree, well over six feet and of athletic build. He proudly told us that he was originally of German origin, but came from a big farm in Alberta. He had been a tank driver in the army and his vehicle had received a direct hit during the invasion of northern France. He was suffering from the results of that trauma, although he claimed he was only suffering from shock. His view was that he didn't really belong there in that place amongst all these *'crazy people.'*

His illness was clearly more than simple shock. As if in accordance with a fixed schedule he would go to the sun rooms, which were situated at both ends of the ward, and there he would march back and forth in a military style. Suddenly he would come to a halt and then stand still with his arms spread out. He would then *'telephone'* and also make *'radio transmissions,'*

The sunrooms of Upper and Lower B Wards in which the patients could do their exercise and where the patient, Peter, would recieve his 'radio and telephone' messages. The lower most row of windows, at cellar-level, belong to C Ward.

not only verbally, but also in morse code, generating his own beeps as he went. His main interest was to find out how the war was going to progress. For this he spoke, by telephone and radio of course, with Franklin Roosevelt, Josef Stalin and Winston Churchill. And, of course, to get a balanced view from the other side, with Adolf Hitler, Benitto Mussolini and Hideki Tojo.

During these *'radio'* connections, he was demonstrably very concerned about us German prisoners of war. Again and again he came into our room and brought the most up-to-date news for us, completely normally telling us which exchanges or special treatment would soon be affecting us. In his own way, he also found out how the war was continuing and which battles had come to an end. He was actually always very well informed, although it was obvious all his knowledge originated from the newspapers he had read. He was, for all his strange behaviour, a real source of good information for us.

On Sundays I always watched from one of the windows in the sun rooms as the people were going to church. Many came from outside the mental hospital to attend the services in the beautiful little hospital chapel. On one occasion I heard that Peter was going to be having important visitors. Apparently his wife had decided to come all the way from Alberta to visit him and to show him their baby, who had been born while he was away. The visit was so important that even Dr Rogier wanted to be present, even though it was a Sunday. I watched from the sun room as the young woman was driven to the main entrance in a taxi. Shortly afterwards she appeared, smiling, with the baby in her arms. She then laid it on a beautiful white, lacy cushion in our department while she went to meet Peter.

The meeting with her husband had been arranged to take place in the sun room. He almost had to be dragged there and was, right from the beginning, terribly awkward and stubborn. The young woman looked at him obviously dismayed; externally he looked so healthy and normal, but that appearance was soon shattered. Peter erupted suddenly in a violent explosion of anger, almost lashing out at her, "Go away, you whore!" he shouted at her, "That child, that bastard is not my child! I've heard everything in detail over the radio and read it in the news!" The meeting lasted hardly a minute. With great effort the orderlies managed to keep that great tree of a man under control as he tried to get at his wife. He was immediately taken to C Ward where he was put in one of the cells.

With tears streaming down her face, the young woman was accompanied back to the taxi by Dr Rogier and a nurse. It was clear how upset she was and luckily there were several people with her, most probably relatives, to rally around as she left. It took a long time before Peter returned from C Ward and he was a little groggy for a long time after that.

My head swam as I thought about scenes like that. My thoughts just roared around in my mind. So this was the world of the genuine patients, and here we were *'playing'* the same game. Wasn't that an abomination? Wasn't that a profanity - an affront to God and one's self? Wasn't it about time I thought again?

Notes on Chapter Twenty-one:

¹ Later I was to find out that the *Gripsholm* was in dry dock having damage repaired.

² Essentially I had begun the early stages of anorexia nervosa.

Note: *'...und Gott Lenkt'* - the title of this chapter is also the title of my last book in German. It is derived from the old German expression, *'Der Mensch denkt, und Gott lenkt!'* ('Man thinks but God decides'). If it is not already clear why I chose that expression to represent my case I believe it will be before the end of my story.

CHAPTER TWENTY-TWO

THE SITUATION GETS DIFFICULT
... DOUBTFUL.

Around this time in Germany, my mother had received a letter from Gerhard Hog, a ship's officer from Danzig:

Danzig, 26th September 1944.

Dear Mrs Steinhilper,

Please allow me to introduce myself. My name is Hog, I had the honour of meeting your son Rudi (this was the name he used when we had briefly met in Upper B) in Canada.
We were both in the same Mental Hospital, with the hopes of a possible exchange from there (Hog had been put on the list in the last minute instead of myself) and I returned to Germany on 10th September of this year. Your son, the same as ten other Germans who simulated a mental illness, had been put in a mental hospital from where the chances of being exchanged back to Germany existed. Sad to say only four of us were the lucky ones. The others, including your son, are still there today. I was asked to write the following to you:
Your son has been there since 15th March of this year, he is completely healthy and mentally fit. It is a pity that, due to his illness (which he is simulating for the Canadians) he cannot write letters. Please understand this correctly, 'simulating'! This is the only way that a healthy man can make his way home. He has further German comrades there, amongst them a Major von Casimir, who is doing exactly the same. There is definitely no danger for your son. I played the same game and was one of the lucky ones. There I couldn't write and was not able to read and have now been exchanged completely healthy. Should your son be successful at the next visit of the International Commission of Doctors, then he should be home next year, perhaps January or February. I do not want to go into more detail in this letter, concerning the mental hospital, but I am prepared to give you as much information as I can, should you be interested.
Please continue to write to your son as in the past, but never ever make

mention of my letter or of your knowledge of his whereabouts. Each letter from home for your son is now receiving extensive censorship and could be a disadvantage for him.
With German greetings,

Gerhard Hog.

Whether there were any other contacts with Ship's Officer Gerhard Hog after this letter, I do not know. I didn't get to see him after the war; who knows what happened to him in Danzig?

In November, with date 8.11.1944, my father received an official answer to his inquiry to the International Red Cross from the Presidency in Berlin:

Mr. Wilhelm Steinhilper,
Heutingsheim near Ludwigsburg
Württemberg.

The delegates of the International Committee of the Red Cross in Canada requested we forward the following health report to you:

7.8.44

Dear Mr. Steinhilper!

I had visited your son, Captain Ulrich Steinhilper, in the Westminster Mental Hospital near London (Ontario), Canada, and am sorry to have to inform you that his state of health was such that a normal conversation with him was not possible. Your son is suffering under a persecution complex and believes that everybody who is taking care of him wants to do him harm.

The physical state of health of the patient is good. I am very sorry that I cannot give you any better news, but I assume it is at least comforting for you to know that I have spoken with your son and that the treatment he is receiving is, under these circumstances, correct.

The German Red Cross is also very sorry that the information forwarded is of such negative content.

The Special Representative...by order....Kucher.

As my parents told me after the war, this news was reason for great concern on their side; especially because, after this letter, there was no correspondence from anybody for a long time, although there was still Hog's mention of a further exchange. Later, when looking at the above date, it made me think. At the time when the Red Cross delegate visited me in the C Ward, 11th July 1944, I had been there for three months and three weeks, and was alone among patients who were genuinely ill. Nevertheless I had resisted the temptation to talk normally in German with the Swiss Red Cross representative. On 7th August, precisely the day on which the report of the visit was prepared in Ottawa - exactly a month after it had taken place - I stupidly talked to the Hospital Director, Dr Rogier. In this manner I managed to bungle my exchange in August 1944, just for the sake of two days! Was it *'stupidity'* or was it fate? What would have happened to *Hauptmann* Steinhilper of the *Luftwaffe* if he'd returned home in September of 1944?

Spending the winter in an *Irrenhaus* was worse than any of the preceding winters; even the Canadian patients suffered the effects of winter. During the summer months they were sent to the farm that belonged to the hospital. There they could not only recover physically but begin the transition from institution back to society. Again and again they were reminded: "Don't escape! Don't run away." For many young soldiers however, this type of recovery from their mental illness was too boring. They just took the opportunity to travel home on their own. During the winter the boredom factor increased and many more of them went *'over the wall.'*

It wasn't going to work like that, either they were caught *enroute*, or at the latest when they reached home, and back they came. When they resisted violently while being recaptured they would land up in C, otherwise they were returned to us, to Upper B, and were again reminded: without official release documents there was no way they could get away and stay away. Some of them got so upset and annoyed over this that they had to take a *'cooling bath'* downstairs in C. There was no way to *'buck the system'*. It was only with much patience that a final release could be achieved and appeared to be a lot easier during the summer than during the winter, perhaps the farm was a good halfway house.

February 1945, we heard through Jenny that once again a neutral exchange commission was under way in Canada. They were also to come and look at a few cases here in the hospital. Now a little alarm bell began to ring in my mind. Hadn't I, in the meantime, just been taking it too easy? Had I, *'an old escaper'*, played away all my chances? We didn't know and couldn't speculate if there was a chance for us but we wanted to take all necessary precautions... *'special provisions'* were prepared... just in case.

Both Hans Hein and myself were recorded as being violent, it was part of how we saw our illness. We wanted to underscore it for the benefit of any visiting commission and this time, so that it looked completely genuine, the Germans were going to get into a fight amongst themselves. Of course we didn't plan a fight in public, that might bring serious reprisals, but we wanted to look like we'd been 'in the wars'. Hans and myself were of the same opinion, our main aim was that both of us would have at least one black eye after our scrap.

We would do it in our room without spectators if possible. Seifried was to stand guard at the door, Gehrke and von Casimir would not be able to avoid being witnesses. The 'punch-up' was planned so that we punched each other on the eyebrows, a well aimed but glancing punch would, we agreed, do the trick. A fat black eye should be the result and would last, by our calculations, for the duration of the visit by the Commission.

The next question was who was to punch first? We quickly agreed that whoever was judged to have the better nerve should be second to punch. Everybody in the room was now involved in the planning and even Seifried and von Casimir were giving us their best advice. Gehrke, predictably, prophesied doom and gloom for our enterprise but notwithstanding that we went ahead. It was decided I should punch second and that was not only the decision of the advisors, Hans himself recommended it. He said he was frequently nervous and shaky as a result of having been in the hospital so long and felt that the effects of his smoking did little to steady him. He said he would like to land the first blow, especially because I'd had boxing instruction and, consequently, more experience. They said they trusted me to land an accurate blow, even after having been hit myself.

The exchange of blows was set for the morning and Seifried stood in the door, waving the Canadians past down the corridor. I was set and the first blow came quickly and effectively, Hans landed a wonderful punch. My right eyebrow burst open and blood began flowing down my face. There were no doors on the room and someone must have heard the impact because some of the Canadian patients immediately stopped in the corridor. Seifried couldn't get rid of them any more and it was my turn. With power and precision I aimed at Hans' right eyebrow, but just in the last fraction of a second I saw the doubt in his eyes and sensed a movement of his head. It was too late, I couldn't stop it, the punch had gone past the point of no return. He had defensively swayed backwards a little and in so doing he'd raised his head enough for me to hit him full on the nose. I had recovered some of my strength and having trained to box I delivered a substantial blow to poor Hans who was knocked backwards by the force of the impact.

Again the noise was heard and attracted the young Canadians to the doorway and, recognising that a fight was in progress, some of them darted away shouting, "The Germans are fighting! The Germans are fighting!" We could hear it spread as they ran through Upper B and in no time the orderlies were in our room. A glance at Hans, his nose bleeding profusely, and another glance at me told them all they seemed to want to know and the alarm bells were actuated. More orderlies came swarming up from C Ward and seeing me, assumed they knew who was at the bottom of things. Literally before I knew what was going on, I was being carted off down one floor and I ended up in a well known cell.

As in old times, I was given an injection and awoke in the middle of the night to find myself on the familiar old leather mattress. Through the peep-hole, in the weak light of the night-lights, I could see that C Ward was well occupied and, consequently, had to spend the next few days in the cell because there was no room; they even pushed a bed into the cell for me. This was actually to my advantage because Harry and Lieutenant Kean were trying to re-establish contact with me and I really didn't want that. It wasn't easy for them, as long as I was in the cell, and that suited me fine. I couldn't take part in the polishing, but that was also alright by me, I wasn't intent on staying long enough to worry about my fitness. Although it had been *'home'* for me for over five months, life in C Ward still had a totally alien feel to it. I found it very unsettling even though the orderlies frequently spoke with me and commented on how good I looked, now I'd put on a little weight again.

Within a few days I was back upstairs again in our room in the same bed. The Commission had been there and had quickly checked their lists and I was told that all the Germans were to be exchanged as soon as possible. They hadn't wanted to see me, the X-rays of Hein's nose had apparently been enough to convince them. Hans harboured no bad feelings towards me for my boxing prowess. Not only the witnesses, but he himself were certain I had only hit him dead-centre because he had ducked away backwards. Of course, after returning to our room, I tried to apologise but he always just waved it away.

My physical condition had improved tremendously in the meantime, I was almost gaining weight too fast, but was that actually of any importance any more? Indeed, in March 1945, we heard through Nurse Jenny that vaccine for all of us had arrived, and in the next few days we would be getting our vaccinations before being exchanged. But would it actually happen we wondered? The war news, which we were getting uncensored by means of the radio, the newspapers and the U.S. magazines, was unequivocal:

Germany was on the point of collapse. There were also reports on the *'wonder weapons'*, the V2 and V1, but would they be of any help we wondered? Wasn't it all too little too late? The question began to arise whether, if we were to be exchanged, there was anything that we could do to help the situation once we got home, or was the war totally and irrevocably lost?

Only defeats were being reported; the offensive in the Ardennes had been stopped, the Americans had crossed the Rhine at Remagen and on the Eastern Front one retreat was following the other. Northern Italy was already in Allied hands and the collapse of the Japanese in the Pacific seemed close, although that was of little direct interest to us. The official statement from Dr Rogier, that the planned exchange was not going to take place, fitted wonderfully into the sequence of bad news. The neutral nations were apparently no longer in a position where they could guarantee the safety of men of both sides in the course of an exchange. The Allies, it was said, still wished to proceed, but without the cooperation of the neutrals it would be impossible.

We discussed the situation whenever we could and as secretly as possible. We agreed that as things stood, with the defeat of Germany apparently becoming inevitable, it was of paramount importance that it should not come to light that we had only been simulating illness. We imagined there would be severe penalties if it could be proved that was what we'd been doing. For the time being we had no other choice than to wait and see. During that time we decided it would be in the best interests of us all to ensure our health didn't deteriorate any further, a holding action until the future became clearer. What might face us we didn't know. Certainly I was worried as all too often I overheard the orderlies and observed them pointing at me and saying, "That one there, he belongs in the category that should never be released." Now Hans Hein's nose stood as very negative evidence in my files. So too did my violent attacks whilst in C Ward - I just might have dug a hole for myself from which I would find it difficult to escape. Perhaps the *'best laid plans of mice and men'* were about to blow up in my face again. What cruel irony.

Sometimes I was so worried about the confused situation I often wondered whether the time hadn't come to attempt another escape, just to survive. I had already recovered the twenty dollars from behind the downpipe in the autumn and had hidden it in a split in the wallpaper in our room. This would probably assist me in getting started if it came to it, I even got Seifried involved in my plans. He, in the meantime, was playing the key role in our German group more and more. His affair with Jenny had the positive side-effect that she was becoming less and less addicted to the narcotics and was even beginning to nurture hopes that she would one day come completely off them. As the war news was always getting better from her point of view, she was slowly letting all security measures slacken and even secretly gave Seifried a key for the fire escape.

With this key Seifried could, through the back entrance of Upper B, reach an iron staircase which led directly out to freedom. On certain days Jenny would be waiting for him in her car and, after a stop at her home for a change of clothes, they would go out for dinner. "After all," said Seifried, "the Canadian patients were allowed out from time to time!" It was amusing in one way, but we all knew Jenny was running a frightful risk.

Whether I wanted it or not, Jenny was informed of my plans. Seifried was conducting his relationship with her on a progressively more honest basis. With this it became clear that this nurse, to a degree, held our fate in her hands. But in this case it was also true that we had knowledge that could make life very uncomfortable for some of the staff, especially Jenny. We all realised this was the case and achieved an unspoken agreement that there would be no blackmail by either side.

Jenny definitely advised against an attempt to escape, although with the help of the key it would have been easy. She wasn't afraid of the consequences of an escape, even if it was Seifried who let us out, she was just certain that we would all be caught again. She sensibly reminded us that not even the Canadian patients had been successful for more than a week before they were brought back 'home'. It wasn't difficult to believe she was right, what could we do once we got out there? Von Casimir assured me that should I actually be retained there in the hospital as a dangerous case he would, after returning to a POW camp, certainly alert the German Camp Commander and the Red Cross. But if all else failed I could then reconsider the idea of an escape. To show her good will, Jenny was even prepared to add a few Canadian dollars to the twenty US dollars I already had. But for the time being I followed their advice, we wanted to see what the future would bring.

It was 8th May 1945 when, in a sort of ceremonial procession, all patients from Upper B were led past a large poster set up in the ward. Printed in large bold letters there in the middle were the words:

UNCONDITIONAL SURRENDER

Above and below it there were further paragraphs, but I didn't want to read them. What 'unconditional surrender' meant I could understand all too well and with it work out what our likely fate would be. Naturally there are diverse opinions on the value of officers in any situation, but in that place I honestly believe von Casimir and myself earned our salt. Although everyone had expected the war to end soon, when it became an inescapable fact it was hard to take. Unconditional surrender was not how we thought things would end, most of us had secretly harboured hopes of a negotiated peace, not another humiliation like Versailles, maybe even worse.

Von Casimir and I held the Germans together as a brotherhood, discussing the consequences as a group and trying to speculate about the future. We would master the expected problems, one after the other, as and when we were confronted with them. The primary consideration was that we must all keep our heads. We were in a very uncomfortable position, in a mental hospital at the end of a war, but things should progress. There would be a way ahead for all of us. We agreed that none of us would be the first to admit that he had been feigning in order to return to the camp. We thought it probable the internees and the merchant navy sailors had the best chances of being sent home first. These sailors, we thought, would probably be needed most now that the war was over. Then NCOs, like Hans Hein, would probably follow but, for us, the two officers, it looked worst of all.

For quite a while the Morgenthau Plan, the document that would determine the fate of the German service personnel, had been the source of discussion in America and comments had appeared in the newspapers. According to early opinion, the first suggestions were aimed at the German intelligentsia, especially the officer corps, who, once and for all, would be put out of action. So obsessed were they that there was something biologically wrong with the German officers that there was even debate about castration to prevent us fathering another nation of *Nazis*. Was this the justice to be meted out after so many had died apparently in the name of freedom? In any event it was clear that we, the officers, would be staying in confinement for some while before our fate was decided.

We naturally followed the debates in the press with great interest and saw the emphasis change from the extreme position of sterilisation to a view that those that had previously held officer rank would not be permitted to study at the universities or to hold managerial posts. They would only be permitted to be employed in manual work, principally menial tasks in agriculture; indeed for a time the sway of the debate seemed to be towards turning Germany into some kind of large farm. Clearly this meant that if anybody was going to be held back it would be *Major* von Casimir and *Hauptmann* Steinhilper. Hard as it was, we both accepted it and were then able to concentrate more on the needs of our charges and to actively support them as best we could.

Interestingly it was the chief orderly, Opel, from whom we got the best advice. It was selfish and the product of self-interest but it was sound: "He who is cooperative; he who, through work, actively supports the hospital, he will be leaving here faster than the others!" That was his contribution and, given his position, we had no doubt it was true. But there were other factors for the Canadians to consider. The number of patients coming in from Europe was ever increasing. It seemed their return transport had been delayed, possibly by the final thrusts on the various battle fronts, but now they were coming back in numbers. I had already noticed the beginning of this during my brief visit to C Ward and it soon manifest itself in the other wards. Beds were being pushed into every available space and it became clear that the Canadians were in need of the space occupied by us.

We had agreed among ourselves that total cooperation would serve us best and launched ourselves into a schedule of work. All except Major von Casimir, who didn't want to get well quite so quickly! We other Germans, I believe, felt the same and after so much lethargy really went willingly to work, it was a pleasure. We took the windows out of their frames, including the iron grills, washed them thoroughly, painted the frames and after everything was back in place, they were shining like new. We painted the walls, stripped the old polish off the floors with steel wool pads and then applied a new coat of polish. The time of the year couldn't have been better for a thorough spring clean the like of which Upper B Ward had never seen. Our work was so well done that even Dr. Rogier appeared, personally, to express his thanks.

I was in charge of a mixed team of German and Canadian patients and hard as it may be to believe, a second team, consisting solely of Canadians, was led by our Freddy. Although the lad was, by then, just twenty years old his natural power of command was such that the mainly older former soldiers willingly volunteered and followed his instructions. Perhaps in us there was the feeling that through our participation and diligent work we could make amends and expect a small amount of forgiveness for the sins we had committed; a kind of penance. In any event it wasn't too long after we'd brought both sun rooms in Upper B up to scratch that the Merchant Navy sailors were able to say farewell. Of course the farewell from Seifried was especially hard for Jenny, it was also terribly hard for Seifried as well and they agreed they would meet again as soon as possible. Seifried promised that when he got back to Germany, if he was released, he would try to emigrate back to Canada. Whether he did or not I don't know.

Hans Hein and von Casimir followed next and I was left alone. I didn't know if I should worry about that though it wouldn't have helped - I would still have to sit it out but, as I was soon to discover, I wouldn't be bored. Now there were no more German working teams I was approached from all sides, the doctor, the orderlies and even from the *unnahbaren* (unapproachable - remote) Head Nurse Victoria and encouraged to continue in my roll as the team leader; I had apparently done so well they said. I wondered to myself if this was in my best interest. On the one hand I had the Chief Orderly's words in the back of my mind, and that had certainly seemed to work for everyone else, but on the other hand was I making myself indispensable? Again there was no real choice and I carried on my role as unpaid organiser of the ward work details and was soon in charge of a group of twelve Canadian patients. With them I soon had the spring cleaning done in the wash-rooms and our two small rooms, followed by painting work throughout.

Meanwhile, time had slipped us by and it was June 1945. More than a month had elapsed since we had paraded before the 'unconditional surrender' notice and I found myself left alone there and returning to the question of whether I should attempt an escape from my apparently hopeless situation. The US dollars were still safe and I even had some additional Canadian dollars which had been given to me by the sailors upon leaving, and Seifried was able to give me the spare key for the emergency exit. However, I wanted to wait before trying an escape, the summer had to pass further, then there would be sufficient berries in the woods and other fruits on which I could sustain myself while in hiding.

I keenly felt the lack of good comrades with whom I could discuss my plans and my dilemma, although I could have approached Nurse Jenny I suppose. I could talk with Tom, the soldier, who'd shot his comrades in North Africa, about most things, we even spoke about the Morgenthau Plan. He said it was disgusting and doubted the Americans as a whole, and especially the English, would be agreeable to it; he reassured me that I need not worry about it too much. It was astonishing how educated this man was and how lucid, but then still in the background was the memory of when God had spoken to him and he had acted on God's word. Later on I was to get the impression that he had buried this whole event deep in his mind and avoided any reference to it. Perhaps that was the reason even he was being sent out to the farm with a working group. Maybe he was to get his chance, and I wouldn't have begrudged him that, but I didn't want to talk to him about escaping or returning to the POW camp.

Peter, the tank driver and German farmer from Alberta had, until he was transferred to another hospital, remained the same. As always he marched back and forth in both sun rooms but, surprisingly, he no longer transmitted radio calls to Mussolini and Hitler. Hirohito, the Japanese Emperor, was the recipient of his undivided attention. While the war in Pacific still raged on he kept up his contact. I would have been especially pleased to see an improvement in his case, I just could not forget his wife and the baby. His being transferred to the west was to bring him closer to his family and it was hoped that through more frequent contacts he could, in time, be brought back to some degree of reality and normality. I earnestly hoped so.

CHAPTER TWENTY-THREE

HEALED? - DISCHARGED INTO A NEW WORLD

It was the middle of June when Dr Rogier personally brought me the good news: I had improved so tremendously and he had been so particularly encouraged by my good cooperation that he was going to discharge me, on probation, to an officers' camp. Once there, he advised, I shouldn't do stupid things any more or I might endanger my prospects of ever returning to Germany.

The good news was soon to be followed by positive deeds as Nurse Jenny brought my uniforms to the room and showed me all of my *'valuables'*. I was really pleased, there was not only my forage cap, two pairs of trousers, flying jacket and my undress uniform jacket, but also all my underwear, shirts and even my tie had been forwarded. My room-mates had certainly done a very thorough job when they collected my kit and sent it on. What surprised me most was that among my valuables was my good old wrist-watch. It had been taken away from me in England, when I was in the first interrogation camp and I hadn't seen it since.

All those years before in October 1940, during the Battle of Britain, I had made my abrupt and unplanned arrival in England and had begun my life as a POW. When I'd arrived at the interrogation camp I had been taken to what would be my room and then, later, marched off to my first interview. In front of the interviewing officers and flanked by soldiers with bayonets fixed I had to strip naked for a medical inspection and during the course of this my watch had been taken from me. It had been a valuable birthday present from my girl friend, Gretl, but that in itself was actually unimportant at the time. What really concerned me was that from then on I wouldn't easily know what the time was. After my persistent refusal to say anything other than, "No!" I was allowed to get dressed, but was not given the watch back, I had wondered quite a bit about this incident - was that English fair play? Almost five years later the precious piece found it's way back to me. Wasn't that a good sign? Were things now, at last, going my way?

Getting my watch back seemed to crystallise everything for me and I cheered up no end. I decided it was a good sign, a new beginning for me. The war had been lost, but with that also came the end. Perhaps the imprisonment would also end as well? Perhaps I would be released into the world outside - dare I believe the nightmare was drawing to a close? The anxiety that I could be held there for years, as a patient and not a prisoner of war, had gone. Why shouldn't my heart beat faster and feel lighter? First I decided to get out of my hospital clothes and back into my uniform, see how that felt. I soon realised that although I had gained quite a lot of weight again, my uniform was still very loose, flapping around on me. I quickly decided to wear my flying blouse which had been tailored a little tighter.

Without much ceremony I finished dressing in Nurse Jenny's room, packed my other belongings into a cardboard box and an orderly took me to the outside steps at the main entrance where I was received by a young officer of the army. There to see me off was Sunny, who could not resist saying farewell to Steenie and to wish him all the best, especially a healthy return journey to Germany. How she'd heard I was to be discharged I didn't know, was it the talk of the hospital? It was easy to see she was very pleased to see me in such a good condition and my bad conscience bothered me again. I'd hated the idea I was deceiving people who seemed to care so much about my welfare.

We drove in a station-wagon to the station at London, Ontario, and travelled on the train amongst all the other passengers to Hamilton and from there to Toronto. How I enjoyed that, the first time I had been outside when there was no war. And what beautiful countryside we were travelling through; bathed in sunshine it spread out as far as I could see, resplendent in the full blush of June; the green fields, some trees in blossom, herds of cattle on the meadows and the beauty of the great lake on the right hand side. I found it easy to readjust to the new situation, it didn't overwhelm me as I'd feared it might. Yes, we had lost the war, but wasn't there going to be a new beginning for me, for all of us prisoners of war. Wasn't the phoenix going to rise from the ashes of Germany to fly again? But when? How much longer would we remain in Canadian custody? How long would it take to finish drafting the Morgenthau Plan and what would it bring for us? Although as I thought of that icy fingers clutched my heart, I buoyed myself up by looking around and taking in the beauty of the day and counting my blessings.

I was still young so what was the point in being bitter about the years I'd lost in prison: I had survived. As we travelled through the countryside I thought over what I had lived through; the accidents during pilot training, the collision in the air with Siggi Voss, over one hundred and fifty sorties over England, the near fatal abandoning of my aircraft at very low level, the interrogation, the escapes and worst of all the *Irrenhaus* (loony-bin). I regretted nothing from my past and would have, if it had been necessary, done it all again - all, that is, except the last part. That was undoubtedly the worst mistake I'd made in my life and nothing would have induced me to relive it.

At least I could congratulate myself on being able to survive that as well. I could forgive myself that big mistake so that I could see the future clearly, the most important thing was to think ahead and to think positively. What I had been through had at least taught me how much I could take when required and that was important knowledge. It gave me the security of thinking there would be little in the future that could be so demanding and I therefore felt I could take whatever life decided to throw at me. I would face up to it and not despair! As an old flyer, even if my wings had been clipped, I should be able to keep control of things.

As the journey wore on I had time to mull many things over in my mind. It was surprising to me that nobody, not even my officer guard, had any objections to the swastikas on my uniform; on the emblem on my forage cap, on the right side of my breast under the spread eagle and on the left side on my pilot's Wings. Some people looked but I didn't detect any hostility - were they being magnanimous in victory? While we were sitting in the cafeteria of the main station in Toronto, the Union Station, waiting for our connection to Gravenhurst, an officer of the RCAF approached us. The Canadian flyer did draw our attention to my swastikas although in a friendly manner; he was of the opinion that I should remove the swastikas from my uniform so we wouldn't have problems with *'certain people',* as he put it. My accompanying officer was of the opinion, however, that if I removed everything from my uniform I would look like a civilian and that wouldn't do. We amiably discussed a compromise: the emblem on my forage cap would remain where it was, my pilot's Wings combined with my shoulder straps would still show that I was a *Hauptmann* and a former German pilot. After all it wasn't every day that my guard had the opportunity to travel with somebody special and I rather think he enjoyed the attention we drew.

He gave me his pocket knife and I went off to the toilet and picked off the eagle and swastika from my right breast and unpicked the white cotton of the swastika which was part of my pilot's wings. That's all that was necessary in the view of my guard, the cap could stay as it was because I took it off while indoors. What a difference, instead of cold inflexible orders, a debate as to what would be the best course. The atmosphere was so relaxed because there was no question that he was preventing me running away, he even let me go to the toilet unaccompanied. Occasionally we got into conversation with the civilians and military personnel around us and they were all surprisingly friendly, especially when they heard that I was on my way from a hospital back to the POW camp. Many even wished me a safe return to Germany, a wish I also subscribed to with all my heart, but there was a long way to go before there was any question of that.

Later that day I arrived back at Gravenhurst and found a space had been allocated for me in my old room. My room-mates could hardly believe I was still normal after so long away in the *Irrenhaus*. The whole camp was apparently of the opinion that I had gone too far, exceeded Dr Eitze's warning and had actually *'übergeschnappt'* (*'gone round the bend'*). This opinion had been supported when the Red Cross representative's report became known in the camp, the same report that reached my parents. Although he was no longer Camp Leader, *Oberstleutnant* Meythaler wanted to speak to me immediately. I duly reported to him and we had a conversation during which he was clearly very relieved when I was not only able to assure him that I was normal, but he himself could witness there was nothing really wrong. He advised me in the most serious tone not to mention my simulated illness to anyone, but to talk about having recovered. The conditions in the camp and the attitudes of the Canadians, he cautioned, had changed tremendously and that made me pause for thought.

Immediately after my talk with *Oberstleutnant* Meythaler I saw Dr Eitze and the relief he felt was obvious. "My God!" he said, "You just don't know what a burden you laid on us all here, Steinhilper." He told me how they'd wondered what to do, whether to try to act from the camp, especially when the Red Cross report became known. It had been something of a dilemma and he was glad things had actually turned out OK. Everything had changed tremendously and once we got over the brief euphoria of meeting up again it was clear most of my comrades were very depressed. Their former ebullient confidence was all but gone and there didn't even seem to be trust between them any more.

My room-mates Döring, Wildermuth and Theopold thought I looked very poorly and was very thin and suggested something would have to be done to correct this. Because the meals were no longer as good as they used to be, although additional supplies were coming from the camp farm by then, the means to help me had to come from their own rations. With that and with the help of the *Zerstörer* (destroyer) - *Obergefreiter* Gutberlet - occasionally smuggling me into the kitchen, I was better off than the average. How glad I was, how unbelievably glad I was, first of all to be out of the *loony-bin* and then to be with my comrades again. Some things had undoubtedly changed and I would have to adapt, but compared with what changes I had experienced in my time away they were nothing. For example, the glass of my wrist-watch had been accidentally broken during the journey and I wanted to get it repaired. In the camp there was a *Luftwaffe Oberleutnant* who had specialised in watchmaking and repairs and he was willing to make the repair, no surprises there. However when we came to negotiate the price he asked for what seemed to me to be a huge cigarette ration. That was a surprise, but not untypical of the changes I was to find. Self interest seemed to be the new culture!

Dr Huppert described our situation like this:

Besides the Camp-Commander, we were talking to Captain Karr, the Swiss-Canadian Hausmann, and the exiled Russian Tschramschenko *(Pferdedieb)*. As long as I held the post of Mail-Officer I was dealing with Hausmann; he was reserved but not unfriendly. As Canteen Officer in 1945, I was dealing with Captain Karr. At first he was very unfriendly, this was because he had been a prisoner of war in the First World War, in the hands of the Germans, and there he'd had the same misfortune as we were experiencing with the kitchen.

I was, however, successful in changing his attitude through politeness. Because I was always the last one to go through when he was counting or when I needed an appointment with him to discuss canteen affairs, my greeting was always 'Morning, Sir' to which he always replied 'Morning, Doc'. I was also successful in further gaining his goodwill through a small Christmas present in 1945, a model of an Olympia class dinghy that I had made of mahogany. This resulted in the supply of sausage, eggs and shoes, etc, being substantially improved.

When saying farewell to him in his quarters, he gave me a box of cigars and a photo of himself. This was exceptional. Later he even gave me a letter of reference for my canteen activities, which I still am proud to have in my possession. Through Karr's assistance I was able to transfer the complete camp finances to England, where they were, however, confiscated.

Summer 1945 Herr Hausmann started the denazification procedure, and was interviewing everybody. There were three groups:

Group 1 (white): Nazi opponents; in Camp 20 there was only one. He had requested Canadian protection and was held in a barracks outside the camp. A staff officer of ours had also requested Canadian protection and when he travelled to England with us he was avoided, especially by the *Afrikanern*.

Group 2 (grey): Young active officers that had not been party members (the bulk of the officer POWs). Some of these were transferred to other camps that were worse than ours.

Group 3 (black): Party members and members of the party organisations like HJ (*Hitler Jugend*), SA (*Sturm Abteilung* - Brown Shirts) etc. This group was actually the luckiest, they were allowed to remain in our good camp, where the food was continually improving, which was partially due to Captain Karr's efforts.

Once in England, in the Sheffield Camp, we were again interviewed, this time the interviews were conducted in part by embittered Polish (Free Poland) Officers.

Group A: As white above.
Group B: As grey above.
Group C: Were *eingefroren* (frozen in - *kept on ice*) and were sent to camps in Scotland.

Among these were some specialists such as, flyers, navy officers (mainly *U-boot* personnel) and engineer-officers who were kept back because the tensions with Russia (the Cold War) had begun. (All of these were discharged 1948, before the Olympic games began in England).

I was lucky, after having been interrogated by a British Captain, I was allowed to be discharged with B minus.

What I especially noticed in Camp Gravenhurst was that an *Obernazi* (a top Nazi), who, in 1943, had shocked us with his horrifying reports from Poland had already successfully affected the democratic style. He had made the change so successfully for the Canadians that they used him for our re-education. That's how they were, these ambitious types, he had been an active party member with the Nazis and in Poland he was in the SS. He had soon advanced to be *Kreisleiter* (County Leader) and earlier he had proudly told us how, under his instructions, Jews and Poles had to parade within two hours of notification with just twenty kilograms of luggage, and were then transported off to the *Arbeitslager* (labour camp). Then, after the war had been lost, people like him were quick to change their colours. They had always been against it, they would swear, and finally they could voice their own free opinion. It was incredible how these really hard-core Nazi Party members and SS men could be held up as shining examples to us. The selection of these shameless opportunists by the Canadians and the British to lead the re-education of the bulk of the officer POWs was, in my view, one of the biggest mistakes they made. Now, nearly fifty years later, people are surprised when a senior government official or prominent person in the diplomatic service is found to have had a somewhat murky Nazi or SS past. Really it's hardly surprising when so many of these *Verrätern* (turncoats) were able to shed their past so easily and embrace the democratic ideals. It was the Allies who set many on the first steps of their new careers.

Naturally this was upsetting to see and affected me badly, but what could I do to resist it? Other than in the course of the interrogations, the opinions of the average loyal officers and soldiers were not asked for or, if expressed, no notice taken of it. Besides that, the Morgenthau Plan and the theories which were being bandied about in its formation were keeping all minds very busy, the newspapers were all full of it. Not only the officers, but the whole German intelligentsia was to be put on ice, it was to be contained and prevented from reproducing. The question that remained was - how? Castration and sterilisation were being seriously discussed, but how could it be accurately decided who was intelligent and who wasn't? That would be determined later - initially we, the officer corps, were an easily identifiable beginning. We would remain in custody until such time as the Morgenthau dilemma was resolved. The theorists returned to their first thoughts of eventually returning us to Germany to carry out menial manual labour on farms.

It is a wonder that during this time of such uncertainty only a few of us really went off their heads. Only a handful were eventually committed to institutions and a very few took their own lives. For me, with my preparation in C Ward, the strain was easier to take. I had gone through much worse and had survived; that, at least, was one positive aspect of my months in the institution. I didn't really care what they gave me to do in Germany, as long as it was at least a worthwhile task. I just wanted to get back and start to build the new Germany, to try to do my bit after having been away so long, ineffectually confined in the camps.

It was by coincidence that I heard that Manni had managed to escape several months before the end of the war using the *Wunderzange*. At the end of hostilities this famous pair of cutters was decorated with an elegant red bow and presented to the last Canadian Commander of Gravenhurst as a souvenir from the escapers when he left the camp. But what had happened to Manni after his escape nobody actually knew. There were rumours that he was fed in a Camp for Internees for quite a while. Another disappointment for me was discovering that my painstakingly written journal which I had entrusted to my comrades had, apparently been destroyed *'for my own protection'*. They had only had my best interest at heart but I was rather upset that so much work had gone up in smoke, or so I thought.

I had hardly got used to life in the Gravenhurst when the news reached me that I was to be transferred to another camp. At that time that wasn't anything exceptional, everything seemed to be in a constant state of flux. Some prisoners were transferred to what was called *das Demokratie Lager* (The Democracy Camp) so they could learn how others, the so-called *'hard core Nazis'* were re-educated. Others, it was rumoured, were sent for longer stays in the west of Canada to fell trees; neither option really appealed to me, I just wanted to go home. But if I had to go somewhere in the meantime I really didn't mind where.

Soon the news of my impending move was translated to fact and I got my travel orders. Again I travelled by train in the company of a single Canadian Captain. I was slowly getting to be familiar with the railway line to Toronto and almost knew the scenery by heart. This time, of course, there were no swastikas left on my uniform; we had, in the meantime, learnt how to remove the patches without damaging our uniforms. Once more we sat in the snack bar in Toronto station while waiting for the train to Montreal. My escort was enjoying the situation more than I was, to accompany a captured *Luftwaffe* officer was something grand for him, especially as it was then only about two months after the end of the war. I couldn't eat and drink everything that he and the other travellers wanted to buy for me; it was really very odd.

We travelled in the direction of Montreal to Grande Ligne, a camp of which I knew nothing. It was located south of Montreal, near Lake Champlain and this time it was a special pleasure for me to travel along the shore of Lake Ontario: Oshawa, Belleville, Kingston (Fort Henry), Brockville, these were all places which had special memories for me, but how much different the situation was for me then. Although my earlier journeys had been in the depth of the freezing cold winters and my transport had been on the open freight cars, at least I'd had a future; there had still been hope for Germany. But what now? I travelled in comfort, but knew with some certainty that, for instance, I would never be able to fly again if the Morgenthau Plan was implemented. Would I ever see Germany, my parents, my friends? Could I ever look forward to a normal life? Germany was so far away... so very far away.

It was already night when we arrived and I spent that first night in the Medical Centre. The next day I was examined by the German doctor, Dr Drees, and was surprised how well-equipped the Medical Centre was. First of all Dr Drees was very concerned about my physical condition and advised me to start with walks and very light sports, to improve my physical condition. He was very soon convinced, or at least acted as if he was convinced, of my normal mental condition. Nevertheless, he told me that there had been a *Fallschirmjäger* (Paratrooper) *Hauptmann* in the camp who'd been mentally ill and that he'd caused him a lot of trouble before he was finally transferred to a mental hospital. I reassured him that I wouldn't be causing him any problems and was released into the camp proper.

I was instructed to report to the German Camp Leader, General Hans von Ravenstein. He had a very long and searching conversation with me. He showed genuine concern about my fate, especially when I told him I would

General Hans von Ravenstein

never regret having attempted to escape, but that the episode in the hospital was a mistake I would never repeat. He was a very cautious man, that was immediately apparent, and he advised me in the strongest terms to keep the fact that I had only feigned illness to myself. Ravenstein himself gave the impression that he'd rather not have known I had been faking my illness. For him, he said, I was just to be someone who had been cured and allowed back into the camps. It was clear to me, especially with this last comment of his, what type of a person he was and how, in this new camp, I had to behave.

I knew hardly anyone among the prisoners, but the camp itself was most impressive. The main building was three storeys high and in a long 'U' form, built of solid stone blocks. The room to which I was assigned lay on the third floor and from the outset my new room-mates were not at all pleased with my arrival. A two-man room was now to become a three man *'association'* or so they felt, too crowded. The two already in residence were, in my estimation, somewhat older than I. Ernst, or 'Ernesto' as he liked to be called, Breiler was a very experienced pilot who had, before the war, flown as a captain for Avianca, a subsidiary of *Lufthansa* in Colombia. He had followed the call of the *Vaterland*, returned to Germany, and as a reserve officer he'd been shot down very early on. The other one was an

Oberleutnant I knew and remembered well. He was Erich Grote, and had been the civilian instructor of the neighbouring group, during the second flight training course held at Werder in 1937. Although I was a newly promoted *Hauptmann* I recognised that in their eyes I was *ein Grünschnabel* (green horn - whippersnapper), but we soon warmed to each other. I developed a particularly good friendship with Ernesto as soon as he realised I wasn't about to start trying pulling rank on him.

Grote, whose home was in the south Tirol, was very depressed and it was only with great effort that we could get him to look at things a little more optimistically. Ernesto was the opposite, he was brimming over with plans and confidence. He was definitely going to fly again, he always said. With the high wages he'd earned as a captain with the Avianca, he had bought himself a big farm in Colombia, and had had enough foresight to transfer it to a Colombian to manage in his absence. "Sooner or later I will be back in Colombia!" Breiler was convinced of this and tried to get other comrades in the camp to agree to go to Colombia and start a new life there. Should Germany be really battened down, as had been indicated it might be in the newspapers, then there would always be room for specialists for his 'Finca' (farm), and mechanics for his aeroplanes which one fine day he was going to buy.

In Grande Ligne, Ernesto had worked a lot on the *Ehrenwort* farm and had learnt much about agriculture. He inspired me to learn how to make German sausage that was, he said, definitely going to be wanted in Colombia; and beyond that, if I couldn't fly, I wouldn't be too bad a mechanic. We soon found we had an excellent Westphalian butcher working in the camp kitchen who understood his trade so well that even with the meagre supplies we had, he was capable of making a good Westphalian quality sausage. I took up an *'apprenticeship'* there and then, learning the skills required. It was best, I thought, to be prepared for all exigencies.

Through amusing encounters I got to know *Landsleute* (fellow countrymen) from my neighbourhood at home. *Faustball* (a variation of volleyball), was the first sport I participated in for my physical rehabilitation. I played in various teams with great enthusiasm wherever an opportunity arose. My preferred position in these games was right back. In one game I had a difficult third hit (as in volleyball three hits are the limit each side of the net) which had to reach the other side with precision and with power. I accompanied the ball with the call, "And that one comes from Ludwigsburg!" Hardly said, the ball returned with equal ferocity and the counter-call, "And this one from Neckarweihingen!" (Neckarweihingen is a village on the outskirts of Ludwigsburg). The game continued with the next volley accompanied with felicitations from Heutingsheim, my actual home town, also on the outskirts of Ludwigsburg, and this was returned by one of the forwards in the other team who slammed it into our midst with the last call, *"Und der sitzt - Und der kommt au von Neckarweihinga!"* (And that one sits! - And it also comes from Neckarweihinga) all said in broad *Schwäbisch* dialect. That's how small the world was, even for the POW in Canada. Every one of them had his home within a few miles of mine.

Through these games I got to know fellow *Schwäbisch* countymen Gerhard Schweizer and Richard Wagenhals, both from the county Ludwigsburg. They had both served with the *Afrikakorps* and been taken prisoners there. Soon further *Schwaben* joined this small circle; Hannes Sinn who, although he had been an active Stuka officer, was in charge of the camp carpenter shop; the chemist, Dr Kurt Löchner, who had originally worked in a leather factory in Backnang; and later after our *'hungry time'*, we received kitchen help from *Obergefreiter* Eduard Wahl, a farmer from Buhlbronn in the Rems Valley. With his help we celebrated many a merry festival, one of which was for my 27th birthday, where I was presented with a wonderful hand carved *Schwabenszepter* (Schwabien sceptre). The close kinsmanship and pride of folk from the same county was very strong then and was a common bond from which we all drew strength.

This contact with so many *Landsleuten* made me feel close to home and I wanted to add something to this *Schwäbisch* culture. I contributed to our bill of fare with some more culinary experiments, extending what we'd achieved in Gravenhurst. One time I tried making *handgeschabte Spätzle* (hand scraped *Spätzle* - a Schwäbian noodle). 'Hand scraped' meant that the dough was scraped from the board with a knife directly into boiling water - in this case the kettle of the glue pot in the carpenters workshop. *Obergefreiter* Wahl, from the kitchen, then provided *Sauerbraten*, an oven roasted pickled beef, and all together that was quite something. *Sauerbraten and Spätzle* - you really couldn't get more traditionally *Schwäbisch* than that. It was a great success and twelve people enjoyed this small treat. For my birthday coffee party I had decided to serve a *Hefe-Kranz* - a yeast cake in the form of a wreath which I even managed to bake successfully myself.

During these times even flour could be bought in the canteen, and egg powder, which most probably couldn't be sold on the market because it tasted fishy. Thanks to the long time I had spent in Westminster Hospital my POW pay had accumulated and I could afford everything. Even ample supplies of beers, that was when the rations of those who had been invited would allow it (everyone had a limit on how much alcohol they could buy). I put the dough with the yeast, egg powder and white flour stirred into the

This picture was actually taken at Camp 30 Bowmanville but is used here to show Gerhard Schweizer, a fellow countyman from Neckarweihingen near Ludwigsburg. It is his camp 'metriculation' certification which was shown earlier.

milk and put it on our window-sill in the sun where it rose wonderfully. I thought plaiting the dough into a wreath was going to be a problem. However, after I had practised long enough with three strings of thick wool, I easily plaited my dough and laid it in a circle on the baking pan. Eduard Wahl baked it to a beautiful golden brown in the kitchen and all the comrades invited enjoyed my *Hefekranz*, another taste of home. It was most likely as a result of this and other activities that I earned my *Schwabenszepter,* a traditional award for services rendered to the county.

Another member of our *Swabian* circle was *Stabsarzt* (staff doctor) Dr von Rauch. In civilian life he'd been a gynaecologist in Heilbronn on the Neckar and soon achieved special distinction in the camp. Shortly after I had arrived in Grande Ligne, the Canadians began continually conducting special actions which had absolutely nothing to do with the Geneva Convention. It was clear that our guards, from the Commander down to the Veteran Guard, were not at all happy with their orders. They were always apologising and explaining that these were instructions from above, orders were orders. Spot searches and apparently unnecessary restrictions on our activities within the camp were all calculated to make life less than pleasant for us. The orders also affected the continuation of our farm, we were still allowed to use the ground, but the animals had to go. Some of these were sold by Canadians and some were slaughtered by our camp butcher. This meat then became a part of our meagre POW rations. A splendid example of a boar, Fritz by name, belonged to our pig breeding programme. With no further facilities for breeding it was senseless to keep him as a boar but his meat would probably be a bit tough and strong. Fritz was, therefore, also integrated into the plan but not for immediate slaughter. As an apprentice in the kitchen slaughterhouse I was informed that the boar was to be castrated, so that after a while he would lose his disgusting male smell. Good advice was rare on this topic, our butcher knew how to slaughter, but didn't know anything about castration. At home it was usually the job of the farmers' wives to quickly remove the testicles of the young pigs with a razor blade. But this was a powerful full grown boar who wasn't going to lose his equipment without a fight. Wasn't this a case for full surgery? Wasn't this a case for a qualified gynaecologist? Naturally it fell to Dr von Rauch to castrate the boar.

I wasn't present during the actual operation, but was called to the battlefield later. Originally the boar had been tied down, held tight and anaesthetized with ether. But he struggled powerfully, resisting the attack by the would-be surgeons. Again and again they thought they'd got him under the influence, but time and again he started snorting and struggling. By the time this huge old pig, weighing in excess of five hundredweight, was subdued the *'anaesthetists'* discovered they had overdone the doses and old Fritz wasn't going to wake up at all. Immediate instructions were issued for an emergency slaughter, hence, as trainee, I became involved.

When I arrived in the kitchen, half of Fritz already hung on the rope and hook and was certainly very impressive. The table was sagging in the middle, almost down to the floor, when half of that animal was lowered onto it. It was almost twice the weight of the pigs that we were used to. The fat was inedible but the meat was used for a very special purpose. For over a week it lay in a bath full of pickling vinegar and, when *saurer Rehbraten* (sour roast venison) was served for the midday meal, the majority of the officers were making the appropriate noises of appreciation for this rare treat. The kitchen team however, managed to control their appetites.

Numerous stories made their rounds in the camp concerning the castration of Fritz, the tremendous boar. Of course there were many attempts to pull Dr von Rauch's leg but he adopted a certain regal air and rose above it in a good-natured way. It is certain that during later times he must have laughed to himself over the disastrous operation.

CHAPTER TWENTY-FOUR

THE WAR WAS LOST...

BUT WHAT HAPPENED TO THE GENEVA CONVENTION?

We were ordered to the cinema to look at film scenes of the liberated concentration camps and were sickened by what we saw. This was the undeniable confirmation of what we'd read in the newspapers. I could see the former *Kreisleiter* from Poland had not exaggerated, certainly he'd seemed almost proud of what they'd achieved; that's the type of people they were. To rub salt in the wound, they were the very ones who were being proposed to us as shining examples of the new democratic German. That aside, what we were shown was worse than we could have ever imagined; it was appalling. A huge feeling of guilt swept over us and I wondered if we would ever be able to hold our heads high in public again.

Obergefreiter Wahl came to me and asked whether the films could be believed or whether they were just propaganda from the other side, carefully made and edited films. Sad to say I had to tell him I thought it was the truth, we Germans would have to wear that pair of shoes, as hard as it was, for at least the life of our generation, if not longer. There would be no ducking the issue for most of us, no excuses that we had been far away in Canada when it all happened. No, this would be a cross that all Germans would have to shoulder for as long as necessary. The only thing we could say in our defence was that none of us had thought such diabolical atrocities would be the result of us going to war.

The emotive pictures of those awfully emaciated bodies being bulldozed into crude mass graves were excuse enough for the Canadians to explain to us that we, there in that country of plenty, would feel what it was like to live with hunger. Questions put by our German camp leaders as to how far this was in line with the Geneva Convention had no effect whatsoever. All we got was scornful laughter, all the Allied prisoners had been released, they had no reason to fear retaliation any more; as far as they were concerned the Geneva Convention was as dead as the millions in the camps. Outside our camp gates the white bread that had been available in unlimited quantities was burnt in front of our eyes, and all other rations, which to date had been equivalent to what the Canadian armed forces were receiving, were also reduced tremendously.

The camp farm was terminated although, at first, we could still use the harvested crops and slaughter the animals of the farm to supplement our reduced rations in the kitchen, but later the farm was completely closed down (it was at this time that Fritz the boar was used to supplement the meat supply). Things quickly got worse, but my room-mates and I were a little better off than the majority. We at least had the foresight to go out gleaning in the potato fields that had already been harvested. We collected all the small and damaged potatoes that had been left, just like we'd done with our mothers after the First World War; well I remembered those days in stony fields of the *Schwäbische Alb* (Schwabian Mountains). After a few days we had a sackful of potatoes weighing about 40 kilograms standing in the corner of our room.

When our hunger had got to it's worst we also found the oil we needed to do some frying; it was now a great advantage for me to have the spare cash I had. The Canadians had taken all items out of the canteen that could have been bought to supplement the normal provisions. But they left the hair oil on the shelves - who'd have thought hair oil would be of any use in sustaining us. Violet, lilac, and rose-scented bottles of oil were soon finding their way to our room. There Ernesto had constructed an electric cooker by using the thinner wires from the bed springs. We were able to borrow a frying pan from the kitchen and, somewhat surprisingly, the base for the hair oil turned out to be good quality olive oil. The bottles were poured into the pan and heated and we wondered about the wisdom of what we were doing as the mixed aroma of the oils boiled off, but as soon as the aromatic additives had gone we could fry our potatoes as we wished.

We soon learned to put the pan out of the window while the additives evaporated burned off so as not to lose our appetites before we tasted our *Pommes frites*. But then, depending on the direction of the wind, our neighbours complained and through this found out that we had *'extra rations'*, which of course did not endear us to them. As a more delicate supplement I was able to provide honey because immediately after my arrival at Grande Ligne I had become a shareholder in *Oberleutnant* Simon's beehives. Simon had studied literature on bees and honey and been allowed by the Canadian camp command to buy and set up several beehives on the camp farm. Because he didn't have enough funds at the time he was in need of shareholders to participate in his venture; the dividends were paid in honey in proportion to the number of shares held. It astonished us to find that the amount of honey produced in Canada was three times as much as the average expected yield in Germany. This was, apparently, the result of the greater number of longer sunny days which offered the industrious insects much more flying time.

Simon was ingenious and made mead (honey wine) as a by-product, by using the water he'd used to wash the honeycombs after the honey had been extracted. He diluted the various mixtures and then, after the fermenting process had taken place, he had a choice of dry to very sweet dessert wines. The beehives also served as a pharmacy for our doctor. Dr Drees was a strong believer in natural therapies and not just because conventional medicine was in short supply. If an inmate complained that he had severe rheumatic pains he was prescribed *Bienenstich* (that is bee stings and not the popular cream cake of the same name). It was amusing to watch how many patients spent days walking around the beehives so as to get stung. According to Dr Drees, bee stings had a potent healing effect on rheumatic pains. Those patients who didn't have the courage to go close enough and so didn't get stung, by some strange quirk also seemed to be healed - or least they didn't visit Dr Drees again complaining of rheumatic pains!

As humorous as it may be to read these pages on hunger and the innovative measures we undertook to get nourishment it was actually no joke. I was really very lucky, once a week I participated in the sausage making overnight in the kitchen. At the end, mostly early in the morning, as a wage for the *'butchers'*, a roast pork fillet was prepared by the trained butcher, Bertram. Other than that we couldn't eat much throughout the night because everything was laden with fat and we would have needed a piece of bread to soak some of it up to make it digestible and bread, of course, was strictly rationed. We only ate small slices of the fillet without bread as eating the fatty sausage fillings resulted in immediate and rather horribly upset stomachs. Mostly I was assigned to tying up the *Leberwurst* (liver sausages) or other short sausages. During this work the skin on one's hands became so soft in the fat and water that when tying the knots in the sausage skins pieces of one's own skin would tear off and leave very painful raw patches. Before the next night's slaughtering came around these patches had hardly healed and the hands could become covered in suppurating wounds. After a time I learnt how to protect my fingers using insulation tape.

As the hunger got worse and worse, something like six weeks into our *Hungerzeit* I wanted to get some extra bread from the end slices after the bakers had cut the bread. Every evening our kitchen team would cut the bread ready for the next day. Punctually at seven p.m. they would open the back door of the kitchen, and three men of the baker's team would carry the end slices of the loaves to the lower staircase in woven baskets. There the officers gathered and the mob would pounce on the bread baskets like locusts. I only went once, that was enough, what took place down there was dreadful to behold. Even senior staff officers would forget all dignity and punch, elbow and gouge their way greedily to the scraps of bread, even while they were still being carried overhead in baskets. They were grabbing so greedily that they tore each others hands until they bled. That was enough for me - my room-mates had warned me!

The jealousy over the food started early in the morning. At an eight or ten-seat table someone would draw small lines across the butter, which was for the whole table, marking the portions. Then the small pieces were distributed with particular attention being paid so that nobody had more than anyone else; woe betide someone distributing a slightly short measure. When we served *Eintopf* (hot-pot), which happened a lot at that time, it was a standing privilege for the higher ranks to ladle theirs out first. By the time it was the youngest *Leutnant's* turn there weren't many lumps left to fish for.

Another odd phenomenon was when Australian mutton was being cooked. It could be smelt throughout the whole building, long before it was time for the midday meal. This affected some people in a strange way and, although they were starving hungry, they just couldn't swallow the meat when it was served, it just stuck in their throats adding more distress to their already pathetic state. I could sympathise because as I had reached my lowest weight in the hospital I too had been unable to eat, even though I wanted to by then. It really rubbed salt in the wound when the Canadians started looking for results to measure the effectiveness of the regime they'd introduced. They actually started weighing us after approximately thirty days and once a week this was conducted under the supervision of the Canadian Camp Doctor. On the appointed weighing day the weight of each POW officer was recorded on a list against his name and in alphabetical order. It wasn't until an average of sixteen kilograms had been lost by the prisoners (and for some this would have been much, much more), over a period of something like three months, normal rations were issued again.

During this time it seemed that they wanted us to freeze as well, during the September and October nights that were already very cold the heating was reduced to a minimum. The ingenious POWs even had a remedy for this, Breiler quickly solved the problem by using the thicker coil springs from the beds, converting them to electric heating coils for our room. But this, as with everything else, quickly made its rounds in the camp and the fuses soon blew. When we then jumped these blown fuses with heavy gauge wire the complete electrical system of the camp went down. That wasn't very convenient for the Canadians, especially at night because it meant that the fence lighting also went off.

But our guards were also very ingenious and for a limited time the heating was turned up again and during this time, under threat of punishment, the German electricians were instructed to wire the fence lighting into an independent circuit secured with separate fuses. That done, they then showed us for quite some time what it meant to feel the cold.

Only our Austrian comrades escaped this treatment, they were exempted from these oppressive measures. The Allies, and principally the Canadians as our custodians, had remembered that Austria had actually been invaded, or at least annexed, by Germany and had been forced to participate in the war. The Austrian officers were also then separated and could look forward to being sent home earlier. These hopes were not in vain, during the summer many of them were transferred to Europe and from there released to their home country. Some of the Austrians wanted to apologise to us and were willing to waive this special treatment in a gesture of true comradeship and solidarity. We were grateful for the effort but had to explain to them how ill-advised it would be. Gestures of that sort, however well meant, would do little to change things for us who remained.

Of course there were exceptions on both sides, some of the Austrian officers suddenly saw clearly how they had indeed been forced by the Germans, totally against their will, to participate in the war. Then, in the course of the re-education we were going through, they suddenly wanted to give speeches on this subject. As a reaction to this there were some German officers who became free with the word *Verräter* (traitors) but these were, fortunately, the exceptions. How the German-Austrian officers' comradeship actually was in those days can still be experienced today when, every year at the Austrian *Kanadiertreffen* (Canadians meeting), the former inmates of the officers' camps gather for a reunion. In the speeches held during these gatherings one can still easily recognise how strong the mutual bond was in those days.

During those times there were many *Umschulungsvoträge* (re-education speeches) held in the camp. At the entrance to these events there always stood those Canadian officers who had conducted the interrogations which, in turn, had led to our political grading. One could never get away from the thought that they were standing there making secret lists that would additionally underline the grading black, grey or white. However, I must admit that one speech held on the subject of capitalism, to which I had gone full of scepticism, gave me cause for thought.

An elderly Canadian officer of the reserves who had, in civilian life, been a banker first of all clearly pointed out how wrongly communism still condemned capitalism and how our recently demised *Third Reich* had made the same mistake. The man explained very clearly that without personal property one could never really be free. It was only when one possessed something, and the State recognised and accepted its accountability to preserve and protect the property of the citizen, that a balanced society evolved; even when the citizen, although subordinate, rebelled against this State. He convinced me especially, because he knew and quoted a story of the Prussian King, Friedrich the Great. The King could not, even after having gone through the court, forbid the grinding of corn by the miller of Sanssouci even though the clatter of the millstones and the rattling of the sails disturbed the King tremendously in the neighbouring castle.

I easily identified with what he had to say because of my position; what was the use of my impressive bank balance, following my term away, if I didn't have the right to dispose of it as I wished? It was capital, it was money, but it was only paper money. Real capital, I began to learn, was measured in possessions; whether it was money, shares or other investments, or more substantially - real estate. It all made one independent of suppression when one lived within a State which made laws to guarantee the citizens these possessions and the right to freely dispose of them. I had begun to realise that this would ultimately be the downfall of communism, although I didn't know it was to take decades for it to come about. There is a saying: *'There are none so easily dispossessed as those who have nothing'*. I suppose that summed it up.

My POW account was still well filled and with the little available for us to buy, it was only reducing slowly, even after the *Hungerzeit* when we returned to business as normal. I threw several parties where I picked up the bill for the beers, but it wasn't until I successfully managed to order a small portable Remington typewriter from Eaton's that my account reduced appreciably. However, that still left me with over $300 for my *'almost free'* disposal (no mean sum in 1945). I almost made a habit of staging parties and that didn't surprise anyone after such a long stay in the *Irrenhaus* - I suppose they thought I was entitled *'to blow off some steam!'* But it was my friend, Breiler, who really made me reconsider. He said I should think about whether all the willing guests that came were actually friends, or were they only coming because it was free? Having thought it over I could see he was right and that it was time for a change.

In those times we were allowed to transfer as many *'camp-dollars'* as we could afford from our POW account to the private accounts of American or Canadian relatives. These relatives could then be asked to send *'comfort'* parcels containing the equivalent in scarce goods to the relatives in Germany. I didn't have relatives in the USA any more, so I transferred my camp dollars to friends' accounts on the understanding that their US relatives would then send parcels to my parents while they were sending their own. I transferred quite large sums in this manner, but sad to say my parents only received very few parcels. Later, back in Germany, I rarely received the promised balance even though the parents of the comrades concerned had managed to rescue either substantial amounts of money or property. Was it thoughtlessness or selfishness? Slowly, personal self-interest replaced comradeship - was this perhaps the other face of capitalism?

For the duration of the *Hungerzeit* the craving for bread was the worst although the *Schnapsbrenner* (illicit liquor distillers) still had wheat by the sack, which they had accumulated through secret exchanges with the Canadians. It was surprising that, given the craving and the means to overcome it, it took so long to begin to make our own bread. It was *Oberfähnrich* Graf von Schwerin, who had been taken prisoner with the *Afrika Korps,* who developed a method by which he was able to bake *Vollkornbrot* (wholemeal bread) for himself and some comrades. On his allotment (small patches of garden which were allowed to be cultivated before the *Hungerzeit*) he had built himself a small baking oven made of clay. From the *Schnapsbrenner* he got the grains of wheat in exchange for finished flour, ground it in a home-made mortar and pestle, added yeast to it, and then baked a wholemeal bread. The finished product was not too wonderful, you needed very good teeth to eat it, but it was nourishing. For him it was as good an item for barter as any, but his enterprise could not help the majority.

I didn't lose a single kilogram in weight, I had always metabolised my food well, that was one reason why it had been so hard for me to lose weight in hospital. It therefore didn't justify my taking risks and my friends were critical when I did. Together with Gerhard Schweizer I was, hungry or not, going for many walks around the farm property to keep up my physical training. I still had a long way to go before I could judge myself fully back in shape. In autumn, at the time of the greatest hunger, we discovered a lot of yellow mushrooms in the woods within the farm boundary. They looked very much like *Pfifferlinge* (chanterelle - a yellow edible fungi) and we took a few samples with us back to the camp and there we asked the *'experts'* for their opinion whether these were edible. Nobody could clearly identify them but they were so numerous and looked so nice that I felt I had to take the chance.

Although everybody, including my room-mates, advised me against it, I performed the experiment and ate a small quantity after they had been boiled. The next day, when no ill-effects seemed apparent, I ate a good portion and again felt very well. Both Schweizer's room-mates and my own then ate the rest of the mushrooms we had collected. Something like that could only be successful once because the following day, as soon as word of the new source of nourishment spread through the camp, the woods were swept clean. Although the fungi were probably of the species known as *'false chanterelles'* they were not poisonous, nor as tasty as the real ones. At least some nourishment was provided by my single-mindedness.

I have previously mentioned my acute allergy to iodine. Whilst in officer school I'd had badly blistered feet treated with iodine which had resulted in my actual transfer to *Luftkriegschule* being made on a stretcher. Some people seem to be sensitive to common substances and I, unfortunately, seem to be one of them. My allergies were causing me great problems in the camp. Most probably it was a result of the change from total physical inactivity in the hospital to my active programme of physical exercise. Every now and then my body would be covered with a rash similar to smallpox but, fortunately, they didn't weep or leave the same terrible scarring of real smallpox. The itching, however, was terrible and could hardly be tolerated. As time passed Dr Drees found a way of treating me and that helped. But when it happened at night, and a feature of the rash was that it usually erupted very suddenly, I was left to help myself until the morning dawned and our medical station was occupied again. I had no other choice than to go through the connecting corridor across to the sports hall and there I could work it off, boxing the heavy bag until the itching ceased. Once one of the Canadian *Frettchen* caught me in the early hours of the morning and I was almost *einen zacken weg* (ear-marked for punishment). However, the next day Dr Drees intervened and after he'd explained the situation I was given official permission for my night excursions.

Extracts from postcards that were sent home in those days clearly betray the atmosphere that prevailed in those times, except that one could not write about the hunger we were suffering! One more letter had been allowed, but otherwise we were only allowed to write postcards.

Extracts from cards to my mother:

30th June 1945:

'Now you are to hear from me (first postcard after months in the hospital)...I am now in the same camp here with Schweizer and Wagenhals from Neckarweihingen. I have no worries about you...'

320

13th July:

'...As long as the weather stays fine, I mostly go to the farm and work there or in the garden - the 'Wilhelmshof' ('Wilhelm's Farm') or the 'Schlossgut' ('Castle farm') in Heutingsheim would most probably be glad to get a good worker...'

30th August:

'How longingly I await a sign of life from you! You were most probably in the same situation when I was reported missing...'

21st September:

'Still no mail... Now the first sign of life would be a relief. Health wise I am well. I have energetically recovered both physically and mentally...'

8th October:

'We have already had the first snow! Thoughts are now again directed towards Christmas - whether we can experience it together? A miracle would be needed... Dr Löchner of Backnang has already received two letters. Perhaps I can soon be hearing something from you; or Wagenhals; or Schweizer of Neckarweihingen will receive mail. One would like to have some inkling of the future.'

29th October:

'...if one could just somehow get involved in some practical work, but in this respect things still look very bad. We will most probably just have to stay behind the barbed wire until the very end... How are you going to manage to survive this coming winter?'

5th November:

'My comrades Schweizer and Wagenhals of Neckarweihing have both received very brief news from home, stating that the war had caused very little damage in their community. Now I hope that this is the same with us. By Christmas I should be hearing what's going on.

Should Father have been in Karlsruhe to the very bitter end, then things certainly didn't go that well for him. I have now bought myself a small portable typewriter and am learning to type. One never knows!...'

28th November:

'... What are you thinking about and doing? ...If only a sign of life would come from you!'

Whether or not this *totale Abgeschiedenheit* (total isolation) had deliberately come about we couldn't say. All that was certain was that we were in a western country whose communication and post system seemed to be in working order, but through which communication to us from home was denied. The effect on our morale was devastating. Of course we knew everything was a lot worse for those in Russia, but there it was the same for everybody, even the Russians didn't have it any better themselves. But was it really necessary in the West?

It was a terrible time for all of us, living with uncertainty on all fronts and being able to do nothing about it. So many asked the same question; are they still alive? In my case the elder of my sisters was last heard of by me when she was somewhere in the Baltic - father was an active soldier at the end and again and again different stories emerged in the newspapers concerning the fate of the soldiers at home. There were reports of famine in Germany and we could only imagine how the women felt being left alone to cope. We could only endlessly speculate about what they had survived, compared with us, and our guilt about this on top of everything else was hard to bear.

I didn't know that my father had, in the meantime, also been imprisoned, He wrote to my mother from Internment Camp 71 Ludwigsburg (only 6 kilometres away from home):

13.12.45.

'Dearest Mother, Trude and Helga!

I am in good health... do you have your daily bread? Has mother returned to school duty again? Has Trude found a job? Is Helga attending the Mittelschule? (secondary school) Do you have any news from Uli and what kind of news? I could do with: a lighter and flints, without lighter fluid, some knitted gloves, one book for English, a pen and a pencil holder. Forbidden are: visits, formal requests, sending groceries and tobacco products. Don't worry about me, everything can be tolerated...I wish you a happy Christmas...!'

One letter a month was all they were allowed to write, that is why he had to wish them a happy Christmas that early although he was so close. Could it get worse?

We in Grande Ligne could not imagine that this was the situation in Germany and we knew nothing about it at the time. We were worrying about the Morgenthau Plan, we were continually being politically interrogated as well as being starved and frozen. I am sure nobody believed then, and I know that few believe now, that the civilised Americans and Canadians behaved in such a manner. However, when one nowadays looks back to the times immediately after the war and sees the evidence emerging of the terribly inhuman hunger in the camps in Germany and France, then one has to be glad that a person like my father, at fifty-three years of age, managed to survive this living hell of starvation, interrogation and beatings.

Not only was I to hear many stories from the American and French mass camps near Heilbronn and the Rheinwiesen Camp near Sinzig, but much of it has now been published in the book 'Other Losses' by James Bacque published by Stoddard of Toronto. James Bacque, born 1929 in Toronto, studied history at the University of Toronto. He has researched how between eight hundred thousand and one million German prisoners lost their lives, mainly due to starvation and disease, in the American and French camps at the end of the war 1945. Bacque alleges that General Eisenhower had a particular hatred of Germany and did little or nothing to provide adequate facilities for the huge mass of POWs who fell into Allied hands when Germany finally capitulated.

Nor was the hard treatment only meted out to the military personnel, in those days everyone was treated alike by the armies of occupation. The American troops and, notably, General Patton, came to have their fling. Now Germany had her Quislings, the *Helfershelfer* (helpers' helpers) who saw that there was indeed profit in confusion. They opportunistically sought any advantage that could be had, doing anything to ingratiate themselves to the occupying powers. Either they were camp supervisors or served as enthusiastic *'official representatives'* of the Occupying Forces. It was going to take a long time to sort the wheat from the chaff.

Therefore, a woman like my mother, fifty-four years of age having led a *Volkschule* (elementary school) throughout the whole war, even given lessons herself, now had to fight for her existence with twelve and twenty-five year old daughters, a twenty-seven year old son in a camp on the other side of the world and a husband just six kilometres away who could only write once a month. For her, there was no other option than *die Zähne zu beißen* (grind her teeth - to grin and bear it). She was one of the true *Trümmerfrauen* (rubble women) to whom Germany owed such a debt after the war. Many of them had heavier burdens to carry than my mother, but they were all found sorting through the mounds of rubble that had once been our towns and sorting the bricks, tiles and beams that would be used to rebuild the nation. Until the men began to return in dribs and drabs they did everything to keep what was left of the nation together.

CHAPTER TWENTY-FIVE

DO WE STILL HAVE A CHANCE?

After the *Hungerzeit* was over we lived as well as we could, under the circumstances. The *Schnapsbrenner* (liquor distillers) were a guild that helped to make life more bearable; first of all because the camp residents found that their products tasted very good and, secondly, because their exchange trading did more than improve on the goods offered in the canteen. Since the end of the war the Canadian guards were obeying their orders with less interest than they had earlier and were showing more and more appreciation of our good products. The *Kornschnaps* was cheap but good, because, after all's said and done, it was being made by experts; as were the other *exports*. The beer was brewed by Bernhard Schels, who owned his own brewery in Tirschenreuth, and was the one who knew how to make the mash for *Schnaps* and ferment it. Then our chemist, Dr Löchner, had the technical know-how to distil it and refine the young *Schnaps*. He then obtained additives through trading with the guards and, with these necessary essences, the raw liquor was given the aroma of *Williams Schnaps, Zwetschgen*[1] or even whisky. It was very seldom we had drunks in the camp, and the Canadians didn't drink everything themselves, they sold it on. Trading must have been good all around the camp.

The mash was made of wheat which was spread out on a board in a layer approximately three centimetres thick. This was then watered and laid out in the sun until it germinated and the seedlings were a few centimetres long. This woolly mass was then turned through the kitchen mincer, very laboriously, and then it was transferred to a large porridge boiler of about eighty litres capacity and filled with water. In the heating process the conversion of starch was monitored by the use of litmus paper and a sweet mash was obtained which fermented very quickly. Distillation was done overnight, both in the kitchen and on the glue stove in the carpenters' workshop. A cooling spiral made of copper tubing with the necessary flow of cold water to condense the alcohol was no problem for our handicraft experts. Clearly this was a huge enterprise and was only really possible because the Canadian *Frettchen* found it to be in their interest to close their eyes to what was being done.

During this time I was called urgently to see Dr Drees. He had some interesting news: "Steinhilper, in a few days a commission of doctors will be coming here. They want to see all the individuals in the camp who couldn't be exchanged in the spring when the exchanges stopped. They also want to see you!" "My God!" I said "As much as I would like to go home I'm glad I got off so lightly. Please leave me out of it, tell them I'm healthy and it won't be necessary for me to appear for the medical examination." Though less than completely happy with my reply he just said, "That's your business!" and I returned to what I was doing.

The day came and in a building outside the fence the Commission looked at case after case. About midday Dr Drees appeared saying, "It won't help, they have your medical file with them and definitely want to see you this afternoon!" "My God, Doctor," I replied, "what can I do now? I can't start playing crazy again, you can see how physically fit I am!" "Do exactly that," he said very calmly, "do what all people do who have been discharged from the mental hospital - complain about why you were put there in the first place!" That sounded good, I thought I'd give it a try.

At approximately three in the afternoon, I was escorted out of the camp and introduced to the doctors. The Commission consisted of one Swiss, one English and two or three Canadian doctors. The English doctor asked me how I was feeling, how things were going, and I could see the well-known green folder that lay on the table. I immediately got into my act. "It's an affront to ask me to come here," I said high handedly, "can't you see how well I am, physically and mentally! Don't you notice how well I speak English? Just because I once had an accident while playing hockey and for a time I could only speak German, was it really necessary to lock me up in a mental hospital for several months!" It was unbelievable, the doctors were grinning and nodding at each other in silent but mutual agreement. I couldn't believe what their gestures and mumbled exchanges were indicating '... *here is a genuine case, poor fellow, he really does have a screw loose!'* There was not a single question more put to me, I was dismissed and wandered back to the camp more confused than ever.

That evening Dr Drees approached me, very dryly he said "You're travelling!" I could hardly believe it, but together with ten others of the *Übriggebliebenen* (left-overs) I was to go home. I slowly began to look forward to my journey and started to wonder if the suffering had been worthwhile after all. I was still uneasy about the whole affair, but hadn't the exchange cases from the other side all been liberated, why should I be so reserved?

The day of departure was set for 10th December 1945. A hospital train was to start in the West of Canada, pick up all the sick prisoners in the camps in Alberta, Ontario, Quebec and then the last ones in New Brunswick; all the cases it had not been possible to exchange in spring. In Halifax the time-tested *Gripsholm* would be waiting and would transport all of us to Europe. It was always said 'Europe' but nobody actually knew where the journey was to end. On the evening of the 9th the whole of camp Grande Ligne staged a huge party, complete with the camp orchestra, specially for the eleven lucky ones who were to be repatriated. At this time our POW Camp Orchestra stood at the zenith of its cultural maturity. Not quite the stature of the Symphony Orchestra at Bowmanville which, led by Hans Poser, could often be heard on the Canadian radio but our *Abschiedsabend* (farewell evening) in Grande Ligne had style.

The day before I had plundered my POW bank account and generous sums had been transferred to friends. A good portion of the remaining camp money went for beer before the evening was over. The rest I gave away with *Grandezza* (grandeur), the *camp dollars* could not be transferred and would be of no use to me so it was best to enjoy them there and then. My friends still remind me of this party nowadays when we get together. On the morning of the 10th, Breiler and Grote let me have the room alone; was it that they didn't want to disturb me while packing, or was it melancholy that overcame them? I don't think anyone held our good fortune against us, but everywhere you looked you could see on the faces of those who were to remain that they wished they could change places.

I finished my packing and wanted to leave the room clean and tidy and decided to sweep the floor. I gathered up the sweepings, together with some rubbish I had put on the window-sill and took it out to the yard with the idea of burning it in the incinerator. Once a little fire was established, I returned to the room and decided to replace my wrist-watch now that the work was done, but it was no longer on the window-sill where it had been. In my eagerness I had gathered it up with the other rubbish and it had found its way to the incinerator. Dashing down the stairs, I tried an emergency rescue but it was in vain, the fire was burning beautifully. The watch I had missed for so long and which made me so happy when it was returned was lost again. Was this another little price I had to pay for my early release? Favours from fate were never cheaply bought - that was for sure!

After ten o'clock it was time to have our luggage searched on long tables out in the yard. The guards search our baggage, piece by piece, and then it was loaded into a Canadian twin axle army lorry. It was a tremendous amount of luggage, astonishing what quantities the Canadians were allowing us. There was sugar, coffee, tea, cigarettes, books, clothing and everything one could imagine, all packed together. It was partly for ourselves and partly for the relatives of our friends, all packed in suitcases and kit bags. The two and a half ton truck was soon loaded up to the tarpaulin - just for us eleven people.

Before the end of the luggage search, which had taken place out in the open, it started to snow but we didn't worry, we were just overjoyed that we were about to embark on the last leg of our long, long journey. Then snow began to fall faster and thicker and finally the Canadians began to panic, a blizzard was coming. I felt the knot of fear form in my throat, was something going to happen at the very last minute again? Surely God couldn't be so cruel. Another two and a half tonner, this time with a snow-plough mounted at the front drove out of the camp to clear the road and at long last, at about midday, we were allowed to climb aboard our lorry and with four wheel drive engaged and wheels spinning we drove out through the camp gate, accompanied by loud cheering and the farewell waves of our comrades.

Immediately outside the camp gate the road, which was parallel to the camp fence, led straight to the railway line and the station, but it looked terrible. It was unbelievable how quickly a blizzard could completely alter the outlook. The ditches on either side of the road were lost under snow-drifts and huge banks of snow lay across the road. In minutes the wind began shrieking around the canvass cover of our lorry, buffeting it from side to side with amazing force. The lorry with the snow-plough returned and it was arranged that it would lead the way, followed by the luggage lorry and then we would bring up the rear. But just then, as the snow-plough lorry was turning in front of us, the luggage lorry slipped over at an angle as its wheel dropped into one of the ditches. "Carry on, just leave the luggage behind!" was the next instruction, but it was even too late for that. The snow-plough was dwarfed against the masses of snow that were being blown against it at speeds of over one hundred kilometres per hour.

Only two hundred metres away from the camp our lorry was also blown into the ditch. On the orders of the Canadian guard team, we tried to reach a farm house that was on the left of the road, just twenty metres across a field. We were all blown over on the icy ground and only by crawling on all fours did we reach the protection of the house. One of our injured, who'd had a leg amputated, was blown away on the ground and it was only with the last grains of strength that the Canadians managed to grab him and pull him into the farmhouse.

The house was well heated and there was also a telephone connecting us with the camp and soon the dreadful news reached us. The hospital train had passed through at about two p.m., had stopped for a short while, and then continued its journey. Apparently there were hundreds on board, serious

Camp Grande Ligne. A water-colour painted by Luftwaffe Oberleutnant Hubert Tscheplak. The track that is leading forward is the one on which we left the camp on 10th December 1945, only to get stuck in a blizzard after 200 metres.

cases, what else could they have done? The storm was still blowing full force and with no sign of it letting up they had no choice but to leave without us. I don't think there are any words which could adequately describe the bitterness and depression which swept over us. It was cruel, unthinkably cruel, to have brought us so close to hope once more and then to have dashed it to fragments before our very eyes!

We remained in the security of the farmhouse until about five in the evening and then our small, very sad, band was driven back into the camp, which we had left only a few hours early amidst the cheering of comrades. The room was once again willingly rearranged to make room for three instead of only two but even the best of friends were, concerning the money, of the opinion *'Geschenkt ist Geschenkt'* ('a gift is a gift'). On the other hand there was so much sympathy for us from the camp as a whole that small donations from the majority meant that my account almost reached its former very healthy balance.

The postcards - all to my mother - best reflect the thoughts of the time after this episode, brackets again to explain what my family would have easily understood:

25th December 1945:

'Christmas has now come, and I still don't know anything about you, or about father nor have I heard from the Schorndorfer (Uncle Karl Bay in Schorndorf was always an opponent of the Third Reich). Nevertheless I am not going to let my courage sink and will search for a new path in life...'

The next letter of January 1946, probably because mention was made of the disastrous attempted journey home, was probably put aside for a while by the censor. The envelope has the Canadian postmark 25th March 1946:

'Today I received your letter of 19.4.45, from the days of combat. If only I could help you in some way. Fate is omnipotent: last month I was to be transported home on a hospital ship as a result of the long passed nervous illness I'd had. Everything was already loaded and the lorries were leaving the camp with us. Two hundred metres down the road we got stuck in a blizzard, missed the train, the boat and... Perhaps there is a reason for everything, life just goes its own way. We will just have to wait. The nerves will have to hold!'

23th January 1946:

'How glad I am my state of mind has changed, you can't imagine. Your Red Cross card of 27th July was a relief. Everything has come, just as I had hoped it would happen in my most optimistic hours. Trude must have gone through a lot (together with the fleeing troops she had made her way from East Prussia in the severe winter months, and then she walked from Schleswig-Holstein to Stuttgart)... When reading the newspapers, one gets the shudders... but we will make it as time goes on!'

31st March:

'I thank you for your letter of 26.3.45. It took its time to get here... I hope that for the time-being you are allowed to stay living in the schoolhouse... One continues to hope...

21st April:

'Great joy over your two cards from February 46! Now I can at least be a little calmed... On the other hand I find it doubly painful that the snowstorm held me back. You could definitely use my help in one way or another. Instead we have again changed camps. Please try and find out what you can of the parents of Oberfähnrich Mann, Oberpauer (clothing shop), Ludwigsburg; he is most distressed, having had no mail...'

16th May 1946:

'If the signs are not deceiving us, we will be leaving this continent in a few days. All we know is that our next destination will be Europe. What that means we don't know. The most vital question here is whether one should, right here and now as prisoner of war, prepare for a new existence in this country... Many times one gains the impression from newspapers and letters that Germany has no room for us... Don't be afraid, since I have been getting your mail, it is firm in my mind we will make plans for the future, once we have discussed them together. I hope father doesn't have to stay too long in the prisoner of war camp. For you women it must be dreadful, always being alone, to manage your way through life without the male support.
Nevertheless I hope that our custodian state sees the hardship and, I believe, that I will soon be with you. Then we will finally start to live again...'

That's how suddenly things had happened. The last two postcards were from Camp 40, Farnham, near to Grande Ligne. Actually I could have written on the first postcard *'once again have changed camps'* and that this was a very important event. Farnham was, at this time, known to be the last *'port of call'* before departure from Canada. But with my prevailing bad luck I only made mention of this a few days before our actual departure for Europe. I didn't want to tempt fate to hurt me even more. Even in Farnham it was possible that in individual cases things could go wrong. Again and again, comrades were separated and without explanation travelled not to Halifax, but to the far west of Canada where an arbitrary accumulation of *'black'* and *'grey'* POWs were employed as lumberjacks in Camp Seebe. Apparently I had, at last, had some luck and as a result of my *'illness'* I was neither interrogated nor *'graded'*.

The mention of starting a new existence *'there in that country'* had reached an advanced stage with more than a few. This was especially the case where comrades had received the sad news that their families in Germany had been killed, and also those whose *Heimat* (homeland) was in the Soviet occupied zone.

Because my home news didn't reach me until 23rd January 1946 I was among those applicants seeking permission to settle in Canada. On 18th December 1945, eight days after the unlucky attempt to return home, I had applied for permission to remain in Canada after my discharge from the status of prisoner of war. On 14th January 1946 there followed a further application so that in the event I was repatriated first I would have that angle covered too. In the meantime we had learned that both the Canadian and also the US rules would not permit immigration before actually having returned to Germany. But one could never be ceratin whether, in the strange circumstances, a rule like this might possibly be changed. To make sure I had a foot in both camps I had both applications stamped by the Canadian censor.

After I knew that my family were all alive it was clear for me that the subject of immigration was not going to be finalised before I had got home and received the full consent of the whole family. Later on it was revealed that emigration to Canada was only possible when the application was submitted in Germany.

In Farnham I was sure our destiny was clear from the beginning and therefore only unpacked the bare necessities out of my kit bag and arranged the room for a temporary stay. During the weeks we spent there we were vaccinated several times and we began to form the impression that Germany must be a hotbed of disease. We were vaccinated against malaria, yellow fever, typhoid, cholera, smallpox and whatever else there was. The best thing, however, about the whole scheme of medical care were four young Canadian dentists who were eagerly repairing our teeth before we went off to Europe.

My teeth had suffered exceptionally badly while in the mental hospital because I hadn't cleaned them for the entire four and a half months I was in C Ward. I have to compliment the young Canadian dentist who did the filling and pulling, even making a bridge out of gold. Some thirty years later my German dentist, who had to remove the bridge, was full of praise for the quality of the work. The special rules which prevailed for this whole treatment was that we only had to pay the costs of the materials which, in most cases, was a real bargain. However, as my treatment involved the use of substantial amounts of gold I was lucky that my account was still full and allowed me to have the treatment; but when we finally left Canada my account was empty.

To the situation at home: extracts from letters from my father, still in the Internment Camp 71, Ludwigsburg:

10.1.46

'Uli will be home before me (my mother had reported)... I am glad for him from the bottom of my heart... We can now have grocery parcels sent... not too much... My greatest wish: a loaf of black bread so that I can eat until my hunger is stilled. Then, when weather permits it, fruit that I have had to do without and whatever else you can spare... You can always write, we can only write once a month. Visits and approaching the camp are forbidden. Applications for discharge are also forbidden...'

8.2.46

'...Although I only weigh ninety-nine pounds, I am healthy, I have even gained three hundred grams weight. Uli's choice of career (farmer or gardener) is definitely not final... I am preparing... Your duty (teaching) is difficult. I hope you manage to survive this... Will we have to separate again?... What does the future look like?...'

1.3.46

'Although I had flu a whole week, I now weigh one-hundred and four pounds... How is Uli? Is he healthy? When did you hear last from him?... The comradeship is helping us to get over a lot. We have good table and social manners, we help each other... Two weeks ago I applied for my discharge. Is it going to help? I'll manage to find some kind of work. How much I would like to correct exercise books. (How much had he hated doing that in the past!)'

3.4.46

'...I am now informed on gardening. How much would I have liked to help you, at least the heavy work..? My application has been positively decided. It is now a matter of time. We have learnt to

wait... We have finished our agricultural school and have now reached the same as if we had attended a two year winter school. Now we start the practical training on a farm... I think I will manage to survive this because I am feeling well and now weigh approximately one hundred and nine pounds. Much of the work is still familiar to me, I am used to working with horses and cows... Is Uli writing regularly and many greetings...?'

That should have been the last letter from my father from Internment Camp 71. Soon after that date good sense was to be applied in his case. He had many who were putting in a good word for him, especially the Community Council of Heutingsheim. But *Strafe mußte sein* (punishment must be) was the decree of the higher school administration. Father had been, as had all teachers and public servants *'PG'* - *Pareteigenosse,* a member of the *Nazi* party, there had been no choice at the time. Although there were specific background reasons why my father's case could perhaps have been viewed in a more positive light, the prevailing view was that 'justice' had to be seen to be done. For over a year he had to commute to the neighbouring community of Eglosheim, mostly walking the six kilometres, after that he was allowed to teach again in his home community. For him to have been required to do anything other than resume his job as a teacher would have been a bad joke, in those times good teachers were in short supply.

Of course at the time I only knew fragments of these events but I was sure of one thing: my energy could be better employed at home rather than sitting around in Canada doing nothing, waiting for some politicians and diplomats to decide our future. But soon enough great events were to begin. My letter dated 2nd June 1946 already had the mailing address:

No. 17 POW Camp, Lodge (Moor), Sheffield 10, Yorkshire, Great Britain

2nd of June 1946.

'Liebe Muttel,

The first letter for quite a long time - from England! (immediately post-war in Canada we were only allowed to write postcards.) Approximately five and a half years ago I travelled across the ocean... on 22nd May we left Camp 40 (Farnham), had a very calm crossing

and reached this location, in the middle of England, on the morning of 30th May. By Christmas I hope to be at home. The first leg of my journey is over. I have met new countrymen in this camp. One of them Leutnant Lutz from Beihingen, saw father in March 1945 in Crailsheim. There is a lot to talk about and to wonder about. One thing I must repeat and that is that the war reached dimensions we knew nothing of in Canada. I am so glad that I have you all, and that, as if it were a wonder, we will soon be together again. We took a straight path and we will continue that way... Especially now, it must be difficult for you at home to persevere under this mental burden... I trust the good will of our custodian state and hope that I can soon take over the hard work that you women are now doing... Remember that only one thousand five hundred kilometres separate us now. Perhaps it will happen faster than one expects...'

Only a change of scenery? No, everything had just gone too fast and too easy; we got onto the boat, huge numbers boarded with us: officers, enlisted men, non commissioned officers, *Afrika Korps*, flyers, *U-boot* crews, prisoners from Normandy, all mixed up in that huge boat, the 42,000 ton *RMS Aquitania*. Once embarked we prepared for a long crossing but we were across the Atlantic in a few days. Much faster than when we went to Canada and we didn't have to travel zigzag any more, nor did we have the great grey bulk of the *Ramillies* crashing her way through the sea beside us.

Enroute I was together with Wildermuth a lot, he had also managed to make it onto this boat. People were beginning to group more and more with their *Landsmanschaft* (fellow countrymen) rather than remain in their former units, arm of the services or even among their rank peer group. We knew only too well that once at home we would certainly need mutual support rather than comrades in arms. Altogether I was treated with *deutlicher Distanz* (obvious distance) by many other officers. My *'case'* was apparently known in all the officers' camps and who would regard me as being normal after spending fifteen months in the *'loony-bin?'* It didn't worry me in the slightest, after the lost war it was easier to live with the reputation of being *'bats'* than having to be the *Ausbrecherkönig* (the king of the escapers).

We became excited when we sighted land for the first time. We had harboured doubts because although we knew our destination was Europe there was still great secrecy and that always made us suspicious. With the landfall we had and the direction we were sailing it was clear we were not in the Irish sea. Soon both the former bomber crews as well as our own navy men recognised the landmarks which confirmed we were sailing straight into

*RMS Aquitania. We were quickly moved on this
42,000 ton ship from Halifax to Southampton.*

the wide mouth of the Channel. In what seemed to be no time we had
negotiated the Isle of Wight, passed the grey British ships lying at anchor off
Portsmouth and docked at Southampton.

It was a beautiful sight on a wonderfully sunny day as we elegantly slid
into the harbour in that monstrous vessel. Disembarkation started without
delay and the British were especially surprised to see the large kit bags we
were carrying, full to the brim. Compared with the luxurious Pullman and
express train coaches in Canada, the small English goods wagons and
passenger coaches looked like toys. So did the patchwork landscape after the
rolling prairies and vast lakes of Canada. The tiny villages we passed through
on the train had a fairy-tale quality about them and even the towns looked
small.

After several hours travelling we reached a camp that consisted of rows of
Nissen huts and we were to learn we had arrived at Lodge Moor, near
Sheffield. At first nothing happened after our arrival apart from a very casual
allocation of beds and cursory inspection by us of the facilities, such as they
were. In the compound right beside us was another section from which we

were separated by means of very high barbed wire fence. If we felt hard done by there was a salutary sight for us; German POWs in a shocking state of malnutrition, their haunted eyes following us about as we arrived. We soon discovered that the British had stepped in and taken these POWs out of the hands of the French and Belgians and taken them to England before they starved to death. So many, many more had already died and would still die in those camps.

Through conversations across the fences we learned from these bare shells of men how they had been driven together in Belgium by the thousands in the mud: starvation, epidemics and the cold had snatched away their comrades by the hundreds. Whatever we had left over, or could spare from our meals and could be thrown, flew across the fence to them. We didn't have that much for ourselves, but none of us were anywhere near starving. For those on the other side every loaf of bread that went flying like a discus was a blessing. With us all in our good uniforms and, for the most part, healthy it was hard for them to understand that we had gone through the *Hungerzeit* too. For us it was just unbelievable that the armies that had beaten Germany into submission in the name of freedom had done what they had done to defenceless prisoners. We could understand the anger and revulsion the Allies must have felt as the true scale of what Hitler had perpetrated in the name of the German people came to light, but was reciprocal inhumanity any solution?

It was during this time that an English Major said to a former German *Panzeroffizier*, "Soon we'll join shoulders!" by which he meant that we would possibly soon be fighting the Russians side by side. How much truth there was in that statement we didn't know at the time. My personal opinion was many a time also going in that same direction.

At the end of the chapter a suitable letter:

21st June 1946:

'...As far as coming home is concerned, I can't give you any new hopes. The newest report we have received is that soon it will be possible for us to overcome the barbed wire, so that we can report for work in the farms...
Now my plans for the future: our old plan was to own our own ground and property. To achieve this, under the present circumstances, I will have to emigrate... Should Canada not allow me to enter the country, then it will have to be South America... Now that is the plan...'

And if all else failed, there were still the thoughts of Colombia, of Ernesto, his farm and his aircraft. He seemed so confident he would one day buy and operate these and I wondered how sincere his invitation was. Perhaps they would need a good mechanic / sausage maker and one day a good German schoolmaster and schoolmistress, a well as a trained telex operator and typist and a twelve year old for the future.

Notes on Chapter Twenty-Five

[1] Williams is *Christ-Williams-Birne* a pear liquor - the pear in the bottle. *Zwetschgen* is plum liquor. All colourless liquors.

CHAPTER TWENTY-SIX

FORLORN - FORGOTTEN - BUT HOMEWARD

Herbert Mann, the *Oberfähnrich* on whose behalf I had asked my mother to make enquiries about his parents in Ludwigsburg, reported on the beginning of the homeward bound journey:

'I was only in Camp Gravenhurst in Canada. I was amongst the last that left for England on 10th June 1946. In the course of the political grading that was conducted after the end of the war I was graded in the group 'black' (unconvincible) because I would not answer the question whether Hitler was a criminal without being given proof.

We were transported by railway via Montreal to Halifax... the boat, with which we sailed to Southampton, was very large, it could have been the Aquitania. I also found that the railway coaches, in which we travelled to Sheffield, were very small.

Camp Sheffield was, in all respects, worse than the one at Gravenhurst. Because of our large amount of luggage, the comrades we met there envied our wealth, and the most noticeable difference between us was that we had not experienced the collapse of the Wehrmacht and the Reich and were still trying to maintain a certain amount of basic military discipline.

It was for that reason that during the first political questioning by the English we were not prepared to admit even the slightest guilt. What annoyed me most was the question whether it would have been better for the nations of Europe if Germany would have won the war. My response to this, was my own question, "Am I a clairvoyant?" I was then, for this reply, locked up in a dirty enclosure together with numerous other recalcitrant comrades. Shortly after arriving there one of the Generals had us gather around him. The Generals had been in the camp before we arrived and had attracted our attention because they were already dressed in a very sloppy manner. This officer then told us to 'be reasonable,' he said he had always been against the NS Regime (NS - National Sozialistische - Nazi). We then yelled the question to him, how then had he managed to be promoted to General! He then left us alone.

The English then changed their approach. In the next, verbal questioning, the English officer explained to me that he would ignore the past irrespective of what had happened, and wanted to know from me how I saw Germany's future. I pointed out to him that Germany only had the choice between communism or democracy and that it would decide for the second of the two, and that it would have to cooperate with the west powers. For myself democracy was nothing strange because where I came from - the Pfalz - as a result of the French revolution and the Hambacher Fest (1832) a democratic union had long been founded. Result: I became 'grey' - that is I could be convinced.'

That much from Herbert Mann, later on we will be hearing of him again. For myself, it appeared that the *Irrenhaus* was still casting its shadow. 7th July:

'...I am still waiting for mail... personally I experienced another disappointment last week. I was driven to see the doctor, he spoke about twenty minutes with me. I asked him to support my request to work on a farm because, I said, that would be a good therapy for my nerves. But he refused. (He said) The illness that I had, had not healed completely.
I would have to wait several months... otherwise the most peculiar coincidences happen here. Within the barbed wire it happened that father-in-law and son-in-law got to know each other... As far as coming home is concerned, there is nothing new to add to my thoughts. One can only hope.'

Indeed, I had filled out an application form in which I requested that I be permitted to work on a farm. The result was a trip to Manchester on a train, accompanied by an English sergeant, where a psychiatrist gave me a check up. The famous green folder, I noticed, lay again on the table and after it had been studied, he made his decision. Would I have to start worrying that my history in the *'loony-bin'* would follow me when I returned to Germany?

Again, to get an accurate feel of those times, I will quote from more letters but what one has to bear in mind is that we knew our letters were being censored and were conscious that our custodians drew conclusions from what we wrote. Therefore it was left to our families to *'read between the lines.'*

10th of July 1946:

'Liebe Muttel,

Yesterday I received Trude's letter of 21st June. I am glad to hear that father has now been discharged from the prisoner of war camp. I would be pleased to hear from him myself. Although for the time being he is not working in his occupation, he is most probably glad that he can do some productive work on a farm... This week I requested work in the coal mines. Should this materialise, then we should be going to the Ruhrgebiet (the coal mines of the Rhur) and there our working power would be put to a better use than here behind barbed wire. Whether this will be authorised for officers or whether my past illness will annul all my hopes, I will have to wait and see...'

7th of August 1946.

'My dearest ones,

We are off to work on farms. I will be glad when the work exhausts my body so that I will be, to an extent, fully occupied. You have to be lucky in these matters. For this reason we are being sent to a work camp, from there we will be employed on the farms. Afterwards, we will be coming back here again...

13th August 1946:

'...You are against my settlement plans. You will see what will result, once we sit down and discuss it all... After six years of theoretical life one would like to get involved in the action of life... So you think I will be coming soon, but for the next two to three months there is certainly no way. In the meantime you could get a good wrist-watch and some carpentry and locksmith's tools, then I would be equipped for the start. If I'm not home by spring, then you will have to add to your rabbits, bees (a reference to the bees which supplied honey in the camp and of which I then had experience. The angora rabbits had been reared by my parents for meat and their skins/fur). ...You will see, once I'm at home, I'll find my way...'

'Now I have been here in the work camp for exactly eight days and I can report to you that life is a lot better here. For the start we are in a mass assignment (fifty men on a flax field, picking the flax and binding the stalks) but the work that one is doing with pleasure is easy work. Perhaps other opportunities will be offered at which one has less the impression that one is one of a mass. The area surrounding the camp is beautiful, it reminds me of the rauhe Alb (ragged - rough mountains)

...Eberhard Wildermuth and Lutz are living with me here. If you could, at some time, invite Mrs Wildermuth that would be nice... I see now that I can carry out as much physical work as the others (even after my illness).

The question concerning our coming home is best answered in the newspapers... It is bitter but the truth, quite some time will certainly pass yet.'

8th September 1946:

'...presently I am working as an electrician... That will be accepted as it comes... You are still of the opinion that I should study, but who can tell, whether after studying I am able (permitted) to practice the occupation I choose?

Because the conditions in Europe are still not calming down... Altogether I advise you to take the advantage of the freedom of decisions. But I hope you are not becoming uncertain because of my theoretical activities...

What beautiful times we experienced together. And it will be exactly the same again this time...'

In the meantime our work assignment had been changed and we were now, that is Wildermuth and I, working at RAF Finningly. There we were working under the supervision of Sergeant Don Bostock, a very pleasant person who was just as unhappy as we were that we had not yet been discharged and could go home. He was responsible for the maintenance of the batteries, in other words he was responsible for all accumulators and batteries for the whole airfield, whether large or small.

The batteries were brought to our workshop which was located in one of the hangers. Before too long we were doing it completely independently, that is the batteries were checked by the POWs Captain Wildermuth and Captain Steinhilper. The acid was topped off with distilled water and they were recharged as required. Every morning and evening we were transported between the camp and the airfield in a RAF bus. The work was fun and the food was ample.

15th September 1946:

'...Yesterday I was twenty-eight years old! Last year I had said, "Well that's the last birthday that I'm going to celebrate behind barbed wire (how many times hadn't it been the case in the past!), and this year I am going to be a pessimist... I hope that the American Minister of Foreign Affairs (the Marshall-Plan) will really bring some improvements to the economic situation...'

1st October:

'...I was very pleased to hear about father's political opinion. My resolution for the future is that I will only once in my life let propaganda lead me up the garden path. In the future I am going to 'believe' less, however, I will exercise more realistic criticism against the political leadership.
...To mother's problem: She is hoping to be relieved soon (as teacher and in charge of the school by my father being able to take over). For the near future I imagine that it is going to remain a major problem... and she also wants to make life at home as easy as possible... that is going too far! Believe me, I don't need any kind of lure to get me out of imprisonment. If I could, I would immediately start walking now... There is nothing worse for an Alten POW (an old POW - one of the longer serving ones like me), than having nothing to do!...I will be at home as fast as possible, as soon as I am released, no matter how! - My work assignment is still as an 'electrician'. I enjoy this work especially, because I am learning (English) while talking... our food is all in all sufficient. I am such a good Futterverwerter (food utiliser - someone with an efficient metabolism) that while others begin to complain it's always enough for me. You have both put a good piece of health into my crib.'

And now follows my last letter from my imprisonment. At the time I wrote it I didn't know it would be my last letter from the camps. An important change had taken place before this letter was written. In the meantime we were on a real farm assignment: the potato harvest.

19th October 1946:

'My Dears,

Thank you very much for your letter of 24th September. Your frame of mind is not the best: is it a result of father's rating ('political' from the Internment Camp). But father shouldn't relax (his views), he has an absolutely clear line behind himself and in earlier days he was always capable of showing unwanted elements the door. Now, today, he shouldn't let himself be suppressed, back in those days he had almost been forced out of his position.[1] And should it be of importance that he was an officer, then I would make mention of the fact that the only type of opposition that was possible against the Herren Ortsgruppen - und Kreisleiter (NSDAP community and county leaders) was when one was an officer and had some kind of backing. That's how it was, and those are the facts that count today... You might believe, I don't know what I want... When I am at home and have to make up my mind as to which occupation I am going to choose... then it is only the question, how far do the outer circumstances allow an approach to the goal..? Here I am presently involved in harvesting the potatoes. There's not much to be learnt on this job, one just has to regard it as a physical training exercise... It's a pity that we hardly have enough time to keep our clothes clean.

I won't forget this potato harvest for the rest of my life - not that it was hard work, but because it rained the whole time. It rained for days on end and the English farmer's people, to whom we were assigned, offered us the opportunity to take a break whenever our fingers were stiff from the cold wet earth in which we were burrowing in search of the potatoes that the special shovel wheel of the tractor had already turned over.

The whole time the farmers were offering us a thick, sweet tea with milk and it tasted wonderful. What a relief it was on those cold wet mornings to hear the clanking of the large enamelled tea jug as it was brought out. Whenever it was possible we all wanted to lift potatoes, it was hard, it was wet, it was cold, but it was better than doing nothing! Inactivity for us old POWs was a real horror. Finally we were again capable of doing something that was to the benefit of mankind, even if it was only the potato harvest in pouring rain.

The worst part of that work was trying to keep ourselves, and the clothes we wore, clean. When we left the camp in the backs of lorries early in the morning, still in darkness, our clothes were clammy and wet, and in the evening it was already dark when we returned and our clothes were even wetter. We lived in tents at the work camp and there were only rows of taps out in the open with which to wash, but at least they had a roof over them, but there was no warm water. First one washed one's hands and then boots, and then followed our blue working clothes. We were so well covered with clay that we had no choice other than to strip down to our underwear. Jacket and trousers were then washed and last to be washed was our underwear. The pyjamas that we wore at night were kept in the tent and weren't completely dry either. Next morning we got back into those clothes that had hardly dried overnight in the tent, but because we then went out to the fields, where it was raining anyway, wet clothes were the norm. Mostly we only felt the cold when sitting on the back of the lorry travelling to and from the farm. It was surprising how few colds were caught, perhaps this was because we were really enjoying it, at long last being able to do some worthwhile work.

Before I continue with my own story of my coming home, some other impressions which were reported to me by some of my comrades:

Once again, Herbert Mann:

'Together with other comrades, I was transferred to the Camp Abergavenny in South Wales. There the preparations for the repatriation began. Of great importance to us was the choice of the Occupied Zone to which one wanted to be discharged...

At this camp there was a shortage of food. During the daytime, we were not allowed to heat the barracks because the British were not allowed to and, in accordance with the Geneva Convention, we were to be treated alike.

Beginning of November, we were taken by railway to Hull and from there by boat to Cuxhaven, and then by train via Hamburg to Munster-Lager. I belonged to that group who had decided to be discharged into the French Zone, although the English had warned us of the danger that the French would very likely imprison us again. I have a very high esteem for the British, that they not only warned us of this danger, but also took measures that the French would release us on the day of arrival from their ill-reputed Camp Bretzenheim near

Bingen. They gave us an accompanying group of soldiers whose instructions were not to return until we had been released by the French. The Camp Bretzenheim had originally consisted of a fenced-in field, in which thousands had starved to death, and was at that time, in November 1946, still a dreadful sight.
That is how I very luckily returned home middle of November 1946. How much luck I'd had became clear to me when a woman spoke to me, who was well acquainted with the camp under French occupation: "Ei, dass Du noch do bischt...!" ("My goodness, that you're still here!") was her comment. For my survival I also thanked the fact that while I had been in Canada, I had polished up my French sufficiently so that I was able to talk to the French Capitaine who had been quartered in my parents' house...'

'Tönnes' Stangl, today a Doctor of Psychology, got home three months after myself, but his report also describes the atmosphere and situation to the point:

'During my transport from Munsterlager to Dachau, middle of March 1947, my brother Konrad, who had been discharged earlier, visited me in Munsterlager. He was Major i.G. (im Generalstab - General Staff) and had been Adjutant to General Oberst Stumpff and had therefore been present at the signing, in Reims and Pankow. He had come from Kiel, where he was 'illegally' studying Law. He had telephoned my other brother in Karlstadt on the River Main, he was vicar there (later from 1957 to 1979 Bishop of Würzburg), and had informed him of the approximate time when we should be travelling through Karlstadt. The vicar, my brother Josef, organised five strong young men to be on the platform. We presented the locomotive driver with cigarettes so that he would make a short stop at Karlstadt. My brother, Josef, had also spoken with the Station Master so that he would set the signal against the train helping the locomotive driver to stop.
I was able to inform about ten other comrades of these preparations and they then, as fast as possible, threw or handed their luggage out of the train, during its short stop. My brother and the five young men then grabbed the luggage and quickly packed it onto waiting luggage carts. Amongst all these young men who were rushing around stood my old mother on the platform, all alone, and waving a big white handkerchief as the train slowly passed by. The windows of the train

were full of inquisitive POWs hanging out, eager to know the reason why the train had stopped. It was a very moving scene, and many had tears in their eyes; myself as well, especially now that, after almost seven years, I saw my mother for the first time again. Everything went so fast and later the comrades, after their discharge from Dachau, picked up their luggage from the Vicarage, where it had been stored...'

Together with Wildermuth, I first of all had to return to the camp at Sheffield, where we found our brim-full duffle bags safely waiting for us. We shouldered them, and initially went in the wrong direction, namely to Abergavenny in Wales. If I had ever been hungry and freezing cold in a camp, then it was there; we had to be grateful we were at least dry. This camp was only a *'holding tank'* and before long we travelled by train back to Hull on the east coast of England.

The journey from Hull to Cuxhaven was on a smaller boat where, just in time, I managed to secure the job of kitchen help. Duty in the ships galley was much desired, while one worked there one could also eat until really full and it was wonderfully warm. In Wales we had all wondered if we would ever feel warm again. Working in the galley and 'topping up my batteries' like that stood me in good stead because afterwards in Munsterlager, on the journey and whilst in the discharge camp in the British Zone, food was again very scarce.

The journey from Cuxhaven, by train to Munsterlager, was a terrible but beautiful experience. We only travelled along rows of houses that were facing the railway, but the residents had realised that there were prisoners of war coming home in the trains. They were waving to us with large pieces of cloth, but what did these rows of houses, those backyards look like! Just heaps of rubble and debris! We hadn't expected it to be that bad, although we had read the most dreadful reports in both the English and the Canadian newspapers. Could that ever be rebuilt we wondered? And worse than the devastation we now saw was the fact that all of us were returning to our own country as prisoners. For that I had tried escaping five times and had spent that awful fifteen months in the *Irrenhaus!*

In Munsterlager I experienced a sad incident; we were scolded bitterly by a young German women because we were still wearing uniform. That was the last straw really, we couldn't even come home in our uniforms without being further rejected. Some of the comrades finally removed the national emblems from their uniforms in this camp so as to avoid any further confrontations.

Our contact with the local residents was only possible through the fence, in the course of trading. We had all kinds of goods to offer, but mostly it was cigarettes, coffee or tea that we were exchanging for bread across the fence. Naturally the locals were, by then, used to the POWs passing through and had their trading very well organised. It really is an ill wind that blows nobody any good! We stayed for approximately two weeks there, by which time it was decreed the southern Germans, myself included, were to travel by rail to the American Zone. That was our Fatherland then - Zones!

The journey went by way of Würzburg, where we had a short stop and were allowed to take a look around. It was unbelievable how this ancient city, which I had known quite well from earlier days, had been destroyed. My father had always taken the newly confirmed children on a day's outing to Würzburg when we lived in Creglingen. As long as I was a schoolboy I was always allowed to go along and so my memories of how it had been were clear. All around the station, nothing but ruins, ruins and more ruins! And this nearly a year and a half after the end of the war! We could not imagine what conditions must have been like towards the end of the war. But on the heights, untouched and magnificent, stood the Marienburg (the hilltop castle overlooking Würzburg); was that an indication that the solid heart of Germany, the bedrock, was untouched by the squabbling and violence of men?

We then continued our journey along the River Main as far as Ochsenfurt, seeing more and more of the American trucks with their white stars which, to us, looked so incongruous in the landscape we knew. If as a young schoolboy I had heard this prophesied by someone - American military trucks as occupiers along the embankments of the River Main - I, like so many, would have laughed in the face of the person who would have been dismissed as a madman. But there it was, the inescapable reality, the destruction, the bitter civilians, the light tan uniforms and the big trucks with the white stars.

Just the same as 'Tönnes', who was to follow us later on, we had the same idea of getting our precious kit bags to safety. Rumours that we would be searched again in Dachau were numerous, as was the use of words like *Beschlagnehme* (confiscation)! We hadn't carried our goods halfway around the world to lose them so close to home but there seemed to be little we could do, other than to hope for the best. More than anything we hoped that Dachau would be our last camp, perhaps our discharge camp?

Our guards, who by then had been changed to black American soldiers, every now and then very generously allowed us to go to the station building and to get a drink of water whenever the train stopped. By this contact we realized that the German railway system was already fully functional. At one of the stations I went and collected some *Expressgutscheine* (express parcels forms) from one of the railway officials and also asked him what could we do with our kit bags. Very matter-of-fact he said, "Send them home!" Of course! That was the simple answer, we had German money in our pockets and sufficient goods for trading so we stuck dispatching documents on our bags and deposited them at the stations along the way. They would then be sent on as *Expressgut* (express goods) by rail to stations we specified. Gerhard Schweizer even telephoned home to announce the arrival of our valuable freight. The railway officials were very helpful and not only because of the Camel, Lucky Strike or Chesterfield cigarettes which were offered as tokens of our thanks. Our guards were amused to watch our activities; they were pleased that with every kit bag that disappeared from the luggage racks more space became available in the overcrowded coaches.

Not all our comrades were as lucky as we were as our journey continued via Crailsheim, Ellwangen and Aalen where there were connections to Stuttgart, Backnang and Ludwigsburg. Later on we were to find out that our *'freight'* had arrived long before we did and had been picked up from the stations and safe-guarded as a result of Gerhard Schweizer's telephone call.

We reached Munich early in the morning and were shunted into a huge yard. I was just in the process of rubbing my eyes and waking up when I heard a call along the outside of our long train. *"Steinhilper! Steinhilper!"* Again and again, then *"Uli! - Uli Steinhilper, wo ist Steinhilper?!"* What was the meaning of all this, was it bad news again? Was I to be taken away from my comrades at that last moment so close to home - surely not? To the left and the right of our train stood other passenger and goods trains and it would have been easy to have got out there and just run away, but that was sense? We had learned from the railway workers that without an *Entlassungsschein* (discharge document) absolutely nothing could be done. One would be caught, first locked up, and then sent to one of the labour camps, who knew where?!

At the front end of the coach a door opened and then I recognised the voice *"Uli wo bist du denn?"* ("Uli where are you then?"). It was my father! Other comrades had brought him to the coach in which I was travelling. We fell into each other's arms and put the same question to each other at the same time, "How are you?" Thank goodness, both were well! "Are you hungry?" he asked, he looked so thin and skinny that I at first didn't want to accept the small rucksack that he was pushing into my hands. "Take it," he insisted, "share it with your comrades! You're going to be taken to Dachau," he continued, "and you don't know yet what will await you there!" Our train was already starting to move again and we wondered, was it true? Was it going towards Dachau? Things were now taking too long for our guards and they urged my father to get off the train. I just managed to ask him, "How did you find out when and where we would be arriving?" "Don't forget," he shouted over his shoulder as he made his way to the door, "I was on Railway Patrol duty, there you get to know everything!" I just managed to shout, "Greet all at home, don't worry, just a little more patience and things will work out!" Then I watched as my terribly thin but still very agile father jumped from the train that had already gathered speed. It was clear he'd had some practice at that.

Many comrades congratulated me on having such a resourceful father and while we talked we unpacked the rucksack. There was bread, smoked ham and a hard sausage in it. Together we ate everything there and then, it tasted wonderful. That was the best way to secure it before we marched through the camp gates at Dachau to be, once more, searched and to have DDT powder blown into our trousers.

Notes on Chapter Twenty-six

[1] My father had actually joined the NSDAP before it became compulsory for all public servants. This was very early on when it looked clear that Hitler and the NSDAP were intent on returning Germany to some of her former status after the Treaty of Versailles. The incident being alluded to in my letter was in 1937 when the local NSDAP *Ortsgruppenleiter* (Community Group Leader), who was also a teacher and thought, because he was senior in the party, he should supersede my father as headmaster. He therefore manufactured a story about my mother having an affair with one of the younger teachers at the school and this was, in the end, to have a significant effect on my life (see 'Spitfire On My Tail' p.46).

CHAPTER TWENTY-SEVEN

DISCHARGE - RETROSPECTION - PROSPECTS

Dachau was indeed the original concentration camp and we had imagined much worse than what we actually found. It looked to all intents and purposes like a normal camp, consisting of barracks which were situated on slightly rising ground. Our part was at the very front but further back, and a little higher up and separated by barbed wire, were said to be the extermination facilities. We had all expected there we would, once again, be confronted with what had been done in the name of the German people, but in the event nothing of the sort happened. The American soldiers who were there to guard us were in the minority and stayed well out of sight. To a great extent we were left to ourselves, a freedom we had never experienced before in a camp.

Food was very scarce though better than in Munsterlager and everything had to be organised. Woollen blankets had to be distributed, the cooking and the occupation of the barracks had to sorted out by us. It soon became clear that we were one of the first bulk transport of POWs to arrive and for what we earnestly hoped was to be the last time, we formed our own camp leadership, but this time in a very informal manner. What was the sense of it all this, we wondered? We were at home weren't we, so when would we be discharged?

We asked the American soldiers, we hardly ever saw an officer, but they avoided committing themselves, apparently they had no idea on how things were to proceed; apparently about as little idea as we had of our own fate. Questions were usually met by a shrug of the shoulders and a non-committal, "Don't ask me, buddy!"

The years in the camps had taught us to put our questions carefully and we had become expert interrogators in our own right, learning to couch the most crucial inquiries in the most casual question. According to rumours, we were to be sieved again, and those who were caught in the mesh would go to labour camps in France for reparation. That was a terrible prospect after having been in camps for so long and now so close to home. There was nothing to be done but to wait and see, wait and see.

Anything different broke up the routine and was, therefore, of interest to us. In the evening the camp gates were opened and a sort of *Jugendbande* (youth gang) were let in to the camp where we were; this was to give them a place to sleep and to get some food. These lads and girls didn't want to talk much to us former officers, I suppose they thought they had little for which they should be thankful to us. They were a mixed gang, aged between six and sixteen, apparently war orphans from different parts of Germany. Even one and a half years after the end of the war they were still roaming around the country side and the cities. They seemed to be very happy with their situation; they always managed to find something to eat; they avoided compulsory school attendance; and occasionally they would brag when they'd had a 'gute Beute' (good catch - they found somewhere comfortable to stay or had been well fed). We didn't know if the food given them was taken from our rations but wouldn't have begrudged them if it had, we were short on food but it was sufficient, we had known much worse.

We had been in the camp for ten days and every day a few were discharged, one could watch it. At the front, along the fence outside the camp gate, they had to stand in long lines and, as in a clothing inspection, had to spread everything out on the ground before them. Those still in possession of a duffle bag, when asked, had to open it for inspection. Some of them were stupid enough to try to take one of the good woollen American blankets out of the camp. How could they be so stupid! Even though in those times this blanket material, the *Amidecke*, was very sought after as a material from which to tailor jackets, it was incredibly stupid to run the risk of being caught. Those that were caught first remained in Dachau and some were sent to labour camps in France.

Every day approximately thirty lucky comrades left the camp and we soon worked out that at that rate we would have to wait weeks. Nothing seemed to stick to a discernable pattern, sometimes things were going in alphabetical order, which was bad news for Wildermuth and myself, but then it would seem to become arbitrary. Sometimes a new troop would arrive in the camp and they were dealt with immediately, but there was nothing to be done other than sit and wait, sit and wait.

What happened to change things we never knew but suddenly we were asked to help fill in the discharge papers. That was great but with only one typewriter in the camp there was still a significant bottleneck. At last I got a turn on the typewriter and I suddenly realised that the time I had taken in Canada to learn to touch-type was to be of value. Nor did I realise at that time how significant typewriters and the processing of words was to become in my future. It was unfortunate that my portable Remmington was in my kit bag and hopefully, by that time, in safe keeping. Limited to the one machine we were making progress but it was still not fast enough for us.

As soon as the Americans realised that our work was reliable we were also allowed to fill out the discharge documents by hand, using block capitals. That helped more and soon fifty men per day were marching away to their homes. After I had completed my medical inspection, around the third of December, I expected my turn any day and, indeed, on the evening of the fifth of December Gerhard Schweizer, Hannes Sinn and myself, all names beginning with 'S', were informed that we should report for discharge in the morning. I had only one matter to resolve and that was whether to try to keep my blanket which I had legitimately bought in Canada. That decision was easy, it wasn't worth the risk of being accused of theft so in the morning it was duly donated to one of my friends.

Roll-call was at nine o'clock in the morning and with our luggage laid out in front of us on the gravel for inspection, we mustered for what we earnestly hoped would be the last time. Even at that late stage some were held back because of their documents or because of something in their kit; it was heartbreaking to watch them gather up their belongings and turn back towards the barracks. Each and every one of us stood there hoping against hope it would not be us, could we stand it if it was? The Americans would not accept any debates on their decisions, perhaps a certain number had to be 'caught' to give the impression that they were doing their job, we didn't know, we just stood and prayed it wouldn't be us.

At last came the order to dismiss and together with Schweizer and Sinn I walked out of the gates. We were just so grateful that in the last minute we hadn't fallen victim to some stupid coincidence or quirk of fate. As we marched through the gate knowing we had our discharge documents in our pockets, we felt like kings! Finally, after six years, we were free human beings, and could now do what we thought was right.

Before leaving the camp we had been issued ration cards for three days and eighty Reichsmarks as discharge money. We made our way to the centre of Munich, where we could hardly find the railway station because everywhere was rubble and ruin. But the station still existed, or at least it had been partially rebuilt. We enquired about a train to Stuttgart and were astonished at how well the railway was already functioning. We could even ask about the connecting train to Ludwigsburg, and Gerhard Schweizer then telephoned home, to announce his coming. Beaming broadly he announced that his sister, Marianne, would be at the station waiting for us.

That was simply great! The rubble heaps around the main station of Munich were enormous, but for us nothing was going to depress us too much. It was a cold sunny day in December and everybody was so helpful to us. Everywhere we were recognised as prisoners of war and when we got

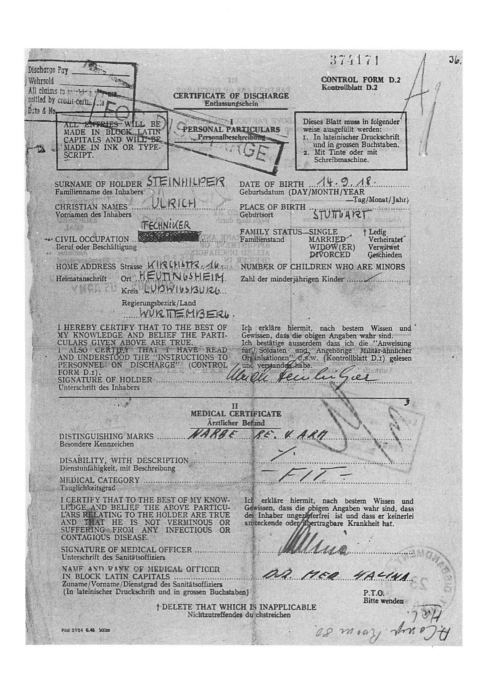

My certificate of discharge. The last act in the six-year odyssey.

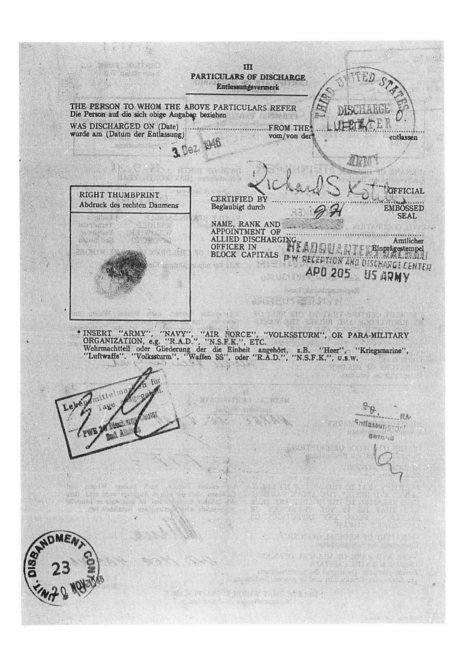

into conversation they seemed to know we'd come from Canada. A restaurant was pointed out to us which had been built up between the rubble heaps, without help we wouldn't have found it. You could have a beer there and they even had a small choice of meals, and no they wouldn't accept ration cards from prisoners of war that had just been released, what we had was *'on the house.'* Our hopes climbed from hour to hour, with so much helpfulness and cooperation our future already looked a lot brighter.

The train travelled very slowly by way of Ulm to Stuttgart, and made many stops on the way. Once in Stuttgart, although it was already dark, we caught the connecting train to Ludwigsburg, which we reached at around ten o'clock at night. Marianne Schweizer, Gerhard's sister, was there waiting for us and she told us that there was no connection to Öhringen (where Sinn came from) that night; nor to Heutingsheim, my destination, that could only be reached on foot. That was absolutely no problem, I would manage those six kilometres before midnight.

At the turn-off to Neckarweihingen, at the *Favoritenpark* in Ludwigsburg, our paths separated. Sinn had decided to spend the night with the Schweizers and I, therefore, marched on alone through the darkness, pleased with the fact that I only had light luggage to carry. How much foresight we'd had, how grateful I was that my kit bag would arrive complete and without my having to lug it the last six kilometres of my journey.

Before midnight, I reached the old schoolhouse in Heutingsheim, across from the church, and saw the light still burning, mother and father were still awake, they had been informed somehow that I would be coming that very night. And what a *Wiedersehen*, what a reunion that was we experienced in the middle of a December night at the end of 1946. After six years and so many adventures I was home.

EPILOGUE.

There was not much time to celebrate as the small flat that my parents lived in, in the schoolhouse, was full of refugees. There was no room left for me. *Wohnungsberechtigung* (Residence Permits - a permit to reside at home) were only issued once one had found work. Therefore I couldn't be too choosy. Saturday night I had arrived and already on Monday morning, just two days later, I sat at the wheel of an American truck and was driving equipment for the US Army to Nuremberg.

Maybe it was this modest beginning that was to determine my outlook for the rest of my life; it was to become filled with work. Mostly I took pleasure in the tasks I was confronted with. I worked at all levels, beginning with the US Army as driver, driving trucks, buses and jeeps. I was able to help in the rebuilding work as well as I'd always wanted to. Although I had only attended POW courses, thanks to my good knowledge of the English language, a position in charge of a sort of planning office was soon forthcoming. I worked there together with graduate architects and engineers, allocating the required quantities of building materials for schemes like the large American construction sites and the refurbishment of other damaged ones. Amongst these projects were such buildings as the Head Office of the *GDF Wüstenrot* (Building Society), at the time a requisitioned building and the factory-like repair workshops for the maintenance of US vehicles in Schwäbisch Gmünd and Böblingen (my airfield in the early days). Because the construction work was in the hands of German firms which had risen out of the ashes again, the allocation of building materials was a very important matter, because one could easily divert the materials to private users or even to 'illegal' building sites. In my position I had to withstand several attempts at bribery. I made up my mind I would never be open to bribery and was, therefore, never in anybody's hands. However, whenever it was possible to make a choice between a German project and another I willingly carried the responsibility of bias.

At the time of the Währungsreform (the currency reform) I was a probationer and stores worker with the firm of Franck und Kathreiner in Ludwigsburg. With an hourly wage of one Mark, one couldn't, at the start of the new *D-Mark (Deutschmark)*, exactly leap ahead. Instead we used to 'brush' coal, a very valuable heating material, off the goods trains that passed the loading ramp of the firm and have a warm home. I was the first

German employee to start with Pan American Airways in Stuttgart when, in October 1948, they began commuter flights to Frankfurt, Munich, and Vienna, all in DC 3s.

January 1953 I started working for IBM (Germany) as a travelling salesman for electric typewriters. That was one of the most difficult and demanding jobs I have ever done in my life but I succeeded in the end. I was one of the few salesmen who consistently remained in 'The 100% Club'- that is I met my monthly sales targets or exceeded them, but for that success I needed to draw on every gram of my six years POW experience: resolution, self confidence, foresight, planning, human relations, wealth of ideas and, last but not least, the courage 'to open new doors'!

At first it was less for professional success than a hobby that I began to develop an idea that the widespread term 'Data Processing' could be complemented with the idea of another system called 'Word Processing'. Word processing was, in Germany, later known as *'TV'* *('Text Verarbeitung')*. In my original draft ideas I described it as 'Making a thought audible, visible and distributable'. By 1966, I was the German guest speaker at Miami, at the worldwide IBM meeting and there I brought forward my idea in English, in the formulation above.

The idea of rearranging 'the office' was, at first, met with great resistance. In the office someone did the 'thinking' - how could a machine be employed? However my vision became more and more a reality; in exchanges of ideas with IBM Chief of Development, Bud Beatty, responsible for Lexington/Kentucky and Austin/Texas and the energetic support of Chief of Products, Claire Vaugh, it was possible to develop new products which fitted into the concept of 'Word Processing.'

New equipment like magnetic tape and magnetic card machines were developed to store text and the ink-jet printer was developed. Not only machines were developed but, thanks to progressive customers and excellent IBM employees, we were able to develop new organisations in the office world and also new career structures. In 1969 I was the guest of IBM in South America, and was able to further develop my thoughts on 'Word Processing'. Then, when I gave my speech in Spanish, which I had learnt in preparation for one of my escape attempts, enthusiasm was great. Although the common language of the country was Portuguese, almost all present had come from Spanish speaking areas. The Americans present were almost ashamed; there came a German who went to the trouble of speaking the language of the country.

At last IBM recognised my inception of the idea of 'Word Processing' and offered my wife and I a journey around the world in 1972, in recognition of my achievements. In 1973 I was invited to attend the great international 'Word Processing Convention' to be held in Boston/Mass as 'Keynote Speaker.' There, in front of six hundred competent experts, I was able to talk about the development of my ideas on 'Word Processing' and develop plans and themes that were to be guide lines for the future.

Before I retired, I put my valuable experiences on paper, and published the book *'ABC der Textverarbeitung'* (ABC of Word Processing - ISBN 3-921439-05-1). However at IBM-USA my thoughts were never fully accepted. In my opinion there were two reasons for this: first of all there was the NHI factor - Not Invented Here (nicht hier erfunden) - and then there was the big brother 'Data Processing.' In retrospect it can be seen that this was to the disadvantage of the firm. They never wanted to recognise it as being an equal partner even though, in general, much more word processing is done in offices than data processing. Even as late as 1988, during a private trip to the USA, a 'big brother' (senior American IBM colleague) proudly announced to me: "In IBM we have eliminated the term 'Word Processing'!"

My personal commitment brought me my own success with IBM 'D' (IBM Germany). I was promoted into a senior executive position and international recognition came at the very end of my career. Together with my wife, I visited IBM Corporations in Scandinavia, England, France, the Benelux countries, USA, Mexico, Venezuela, Spain, Italy, Austria, stopping at a 'danger-point' at that time, Teheran, the troubles having just started there. Before that we had also been in Singapore, Australia and Japan. The purpose of the journey was to see how the IBM Corporations themselves were employing the medicine 'Word Processing' in their own offices.

I wrote what I thought was a very accurate report on my observations in all countries I had visited, only to feel the NHI factor again. The missed opportunities can be tolerated, I have achieved nothing if I am not more philosophical now, just like the experiences during my imprisonment; ultimately God decides: "...und Gott lenkt"

After my retirement 1987, I was able to visit 'old hunting grounds' in Canada and the USA with my wife, Lore, in a mobile camper. During this visit I was able to meet policeman Bill McIntyre who had arrested me with Hinnerk Waller in 1942 in Watertown/NY. He and his wife Gerry were very pleased over our *Wiedersehen*, our reunion, after forty-five years. Bill has since died, but we are still corresponding with his wife.

What control do we actually have over our life? For myself I can say that it is not until now that I have been able to find a fatalistic justification for many things that happened. As unhappy as I was at the time, being recaptured five times, the more I realise now how lucky I really was. My attempts to feign mental illness were a terrible and tragic mistake for me, something I need never have done.

It did actually happen that some POW comrades emigrated to Canada. Ekkehard Priebe, former *Oberleutnant* in JG 77, lives today in West Vancouver. He managed to get hold of secret reports of the Royal Canadian Mounted Police, which have now been released. A real *Fundgrube*, a rich source, of information for my readers and myself. On page 371 of "Noch zehn Minuten bis Buffalo" (ISBN 3-7628-0465-6 - the German edition of "Ten Minutes To Buffalo") I wrote how, according to Manhart, the *Puppen*, the manikins dressed as soldiers that had 'stood in' for us, were withdrawn on Saturday, 21st February 1942. With that the search along the Canadian/American border was started. It was probably a slip of Manni's memory, as the *Puppen* were, in fact, withdrawn from counting on the evening of Friday, 20th February, and with that our escape was declared.

At the time we climbed over the fence on the 18th at midday. According to the report of RCMP dated 21.2.42, I now know, that not only the Canadian, but also the American police started searching for us early on Saturday morning. Where it is necessary to add comment it is in brackets. To quote:

Royal Canadian Mounted Police,
Detachment Kingston/Ontario 21-2-42.

Reference Ulrich STEINHILPER and Alfred WALLER, Escaped P.O.Ws, Bowmanville.

1. After telephonic instructions, which he had received this morning at 3.30 a.m. from Insp. R.S.S. Wilson, the undersigned went to the duty station, where at 4.15 (a.m.) he received a full description of mentioned prisoners from the Department "O".

2. The Duty Station Belleville was not informed by us, because Toronto had done this themselves. However the local railway, city, and provincial police were informed of the two escaped prisoners at 4.30 a.m.

3. Brockville was called at 4.35 a.m., they said they would immediately get their squad car on the road... they would

control all trains travelling eastward... the Detachment Cornwall, especially Sgt. Smaridge wanted to control all roads and the river embankments, during which Constable Sinnema took over the local controls...

3. The writer contacted Inspector Cousins, the Provincial Police at 4.40 a.m. and at 4.50 a.m. Inspector Benjamin of the U.S. Immigration Border Patrol, Ogdensburg, U.S.A. (How accurately I had recorded times and names in my hand written manuscript). He was given exact information and promised that he would immediately alarm his squad cars. (Therefore they had already been searching for us since early Saturday morning!)

4. All traffic travelling east, whether truck or car, was controlled by our department at the LaSalle Main Street in Kingston, from 3.55 a.m. in the morning until 9 p.m. Many a driver reported that they had, since 5 a.m. between Bowmanville and Kingston, been stopped up to three times and searched. This proves that we have this route under control.

Both policemen of the local Police Station, promised to keep Highway No. 2 (well known) under control on both sides of Kingston, because it is assumed, that STEINHILPER will attempt to reach the USA by way of the frozen St Lawrence River, which he already knows very well. (How could they assume that so precisely? They were, in any event, three days too late!) River embankment controls are now effective. - Signed C.W.Bishop Cpl., Reg.No. 10734. - Received Ottawa 25-2-42.

This 'secret' report is today not only interesting because of the search for Waller and myself, but because it shows how big an 'alarm' was generated when German POWs were *unterwegs* (on the road). In fulfilling our duty as officers in escaping I honestly believe we had contributed to the war effort.

From having been shot down to the return home - this is all now contained in the last two books of this trilogy. Many people keep saying that imprisonment in Canada was *Honigschlecken* (licking honey) when compared with Russia and the conditions in most of the Allied Camps. Even as the war was coming to an end, our life was certainly better. Nevertheless I would like to express with emphasis that even a 'Golden Cage' is still a 'Cage!' Those who believe that the Canadian POWs, after being shot down, rescued out of the cold water, or otherwise avoided death, felt that they were safe and secure and happy to stay there should think again.

THE LAST BATTLE

In 1980 the remains of my old Me 109 were recovered from the marshes near Canterbury and preserved by the dedicated staff of the Kent Battle of Britain Museum at Hawkinge. Later, in 1983, I was asked to participate in the making of the Yorkshire Television programme 'Churchill's Few.' For this I was brought to England and after forty-six years remade my acquaintance with 'Yellow 2', then just a mass of wreckage. When I saw it I was moved far more than I had expected. There I saw the guns, the thousands of rounds of unfired ammunition and the horribly mangled cockpit area where I so nearly ended my life.

Thus began a happy association with the museum at Hawkinge and notably with its outstanding director, Mike Llewellyn. In 1990 the airfield which had once been RAF Hawkinge, the front line for the RAF in 1940, came under threat from developers who wanted to bury it under houses and factory units. The battle for Hawkinge began and I was able to help in my small way. Reproduced overleaf is an article which Peter helped me write, expressing the thoughts of a former *Luftwaffe* pilot on the preservation of this old airfield. Extracts from the article have been published in newspapers and magazines and have provided a different slant for the preservation cause.

At the time of going to press we don't know if our appeals will be successful but many, many people have now joined the cause including a lot of *Luftwaffe* personnel who share my views. We have also made a good quality video film which will be distributed to all interested parties to help the campaign. It features people like myself, Paddy Barthropp, Jimmy Goodson and is narrated by Raymond Baxter. I hope that we are successful.

Here follow some photographs of the making of the video in and around the Museum at Hawkinge.

Filming inside the main hangar by the tail of a Spitfire

SAVE HAWKINGE FOR FUTURE GENERATIONS

I imagine that there will be many people who will find it difficult to understand why an ex-*Luftwaffe* pilot should want to be associated with an attempt to save an RAF airfield. I imagine there will be those who would resent my offering to speak out for it, condemning the German airmen as evil, associating what they did with the events of the latter days of the war. But I would ask them to read what I have to say and, perhaps, to reconsider.

In England your 'Battle of Britain' pilots are celebrated as the real heros of World War II and quite rightly. They did stand alone against a numerically superior force and they fought us to a standstill - they won the 'Battle of Britain' at terrible cost for both sides. Without them, operation *Seelöwe* would probably have succeeded and perhaps history may have been very different, we can only speculate. In my book "Spitfire On My Tail" I have stated that it is my conviction that the RAF broke the back of the *Luftwaffe* during the 'Battle of Britain', a blow from which it could never really recover. This view has not won me many friends in Germany but I still believe it to be true.

*Again filming inside the main hangar, this time inspecting the
Me. 109 which represents the fighter flown by my friend Franz von Werra.*

My own fighter *Gruppe* is a good example: we joined the Battle in August 1940 with thirty-six experienced pilots, none of them with less than three years flying experience, many with more. By 27th October, the day the Battle ended for me, we could only muster six. By far the most experienced pilots were those who flew the Me. 110 *Zerstörers* (Destroyers), they had blind flying experience, multi-engine training and were really the cream of our crop. Students of the 'Battle' will be aware of how many of them were sacrificed to prop up Hermann Göring's mistaken belief in the aircraft's potential.

In Germany it is forgotten, lost in the victories and massive scores of the 'aces' in Russia. It was also the first real reversal for the *Wehrmacht*, so it is not celebrated and for the majority in Germany the brave men who died fighting for what they thought was right are largely also forgotten. But not by widows, brothers, sisters, parents or the children who never really knew their fathers.

In Germany, for a long time after the end of the war, it was not mentioned. We, as a nation, reeled under the shock realisation of what Hitler

Filming outside with David Brocklehurst, one of those dedicated to saving Hawkinge

had done in the name of the German people. But now people are more honest and open about it and painful as it is we accept it as part, albeit a terrible part, of our history. Young people are growing up and have to come to terms with what was once done by the Germans and want to know how such a thing could ever have happened. And this is where Hawkinge and museums in England have a role to play for us - they are the custodians of a significant piece of German history.

As a united Europe comes closer and closer, so the nations are growing together and in many instances old wounds are healing. That should not mean that the past is buried; it should be on display for future generations - as the Greeks observed, *'Those who do not understand and revere history are doomed to repeat it'*. It is to the future we should look with resources like Hawkinge, we are the custodians of history for future generations. It is just a matter of a little more time before sites like Hawkinge would achieve the status necessary to **require** their preservation. Who would build on the site of your Battle of Hastings or on the field of Waterloo? The only difference is that more time has passed. And when time has passed how will we be judged? Will the young enquiring minds then say why did they let it

*A very moving experience for me was our filming visit to the cemetery at Hawkinge.
There German, British, Canadian, Polish and American airmen who died in 1940 lie
buried side by side. Herbert Kunze, born the same year as me and died on my 22nd
birthday, September 1940. I also found the grave of Hans Carl Mayer who died on
the 27th October 1940, the day I was shot down and lived. A graphic reminder to me
that it could so easily have been me in one of those graves.*

366

happen? Why did they let the last one go to the digger and bulldozer? Or will they praise the foresight which preserved a unique example of what was the British Front Line in 1940?

Many British writers have made the protests about unrequired industrial capacity being built on the site and bringing hundreds of families to an area with insufficient schools, shops, roads and recreation facilities - that is not my argument as a foreigner. What I did witness first hand at Hawkinge was the enthusiasm with which hundreds of people signed their names to the petition to preserve the airfield. I merely want to speak out to appeal to you to preserve something as a memorial to many of my friends and good comrades for whom there is no other marker.

I now count as friends many British pilots against whom I once flew. The more of them I meet the more I realise how very, very similar we were and what a tragedy it was that politicians should have pitted us against each other. My friends were not Nazis, Huns or Bastards, they were bright young men who died fighting for their country at a time when the world was very confused. Please don't let them be so easily forgotten, remember them and 'The Few' by preserving Hawkinge as it was, a grass airfield and a quiet place to remember and think.

So there we are. After fifty-two years ex-*Luftwaffe* pilots join a campaign to save an RAF airfield which we once tried to annihilate! After a full and demanding life I can say now with some certainty that there is something called destiny and things do tend, in the end, to come *zum Ausgangspunkt zurück! - Full Circle!*

APPENDIX ONE

THE FARM

After we had gone through and around the farm many times on our walks we heard that it could be let for an annual rent amounting to one-hundred and ten dollars. Negotiations began through *Pferdedieb*, he knew the farmer who had previously managed it and who was, curiously enough, an ex-patriot German, Herr Grothe. He came, originally, from Hamburg and had emigrated with his parents as a young lad. In the fire that destroyed the farm he tragically lost his family, his wife and two daughters. Mr Grothe had then moved into Gravenhurst and was running a small saw mill there. We knew him quite well because he had a small band saw in his mill which was always

The remains of the farmhouse as we first saw it. Excavation of the cellar and foundations had just begun.

Another view of the foundations of the house that fire had destroyed

breaking down. He would come to the camp and ask for help and some of our technicians were allowed out of camp to fix the ancient motor.[1] During these visits he always produced his few remaining words of German, actually only one sentence: *"Ick kann ook Platt snacken"* - phonetically spelt north German *Platt Deutsch* dialect meaning: "I can also speak Platt." Mr Grothe was a real character and always got along well with 'his prisoners'.

The rent for the farm was deducted from the *Wehrsold*, the pay of the Gravenhurst officers as a whole and, of course, the prisoners could only 'work out' on the farm 'on parole'. The Canadians were very pleased with the initiative and for the POWs it was an individual matter of conscience whether he could be trusted to go and work on parole on the farm and not run. Our *'Ehrenwort'* was, in the meantime, so well recognised by the Canadians that they sometimes, in our view, over did it and became too trusting in a way; for someone to break the code of the *Ehrenwort* would been unthinkable. We started worrying whether they were taking their guard duties too easy and questioned whether we weren't restricting ourselves with our escape attempts. The problem was that policing ourselves in the way we were was allowing the Canadians to effectively reduce the level of personnel

The new house close to completion. All the timber for the construction was felled and prepared on the farm itself. Obltn. Bubenzer (third from left) was one of the dedicated carpenters

Some of the builders muster outside the finished house. 'Maxi' the first house pulls the cart towards the gathering

The log stables. Built from rough-hewn timber but of fine construction. Third from the left Hinnerk Waller and next to him Eberhart Wildermuth and von Gablenz. Sitting on Maxi is Hauptmann Donike and the horse is being held by Piepel Rapmund who came from South West Africa.

required to guard us and, in that way, we were not performing our role as POW officers completely (keeping as many as possible of the enemy involved in guarding us). There were many serious discussions on this theme in the *Ältestenrat*.

The reasoning behind the work on the farm was very simple: *Gesundheit für Leib und Seele* (health for body and mind) during this lengthy and unnatural imprisonment. Before we got round to the agricultural work, with typical German thoroughness and in the spirit of the first settlers, the original buildings were reconstructed. The quality and volume of work produced there was surprising, but the photographs of the topping-out ceremony, those of the horses and those of the rest of the farm give the right impression. The *experts* in charge were *Hauptmann* Neumann, whose father owned an estate in Pomerania, and the building engineer, Schwarz. The following buildings were reconstructed: the previous farm house in the form of a log cabin, using the trees that had been felled on the farm premises, a chicken pen, stables, and 'last but not least' a pigsty.

The real *Baumeistern* (master builders), as far as design and construction

Vegetable production on the farm. The woodland in the background was also part of the farm and the new sports field can also be seen in front of the trees.

were concerned, were *Hauptmann* Koch and *Oberleutnant* Bubenzer (both were excellent carpenters). They, together with many helpers, constructed practical buildings of great longevity. As a bonus for more of the camp's inmates an additional sports ground was also built in the area of the farm at a later date. Having completed the construction it was time to purchase some animals. At first this was restricted to chickens, rabbits and the horse, Maxi, who was mentioned earlier. Later additions were a team of two brown ploughing horses and, once the various stables and ancillary buildings had been completed, there followed pigs and sheep which were bred and reared.

Fields were ploughed with the assistance of the two horses in preparation for the sowing of potatoes and other vegetables, herbs and cultivated berries. All of this served to supplement the daily rations being served in the camp but this, however, was not the main reason for all this work. It was the experience of becoming creative again which was of such special importance to the prisoners, to regain some sense of worth. To many it became more important to join the community effort at the farm than to burn their energy in the pursuit of sports.

The small animals were cared for by Hauptmann Hué and Stabszahlmeister Klein.

So as not to stress the animals by numerous changes of keeper, volunteers were accepted to care for specific animals. Maxi, the white horse, was placed under the care of *Hauptmann* Wildermuth and *'Piepel'* Rapmund. The brown ploughing team were willingly cared for by *Major* Wüstefeld, after he had relinquished the position of German camp administrator. All of them in the course of their military training been schooled in the care of horses. So the animals were in good hands and there was a vet on hand. Other individual responsibilities were *Hauptmann* Hué as *Hühnerbetreuer* (chicken keeper), the rabbits were in the hands of *Stabszahlmeister* (Staff Payroll Master) Klein and there was also a *Schweinemeister* (pig master) with assistants, but I regret I have forgotten their names. On Sundays and Holidays there was no work on the farm, except for a small group that went there to feed the animals and 'muck out'. On these days there were no parole walks either. The farm proved to be a real blessing for those who had the benefit of it. It not only gave them a chance to exercise skills previously left dormant and to hand them on but, also to cultivate something of real value. I have been told by some of those who worked on the farm that it was their saviour as the years of imprisonment wore on.

The plough team at work guided by their groom, Major Wüstefeldt.
Hauptmann Neumann is handling the plough.

Major Wüstefeldt with the ploughing team.
'Blacky' the dog is also taking an interest.

Long before the farm time, there had been a small zoo in the camp, constructed in the form of a stone grotto. There were snakes, striped squirrels, frogs, toads and a pool with fish, all of which had been caught during our walks or when we went swimming which brings us to the story of 'Elvira', a *Riesensumpfkröte* (giant swamp turtle). *'Stickel'* Stirnat almost had a bad accident with her when he was diving into the lake from the five meter board. Exactly where he was to enter the water Elvira appeared on the surface with her thick shell above the surface. *'Stickel'* just managed to turn away and avoid Elvira, otherwise he would have hit his head on her back and both would have been badly injured. That was the camps first encounter with Elvira and thereafter everybody was on the look out for her until she was finally caught by our long distance underwater swimmer Wildermuth. He located her home in the swimminmg zone and a very courageous group tugged her on land. Elvira was, after her capture, kept in the terrarium, and *Korkweschte* together with Paul Engelen put her under their personal protection. This however did not prevent her disappearing during the *Hungerzeit* (the hungry time)[2], where it was assumed that she landed in the cooking pots of the Pfundtner room.

Notes

[1] When Walter Stirnat paid a visit to Gravenhurst in 1976, he not only saw the grave of Major Bach, but also found Mr Grothe's old locomotor on his premises, restored and newly painted.

[2] More details of the *Hungerzeit* (hungry period) have been given in the book, the weeks after the war had been lost. In the begining the originally 1100 calories daily were supplemented by being allowed to go fishing from our swimming pier. From there a seagull was also once caught and prepared for eating but it was not edible. The chickens tasted much better at that time, and they all froze to death sitting on their perch. It wasn't long before the Canadians even stopped these meagre supplements to our rations.

APPENDIX TWO

Escapee Told Story to Times
Downed Pilot Takes Issue

Long after the guns of World War II were stilled, suspicions and beliefs perhaps fostered by the propaganda machines of the time leave impressions which hurt the survivors of that conflict.

Ulrich Steinhilper, a former Luftwaffe pilot who was shot down over England after an attack on London and later escaped from a prison camp in Canada only to be apprehended in Watertown, resents being called a Nazi and claims he never was one.

Mr. Steinhilper has been corresponding with retired Watertown policeman William J. McIntyre, once a deputy, police chief, who assisted in his capture on Arsenal Street on Feb. 22, 1942. Mr. McIntyre and the late Patrolman John A. Berow captured Mr. Steinhilper and another escapee from a camp near Toronto, Ont.

Mr. Steinhilper's escapades, including his own graphic account of his last flight over Great Britain,

were recounted in a series in the Watertown Daily Times last December.

The former pilot, who assisted in a British television project after his Messerschmitt was found buried in a Kent field, has read the series and is disturbed at being labelled a Nazi.

Mr. Steinhilper wrote The Times: " 'Nazi Recounts Story' to me is disturbing as a headline. Even during the war when we were still prisoners of war, we were smiling when reading in the Canadian or American press about 'Nazi' officers, 'Nazi' pilots, 'Nazi' submarines, and so on.

"Then we understood that it had to be the official propaganda tone that then we were all 'Nazis'."

"But today?" Mr. Steinhilper asks. "At least I now can try to speak up. Then, this was not possible."

Mr. Steinhilper then defended

the stance of the German Officers' Corps.

"Believe me if ever there was one — however small — part of the population in Germany that did not identify itself with the National Sozialistische Deutsche Arbeiterpartei, or in your terms, the 'Nazi' party, it was certainly the German Officers Corps" of the Navy, Army and Air Force.

"So you can imagine being called a 'Nazi' even today is not flattering."

Mr. Steinhilper, who is retired from IBM corporation after a career selling typewriters and word processors, now lives in Stuttgart, West Germany.

The former lieutenant, for the first time, revealed details of his five escapes from Canadian prison camps.

The escapes were:
● Out of Camp Bowmanville, Ont., recaptured at Niagara Falls.

With 'Nazi' Label

"After I had been across the bridge, I did not know that at the border locomotive and crew change. I had been in hiding along the vessel of the locomotive. This was in November 1941 when the U.S. was not yet at war.

● Escaped from Bowmanville again and was recaptured in Montreal.

● Bowmanville escape which ended in Watertown.

● Escapes four and five were from Gravenhurst, Ont., and freedom was brief.

Mr. Steinhilper also took exception to the view of many persons that the "rules of fair warfare" were broken by the Luftwaffe "by deliberately attacking 'residential' areas."

"This was not true," Mr. Steinhilper wrote. "I still know today very clearly under which orders we were then flying.

"When there were no military

targets to be identified, bombs had to be taken back, sometimes to be jettisoned into the English channel for safe landing," Mr. Steinhilper wrote.

"Of course I cannot guarantee what happened in emergency cases or at night. But I still clearly remember the orders that were in place.

"As a fighter pilot, fortunately I never had to carry bombs. For me these orders meant no strafing on the ground, especially civilian trains.

"In August 1940 we had such air superiority above Southern England that we easily could have stopped train traffic in daylight south of London.

"Then we were allowed only to aim and shoot at barrage balloons, gas and gasoline tanks, docks and shipping," the ex-pilot wrote.

"Therefore, in most of my more than 100 missions above Southern England I returned with full

Ulrich Steinhilper

ammunition. This meant two times 1,000 shots in the machine guns and two times 50 shots in the 20 mm. guns in each wing."

376

In December 1984 the *'Watertown Daily Times'* printed a long report (in three parts) on my cooperation in the making of Yorkshire TV's programme 'Churchill's Few', my being shot down in 1940, being a POW and my subsequent arrest in Watertown. I protested, because I was still marked as a *Nazi pilot* in their report. The article reproduced overleaf was a pleasant reaction to my protest, but it did not prevent the newspaper, in 1987 when I visited McIntyre and later when I attended his funeral, to again mark me as a *Nazi*. I wonder if the Americans public ever knew what a *Nazi* was.

SPITFIRE ON MY TAIL

A View From The Other Side

Ulrich Steinhilper & Peter Osborne

Non-fiction   *Illustrated*

ISBN 1 872836 003

Spitfire On My Tail is the detailed account of how one German grew up and joined the *Luftwaffe* as a career officer and airman. It was written by Ulrich Steinhilper who was an *Oberleutnant* with JG 52 (52nd Fighter Wing) based at Coquelles near Calais. He flew over one-hundred and fifty combat missions during the Battle of Britain and saw his *Gruppe* of thirty-six experienced pilots whittled down to just a handful by October.

It is a very personal and human story of the naivety of youth being shaped by the forces of war. Poignant lessons learned by tragic accidents, counterbalanced by anger towards those who saw the war as a means of personal advancement and self aggrandizement.

There is no doubt there is, today, a movement towards a more balanced understanding of events and *SPITFIRE ON MY TAIL*, already being referred to as a classic of the period, presents a rare opportunity for students of this classic air engagement to see The View From The Other Side. In a market where new books on the subject, and many re-issues of classics, offer a bewildering choice *SPITFIRE ON MY TAIL* is in a class of its own.

SPITFIRE ON MY TAIL: 335 Pages, 84 black & white illustrations, hardback only. Price: £14.95

TEN MINUTES TO BUFFALO

The Story of Germany's Great Escaper

Ulrich Steinhilper & Peter Osborne

Non-Fiction   *Illustrated*

ISBN 1 872836 01 1

"Ten Minutes to Buffalo" is long-awaited sequel to Ulrich Steinhilper's highly successful first book, "Spitfire On My Tail". Unlike the first book, which tells the story of how a young German came to fly in Hitler's Luftwaffe and to fight in the Battle of Britain, "Ten Minutes to Buffalo" is a catalogue of courage and determination on the ground. In this way it is set to repeat the successful formula by providing a rare chance to witness how things were for 'The Other Side,' this time behind the barbed wire and in Ulrich Steinhilper's case - all too often outside the wire! It relates a story of remarkable courage and perseverance in the most appalling conditions, braving arctic weather and appalling hardship with one thought in mind - to get home.

In 1940, during the Battle of Britain, Ulrich Steinhilper was an *Oberleutnant* flying Messerschmitt Me 109s against the RAF. On the 27th October, just three days before the official end of the battle, his luck ran out and he was shot down by Sergeant 'Bill' Skinner of 74 Squadron who was flying a Spitfire. Thus Ulrich began a new life as a Prisoner of war, but never a man to take things easy he began to plot to escape and to get back to Germany.

From his first camp in England away to the vastness of Canada he and a select few of his fellow officers were to become known as *Die Ausbrecherkönige von Kanada* (the breakout kings from Canada) and Ulrich was to shine among them. His escapes were innovative and even audacious and it was only bad luck that seemed to keep him from a completely successful 'homerun'. Time and again he got to the other side of the wire and even as far as the USA before the long arm of co-incidence decreed he was to be recaptured.

Very little has ever been written about the conditions of German officers as prisoners of the Allies and practically nothing of their ingenuity and perseverance in planning and executing escape plans so similar to their counterparts in German hands. This remarkable book is entirely written from original hand-written sheets which date from 1942 and which give it a great immediacy and accuracy. Already successful in Germany under the title "Noch zehn Minuten bis Buffalo" this translation is a must for all serious student of the Second World War or just for those who enjoy and exciting factual read.

****

Available from: INDEPENDENT BOOKS, 3, Leaves Green Crescent, Keston, Bromley, BR2 6DN, England. Or INDEPENDENT BOOKS, Freepost, Keston, Kent, BR2 6BR.(Tel: 0959 573360)

Post and packing: £1.95 first class in the UK and all BFPO numbers. £2.50 surface mail anywhere in the world. If quicker delivery is required outside the UK please include additional payment sufficient for the mailing of a 900 gram packet to the destination. e.g USA £7.50 Air Mail, printed paper rate.
Orders outside the United Kingdom: Please note payment cheques should be drawable on a London bank. If not add the value of £5.00 for clearance or use an International Postal Order or International Money Order. *Available from:*

INDEPENDENT BOOKS,
3,Leaves Green Cresc., Keston, Bromley, BR2 6DN
Telephone: Biggin Hill Kent (0959) 73360